ONE SUMMER: AMERICA 1927 –
THE CRITICS

'Few writers of non-fiction, and, let's be honest, few enough writers of novels, can crack the narrative whip like Bryson. *One Summer* fairly whirls along . . . full of exhilarating, fact-filled fun . . . **surely the most sublime distraction published this year**'
Observer

'**Bill Bryson is a true master of popular narrative**. Over the course of his career, he has bestowed a beautiful clarity on even the most recondite of subjects . . . With this book, he proves once again that he is able to juggle any number of different balls . . . while never letting a single one drop . . . **Has history ever been so enjoyable?**'
Craig Brown, *Mail on Sunday*

'**A gripping slice of history with all sorts of reverberant echoes of today** . . . Bryson, the travel writer turned non-fiction impresario, has now invented what may be an entirely new genre of non-fiction: the brief history of an era told through the biography of a summer. It is a book from which you can read many lessons or just revel in the writing'
Matt Ridley, *The Times*

www.billbryson.co.uk

'Immaculately researched and lit up by [Bill Bryson's] **marvellous** anecdotal and descriptive skills'
Literary Review

'Wry but scholarly infotainment . . . *One Summer* wins you over by the sheer weight of its encylopedic enthusiasms . . . **Bryson's winning love of the ridiculous finds a rich seam** in charting the rise and fall of America's great men . . . there is tumultuous energy in this serio-hilarious fan letter. In short, it's a bit like America itself'
Sunday Telegraph

'Bryson writes in a style **as effervescent as the time itself** . . . No one is immune to Bryson's irreverence . . . a wonderful romp'
New York Times

'**Exuberant** . . . he propels his story forward with enviable skill and inexhaustible verve . . . Bryson's summer of 1927 seems like a boisterous American version of the British summer of 1913, another high point of that fabled innocence which America was always doomed to lose'
Elaine Showalter, *Times Literary Supplement*

'The T&Cs of a bank loan could be made eloquent in the hands of Bryson so with this rich material, **the book sings**'
The Times (Books of the Year)

Bill Bryson's opening lines were:
'I come from Des Moines. Somebody had to.'
This is what followed:

The Lost Continent
A road trip around the puzzle that is small-town America introduces the world to the adjective 'Brysonesque'.

> *'A very funny performance, littered with wonderful lines and memorable images'* LITERARY REVIEW

Neither Here Nor There
Europe never seemed as funny until Bill Bryson looked at it.

> *'Hugely funny (not snigger-snigger funny but great-big-belly-laugh-till-you-cry funny)'* DAILY TELEGRAPH

Made in America
A compelling ride along the Route 66 of American language and popular culture.

> *'A tremendous sassy work, full of zip, pizzazz, and all those other great American qualities'* INDEPENDENT ON SUNDAY

Notes from a Small Island
A paean to Bryson's beloved Britain captures the very essence of the original 'green and pleasant land'.

> *'Not a book that should be read in public, for fear of emitting loud snorts'* THE TIMES

A Walk in the Woods
Bryson's punishing (by his standards) hike along the celebrated Appalachian Trail, the longest footpath in the world.

> *'This is a seriously funny book'* SUNDAY TIMES

Notes from a Big Country
Bryson brings his inimitable wit to bear on that strangest of phenomena – the American way of life.

> *'Not only hilarious but also insightful and informative'*
> INDEPENDENT ON SUNDAY

Down Under

An extraordinary journey to the heart of another big country – Australia.

> 'Bryson is the perfect travelling companion . . . When it comes to travel's peculiars the man still has no peers' THE TIMES

A Short History of Nearly Everything

Travels through time and space to explain the world, the universe and everything.

> 'Truly impressive . . . It's hard to imagine a better rough guide to science' GUARDIAN

The Life and Times of the Thunderbolt Kid

Quintessential Bryson – a funny, moving and perceptive journey through his childhood.

> 'He can capture the flavour of the past with the lightest of touches' SUNDAY TELEGRAPH

At Home

On a tour of his own house, Bill Bryson gives us an instructive and entertaining history of the way we live.

> 'A work of constant delight and discovery . . . don't leave home without it' SUNDAY TELEGRAPH

One Summer

Bryson travels back in time to a forgotten summer, when America came of age, took centre stage and changed the world for ever.

> 'Has history ever been so enjoyable?' MAIL ON SUNDAY

The Road to Little Dribbling

Two decades after Notes from a Small Island, Bill Bryson takes a new amble round Britain, to rediscover the beautiful, eccentric and endearing country he calls home.

> 'Clever, witty, entertaining' INDEPENDENT ON SUNDAY

By Bill Bryson

ONE SUMMER

AMERICA

~1927~

BILL BRYSON

BLACK SWAN

TRANSWORLD PUBLISHERS
61–63 Uxbridge Road, London W5 5SA
A Random House Group Company
www.transworldbooks.co.uk

ONE SUMMER
A BLACK SWAN BOOK: 9780552772563 (B format)
9780552779401 (A format)

First published in Great Britain
in 2013 by Doubleday
an imprint of Transworld Publishers
Black Swan edition published 2014

Addresses for Random House Group Ltd companies outside the UK
can be found at: www.randomhouse.co.uk
The Random House Group Ltd Reg. No. 954009

Penguin Random House is committed to a sustainable future for
our business, our readers and our planet. This book is made from
Forest Stewardship Council® certified paper.

Typeset in 10.5/14pt Giovanni Book by Falcon Oast Graphic Art Ltd.
Printed and bound in Great Britain by Clays Ltd, St Ives plc

12

To Annie, Billy and Gracie,
and in memory of Julia Richardson

CONTENTS

Prologue

O N A WARM spring evening just before Easter 1927, people who lived in tall buildings in New York were given pause when wooden scaffolding around the tower of the brand-new Sherry-Netherland Apartment Hotel caught fire and it became evident that the city's firemen lacked any means to get water to such a height.

Crowds flocked to Fifth Avenue to watch the blaze, the biggest the city had seen in years. At thirty-eight storeys, the Sherry-Netherland was the tallest residential building ever erected, and the scaffolding – put there to facilitate the final stages of construction – covered the top fifteen storeys, providing enough wood to make a giant blaze around its summit. From a distance, the building looked rather like a just-struck match. The flames were visible twenty miles away. Up close, the scene was much more dramatic. Sections of burning scaffolding up to fifty feet long fell from a height of five hundred feet and crashed in clattering showers of sparks in the streets below, to the gleeful cries of the spectators and the peril of toiling firemen. Burning embers dropped on to the roofs of neighbouring buildings, setting four of them alight. Firemen trained their hoses on the Sherry-Netherland building, but it was a token gesture since their streams could not rise above the third or fourth storey. Fortunately, the building was unfinished and therefore unoccupied.

People in 1920s America were unusually drawn to spectacle and by 10 p.m. the crowd had grown to an estimated hundred thousand people – an enormous gathering for a spontaneous event. Seven hundred policemen had to be brought in to keep order. Some wealthy observers, deflected from their evening revels, took rooms in the Plaza Hotel across the street and held impromptu 'fire room parties', according to the *New York Times*. Mayor Jimmy Walker turned up to have a look and got soaked when he wandered into the path of a hose. A moment later a flaming ten-foot-long plank crashed on to the pavement near him and he accepted advice to withdraw. The fire did extensive damage to the upper reaches of the building, but luckily did not spread downwards and burned itself out about midnight.

The flames and smoke provided some welcome diversion to two men, Clarence Chamberlin and Bert Acosta, who had been flying in circles in a small plane above Roosevelt Field on Long Island since 9.30 that morning. They were doing so in an attempt to break the world endurance record set two years earlier by two French aviators. This was partly a matter of national honour – America, birthplace of aviation, was now hopelessly behind even the smallest European nations – and partly to confirm that planes could stay up long enough to make long-distance flights.

The trick of the exercise, Chamberlin explained

afterwards, was to squeeze maximum mileage out of the plane by adjusting the throttle and fuel mixture to the point where the plane was just able to remain airborne – keeping it 'on starvation rations', as Chamberlin put it. When he and Acosta finally glided back to earth, shortly before one o'clock in the afternoon of their third day aloft, they were essentially flying on vapour. They had been continuously airborne for 51 hours, 11 minutes and 25 seconds, an advance of nearly six hours on the existing record.

They emerged grinning from their plane to the approving roar of a large crowd. (People really did gather in enormous numbers for almost any event in the 1920s.) The two triumphant pilots were tired and stiff – and very thirsty. It turned out that one of their ground crew, in a moment of excited distraction, had left their canteens filled with soapy water, so they had had nothing to drink for two days. Otherwise the flight was a great success – great enough to be the main story in the *New York Times* on Good Friday, 15 April. Across three columns the headline declared:

FLIERS SET RECORD OF 51 HOURS IN AIR;
DAY AND NIGHT WITHOUT FOOD OR WATER;
LAND WORN, BUT EAGER FOR PARIS FLIGHT

They had flown 4,100 miles – 500 miles more than the distance from New York to Paris. Just as significantly, they had managed to get airborne with 375 gallons of fuel, an enormous load for the time, and had used up just 1,200 feet of runway to do so. All this was extremely encouraging for those who wished to fly the Atlantic, and in the spring

15

of 1927 there were many, like Chamberlin and Acosta, who most assuredly did.

By a curiously ironic twist, the event that left America far behind the rest of the world in aviation was the very one that assured its dominance in so many other spheres: the First World War.

Before 1914, aeroplanes barely featured in military thinking. The French air corps, with three dozen planes, was larger than all the other air forces in the world put together. Germany, Britain, Italy, Russia, Japan and Austria all had no more than four planes in their fleets; the United States had just two. But with the outbreak of fighting, military commanders quickly saw how useful planes could be – for monitoring enemy troop movements, for directing artillery fire, and above all for providing a new direction and manner in which to kill people.

In the early days, bombs often were nothing more than wine bottles filled with petrol or kerosene, with a simple detonator attached, though a few pilots threw hand grenades and some for a time dropped specially made darts called flechettes which could pierce a helmet or otherwise bring pain and consternation to those in the trenches below. As always where killing is involved, technological progress was swift, and by 1918 aerial bombs of up to 2,200 pounds were being dropped. Germany alone rained down a million individual bombs, some 27,000 tons of explosives, in the course of the war. Bombing was not terribly accurate – a bomb dropped from ten thousand feet rarely hit its target and often missed by half a mile or more – but the psychological effect, wherever a large bomb fell, was considerable.

Heavy bomb loads required planes of ever greater size

and power, which in turn spurred the development of swifter, nimbler fighter craft to defend or attack them, which in further turn produced the celebrated dogfights that fired the imaginations of schoolboys and set the tone for aviation for a generation to come. The air war produced an insatiable need for planes. In four years, the four main combatant nations spent $1 billion – a staggering sum, nearly all borrowed from America – on their air fleets. From almost nothing, France in four years built up an aircraft industry that employed nearly 200,000 people and produced some 70,000 planes. Britain built 55,000 planes, Germany 48,000, and Italy 20,000 – quite an advance bearing in mind that only a few years earlier the entire world aviation industry consisted of two brothers in a bicycle shop in Ohio.

Up to 1914, the total number of people in the world who had been killed in aeroplanes was about a hundred. Now men died in their thousands. By the spring of 1917, the life expectancy of a British pilot was put at eight days. Altogether, in four years between 30,000 and 40,000 flyers were killed or injured to the point of incapacity. Training was not a great deal safer than combat. At least 15,000 men were killed or invalided in accidents in flight schools. American flyers were particularly disadvantaged. When the United States entered the war, in April 1917, not a single American military official had ever even seen a fighter air-craft, much less commanded one. When the explorer Hiram Bingham, discoverer of Machu Picchu but now a middle-aged professor at Yale, offered himself as an instructor, the army made him a lieutenant-colonel and put him in charge of the whole training programme, not because he had useful experience – he didn't – but simply because he knew how to

17

fly a plane. Many new pilots were taught by instructors who had only just been taught themselves.

America now made a huge but ultimately futile effort to catch up in aviation; Congress appropriated $600 million to build an air force. As Bingham wrote in his memoirs, 'When we entered the war, the Air Service had two small flying fields, 48 officers, 1,330 men, and 225 planes, not one of which was fit to fly over the lines. In the course of a year and a half, this Air Service grew to 50 flying fields, 20,500 officers, 175,000 men and 17,000 planes.' Unfortunately, almost none of those 17,000 planes reached Europe because nearly all available shipping was needed for troops. So American airmen, when they got to the front, mostly flew in borrowed, patched-up planes provided by the Allies, and thus they were sent into the most dangerous form of combat in modern times with next to no training in generally second-rate surplus planes against vastly more experienced enemies. Yet at no point was there a shortage of volunteer pilots on any side. The ability to climb to 13,000 feet, to fly at 130 miles an hour, to roll and dart and swoop through the air in deadly combat, was for many airmen thrilling to the point of addiction. The romance and glamour of it can scarcely be imagined now. Pilots were the most heroic figures of the age.

Then the war ended, and planes and aviators both were suddenly largely worthless. America terminated $100 million of aircraft orders at a stroke, and essentially lost all official interest in flying. Other nations scaled back nearly as severely. For aviators who wished to remain airborne, the options were stark and few. Many, lacking anything better to do, engaged in stunts. In Paris, the Galeries Lafayette department store, in a moment of unconsidered folly, offered a prize of 25,000 francs to anyone who could land a plane on its roof. A more foolhardy challenge could hardly be imagined: the roof was just thirty yards long and bounded by a three-foot-high balustrade, which added several perilous degrees of steepness to any landing on it. A former war ace named Jules Védrines decided nonetheless to have a try. Védrines placed men on the roof to grab the wings of his plane as it came in. The men succeeded in keeping the plane from tumbling off the roof and on to the festive throngs in the Place de l'Opéra below, but only at the cost of directing it into a brick shed housing the store's lift mechanisms. The plane was smashed to splinters, but Védrines stepped from the wreckage unscathed, like a magician from an amazing trick. Such luck, however, couldn't hold. Three months later he died in a crash while trying to fly, more conventionally, from Paris to Rome.

Védrines's death in a French field illustrated two awkward facts about aeroplanes: for all their improvements in speed and manoeuvrability, they were still dangerous devices and not much good for distances. Just a month after his crash, the US Navy unwittingly underscored the point when it sent three Curtiss flying boats on a hair-raisingly ill-conceived trip from Newfoundland to Portugal via the Azores. In readiness, the navy positioned sixty-six ships along the route to steam to the aid of any plane that got into trouble, which suggests that its own confidence in the exercise was perhaps less than total. It was as well that it took precautions. One of the planes ditched in the sea and had to be rescued before it even got to Newfoundland. The other two planes splashed down prematurely during the journey itself and had to be towed to the Azores; one of those sank en route. Of the three planes that set out, only one made it to Portugal, and that took eleven days. Had the purpose of the exercise been to show how unready for ocean flights aeroplanes were, it could not have been more successful.

Crossing the ocean in a single leap seemed a wholly unachievable ambition. So when two British airmen did just that, in the summer of 1919, it was quite a surprise to everyone, including, it seems, the airmen. Their names were Jack Alcock and Arthur Whitten (Teddy) Brown and they deserve to be a good deal more famous. Their flight was one of the most daring in history, but is sadly forgotten now. It wasn't particularly well noted at the time either.

Alcock, aged twenty-six, was the pilot and Brown, thirty-three, the navigator. Both men had grown up in Manchester, though Brown was the child of American parents. His father had been sent to Britain in the early 1900s to build a factory for Westinghouse, and the family had stayed on. Though Brown had never lived in America, he spoke with an American accent and only recently had given up his American citizenship. He and Alcock barely knew each other and had only flown together three times when they squeezed into the open cockpit of a frail and boxy Vickers Vimy aeroplane in June 1919 at St John's in Newfoundland and headed out over the forbidding grey void of the Atlantic.*

* The Vickers Vimy hangs in the Science Museum in London, but few notice it. A monument to Alcock and Brown, at Heathrow Airport, wasn't erected until thirty-five years after their flight. When I checked out Graham Wallace's classic account of the trip, *The Flight of Alcock & Brown, 14–15 June 1919*, from the London Library, I was the first person in seventeen years to do so.

Perhaps never have flyers braved greater perils in a less substantial craft. The Vickers Vimy was little more than a box-kite with a motor. For hours Alcock and Brown flew through the wildest weather – through rain and hail and driving snow. Lightning lit the clouds around them and winds tossed them violently in all directions. An exhaust pipe split and sent flames licking along the plane's fabric covering, to their understandable alarm. Six times Brown had to crawl out on to the wings to clear air intakes of ice with his bare hands. Much of the rest of the time he spent wiping Alcock's goggles since Alcock couldn't for a moment relax his grip on the controls. Flying through cloud and fog, they lost all orientation. Emerging into clear air at one point, they were astounded to find that they were just sixty feet above the water and flying *sideways*, at a 90-degree angle to the surface. In one of the few spells when Brown was able to navigate, he discovered that they had somehow turned round and were heading back to Canada. There really has never been a more hair-raising, seat-of-the-pants flight.

After sixteen hours of bouncing disorder, Ireland miraculously appeared beneath them, and Alcock crash-landed in a boggy field. They had flown 1,890 miles, only slightly more than half the distance from New York to Paris, but it was still an astounding achievement. They emerged unhurt from their mangled plane, but struggled to get anyone to grasp quite what they had just done. Word of their departure from Newfoundland had been delayed, so no one in Ireland was expecting their arrival, removing all sense of excitement and anticipation. The telegraph girl in Clifden, the nearest town, was not terribly good at her job, it seems, and could only manage to transmit short, mildly befuddled messages, adding to the confusion.

When Alcock and Brown managed to get back to England, they were given heroes' welcomes – medals were bestowed, the king gave them knighthoods – but they quickly returned to their quiet previous lives, and the world forgot all about them. Six months later, Alcock died in a flying accident in France when he crashed into a tree in fog. Brown never flew again. By 1927, when flying the Atlantic Ocean became an earnest dream, their names were hardly remembered.

Entirely coincidentally, at almost exactly the same time that Alcock and Brown were making their milestone flight, a businessman in New York who had no connection to aviation at all – he just liked planes – made an offer that transformed the world of flying and created what became known as the Great Atlantic Air Derby. The man's name was Raymond Orteig. He was from France originally, but was now a successful hotelier in New York. Inspired by the exploits of First World War aviators, Orteig offered a prize of $25,000 to the first person or persons who could fly non-stop from New York to Paris, or vice versa, in the next five years. It was a generous offer but an entirely safe one since it was patently beyond the scope of any aeroplane to cover such a span in a single flight. As Alcock and Brown painfully proved, just flying half that distance was at the very bounds of technology and good fortune.

No one took up Orteig's offer, but in 1924 he renewed it, and now it was beginning to seem possible. The development of air-cooled engines – America's one outstanding contribution to aviation technology in the period – gave planes greater range and reliability. The world also had an abundance of talented, often brilliant, nearly always

severely underemployed aeronautic engineers and design-
ers who were eager to show what they could do. For many,
winning the Orteig Prize wasn't merely the best challenge
around, it was the only one.

The first to try was the great French aviator René Fonck,
in partnership with the Russian émigré designer Igor
Sikorsky. No one needed the success more than Sikorsky
did. He had been a leading aeroplane designer in Europe,
but in 1917 had lost everything in the Russian Revolution
and fled to America. Now, in 1926, at the age of thirty-
seven, he supported himself by teaching chemistry and
physics to fellow immigrants and by building planes when
he could.

Sikorsky loved a well-appointed aeroplane – one of his
pre-war models included a washroom and 'promenade
deck' (a somewhat generous description, it must be said)
– and the plane he now built for the Atlantic flight was the
plushest of all. It had leather fittings, a sofa and chairs,
cooking facilities, even a bed – everything that a crew of
four could possibly want in the way of comfort and
elegance. The idea was to show that the Atlantic could not
simply be crossed, but crossed in style. Sikorsky was
supported by a syndicate of investors who called themselves the Argonauts.

For a pilot they chose René Fonck, France's greatest war
ace. Fonck had shot down seventy-five German planes – he
claimed it was over 120 – an achievement all the more
remarkable for the fact that he had flown only for the last
two years of the war. He spent the first two digging ditches
before persuading the French air service to give him a
chance at flight school. Fonck was adroit at knocking
down enemy planes, but even more incomparably skilled

23

at eluding damage himself. In all his battles, Fonck's own plane was struck by an enemy bullet just once. Unfortunately, the skills and temperament needed for combat are not necessarily the ones required to fly an aeroplane successfully across a large and empty sea.

Fonck now showed no common sense in regard to preparations. First, he insisted on going before the plane was adequately tested, to Sikorsky's despair. Next, and even worse, he grossly overloaded it. He packed extra fuel, an abundance of emergency equipment, two kinds of radios, spare clothes, presents for friends and supporters, and lots to eat and drink, including wines and champagne. He even packed a dinner of terrapin, turkey and duck to be prepared and eaten in celebration after reaching Paris, as if France could not be counted on to feed them. Altogether the plane when loaded weighed 28,000 pounds, far more than it was designed, or probably able, to lift.

On 20 September came news that two Frenchmen, a Major Pierre Weiss and a Lieutenant Challé, had flown in a single leap from Paris to Bandar Abbas in Persia (now Iran), a distance of 3,230 miles, almost as far as from New York to Paris. Elated at this demonstration of the innate superiority of French aviators, Fonck insisted on immediate preparation for departure.

The following morning, before a large crowd, the Sikorsky – which, such was the rush, hadn't even been given a name – was rolled into position and its three mighty silver engines started. Almost from the moment it began lumbering down the runway things didn't look right. Airfields in the 1920s were essentially just that – fields – and Roosevelt Field was no better than most. Because the plane needed an especially long run, it had to cross two dirt service roads, neither of which had been rolled smooth – a painful reminder of how imprudently overhasty the entire operation was. As the Sikorsky jounced at speed over the second of the tracks, a section of landing gear fell off, damaging the left rudder, and a detached wheel went bouncing off into oblivion. Fonck pressed on nonetheless, opening the throttle and continually gaining speed until he was going almost fast enough to get airborne. Almost, alas, was not good enough. Thousands of hands went to mouths as the plane reached the runway's end, never having left the ground even fractionally, and tumbled clumsily over a twenty-foot embankment, vanishing from view.

For some moments, the watching crowds stood in a stunned and eerie silence. Birdsong could be heard, giving an air of peacefulness obviously at odds with the catastrophe just witnessed. Then awful normality reasserted itself with an enormous gaseous explosion as 2,850 gallons of aviation fuel combusted, throwing a fireball fifty feet into the air. Fonck and his navigator, Lawrence Curtin, somehow managed to scramble free, but the other two crew members were incinerated in their seats. The incident horrified the flying fraternity. The rest of the world was horrified too, but at the same time morbidly eager for more.

For Sikorsky, the blow was economic as well as emotional. The plane had cost more than $100,000 to build, but his backers had so far paid only a fraction of that, and now, the plane gone, they declined to pay the rest. Sikorsky would eventually find a new career building helicopters, but for now he and Fonck, their plane and their dreams were finished.

For the time being, it was too late for other ocean flyers as well. Weather patterns meant that flights over the North Atlantic were only safely possible for a few months each year. Everyone would have to wait now until the following spring.

Spring came. America had three teams in the running, all with excellent planes and experienced crews. The names of the planes alone – *Columbia, America, American Legion* – showed how much this had become a matter of national pride. The initial front-runner was the *Columbia*, the monoplane in which Chamberlin and Acosta had set their endurance record just before Easter. But two days after that milestone flight, an even more impressive, and vastly more expensive, plane was wheeled out of its factory at Hasbrouck Heights, New Jersey. This was the *America*, which carried three powerful, roaring engines and had space for a crew of four. The leader of the *America* team was 37-year-old naval Commander Richard Evelyn Byrd, a man seemingly born to be a hero. Suave and handsome, he came from one of America's oldest and most distinguished families. The Byrds had been dominant in Virginia since the time of George Washington. Byrd's brother Harry was governor of the state. Richard Byrd himself was already a celebrated adventurer in 1927. The previous spring, with the pilot Floyd Bennett, he had made the first flight in an aeroplane over the North Pole (though in fact, as we will see, there have long been doubts that he actually did so).

Byrd's present expedition was also by far the best funded and most self-proclaimedly patriotic, thanks to Rodman Wanamaker, owner of department stores in

Philadelphia and New York, who had put up $500,000 of his own money and gathered additional, unspecified funding from other leading businessmen. Through Wanamaker, Byrd now controlled the leasehold on Roosevelt Field, the only airfield in New York with a runway long enough to accommodate any plane built to fly the Atlantic. Without Byrd's permission, no one else could even consider going for the Orteig Prize.

Wanamaker insisted that the operation be all-American. This was a little ironic because the plane's designer, a strong-willed and difficult fellow named Anthony Fokker, was Dutch and the plane itself had been partly built in Holland. Even worse, though rarely mentioned, was that Fokker had spent the war years in Germany building planes for the Germans. He had even taken out German citizenship. As part of his commitment to German air superiority, he had invented the synchronized machine gun, which enabled bullets to pass between the spinning blades of a propeller. Before this, amazingly, all that aircraft manufacturers could do was wrap armour plating around the propellers and hope that any bullets that struck the blades weren't deflected backwards. The only alternative was to mount the guns away from the propeller, but that meant pilots couldn't reload them or clear jams, which were frequent. Fokker's gun gave German flyers a deadly advantage for some time, and made him probably responsible for more Allied deaths than any other individual. Now, however, he insisted that he had never actually been on Germany's side. 'My own country remained neutral throughout the entire course of the great conflict, and in a definite sense, so did I,' he wrote in his post-war autobiography, *Flying Dutchman*. He never explained in what sense he thought himself neutral, no doubt because there wasn't any sense in which he was.

Byrd never liked Fokker and now in April 1927 their enmity became complete. Just before six in the evening, Fokker and three members of the Byrd team – the co-pilot Floyd Bennett, the navigator George Noville and Byrd himself – eagerly crowded into the cockpit. Fokker took the controls for this maiden flight. The plane took off smoothly and performed faultlessly in the air, but as the *America* came in to land it became evident that it was impelled by the inescapable burden of gravity to tip forward and come down nose first. The problem was that all the weight was up front and there was no way for any of the four men on board to move to the back to redistribute the load because a large fuel tank entirely filled the middle part of the fuselage.

Fokker circled around the airfield while he considered his options (or, rather, considered that he had no options) and came in to land as gingerly as he could. What exactly happened next became at once a matter of heated dispute. Byrd maintained that Fokker abandoned the controls and made every effort to save himself, leaving the others to their fates. Fokker vehemently denied this. Jumping out of a crashing plane was not possible, he said. 'Maybe Byrd was excited and imagined this,' Fokker wrote with pained sarcasm in his autobiography. Surviving film footage of the crash, which is both brief and grainy, shows the plane landing roughly, tipping on to its nose and flopping on to its back, all in a continuous motion, like a child doing a somersault. Fokker, like all the other occupants, could have done nothing but brace and hold on.

In the footage, the damage looks slight, but inside all

was violent chaos. A piece of propeller ripped through the cockpit and pierced Bennett's chest. He was bleeding profusely and critically injured. Noville, painfully mindful of the fire that had killed two of Fonck's men, punched his way out through the plane's fabric covering. Byrd followed and was so furious with Fokker that he reportedly failed to notice that his left arm had snapped like a twig and was dangling in a queasily unnatural way. Fokker, uninjured, stood and shouted back at Byrd, blaming him for overloading the plane on its first flight.

The episode introduced serious rancour into the Byrd camp and set back the team's plans by weeks. Bennett was rushed to a hospital at Hackensack, where he lay close to death for the next ten days. He was lost to the team for good. The plane had to be almost completely rebuilt – and indeed extensively redesigned to allow the weight to be distributed more sensibly. For the time being, the Byrd team was out of the running.

That left two other American planes, but fate, alas, was not on their sides either. On 24 April, eight days after the Byrd crash, Clarence Chamberlin was prevailed upon to take the nine-year-old daughter of *Columbia*'s owner, Charles A. Levine, and the daughter of an official from the Brooklyn Chamber of Commerce up for a short flight above Long Island. Chamberlin's young passengers got a more exciting flight than they expected because the landing gear fell apart during takeoff, leaving one wheel behind, which meant he had only one wheel to land on. Chamberlin made a nearly perfect landing without injury to himself or his passengers, but the wing hit the ground and the damage to the plane was sufficient to set back the *Columbia*'s plans considerably.

Hopes now turned to two popular naval officers at the Hampton Roads Naval Airbase in Virginia, Noel Davis and Stanton H. Wooster. Davis and Wooster were smart, able aviators, and their plane, a Keystone Pathfinder built in Bristol, Pennsylvania, was gleamingly new and powered by three Wright Whirlwind engines. What the outside world didn't know was that upon delivery the plane weighed 1,150 pounds more than it was supposed to. Davis and Wooster took it up in a series of test flights, each time cautiously increasing the fuel load, and so far had experienced no problems. On 26 April, two days after Chamberlin's emergency landing, they scheduled their final test flight. This time they would take off with a full load of 17,000 pounds, nearly a quarter more than the plane had attempted to lift before.

Among those who came to cheer them on were Davis's young wife, their infant son in her arms, and Wooster's fiancée. This time the plane struggled to get airborne. At length it rose into the air, but not enough to clear a line of trees at the far side of a neighbouring field. Wooster banked sharply. The plane stalled and fell to earth with a sickening crash. Davis and Wooster died instantly. America, for the time being at least, was out of contenders.

To make matters worse, things were going rather well for foreigners. While the American flyers were investing all their energies in land planes, the Italians saw seaplanes as the way of the future. Seaplanes had much to commend them. They eliminated the need for landing fields since they could put down on any convenient body of water. Seaplanes could island-hop their way across oceans, follow rivers deep into jungly continents, stop at coastal communities with no clearings for airstrips, and otherwise go where conventional aeroplanes could not.

No one demonstrated the versatility and usefulness of seaplanes better than the Italian aviator Francesco de Pinedo. The son of a lawyer from Naples, Pinedo was well educated and headed for a career in the professions when he discovered flying. It became his life. In 1925, accompanied by a mechanic named Ernesto Campanelli, Pinedo flew from Italy to Australia and back via Japan. They did it in comparatively short hops, always sticking close to land, and the trip took seven months to complete, but it was still a voyage of 34,000 miles, epic by any standards. Pinedo became a national hero. Benito Mussolini, who had come to power in 1922, showered him with honours. Mussolini was enthralled by flight – by its speed and daring and promise of technological superiority. All of those qualities were magically personified, in his view, by the stout little Neapolitan, who became his emissary of the air.

Time magazine, four years old and enchanted with stereotype, described Pinedo in the spring of 1927 as a 'swart Fascist ace'. (Almost anyone from south of the Alps was 'swart' in *Time*.) Pinedo was in fact not especially swart and not at all an ace – he had spent the war flying reconnaissance missions – but he was indeed a loyal fascist. With his black shirt, brilliantined hair, thrusting jaw and habit of standing with his fists pinned to his hips Pinedo was, to an almost comical degree, the very model of a strutting, self-satisfied fascist. This was not a problem to anyone so long as he stayed in Europe, but in the spring of 1927 he came to America. Worse, he did it in the most heroic way possible.

While America's Atlantic hopefuls were struggling to

get their planes ready, Pinedo efficiently made his way to the United States via coastal Africa, the Cape Verde Islands, South America and the Caribbean. It was the first westward crossing by aeroplane of the Atlantic Ocean, a feat in itself, even if it was not done in a single bound. Pinedo reached the United States in late March at New Orleans and began a lavish, if not always wholly welcome, progress around the country.

It was hard to decide what to make of him. On the one hand, he was unquestionably a gifted flyer and entitled to a parade or two. On the other, he was a representative of an obnoxious form of government that was admired by many Italian immigrants, who were thus deemed to represent a threat to the American way of life. At a time when America's air efforts were suffering one setback after another, Pinedo's prolonged victory lap around the country began to seem just a little insensitive.

After New Orleans, Pinedo proceeded west to California, stopping at Galveston, San Antonio, Hot Springs and other communities along the way to refuel and receive ovations from small bands of supporters and a rather larger number of the merely curious. On 6 April, en route to a civic reception in San Diego, he landed at a reservoir called Roosevelt Lake in the desert east of Phoenix. Even in this lonely spot a crowd gathered. As the observers respectfully watched the plane being serviced, a youth named John Thomason lit a cigarette and unthinkingly tossed the match on the water. The water, coated with oil and aviation fuel, ignited with a mighty *whoompf* that made everyone scatter. Within seconds, Pinedo's beloved plane was engulfed in flames and workmen were swimming for their lives.

Pinedo, having lunch at a lakeside hotel, looked up from his meal to see smoke where his plane should be. The plane was entirely destroyed but for the engine, which sank to the lake bottom sixty feet below. The Italian press, already hypersensitive to anti-fascist sentiment in America, concluded that this was an act of treacherous sabotage. 'Vile Crime against Fascism', one paper cried in a headline. 'Odious Act of Anti-Fascists', echoed another. America's ambassador to Italy, Henry P. Fletcher, made matters even worse by dashing off a letter of apology to Mussolini in which he described the fire as an 'act of criminal folly' and promised that the 'guilty will be discovered and severely punished'. For days afterwards, a *Times* correspondent reported from Rome, the citizens of Italy talked of little else but this catastrophic setback to 'their hero, their superman, their demigod, de Pinedo'. Eventually, all sides calmed down and accepted that the act was an accident, but suspicions simmered and henceforth Pinedo, his crew and his possessions were guarded by menacing *Fascisti* volunteers armed with stilettos and truncheons.

Pinedo left his lieutenants to haul the dripping engine from the lake and get it dried out while he headed east to New York to await delivery of a substitute plane from Italy that Mussolini promised to dispatch at once.

He could have no idea of it, of course, but his troubles, in life and in the air, had only just begun.

The world's attention moved to Paris, where at dawn on 8 May two slightly ageing men in bulky flying suits emerged from an administration building at Le Bourget airfield to the respectful applause of well-wishers. The men, Captain Charles Nungesser and Captain François

Coli, walked stiffly and a little self-consciously. Their heavy gear, which was necessary because they were about to fly 3,600 miles in an open cockpit, made them look almost uncannily like little boys in snowsuits.

Many of their well-wishers had been out all night and were still in evening dress. The *New York Times* likened the scene to a garden party. Among those who had come to see them off were Nungesser's pal the boxer Georges Carpentier and the singer Maurice Chevalier, with his mistress, a celebrated chanteuse and film actress who went by the single sultry name of Mistinguett.

Nungesser and Coli were war heroes, and normally sauntered about with the smooth and cocky air of men at ease with danger, but today was a little different. Coli, at forty-six, was a venerable figure: not many airmen were still alive and flying at forty-six. He wore a rakish black monocle over a missing right eye, one of five wounds he had sustained in combat. This was nothing compared with Nungesser's extravagant affinity for injury, however. No one in the war was injured more; or at least got up again afterwards. Nungesser had so many injuries that after the war he listed them all on his business card. They included: six jaw fractures (four upper, two lower); fractured skull and palate; bullet wounds to mouth and ear; dislocations of wrist, clavicle, ankle and knees; loss of teeth; shrapnel wound to upper body; multiple concussions; multiple leg fractures; multiple internal injuries; and contusions 'too numerous to list'. He was also gravely injured in a car crash in which a companion died. Often he was so banged up that he had to be carried to his plane by crew members and gently inserted into the cockpit. Despite his injuries, Nungesser shot down forty-four planes (he claimed many more), a number exceeded among French aviators only by René Fonck, and received so many medals that he all but clanked when he walked. He listed those on his business card, too.

As with so many airmen, armistice left him at something of a loss. He worked for a time as a gaucho in Argentina, gave flying demonstrations in America with his friend the Marquis de Charette and starred in a movie called *The Sky-Raiders*, filmed at Roosevelt Field in New York, where the Orteig Prize competitors were gathering now.

With his Gallic charm and chestful of medals, Nungesser proved irresistible to women, and in the spring of 1923 after a whirlwind romance he became engaged to a young New York socialite with the unimprovably glorious name of Consuelo Hatmaker. Miss Hatmaker, who was just nineteen, came from a long line of lively women. Her mother, the former Nellie Sands, was a celebrated beauty who proved too great a handful for three husbands, including the eponymous Mr Hatmaker, whom she discarded in a divorce in 1921. This bewildered but well-meaning gentleman opposed his daughter's marriage to Captain Nungesser on the grounds – not unreasonable on the face of it – that Nungesser was destitute, broken-bodied, something of a bounder, unemployable except in time of war, and French. In this, however, Mr Hatmaker was unsupported by his former wife, who not only endorsed the marriage, but announced that she would at the same time marry her own latest paramour, Captain William Waters, an American of amiable anonymity who seems to have aroused the passing interest of the world just twice in his life: once when he married Mrs Hatmaker and once when they divorced a few years later. So mother and daughter were wed in a joint ceremony in Dinard, in Brittany, not far from where Charles Nungesser would get his last glimpse of his native soil, in the spring of 1927.

Consuelo and Charles's marriage was not a success. She declared at the outset that she would not live in France, while he disdained to live anywhere else. They parted swiftly and were divorced in 1926. But Nungesser clearly had second thoughts because he now mused aloud to friends that a heroic gesture might help to reunite him with the luscious Consuelo and her no less luscious fortune. Nungesser was aided in his ambitions by the misfortunes of Fonck, whose crash the previous autumn had helped Nungesser persuade Pierre Levasseur, an aircraft manufacturer, to provide him with a plane, as a restorative to French pride. A prize endowed by a Frenchman and won by French flyers in a French machine would obviously be a boost to French prestige. Coli gladly joined the enterprise as navigator. They called their plane *L'Oiseau Blanc* – the *White Bird* – and painted it white so that it would be easier to find if it came down in the sea.

Starting in Paris was a piece of patriotic vanity that many were certain would prove their undoing. It would mean flying into prevailing winds that would slow their speed and cut their fuel efficiency dramatically. The engine was a water-cooled Lorraine-Dietrich, the same make Pinedo had used to fly to Australia, so it had a pedigree, but it was not an engine built with long ocean crossings in mind. In any case, they could carry no more than about forty hours' worth of fuel, which left them almost no margin for error. Nungesser seemed to know that what they hoped to achieve was probably not possible. As he moved around his plane on 8 May he smiled weakly at well-wishers and seemed distracted. To boost his alertness he accepted an intravenous injection of caffeine, which cannot have done his nerves any good.

Coli by contrast appeared entirely relaxed, but agreed with Nungesser that the plane was overloaded and should be lightened. They decided to discard most of their rations, as well as their life jackets and an inflatable dinghy. If forced down, they had nothing now to aid their survival but a contraption for distilling seawater, a length of fishing line and a hook, and a small, curious assortment of food: three cans of tuna and one of sardines, a dozen bananas, a kilo of sugar, a flask of hot coffee, and brandy. Even after unloading supplies, their plane weighed almost 11,000 pounds. It had never taken off with that much weight before.

When preparations were complete, Coli and his wife embraced, then he and Nungesser waved to their well-wishers and clambered aboard. It was 5.15 a.m. when they assumed their takeoff position. The runway at Le Bourget was two miles long and they would need nearly all of it. The plane crossed the grass expanse with fearful sluggishness at first, but slowly gathered speed. After some time, it lifted briefly, but came down again and bouncily proceeded another three hundred yards before finally, and agonizingly, barely getting airborne. The chief engineer, who had run along beside the plane much of the way, fell to his knees and wept. Just taking off was a unique triumph. No plane in the Atlantic race had done even that before now. The crowd roared its approval. The *White Bird* climbed with painful slowness into the milky haze of the western sky and set a course for the English Channel. One hour and twenty-seven minutes later, at 6.48 a.m., Nungesser and Coli reached the chalky seacliffs of Normandy at Étretat. A squadron of four escort planes tipped their wings in salute and peeled away, and *L'Oiseau Blanc* flew off alone in the direction of the British Isles and the cold Atlantic beyond.

All France waited breathlessly.

The following day came the joyous news that the two airmen had made it. 'Nungesser est arrivê,' the Parisian newspaper *L'Intransigeant* announced excitedly (so excitedly that it put a circumflex rather than an acute accent on 'arrivé'). A rival publication, *Paris Presse*, quoted Nungesser's first words to the American people upon landing. According to this report, Nungesser had made a smooth and stylish landing in New York Harbor and brought the plane to a halt before the Statue of Liberty (also from France, as the paper proudly noted). Once ashore the two aviators were greeted by a deliriously impressed and jubilant city and showered with ticker tape as they paraded up Fifth Avenue.

In Paris, the happy news all but stopped the city. Bells rang out. Strangers weepily embraced. Crowds gathered around anyone who had a newspaper. Levasseur sent a telegram of congratulations. At Coli's mother's home in Marseilles, champagne was broken out. 'I knew my boy would do it because he told me he would,' Coli's mother said, tears of joy and relief shining on her cheeks.

Soon, however, it emerged that the two news stories were not just mistaken but sadly imaginary. Nungesser and Coli had not arrived in New York at all. They were in fact missing and feared lost.

An enormous ocean manhunt at once swung into action. Naval ships were dispatched and merchant vessels instructed to keep a sharp lookout. The navy dirigible USS *Los Angeles* was ordered to search from the air. The passenger liner *France*, en route to New York from Le Havre, received instructions from the French government to take a more northerly course than normal, despite the risk of icebergs, in the hope of coming across the floating *White Bird*. At Roosevelt Field, Rodman Wanamaker offered $25,000 to anyone who could find the missing aviators dead or alive.

For a day or so people clung to the hope that Nungesser and Coli would at any moment putter triumphantly into view, but every passing hour counted against them, and now the weather, already grim, turned dire. Dense fog settled over the eastern Atlantic and blanketed the North American seaboard from Labrador to the mid-Atlantic states. At Ambrose Light, a floating lighthouse off the mouth of New York Harbor, the keeper reported that thousands of birds, lost on their annual migration north, were sheltering bleakly on every surface they could cling to. At Sandy Hook, New Jersey, four searchlights endlessly but pointlessly swept the skies, their beams unable to penetrate the enshrouding murk. In Newfoundland, temperatures plunged and a light snow fell.

Unaware that the flyers had jettisoned reserve supplies at the last moment, commentators noted that Nungesser and Coli had packed enough food to sustain them for weeks, and that their plane was designed to stay afloat indefinitely. (It wasn't.) Many people took hope from the fact that two years earlier an American aviator,

Commander John Rodgers, and three crewmen spent nine days floating in the Pacific, presumed dead, before being rescued by a submarine after failing to fly from California to Hawaii.

Rumours now put Nungesser and Coli all over the place – in Iceland, in Labrador, scooped from the sea by any of several passing ships. Three people in Ireland reported seeing them, which gave some people heart while others reflected that three sightings was not many in a nation of three million. Sixteen people in Newfoundland, mostly in or around Harbour Grace, reported hearing or seeing a plane, though none could give a positive identification, and other, similar reports drifted in from Nova Scotia, Maine, New Hampshire and as far south as Port Washington, Long Island.

A Canadian trapper came in with a message signed by Nungesser, but on examination the message proved to be suspiciously illiterate and in a hand quite unlike Nungesser's but very like the trapper's own. Messages in bottles were found, too, and were still turning up as late as 1934. The one thing that wasn't found was any trace of the *White Bird* or its occupants.

In France a rumour circulated that the US Weather Bureau had withheld crucial information from the Frenchmen, to keep the advantage with the American flyers. Myron Herrick, the American ambassador, cabled Washington that an American flight at this time would be unwise.

It was altogether a wretched week for French aviation. At the same time as Nungesser and Coli's flight from Le Bourget, another ambitious French flight – now forgotten by the rest of the world and hardly noticed even then – got under way when three aviators, Pierre de Saint-Roman, Hervé Mouneyres and Louis Petit, took off from Senegal, on the west coast of Africa, and headed for Brazil. When just 120 miles from the Brazilian coast, they radioed the happy news that they would be arriving in just over an hour, or so a correspondent for *Time* magazine reported. That was the last anyone ever heard from them. No wreckage was ever found.

In nine months, eleven people had died in the quest to fly the Atlantic. It was just at this point, when nothing was going right for anyone, that a gangly young man known as Slim flew in from the west and announced his plan to fly the ocean alone. His name was Charles Lindbergh.

A most extraordinary summer was about to begin.

May
The Kid

———

'In the spring of '27, something bright
and alien flashed across the sky.'

F. Scott Fitzgerald, *My Lost City*

Chapter 1

TEN DAYS BEFORE he became so famous that crowds would form around any building that contained him and waiters would fight over a corncob left on his dinner plate, no one had heard of Charles Lindbergh. The *New York Times* had mentioned him once, in the context of the coming Atlantic flights. It had misspelled his name.

The news that transfixed the nation as spring gave way to summer in 1927 was of a gruesome murder in a modest family home on Long Island, coincidentally quite close to Roosevelt Field, where the Atlantic flyers were now gathering. The newspapers, much excited, called it the Sash Weight Murder Case. The story was this:

Late on the night of 20 March 1927, as Mr and Mrs Albert Snyder slept side by side in twin beds in their house on 222nd Street in a quiet, middle-class neighbourhood of Queens Village, Mrs Snyder heard noises in the upstairs hallway. Going to investigate, she found a large man – a 'giant', she told police – just outside her bedroom door. He was speaking in a foreign accent to another man, whom she could not see. Before Mrs Snyder could react, the giant

seized her and beat her so roughly that she was left unconscious for six hours. Then he and his confederate went
to Mr Snyder's bed, strangled the poor man with picture
wire and stove in his head with a sash weight from a
window. It was the sash weight that fired the public's
imagination and gave the case its name. The two villains
then turned out drawers all over the house and fled with
Mrs Snyder's jewels, but they left a clue to their identity in
the form of an Italian-language newspaper on a table
downstairs.

The *New York Times* the next day was fascinated but
confused. In a big page-one headline it reported:

ART EDITOR IS SLAIN IN BED;
WIFE TIED, HOME SEARCHED;
MOTIVE MYSTIFIES POLICE

The story noted that a Dr Vincent Juster from St Mary
Immaculate Hospital had examined Mrs Snyder and
couldn't find any bump on her that would explain her six
hours of unconsciousness. Indeed, he couldn't find any
injuries on her at all. Perhaps, he suggested tentatively, it
was the trauma of the event rather than actual injury that
accounted for her prolonged collapse.

Police detectives by this time, however, were more
suspicious than confused. For one thing, the Snyder house
showed no sign of forced entry, and in any case it was an
oddly modest target for murderous jewel thieves. The
detectives found it curious, too, that Albert Snyder had
slept through a violent scuffle just outside his door. The
Snyders' nine-year-old daughter, Lorraine, in a room across

the hall, had also heard nothing. It also seemed strange that burglars would break into a house and evidently pause to read an anarchist newspaper before placing it neatly on a table and proceeding upstairs. Oddest of all, Mrs Snyder's bed – the one from which she had arisen to investigate the noise in the hallway – was tidily made, as if it had not been slept in. She was unable to account for this, citing her concussion. As the detectives puzzled over these anomalies, one of them idly lifted a corner of the mattress on Mrs Snyder's bed and there revealed the jewels that she had reported stolen.

All eyes turned to Mrs Snyder. She met their gazes uncertainly, then broke down and confessed the crime – but blamed it all on a brute named Judd Gray, her secret lover. Mrs Snyder was placed under arrest, a search was begun for Judd Gray, and the newspaper-reading public of America was about to become uncommonly excited.

The 1920s was a great time for reading altogether – very possibly the peak decade for reading in American life. Soon it would be overtaken by the passive distractions of radio, but for the moment reading remained for most people the principal method for filling idle time. Each year, American publishers produced 110 million books, more than ten thousand separate titles, double the number of ten years before. For those who felt daunted by such a welter of literary possibility, a helpful new phenomenon, the book club, had just made its debut. The Book-of-the-Month Club was founded in 1926 and was followed the next year by the Literary Guild. Both were immediately successful. Authors were venerated in a way that seems scarcely possible now. When Sinclair Lewis returned

47

home to Minnesota to work on his novel *Elmer Gantry* (published in the spring of 1927), people came from miles around just to look at him.

Magazines boomed, too. Advertising revenues leapt 500 per cent in the decade, and many publications of lasting importance made their debut: *Reader's Digest* in 1922, *Time* in 1923, the *American Mercury* and *Smart Set* in 1924, the *New Yorker* in 1925. *Time* was perhaps the most immediately influential. Founded by two former Yale classmates, Henry Luce and Briton Hadden, it was very popular but wildly inaccurate. It described Charles Nungesser, for instance, as having 'lost an arm, a leg, a chin' during the war, which was not merely incorrect in all particulars but visibly so since Nungesser could be seen every day in newspaper photographs with a full set of limbs and an incontestably bechinned face. *Time* was noted for its repetitious devotion to certain words – 'swart', 'nimble', 'gimlet-eyed' – and to squashed neologisms like 'cinemaddict' and 'cinemactress'. It also had a fondness for odd, distorted phrases, so that 'in the nick of time' became, without embarrassment, 'in time's nick'. In particular it had a curious Germanic affection for inverting normal word order and packing as many nouns, adjectives and adverbs as possible into a sentence before bringing in a verb – or as Wolcott Gibbs put it in a famous *New Yorker* profile of Luce, 'Backward ran the sentences until reeled the mind.' Despite all their up-to-the-minute swagger, Luce and Hadden were deeply conservative. They would not, for instance, employ women for any job above the level of secretary or office assistant.

Above all, the 1920s was a golden age for newspapers. Newspaper sales in the decade rose by about a fifth, to 36 million copies a day – or 1.4 newspapers for every house-hold. New York City alone had twelve daily papers, and almost all other cities worthy of the name had at least two or three. More than this, in many cities readers could now get their news from a new, revolutionary type of publi-cation that completely changed people's expectations of what daily news should be – the tabloid. Tabloids focused on crime, sport and celebrity gossip, and in so doing gave all three an importance considerably beyond any they had enjoyed before. A study in 1927 showed that tabloids devoted between a quarter and a third of their space to crime reports, up to ten times more than the serious papers did. It was because of their influence that the quiet but messy murder of a man like Albert Snyder could become national news.

The tabloid, both as a format and as a way of distilling news down to its salacious essence, had been around for a quarter of a century in England, but no one had thought to try it in the United States until two young members of the *Chicago Tribune* publishing family, Robert R. McCormick and his cousin Joseph Patterson, saw London's *Daily Mirror* while serving in England during the First World War and decided to offer something similar at home when peace came. The result was the *Illustrated Daily News*, launched in New York in June 1919, price 2 cents. The concept was not an immediate hit – circulation at one point fell to 11,000 – but gradually the *Daily News* built a devoted following and by the mid-twenties it was far and away the best-selling newspaper in the country with a circulation of one million, more than double that of the *New York Times*.

Such success inevitably inspired imitators. First came

the *New York Daily Mirror* from William Randolph Hearst in June 1924, followed three months later by the wondrously dreadful *Evening Graphic*. The *Graphic* was the creation of an eccentric, bushy-haired businessman named Bernarr Macfadden, who had started life rather more prosaically some fifty years earlier as a Missouri farm boy named Bernard MacFadden. Macfadden, as he now styled himself, was a man of strong and exotic beliefs. He didn't like doctors, lawyers or clothing. He was powerfully devoted to body-building, vegetarianism, the rights of commuters to a decent railroad service, and getting naked. He and his wife frequently bemused their neighbours in Englewood, New Jersey – among them Dwight Morrow, a figure of some centrality to this story, as will become apparent – by exercising naked on the lawn. Macfadden's commitment to healthfulness was so total that when one of his daughters died of a heart condition he remarked: 'It's better she's gone. She'd only have disgraced me.' Well into his eighties he could be seen walking around Manhattan carrying a 40-pound bag of sand on his back as a way of keeping fit. He lived to be eighty-seven.

As a businessman, he seems to have dedicated his life to the proposition that where selling to the public is concerned no idea is too stupid. He built three separate fortunes. The first was as the inventor of a cult science he called Physcultopathy, which featured strict adherence to his principles of vegetarianism and strength through body-building, with forays into nakedness for those who dared. The movement produced a chain of successful health farms and related publications. In 1919, as an outgrowth of the latter, Macfadden came up with an even more inspired invention: the confession magazine. *True Story*, the flagship of this side of his operations, soon had monthly sales of 2.2 million. All the stories in *True Story* were candid and juicy, with 'a yeasty undercurrent of sexual excitation', in the words of one satisfied observer. It was Macfadden's proud boast that not a word in *True Story* was fabricated. This claim caused Macfadden a certain amount of financial discomfort when a piece in 1927 called 'The Revealing Kiss', set in Scranton, Pennsylvania, turned out, by unfortunate chance, to contain the names of eight respectable citizens of that fair city. They sued, and Macfadden was forced to admit that *True Story*'s stories were not in fact true at all and never had been.

When tabloids became the rage, Macfadden launched the *Graphic*. Its most distinguishing feature was that it had almost no attachment to truth or even, often, a recognizable reality. It conducted imaginary interviews with people it had not met and ran stories by figures who could not possibly have written them. When Rudolph Valentino died in 1926, it produced a series of articles by him from beyond the grave. The *Graphic* became famous for a form of illustration of its own invention called the 'composograph', in which the faces of newsworthy figures were superimposed on the bodies of models who had been posed on sets to create arresting tableaux. The most celebrated of these visual creations came during annulment proceedings, earlier in 1927, between Edward W. 'Daddy' Browning and his young and dazzlingly erratic bride, affectionately known to all as Peaches, when the *Graphic* ran a photo showing (without any real attempt at plausibility) Peaches standing naked in the witness box. The *Graphic* sold an extra 250,000 copies that day. The *New Yorker* called the *Graphic* a 'grotesque fungus', but it was a phenomenally successful fungus. By 1927, its circulation was nearing 600,000.

For conventional newspapers, these were serious and worrying numbers. Most responded by becoming conspicuously more like tabloids themselves, in spirit if not presentation. Even the *New York Times*, though still devotedly solemn and grey, found room for plenty of juicy stories throughout the decade and covered them with prose that was often nearly as feverish. So now when a murder like that of Albert Snyder came along, the result across all newspapers was something like a frenzy.

It hardly mattered that the perpetrators were spectacularly inept – so much so that the writer and journalist Damon Runyon dubbed it the Dumbbell Murder Case – and that they were not particularly attractive or imaginative. It was enough that the case involved lust, infidelity, a heartless woman and a sash weight. These were the things that sold newspapers. The Snyder–Gray case received more column inches of coverage than any other crime of the era, and would not be exceeded for column inches until the trial of Bruno Hauptmann for the kidnapping of Charles Lindbergh's baby in 1935. In terms of its effect on popular culture, even the Lindbergh kidnapping couldn't touch it.

Trials in 1920s America were often amazingly speedy. Gray and Snyder were arraigned, indicted by a grand jury and in the dock barely a month after their arrest. A carnival atmosphere descended on the Queens County Court House, a building of classical grandeur in Long Island City. A hundred and thirty newspapers from across the nation and as far afield as Norway sent reporters. Western Union installed the biggest switchboard it had ever built – bigger than any used for a presidential convention or World Series. Outside the courthouse, lunch wagons set up along the kerb and souvenir sellers sold tiepins in the shape of sash weights for 10 cents each. Throngs of people turned up daily hoping to get seats inside. Those who failed seemed content to stand outside and stare at the building, knowing that important matters that they could not see or hear were being decided within. People of wealth and fashion turned up too, among them the Marquess of Queensberry and the unidentified wife of a US Supreme Court justice. Those fortunate enough to get seats inside were allowed to come forward at the conclusion of proceedings each day and inspect the venerated exhibits in the case – the sash weight, picture wire and bottle of chloroform that featured in the evil deed. The *News* and *Mirror* ran as many as eight articles a day on the trial. If any especially riveting disclosures emerged during the day – that, for instance, Ruth Snyder on the night of the murder had received Judd Gray in a blood-red kimono – special editions were rushed into print, as if war had been declared. For those too eager or overcome to focus on the words, the *Mirror* provided 160 photographs, diagrams and other illustrations during the three weeks of the trial, the *Daily News* nearer 200. For a short while, one of Gray's lawyers was one Edward Reilly, who would later gain notoriety by defending Bruno Hauptmann in the Lindbergh baby kidnapping trial, but Reilly, who was a hopeless drunk, was fired or resigned at an early stage.

Each day for three weeks, jurors, reporters and audience listened in rapt silence as the tragic arc of Albert Snyder's mortal fall was outlined. The story had begun ten years earlier when Snyder, the lonely, balding art editor of

Motor Boating magazine, had developed an infatuation with an office secretary of high spirits and light intellect named Ruth Brown. She was thirteen years his junior and not notably attracted to him, but when, after their third or fourth date, he offered her a gumball-sized engagement ring her modest defences crumbled. 'I just couldn't give up that ring,' she explained helplessly to a friend.

They were wed four months after they met and moved into his house in Queens Village. Their period of wedded bliss was a short one even by the standards of ill-fated marriages. Snyder longed for a life of quiet domesticity. Ruth – who was known to her intimates as Tommy – wanted bright lights and gaiety. He infuriated her by refusing to take down photographs of a previous sweetheart. Within two days of the wedding she revealed that she didn't actually like him. And so began ten years of loveless marriage.

Ruth took to going out alone. In 1925, in a café in Manhattan, she met Judd Gray, a travelling salesman for the Bien Jolie Corset Company, and they began a relationship. Gray made an unlikely villain. He wore owlish spectacles, weighed just 120 pounds, and called Ruth 'Mommie'. When not engaged in lustful infidelity, he taught Sunday school and sang in a church choir, fundraised for the Red Cross, and was happily married with a ten-year-old daughter.

Increasingly dissatisfied with her marriage, Ruth tricked her unsuspecting hubby into signing a life insurance policy with a double indemnity clause providing nearly $100,000 in the event that he met a violent end, and she now doggedly dedicated herself to making sure he did. She dosed his evening whisky with poison and whisked it into his prune whip (a feature of the affair much dwelt on by reporters). When that failed to slow him, she added crushed sleeping pills to the concoction, gave him bichloride of mercury tablets on the pretext that they were a healthful medicine, and even tried gassing him, but the unwitting Mr Snyder proved obstinately indestructible. In desperation, Ruth turned to Judd Gray. Together they devised what they conceived to be the perfect murder. Gray caught a train to Syracuse and checked into the Hotel Onondaga, making sure that plenty of people saw him, before slipping out a back way and returning to the city. While he was away he arranged for a friend to go to his hotel room, muss the bed and otherwise make it look as if the room had been occupied. He also left the friend with letters to mail after his departure. His alibi thus securely in place, Gray travelled to Queens Village and presented himself late at night at the Snyder house. Ruth, sitting up in the kitchen in her soon-to-be-famous scarlet kimono, let him in. The plan was for Gray to creep into the marital bedroom and smash in Snyder's skull with a sash weight that Ruth had placed on the dresser for the purpose. Things didn't work out quite as planned. Gray's first blow was timidly experimental, and served only to wake the intended victim. Confused but considerably enlivened at finding a strange, small man leaning over him and tapping him on the head with a blunt instrument, Snyder cried out in pain and grabbed Gray's necktie, choking him.

'Mommie, Mommie, for God's sake help!' Gray croaked.

Ruth Snyder seized the sash weight from her floundering lover and brought it forcefully down on her husband's cranium, stilling him. She and Gray then stuffed chloroform up Snyder's nostrils and strangled him with picture wire, which she had also laid in. Then they turned out drawers and cupboards all over the house to make it look as if it had been ransacked. It appears not to have occurred to either of them that it would be a good idea to make Ruth's bed look slept in. Gray loosely tied Ruth around the ankles and wrists, and arranged her comfortably on the floor. In what he considered his most cunning touch, he left the Italian newspaper on a table downstairs, so that the police would conclude that the intruders were alien subversives, like Sacco and Vanzetti, the infamous anarchists then awaiting execution in Massachusetts. When everything was in place, Gray kissed Ruth goodbye, then caught a taxi into the city and a train back to Syracuse.

Gray was convinced that even if he came under suspicion the police would be unable to prove anything because his alibi firmly placed him three hundred miles away in Syracuse. Unfortunately, Gray was remembered by a Long Island taxi driver to whom he had given a 5-cent tip on a $3.50 fare – even in 1920s money a nickel was a paltry show of gratitude – and who was now extremely eager to give evidence against him. Gray was tracked down to the Hotel Onondaga, where he professed astonishment that the police would suspect him. 'Why, I have never even been given a ticket for speeding,' he said and confidently asserted that he could show that he had been in the hotel all weekend. Unfortunately, not to say amazingly, he had thrown the ticket stub from his train journey in the waste-basket. When a policeman fished it out and confronted him with it, Gray swiftly confessed, too. Upon learning that Mrs Snyder was blaming him for everything, he hotly insisted that she was the mastermind and had blackmailed him into cooperating by threatening to expose his faithlessness to his loving wife. It was clear that he and Mrs Snyder were not going to be friends again.

Such was the intensity of interest in the trial that no aspect of the affair, however tangential, was overlooked. Readers learned that the presiding judge, Townsend Scudder, returned home to his Long Island estate each evening to be greeted – and presumably all but overwhelmed – by his 125 pet dogs, which he then personally fed. Someone else noticed, and solemnly reported, that the ages of the jurors exactly added up to five hundred. One of Ruth Snyder's lawyers, Dana Wallace, merited special attention for being the son of the owner of the *Mary Celeste*, the infamous cargo ship found drifting in the Atlantic in 1872, its crew mysteriously vanished. A journalist named Silas Bent made a careful measurement of column inches and found that the Snyder–Gray affair received more coverage than the sinking of the *Titanic*. Analysis and commentary were provided by a pack of celebrity observers, including the mystery writer Mary Roberts Rinehart, the playwright Ben Hecht, the film director D. W. Griffith, the actress Mae West, and the historian Will Durant, whose *Story of Philosophy* was currently a phenomenal bestseller, if not obviously relevant to a criminal trial on Long Island. Also present, somewhat unaccountably, was a magician who went by the single name of Thurston. Moral context was added by three leading evangelists: Billy Sunday, Aimee Semple McPherson, and John Roach Straton. Straton was famous for hating almost everything – 'card playing, cocktail drinking, poodle dogs, jazz music, the theater, low-cut dresses, divorce, novels, stuffy rooms, Clarence Darrow, overeating, the Museum of Natural History, evolution, the Standard Oil influence in the Baptist church, prizefighting, the private lives of actors, nude art, bridge playing, modernism and greyhound racing', according to one partial contemporary account. To this list he was now happy to add Ruth Snyder and Judd Gray; they couldn't be executed fast enough as far as he was concerned. McPherson, more moderately, offered prayers and the hope that God would teach young men everywhere to think: 'I want a wife like Mother – not a Red Hot Cutie.'

The critic Edmund Wilson wondered in an essay why it was that so dull and unimaginative a murder excited such earnest attention, without pausing to reflect that the same question could be asked of his essay. To him it was largely another case of 'a familiar motif' – a 'ruthless ambitious woman who commands the submissive male'. By almost universal consent, Ruth Snyder was held to be the guilty party, Judd Gray the hapless dupe. Gray received so much mail, nearly all of it sympathetic, that it filled two neighbouring cells in the Queens County Jailhouse.

The papers strove hard to portray Ruth Snyder as an evil temptress. 'Her naturally blonde hair was marcelled to perfection,' wrote one observer tartly, as if that alone confirmed her guilt. The *Mirror* dubbed her 'the marble woman without a heart'. Elsewhere she was called 'the human serpent', 'the ice woman' and, in a moment of journalistic hyperventilation, 'the Swedish-Norwegian vampire'. Nearly all reports dwelt on Ruth Snyder's deadly good looks, but this was either delusional or selectively generous. By 1927, Ruth Snyder was thirty-six years old, plump, haggard and worn. Her complexion was blotchy, her expression an iron scowl. Franker commentators doubted that she had ever been attractive. A reporter for the *New Yorker* suggested: 'No one has yet satisfactorily analyzed the interest that attaches to Ruth Snyder ... Her irresistible charm is visible only to Judd Gray.' Gray, with his heavy round glasses, looked improbably wise and professorial, and much older than his thirty-five years. In photographs he wore an expression of perpetual startlement, as if he couldn't believe where he now found himself.

Quite why the Snyder murder attracted such a devoted following wasn't easy to say then, and impossible to say now. Plenty of other, better murders were available to excite attention that year, even without leaving New York. One was the Gravesend Bay Insurance Murder, as the newspapers dubbed it, in which a man named Benny Goldstein devised a plan to fake his own drowning in Gravesend Bay, Brooklyn, so that his friend Joe Lefkowitz could collect on a $75,000 insurance policy, which they would then split. Lefkowitz, however, made one significant change to the plan: he tossed Goldstein out of a boat in the middle of the bay rather than conveying him to a beach in New Jersey, as agreed. Since Goldstein couldn't swim his death was pretty well assured, and Lefkowitz collected all the money, though he didn't have long to enjoy it because he was swiftly caught and convicted.

The Snyder case, in contrast, was clumsy and banal, and didn't even hold out the promise of exciting court-room revelations since both of the accused had already fully confessed. Yet it became known, without any sense of hyperbole, as 'the crime of the century', and exerted a most extraordinary influence on popular culture, particularly on Hollywood, Broadway and the more sensational end of light fiction. The film producer Adolph Zukor brought out a movie called *The Woman Who Needed Killing* (the title was later toned down) and the journalist Sophie Treadwell, who had covered the trial for the *Herald Tribune*, wrote a play called *Machinal*, which enjoyed both critical and commercial success. (The part of Judd Gray in the Treadwell production was played by a promising young actor named Clark Gable.) The novelist James M. Cain was so taken with the case that he used it as the central plot device in *two* books: *The Postman Always Rings Twice* and *Double Indemnity*. Billy Wilder made the latter into the artfully lit 1944 movie of the same name starring Fred MacMurray and Barbara Stanwyck. This was the movie that created film noir, and so became the template on which a generation of Hollywood melodramas was based. *Double Indemnity* the movie *is* the Snyder–Gray case, but with snappier dialogue and better-looking people.

The murder of poor Albert Snyder had one other unusual feature: the people responsible were caught. That didn't actually happen much in America in the 1920s. New York recorded 372 murders in 1927; in 115 of those cases no one was arrested. Where arrests were made, the conviction rate was less than 20 per cent. Nationally, according to a survey made by the Metropolitan Life Insurance Company – and it is notable that the best records were kept by insurers, not police authorities – two thirds of America's murders were unsolved in 1927. Some localities couldn't even achieve that grimly unsatisfactory proportion. Chicago in a typical year experienced between 450 and 500 murders and managed to solve far fewer than a quarter of them. Altogether, nine tenths of all serious crime in America went unpunished, according to the survey. Only about one murder in a hundred resulted in an execution. So for Ruth Snyder and Judd Gray to be accused, convicted and ultimately executed, they had to be truly, outstandingly inept. They were.

Late in the afternoon of 9 May, the lawyers concluded their closing arguments and the twelve men of the jury – it was all male because women were not allowed to hear murder cases in New York State in 1927 – were sent to deliberate. One hour and forty minutes later the jurors shuffled back in with their verdicts: both defendants were guilty of murder in the first degree. Ruth Snyder wept bitterly in her seat. Judd Gray, face flushed, stared hard at the jury, but without animosity. Justice Scudder set sentencing for the following Monday, though that was really just a formality. The penalty for murder in the first degree was death by electrocution.

Coincidentally and conveniently, just as the Snyder–Gray case wound to its inevitable conclusion, another even bigger story began to unfold. Three days after the trial ended and just a short distance away, a silvery plane called the *Spirit of St Louis* swooped down on Long Island from the west and landed at Curtiss Field, adjacent to Roosevelt Field. From it stepped a grinning young man from Minnesota about whom almost nothing was known.

Charles Lindbergh was twenty-five years old but looked eighteen. He was six feet two inches tall and weighed 128 pounds. He was almost preposterously wholesome. He didn't smoke or drink – not even coffee or Coca-Cola – and had never been on a date. He had a curiously stunted sense of humour, and loved practical jokes that veered dangerously close to cruelty. Once on a hot day he filled a friend's water jug with kerosene and mirthfully stood by as the friend took a mighty swig. The friend ended up in hospital. His principal claim to fame was that he had successfully parachuted out of more crashing planes than anyone else alive, as far as could be told. He had made four emergency parachute jumps – one from just 350 feet – and had crash-landed a fifth plane in a Minnesota bog, but clambered out unhurt. He had only just reached the fourth anniversary of his first solo flight. Among the flying community on Long Island his chances of successfully crossing the Atlantic were generally presumed to be about zero.

With Snyder and Gray off the front pages, demand arose now for a new story, and this confident, rather mysterious young Midwesterner looked like he could be it. A single question swept through the reporting fraternity: Who *is* this kid?

Chapter 2

THE FAMILY NAME was really Månsson. Charles Lindbergh's grandfather, a dour Swede with a luxuriant beard and fire-and-brimstone countenance, changed it to Lindbergh when he came to America in 1859 in circumstances that were both abrupt and dubious.

Until shortly before that time, Ola Månsson had been a respectable citizen and, by all appearances, a contentedly married man with a wife and eight children in a village near Ystad on the southernmost, Baltic edge of Sweden. In 1847, at the age of forty, he was elected to the Riksdag, the national parliament, and began to spend a good deal of time in Stockholm, 600 kilometres to the north. There his life grew uncharacteristically complicated. He took up with a waitress twenty years his junior, and with her produced a child out of wedlock: Charles Lindbergh's father. At the same time Månsson was implicated in a financial scandal for improperly guaranteeing bank loans to some cronies. It is not clear how serious the charges were. The Lindberghs in America always maintained that they were trumped up by his political enemies. What is certain is that

Ola Månsson in 1859 left Sweden in a hurry, failed to answer the accusations against him, abandoned his original family, settled in rural Minnesota with his mistress and new child, and changed his name to August Lindbergh – all matters that Charles Lindbergh overlooked or lightly glossed over in his various autobiographical writings.

The Lindberghs (the name means 'linden tree mountain') settled near Sauk Centre, future home town of the novelist Sinclair Lewis but then on the very edge of civilization. It was in Sauk Centre, two years after their arrival, that the elder Lindbergh suffered a famously horrific injury. While working at a sawmill, he slipped and fell against the whirring blade, which tore through his upper body at the shoulder, creating a hole so large that his internal organs were exposed – one witness claimed he could see the poor man's beating heart – and leaving his arm attached by just a few strands of glistening sinew. The millworkers bound the injuries as best they could and carried Lindbergh home, where he lay in silent agony for three days awaiting the arrival of a doctor from St Cloud, forty miles away. When the doctor at last reached him, he took off the arm and sewed up the gaping cavity. It was said that Lindbergh made almost no sound. Remarkably, August Lindbergh recovered and lived another thirty years. Stoicism became the Lindbergh family's most cultivated trait.

Charles Lindbergh's father, who had arrived in America as a Swedish-speaking toddler named Karl August Månsson, grew up into a strapping but cheerless young man named Charles August Lindbergh. Friends and colleagues called him C. A. As a youth, C. A. became adroit at trapping muskrats, whose pelts furriers made into jackets and stoles which they marketed under the more appealing name of 'Hudson seal'. C. A. made enough from the trade to put himself through the University of Michigan law school. Upon qualifying, he opened a law office in Little Falls, Minnesota, married, produced three daughters, and prospered sufficiently to build a large wooden house on a bluff overlooking the Mississippi River about a mile and a half outside town. All was eminently well with his life until the spring of 1898 when his wife died suddenly from surgery to remove an abdominal growth.

Three years later, C. A. married again – this time a pretty, rather intense young chemistry teacher from Detroit who had recently taken a position at Little Falls High School. Evangeline Lodge Land was unusually well educated for a woman, for the time and for Little Falls. She, too, had graduated from Michigan, but was even more academic than her husband and would later do graduate work at Columbia. Beyond physical attraction – they were both extremely good-looking – the new Mr and Mrs Lindbergh had little in common. C. A. Lindbergh was handsome but severe and measured. His wife was brittle and demanding. On 4 February 1902, they produced another C. A. Lindbergh – this one named Charles August*us*, with an extra, more classically refined syllable on the second name. From his father Charles inherited a dimpled chin and perpetually tousled hair, from his mother dreaminess, and from both a tendency to be headstrong. He was the only child they would have together. Young Charles – he was never Charlie or anything more relaxed and familiar – grew up in a household that was comfortable and well looked after (the family kept three servants) but lacking in warmth. Both his parents were almost wholly incapable of showing affection. Lindbergh and his mother never hugged. At bedtime, they shook hands. As both boy and man, Charles signed letters to his father 'Sincerely, C. A. Lindbergh', as if corresponding with his bank manager.

Charles was a shy, rather dreamy boy. He made so little impression on Little Falls that when journalists descended on the town in 1927 looking for anecdotes from his boyhood none of his ex-schoolmates could think of any. Lindbergh himself in adulthood said that he had no memories at all of his daily life as a youngster. In his first autobiographical effort, called *We*, he gave just eighteen lines to his childhood.

In 1906, when Charles was not quite five, his father was elected to Congress as a Republican, which meant that young Charles divided his time between Little Falls, which he loved, and Washington, which he did not. This gave Charles an eventful but disrupted childhood. He enjoyed experiences that other children could only dream of – he played in the grounds of the White House and in the halls of the Capitol building, visited the Panama Canal at the age of eleven, went to school with the sons of Theodore Roosevelt – but he moved around so much that he never really became part of anything.

As the years passed, his parents grew increasingly estranged. At least once, according to Lindbergh's biographer A. Scott Berg, his mother held a gun to his father's head (after learning that he was sleeping with his stenographer), and at least once in fury he struck her. By the time Charles was ten years old, they were living permanently apart, though they kept it secret for the sake of

Charles senior's political career. Charles attended eleven different schools before graduating from high school, and distinguished himself at each by his mediocrity. In the autumn of 1920, he entered the University of Wisconsin, hoping to become an engineer. Charles survived in large part by having his mother write his papers for him, but ultimately even that wasn't enough. Halfway through his sophomore year he flunked out and abruptly announced his intention to become an aviator. From his parents' perspective, this was a mortifying ambition. Flying was poorly paid, wildly unsafe and unreliable as a career – and nowhere were those three unhappy qualities more evident than in the United States.

In no important area of technology has America ever fallen further behind the rest of the world than it did with aviation in the 1920s. As early as 1919, Europe had its first airline in KLM and others quickly followed. Before the year was out, daily flights were introduced between London and Paris, and soon more than a thousand people a week were flying that route alone. By the mid-1920s it was possible to fly almost anywhere in Europe – from Berlin to Leipzig, from Amsterdam to Brussels, from Paris to distant Constantinople (by way of Prague and Bucharest). By 1927, France had nine airlines operating, British airlines were flying almost a million miles a year, and Germany was safely delivering 151,000 passengers to their destinations. In America, as the spring of 1927 dawned, the number of scheduled passenger air services was . . . none.

Aviation in America was almost wholly unregulated. The country had no system of licensing and no requirements for training. Anyone could buy a plane, in any condition, and legally take up paying passengers. The United States was so slack about flying that it didn't even keep track of the number of aeroplane crashes and fatalities. The most authoritative source, the *Aircraft Year Book*, compiled its figures from newspaper clippings. The anonymous authors of that annual tome were in no doubt that the absence of regulation was holding back progress and causing needless deaths. They wrote: 'Since the Armistice, when airplanes were first made generally available and came into hands skilled and unskilled, responsible and irresponsible, it may be conservatively estimated that more than 300 persons have been killed and 500 injured – many of them fatally – in flying accidents which could have been prevented had there been in existence and enforced a statute regulating the operation of commercial aircraft.'

Without airlines to employ them, American aviators had to turn a hand to whatever work they could find – dusting crops, giving rides at county fairs, thrilling spectators with stunts and acrobatics, dragging advertising banners across the skies, taking aerial photographs, and above all carrying mail – the one area in which America was pre-eminent. Of all the aerial employments, delivering mail was the most economically secure but also the most dangerous: thirty-one of the first forty airmail pilots were killed in crashes, and accidents remained common throughout the 1920s. Airmail pilots flew in all weather and often at night, but with almost no support in the way of navigational aids. In March 1927, an article in *Scientific American*, under the heading 'Invisible Beams Guide Birdmen in Flights Between European Cities', noted admiringly how pilots in Europe could fix their locations instantly via radio beacons. Lost American pilots, by contrast, had to search for a town and hope that someone had written its name on the roof of a building. In the absence of that – and it was generally absent – pilots had to swoop low to try to read the signs on the local railway station, often a risky manoeuvre. For weather reports, they mostly called ahead to railway agents along the route and asked them to put their head out of the door and tell them what they saw.

Such deficiencies marked almost every area of American civil aviation. Until 1924, Detroit, the fourth largest city in the country, didn't have an airfield at all. In 1927, San Francisco and Baltimore still didn't. Lambert Field in St Louis, one of the most important in the country because of its position at the heart of the continent, existed only because Major Albert B. Lambert, a flying enthusiast, was willing to support it out of his own pocket. Metropolitan New York had four airfields – three on Long Island and one on Staten Island – but all were privately owned or run by the military, and offered only the most basic facilities. None of them even had a control tower. No American airfield did.

Not until 1925 did the country begin at last to address even peripherally its aeronautical shortcomings. The person chiefly responsible for rectifying these deficiencies was Dwight Morrow, a New York banker who knew nothing whatever about flying but was put in charge of the President's Aircraft Board – a panel charged with investigating the safety and efficiency of American aviation – because he was a friend of President Coolidge. By a rather extraordinary coincidence Morrow would in 1929 become Charles Lindbergh's father-in-law. Had Morrow been told that before the decade was out his shy, intellectual daughter at Smith College in Massachusetts would be marrying an airmail pilot and former stunt flyer we may assume he would have been flabbergasted. Had he been further informed that this pilot would also by then be the world's most celebrated individual his astonishment would presumably have been immeasurable. In any case, thanks to Morrow's efforts, the Air Commerce Act was signed into law by President Coolidge on 20 May 1926 – coincidentally one year to the day before Lindbergh's flight. The act brought in some minimal training require-ments for pilots and inspection of planes used in interstate commerce, and required the Commerce Department to keep track of fatalities. It wasn't much, but it was a start.

This was the casual and high-risk world in which Charles Lindbergh learned to fly. His first flight – indeed, his first experience of an aeroplane at close range – was at a flying school in Lincoln, Nebraska, on 9 April 1922, two months after his twentieth birthday. He was instantly smitten. Almost at once he embarked on a brief but perilous career as a stunt performer. Within a week he was wing-walking and within a month he was – without any prior training – parachuting from giddy heights to the delight of watching crowds. In the course of these duties he also learned, in an entirely informal way, to fly. He proved to be unusually good at it. Like most young men, Lindbergh was capable of the most riveting foolishness. Part of the job of barn-stormers was to impress the locals with their flying skills, and on a visit to Camp Wood, Texas, Lindbergh decided to do so by taking off from the town's Main Street – an ambitious challenge since the street's telephone poles were just forty-six feet apart and his wingspan was forty-four. As he sped down the street, he hit a bump, which caused a wingtip to clip a pole, spinning him sideways and through the front window of a hardware store. How neither he nor any of the spectators were injured is a miracle.

Barnstorming gave Lindbergh a great deal of practical experience – he made over seven hundred flights in two years – but no technical training. In 1924, he corrected that deficiency by enrolling in a one-year course in the army air reserve, which provided the most advanced and challenging training then available. He finished top of his class – the first time in his life he had done well at anything academic – and emerged with the rank of captain. The achievement was muted somewhat by the fact that it coincided with the death of his father, from a neurological disorder, in May 1924. Because no military posts were available, he took a job as an airmail pilot on the St Louis to Chicago route, where he acquired the sort of resourcefulness that comes with flying cheap and temperamental planes through every possible type of adversity. Thanks to this varied apprenticeship, Lindbergh in the spring of 1927 was a more experienced and proficient flyer – and a vastly more gifted one – than his competitors realized. As events would show, you couldn't be a better pilot and still be just twenty-five.

In many ways Charles Lindbergh's greatest achievement in 1927 was not flying the Atlantic but getting a plane built with which to fly the Atlantic. Somehow he managed to persuade nine flinty businessmen in St Louis, among them the eponymous A. B. Lambert, to back him, convincing them that a plane with 'St Louis' in its title could do nothing but good for the city's business prospects. It was an exceedingly dubious proposition. The greater likelihood for his backers was that they would be indelibly associated with the needless death of a young, idealistic flyer, but that thought, if it occurred to them at all, seems not to have troubled them. By late autumn 1926, Lindbergh had a promise of $13,000 of funding from his backers, plus $2,000 of his own – not a lavish bankroll by any means, but with luck, he hoped, enough to get him a single-engine plane capable of crossing an ocean.

In early February 1927, Lindbergh took a train to New York for a meeting with Charles Levine, owner of the aeroplane *Columbia*. This was the same plane that would, two months later, set the world endurance record with Chamberlin and Acosta. Chamberlin was present at the February meeting, as was the plane's brilliant, sweet-tempered designer, Giuseppe Bellanca, though neither said much.

They met in Levine's office in the Woolworth Building in Manhattan. Levine listened to Lindbergh's pitch, then agreed to sell the plane to him for $15,000 – rather a startling thing to do since Chamberlin was, up to that moment, expecting to fly the plane to Paris himself. It was also a very good price for what was unquestionably one of the best planes in the world and the only one capable of taking Lindbergh to Europe alone. Understandably elated, Lindbergh travelled back to St Louis to draw a cheque and confirm the support of his backers, then returned at once to New York to complete the transaction. On the return visit, as Lindbergh handed over a cashier's cheque for the full amount of the purchase, Levine casually mentioned that although they were happy to proceed with the deal as agreed, they of course reserved the right to choose the crew.

Lindbergh could not have been more taken aback. The proposition was ludicrous. He was hardly going to buy a plane so that a pilot of Levine's choosing could make the flight and receive all the glory. Lindbergh had just discovered, as many others did before and after him, that where business was concerned Charles A. Levine had a genius for causing dismay. Almost everyone who dealt with Levine found reasons to distrust and despise him. Bellanca himself would terminate their relationship before June was out. Lindbergh took back his cheque and dolefully made the long, clacketing trip back to St Louis.

Lindbergh could now hardly be in a less promising situation. In desperation he cabled a tiny company in San Diego, Ryan Airlines, and asked if it could build a plane for an Atlantic flight, and, if so, how much it would cost and how long it would take. The reply came quickly and was unexpectedly heartening. Ryan could build the plane in sixty days for $6,000, plus the expense of the engine, which it would install at cost. Ryan, it turned out, needed the work as much as Lindbergh needed the plane.

On 23 February, slightly less than three weeks after his twenty-fifth birthday and three months before he would fly to Paris, Lindbergh arrived at the factory of Ryan Airlines in San Diego. There he met the president, B. F. Mahoney, and chief engineer, Donald Hall, both only slightly older than he was. Though the company was called Ryan, Ryan had sold out to Mahoney a few weeks earlier – so recently in fact that they hadn't had time to change the company name. Donald Hall had also joined the company only a month before, a truly fortunate break for Lindbergh because Hall was a gifted and diligent designer – exactly what Lindbergh needed.

Over the next two months the entire Ryan workforce – thirty-five people – laboured flat out on Lindbergh's plane. Hall worked to the point of exhaustion – for thirty-six hours straight at one point. The plane could not have been built so swiftly otherwise, but then the Ryan employees had every reason to work hard. Ryan had no orders and was on the verge of bankruptcy when Lindbergh arrived. It is hard to imagine what the employees thought of this lanky youth from the Midwest hovering over them, questioning their every move in a manner bound to try patience. Lindbergh and Hall, however, got along extremely well, which was the main thing.

The *Spirit of St Louis* was based on an existing model, the Ryan M-2, but many adjustments were necessary to make a plane suitable for an ocean flight. The inordinately heavy fuel load meant Hall had to redesign the wings, fuselage, landing gear and ailerons, all major jobs. Of necessity, much of what they did was based on improvisation and guesswork – sometimes to a startling degree. Realizing they had no clear notion of how far it was from New York to Paris by the most direct route, they went to a public library and measured the distance on a globe with a piece of string. By such means was one of history's greatest planes built.

Lindbergh didn't want to be sandwiched between the engine and fuel tank – too many pilots had been crushed in forced landings that way – so the main tank was put at the front of the plane, where the cockpit normally was, and the cockpit moved further back. This meant he had no forward visibility, but that troubled him less than you might expect. He couldn't see the ground ahead during takeoff anyway because of the backward slope of a taxiing plane, and once airborne he would be flying over an empty ocean with nothing to crash into. He could get a fix ahead by 'crabbing', a manoeuvre in which the plane is turned slightly sideways while still flying forward, allowing one of the side windows to become temporarily a front window. Even so, one of the mechanics, a former submariner named Charlie Randolph, installed a simple periscope that Lindbergh could use if need be, though he never did.

The finished plane was anything but state-of-the-art. Lindbergh flew with two foot pedals and a stick between his legs. The instrument panel had just ten fairly rudimentary gauges – eleven if you counted the clock. One conspicuous absence was a fuel gauge. Lindbergh didn't feel they were reliable enough. He would compute his fuel use manually, though that was essentially an academic exercise: either he would have enough fuel or he wouldn't. The plane also had no brakes. Planes in 1927 almost never did. That would not matter in most circumstances, but it would prove an unnerving absence when, later, crowds streamed on to runways wherever Lindbergh landed.

The plane's frame was covered in Pima cotton painted over with six coats of aluminium-pigmented dope – a kind of aromatic varnish that made the cotton shrink to fit tight around its wood and tubular-steel skeleton. Although the *Spirit of St Louis* looked metallic, and was often described as such in newspaper reports, only the nose cowling was actually of metal. With only a thin layer of canvas between Lindbergh and the outside world, the *Spirit of St Louis* was deafeningly noisy and unnervingly insubstantial. It would have been rather like crossing the ocean in a tent.

Lindbergh and the other Atlantic competitors were slightly too early for a great unsung invention of the age – Alclad, a new type of non-corrosive aluminium invented by Alcoa and unveiled later that year. For the next eighty years (until the introduction of carbon fibres) virtually every plane built on earth would have an Alclad skin – but not in the summer of 1927. Lindbergh did at least have a metal propeller, which was much more reliable and resistant to cracking than the wooden propellers used until quite recently. The American flyers also had an advantage over their European competitors that nobody yet understood. They all used aviation fuel from California, which burned more cleanly and gave better mileage. No one knew what made it superior because no one yet understood octane ratings – that would not come until the 1930s – but it was what got most American planes across the ocean while others were lost at sea.

The completed *Spirit of St Louis*, as has often been said, was little more more than a flying fuel tank. Though it was vastly sleeker than planes of a few years earlier, it still had a lot of drag built into it: the jutting cylinders on its engine, its many struts and guy wires, above all its fixed landing gear with its two dangling wheels dragging through the wind – all acted like an arm thrust out of a car window. To maximize mileage, every ounce of unnecessary weight was discarded. Lindbergh took nothing he didn't need. He reportedly even trimmed the white margins off his maps.

Because of its many design compromises, the plane was not nearly as stable as it ought to have been – a fact that troubled Hall greatly – but there wasn't time to make it better and Lindbergh was convinced, probably rightly, that having to work harder would help him to stay awake. 'Lindbergh didn't want an innovative plane,' says Alex Spencer of the Smithsonian National Air and Space Museum in Washington. 'He wanted nothing but tried and tested technology.'

Only the engine, a 223-horsepower Wright J-5 Whirlwind, was of a new design. It was the one thing on the plane that was unquestionably of the latest technology. The J-5 was air-cooled, which made it simpler, lighter and more reliable than conventional water-cooled engines, and it had two additional benefits. It was the first machine in the world to incorporate Samuel Heron's sodium-cooled valves, which eliminated the serious problem of burned exhaust valves, and it had self-lubricating rocker arms, which allowed the valves to putter along contentedly for hours without attention. The J-5 was first used on Richard Byrd's North Pole flight in 1926, and did its job admirably. The irony, as we shall see, is that Byrd probably never got anywhere near the North Pole.

Lindbergh made his first test flight on 28 April, two months to the day after placing the order. The plane performed better than he had dared to hope. It was agile and fast – he got it up to 128 miles an hour on its first flight – and it positively leapt into the air from the ground, at least when lightly loaded. Over the next ten days, Lindbergh took the plane up another twenty-two times, mostly in short test flights of between five and ten minutes. In a series of trials on 4 May, he gradually increased the fuel load from 38 gallons to 300, but that was still 150 gallons short of what he would carry at takeoff in New York. He dared not push the plane further because of the danger of landing with full tanks. The only test of the plane's true capabilities would come with the flight to Paris itself.

Lindbergh was now desperately eager to go. From New York came word that Byrd's *America* and Levine's *Columbia* were both ready to depart. Only bad weather was holding them back. Then came the news that Nungesser and Coli had left Paris and were en route to America. Lindbergh, quietly despairing, considered changing his plans completely and trying to become the first pilot across the Pacific, flying to Australia via Hawaii – a very much greater challenge and one that would in all likelihood have killed him. He abandoned that thought immediately, however, when the news broke that Nungesser and Coli were missing and presumed dead. If he could get to New York before the storms across much of the continent cleared, he still stood a chance.

On the afternoon of 10 May, shortly before 4 p.m. California time, Charles Lindbergh climbed into the cockpit of his sleek new plane and took off. Once comfortably airborne, he pointed the nose east and, with the supreme confidence of youth, headed towards St Louis and some of the worst weather America had seen in years.

Chapter 3

Most people couldn't recall a time like it. For months on end, across much of the country, it rained steadily, sometimes in volumes not before seen. Southern Illinois received over two feet of rain in three months; parts of Arkansas had well over three. Rivers almost beyond counting – the San Jacinto in California, the Klamath, Willamette and Umpqua in Oregon, the Snake, Payette and Boise in Idaho, the Colorado in Colorado, the Neosho and Verdigris in Kansas, the Ouachita and St Francis in Arkansas, the Tennessee and Cumberland in the South, the Connecticut in New England – overran their banks. Between the late summer of 1926 and the following spring, enough precipitation fell on the forty-eight United States, by one calculation, to make a cube of water 250 miles across on each side. That is a lot of water, and it was only just the beginning.

On Good Friday, 15 April, a mighty storm system pounded the middle third of America with rain of a duration and intensity that those who experienced it would not forget in a hurry. From western Montana to

West Virginia and from Canada to the Gulf, rain fell in what can only be described as a Noachian deluge. Most places received six to eight inches and some recorded more than a foot. Now nearly all that water raced into swollen creeks and rivers and headed, with unwonted intensity, for the great central artery of the continent, the Mississippi River. The Mississippi and its tributaries drain 40 per cent of America, almost a million square miles spread across thirty-one states (and two Canadian provinces), and never in recorded history had the entirety of it been this strained.

A river approaching flood stage is an ominously fearsome thing, and the Mississippi now took on an aspect of brutal, swift-flowing anger that unnerved even hardened observers. All along the upper Mississippi people stood on the banks and mutely watched as the river paraded objects – trees, dead cows, barn roofs – that hinted at the carnage further north. At St Louis the volume of passing water reached two million cubic feet per second – a phenomenal rate, double the volume recorded during the great flood of 1993. You didn't have to be an expert to see that this was an unsustainable burden. All along the river armies of men with shovels and sandbags shored up flood defences, but the pressures were too overwhelming. On 16 April, on a great bend of the river in south-east Missouri at a place called Dorena, the first levee gave way. Some 1,200 feet of earthen bank burst open and a volume of water equal to that at Niagara Falls poured through the chasm. The roar could be heard miles away.

Soon levees up and down the river were popping like buttons off a tight shirt. At Mounds Landing, Mississippi, a hundred black workers, kept at their posts by men with rifles, were swept to oblivion when a levee gave way. The coroner, for reasons unstated, recorded just two deaths. In some places, the water rushed across the landscape so swiftly that people had no means of escape. At Winterville, Mississippi, twenty-three women and children perished when the house in which they were sheltering was swept away.

By the first week of May, the flood stretched for 500 miles from southern Illinois to New Orleans, and was up to 150 miles wide in places. Altogether an area almost the size of Scotland was under water. From the air, the Mississippi valley looked like – indeed, for the time being was – a new Great Lake. The statistics of the Great Flood were recorded with chilling precision: 16,570,627 acres flooded; 203,504 buildings lost or ruined; 637,476 people made homeless. The quantities of livestock lost were logged with similar exactitude: 50,490 cattle, 25,325 horses and mules, 148,110 hogs, 1,276,570 chickens and other poultry. The one thing that wasn't carefully recorded, oddly, was the number of human lives lost, but it was certainly more than a thousand and perhaps several times that. The numbers weren't more scrupulous because, alas, so many of the victims were poor and black. It is a shocking fact that a closer count was kept of livestock losses than of human ones. It is perhaps only slightly less shocking to note that outside the affected areas the flood received less coverage on most days than the murder trial of Ruth Snyder and Judd Gray.

The nation's inattentiveness notwithstanding, the Mississippi flood of 1927 was America's most epic natural disaster in extent, duration and number of lives affected. The scale of economic loss was so large as to be essentially incalculable. Estimates ranged from $250 million to $1 billion. It wasn't the most lethal catastrophe in American history, but it ruined more lives and property than any other, and it lasted far longer. Altogether the Mississippi would be at flood stage for 153 consecutive days.

Fortunately America had a figure of rock-like calm – a kind of superman, a term that he was not embarrassed to apply to himself in private correspondence – to whom it could turn in times of crisis such as this. His name was Herbert Hoover. Soon he would be the most derided president of his time – quite an achievement for someone elected in the same decade as Warren G. Harding – but in the spring of 1927 he was, and by a very wide margin, the world's most trusted man. He was also, curiously, perhaps the least likeable hero America has ever produced. The summer of 1927 would make him a little more of both.

Herbert Clark Hoover was born in 1874 thirty miles west of the Mississippi (he would be the first president from west of that symbolically weighty boundary) in the hamlet of West Branch, Iowa, in a tiny white cottage, which still stands. His parents, devout Quakers, died tragically early – his father of rheumatic fever when little Bert was just six, his mother of typhoid fever three years later – and he was sent to live with an uncle and aunt in Oregon. These dour relatives, themselves ardent Quakers, had just lost a much-loved son, ensuring that Bert would feel the gloomy weight of death on his shoulders during every moment of his formative years. Whatever high spirits he was born with – and it is by no means certain that there were any – were thoroughly extinguished by the experiences of his youth. Herbert Hoover lived to be ninety, and never in the whole of that time, so far as can be told, experienced anything approaching a moment's real joy.

Though he never finished high school – his uncle, disregarding his brightness, sent him to work as an office boy in Salem instead – Hoover nurtured a fierce ambition to better himself. In 1891, aged seventeen, he passed the entrance examinations for the brand-new Leland Stanford Junior University (or just Stanford as we now know it), which then was a free school. As a member of Stanford's first-ever class, he studied geology and also met there his future wife, Lou Henry, who by chance was also from Iowa. (They would marry in 1899.) Upon graduating, Hoover took the only job he could find, in a mine in Nevada City, California, loading and pushing an ore cart in a gold mine ten hours a day seven days a week for 20 cents an hour – a meagre salary even then. That this was the permanent lot for his fellow miners seems never to have troubled him. Hoover was a great believer in – and living personification of – the notion of personal responsibility.

In 1897, still in his early twenties, Hoover was hired by a large and venerable British mining company, Bewick, Moreing and Co., and for the next decade travelled the world ceaselessly as its chief engineer and troubleshooter – to Burma, China, Australia, India, Egypt and wherever else its mineralogical interests demanded. In six years, Hoover circled the globe five times. He lived through the Boxer Rebellion in China, hacked through the jungles of Borneo, rode camels across the red emptiness of Western Australia, rubbed shoulders with Wyatt Earp and Jack London in a Klondike saloon, camped beside the Great Pyramids of Egypt. He had experiences as rich and memorable as any young man has ever enjoyed, and was moved by none of them. In his memoirs, written towards the end of his life, Hoover rather testily acknowledges that he visited many marvellous places and saw many wondrous things as a young man, but informs the reader that he will dwell on none of that. 'For those who are interested [in romance and adventure] there are whole libraries of books in every geographical setting,' he says. Instead the reader is given an emotionless survey of duties fulfilled and minerals extracted. His life was work. There was nothing else.

After a decade in the field, Hoover was brought back to London and made a partner in Bewick, Moreing. Now a family man with two young sons, he moved into a big house on Campden Hill in Kensington, and became a pillar of the British business community. He socialized a little, but poorly. Dinners at his house often passed in more or less complete silence. 'Never was he heard to mention a poem, a play, a work of art,' wrote one observer. Instead, he just steadily accumulated wealth – some $4 million of it before his fortieth birthday.

He would very probably have passed his life in wealthy anonymity but for a sudden change in circumstances that thrust him unexpectedly into the limelight. When war broke out, Hoover, as a prominent American, was called on to help evacuate other Americans stranded in Europe – there were, remarkably, over 120,000 of them – and he performed that duty with such efficiency and distinction that he was asked to take on the much greater challenge of heading the new Commission for Relief in Belgium.

Belgium was overwhelmed by war, its farms destroyed, its factories shut, its foodstocks seized by the Germans. Eight million Belgians were in real peril of starving. Hoover managed to find and distribute $1.8 million worth of food a week every week for two and a half years – 2.5 million tons of it altogether – and to deliver it to people who would otherwise have gone unfed. The achievement can hardly be overstated. It was the greatest relief effort ever undertaken on earth, and it made him, deservedly, an international hero. By 1917, it was reckoned that Hoover had saved more lives than any other person in history. One enthusiast called him 'the greatest humanitarian since Jesus Christ', which of course is about as generous as a compliment can get. The label stuck. He became to the world 'the Great Humanitarian'.

Two things accounted for Hoover's glorious reputation: he executed his duties with tireless efficiency and dispatch, and he made sure that no one anywhere was ever unaware of his accomplishments. Myron Herrick, America's avuncular ambassador in Paris, performed similar heroic feats in occupied France without receiving any thanks from posterity, but only because he didn't seek them. Hoover by contrast was meticulous in ensuring that every positive act associated with him was inflated to maximum importance and covered with a press release.

In fact, Hoover was almost totally lacking in feeling for those he saved. He refused to visit any relief sites or otherwise interact with the unfortunate victims he was helping. Once when an aide innocently took him to a field kitchen in Brussels, Hoover recoiled. 'Don't you ever let me see one of these again,' he seethed. To those who knew him he seemed to have no feelings at all. One acquaintance noted how Hoover talked of his relief work in Europe without emotion. 'Not once did he show the slightest feeling or convey to me a picture of the tragedies that went on,' the friend related in wonder.

Hoover was also extremely intolerant of anything that

seemed likely to diminish his eminence. When a *Saturday Evening Post* article suggested – incorrectly – that the New York office of the Commission for Relief in Belgium was actually the most important and productive part of the operation and that the real leader of the CRB was its American head, Lindon Bates, Hoover reacted with a certain wildness. He dashed off a long letter asserting that the article contained '46 absolute untruths and 36 half-truths', and carefully addressed each contentious point in turn. He ordered the New York office to cease putting out press releases and to clear all announcements in advance through Hoover's office in London, thus severely hampering its ability to generate donations.

Belgium was just the beginning for Hoover. Solving crises became his role in life. When America joined the war, President Woodrow Wilson called Hoover home and asked him to become national food administrator, looking after every aspect of wartime American food production, to make sure that plenty was grown, every citizen amply fed, and profiteering rooted out. Hoover coined the slogan 'Food Will Win the War' and promoted it so effectively that millions were left with the impression that it was Hoover more than anyone else who secured America's triumph. At war's end, he was sent back to Europe to save millions from starvation again as head of the American Relief Administration. The challenge was bigger than ever. Hoover was responsible for the well-being of 400 million people. He oversaw relief operations in more than thirty countries. In Germany alone, the ARA ran 35,000 feeding centres, which collectively provided 300 million meals to people who would not otherwise have eaten.

Austria was in an especially parlous state when Hoover

arrived. 'The peacemakers had done their best to make Austria a foodless nation,' Hoover noted drily in his memoirs. (For a man who had no sense of humour in his personal life, his writing was often bitingly ironic.) Hoover estimated that Austria needed $100 million of food aid to hold out until the next harvest, but it couldn't raise even a small portion of that. The United States was unable to assist because US law prohibited lending to enemy states, even after they had ceased being enemies. To get around this, Hoover arranged for America to lend $45 million to Britain, France and Italy, and for them to lend the money on to Austria on the understanding that it be used to buy American food. This cleverly averted starvation while helping American farmers dispose of surplus crops, but caused understandable dismay among the three allied nations when Congress subsequently insisted that they repay the loan after Austria defaulted. The allies pointed out that they had only borrowed the money in a technical sense and hadn't benefited from the arrangement, whereas American farmers had been enriched by $45 million. Congress, unmoved, insisted on payment. Such actions fed America's prosperity, but did nothing to enhance its popularity or prestige abroad.

None of this rebounded on Hoover, who seemed to enjoy a permanent immunity from blame. In fact, closer investigation shows that Hoover was not as heroic and noble as most of his contemporaries thought him. An investigative reporter named John Hamill, in a book called *The Strange Career of Mr Hoover Under Two Flags*, claimed that Hoover profited personally, and substantially, from the Belgian food relief programme. That charge was never proved – possibly, it must be said, because it was baseless

– but another, even graver charge was true. During the war as part of his business operations Hoover illegally bought chemicals from Germany. This was an exceedingly grave offence in wartime. Remarkably, he did so not because the chemicals were unavailable in Britain, but simply because the German ones were cheaper. He saw no moral inconsistency in supporting the German economy even as Germany was trying to kill the sons and brothers of the people he worked and lived with. It is extraordinary to think that only a little more than a decade before he became President of the United States, Herbert Hoover, the Great Humanitarian, was engaged in an act that could have led to his being taken outside, stood against a wall and shot.

In 1919, his work in Europe done, Hoover returned permanently to the United States. He had lived abroad for twenty years, and was something of a stranger in his own land, yet he was so revered that he was courted as a potential presidential candidate by *both* political parties. It has often been written that Hoover had been away so long that he didn't know whether he was a Republican or a Democrat. That is not actually true. He had joined the Republican Party in 1909. But it is true that he wasn't terrifically political and had never voted in a presidential election. In March 1921, he joined Warren G. Harding's cabinet as secretary of commerce. After Harding died suddenly in 1923, he continued in the same post under Calvin Coolidge.

Hoover was a diligent and industrious presence in both administrations, but he was dazzlingly short on endearing qualities. His manner was cold, vain, prickly and snappish. He never thanked subordinates or enquired into their happiness or well-being. He had no visible capacity for friendliness or warmth. He did not even like shaking hands. Although Coolidge's sense of humour was that of a slightly backward schoolboy – one of his favourite japes was to ring all the White House servant bells at once, then hide behind the curtains to savour the confusion that followed – he did at least have a sense of humour. Hoover had none. One of his closest associates remarked that in thirty years he had never heard Hoover laugh out loud.

Coolidge kept an exceedingly light hand on the tiller of state. He presided over an administration that was, in the words of one observer, 'dedicated to inactivity'. His treasury secretary, Andrew Mellon, spent much of his working life overseeing tax cuts that conveniently enhanced his own wealth. According to the historian Arthur M. Schlesinger, Jr, with a single piece of legislation Mellon gave himself a greater tax cut than that enjoyed by almost the entire populace of Nebraska put together. Mellon had the Internal Revenue Service send its best men to prepare his tax returns for him with a view to keeping them as small as possible. The head of the IRS even helpfully provided a list of loopholes for Mellon to exploit. As Mellon's biographer David Cannadine notes, Mellon also illegally used his position to promote his business interests – for instance, by asking the secretary of state to help one of his companies secure an engineering contract in China. Thanks to these manoeuvrings, Mellon's personal net worth more than doubled to over $150 million during his term of office, and the wealth of his family, which he oversaw, topped $2 billion.

By 1927, Coolidge worked no more than about four and a half hours a day – 'a far lighter schedule than most other presidents, indeed most other people, have followed', as the political scientist Robert E. Gilbert once observed – and napped much of the rest of the time. 'No other President in my time,' recalled the White House usher, 'ever slept so much.' When not napping, he often sat with his feet in an open desk drawer (a lifelong habit) and counted cars passing on Pennsylvania Avenue.

All this left Herbert Hoover in an ideal position to exert himself outside his areas of formal responsibility, and nothing pleased Herbert Hoover more than conquering new administrative territories. He took a hand in everything – in labour disputes, the regulation of radio, the fixing of airline routes, the supervision of foreign loans, the relief of traffic congestion, the distribution of water rights along major rivers, the price of rubber, the implementation of child hygiene regulations, and much else that often seemed only tangentially related to matters of domestic commerce. He became known to his colleagues as 'Secretary of Commerce and Undersecretary of Everything Else'. When aeroplane licences were introduced, it was Hoover's department that issued them. When a cheesy Broadway impresario named Earl Carroll publicly invited high-school girls to audition for his risqué stage shows, it was to Hoover that a group called Moms of America appealed (successfully) for help. When AT&T wished to demonstrate a new invention called television, it was Herbert Hoover who was put in front of the camera. He even found time in the spring of 1927 to produce an article for the *Atlantic Monthly* on how to improve the nation's fish hatcheries. ('I wish to state a fact, to observe a condition, to relate an experiment, to define a proposition, to offer a protest, and to give the reasons for all,' he wrote in the article's opening passage, proving that there was no matter too small to escape his numbing pomposity.) When not sorting out the nation's problems, he travelled widely to accept honours. In the course of his life, he received more than five hundred awards, including honorary degrees from eighty-five universities.

Coolidge didn't have much regard for Hoover. He didn't like most people, but he seemed especially not to like Hoover. 'That man has offered me unsolicited advice for six years, all of it bad!' Coolidge once barked when the subject of Hoover came up. In April 1927 Coolidge puzzled the world by issuing a statement proclaiming that Hoover would never be appointed secretary of state. The headline on the front page of the *New York Times* for 16 April 1927 read:

CAPITAL MYSTIFIED
ON HOOVER'S STATUS
WITH THE PRESIDENT

WHITE HOUSE DECLARES HE WILL
NOT BE SECRETARY OF STATE,
EVEN IF KELLOGG QUITS

Why Coolidge issued the statement at all, and why with such finality, was a matter that puzzled every political commentator in the country. As Hoover had indicated no desire for the role, and the incumbent, Frank B. Kellogg, no inclination to leave it, they were as bewildered as everyone else.

With withering disdain Coolidge referred to his tireless

commerce secretary as 'Wonder Boy', but, much as he sneered, he was glad to have someone to do so much of his work for him. And now when the Mississippi flooded as it never had before, it was to Herbert Hoover that he turned. One week after making his enigmatic promise not to promote Hoover to the role of secretary of state, President Coolidge appointed him to head the relief efforts to deal with the emergency. Apart from that one act, Coolidge did nothing. He declined to visit the flooded areas. He declined to make any federal funds available or to call a special session of Congress. He declined to make a national radio broadcast appealing for private donations. He declined to provide the humourist Will Rogers with a message of hope and goodwill that Rogers could read out as part of a national broadcast. He declined to supply twelve signed photographs to be auctioned off for the relief of flood victims.

Hoover made his headquarters nominally in Memphis, but over the next three months he was to be found everywhere – in Little Rock, Natchez, New Orleans, Baton Rouge. Wherever a man of dignity was needed, there stood Hoover. To give the commerce secretary his due, he presented an air of statesmanship that the president declined to provide. It was he who addressed the nation by radio. 'It is difficult to picture in words the might of the Mississippi in flood,' Hoover reported to the nation from Memphis.

> To say that two blocks from where I stand it is at this minute flowing at a rate ten times that of Niagara seems unimpressive. Perhaps it becomes more impressive to say that at Vicksburg the flood is 6,000 feet wide and 50 feet deep, rushing on at the rate of six

> miles an hour. Behind this crest lies the ruin of
> 200,000 people. Thousands still cling to their homes
> where the upper floors are yet dry ... This is the
> pitiable plight of a lost battle.

Much worse was to come. Over the next two weeks, the number of homeless would soar to half a million. Hoover, however, was in his element. He had a massive crisis to solve and the authority to instruct and deploy people from a multitude of departments and agencies – the Red Cross, Weather Bureau, Public Health Service, Coast Guard, Veterans' Bureau, Interstate Commerce Commission, national lighthouse service, and at least a dozen more – *and* to interfere directly in the running of four large government departments: Agriculture, Navy, War and the Treasury. No one short of the presidency had ever been in charge of so much at once. No aspect of the operations escaped his concentrated attention. He authorized the setting up of 154 refugee camps and provided exacting instructions on how each should be laid out and operated: tents should be 18 feet by 18 feet and arrayed in ordered ranks along streets exactly 25 feet wide, with 10-foot-wide alleys between each two rows of tents. (In fact, for practical reasons mostly to do with terrain, such geometrical perfection was almost nowhere achieved.) Amounts of food, types of entertainment, extent of medical care and all other details of camp life were similarly prescribed, if not often followed. Rather amazingly, Hoover saw the camps as happy places. For many of the inhabitants, he insisted, 'this was the first real holiday they had ever known'. These were people, remember, who had just lost everything.

As in Europe, Hoover was not comfortable with the people whose lives he had been sent to sort out. He particularly didn't like the Cajuns of Louisiana, who he thought were 'as much like French peasants as one dot is like another'. Hoover was particularly exasperated at the number of Cajuns who repeatedly ignored calls to move to higher ground. One farmer had to be 'rescued' six times. In Melville, Louisiana, when a levee on the Atchafalaya River gave way in the night, ten people lost their lives because they hadn't left when told to – nine from a single family: a woman and her eight children. To Hoover this was not so much a source of tragedy as irritation. 'I concluded a Cajun would move only when the water came up under the bed,' he wrote.

The Cajuns, in turn, weren't crazy about him. Near Caernarvon, Louisiana, a man with a rifle fired on Hoover's party as it passed in a boat, then vanished back into the woods before he could be caught. The man's animosity was perhaps understandable. The party was inspecting a levee that was about to be blown up to divert flood waters away from New Orleans – an action that was widely held to be unnecessary. Levee failures further north had already lowered the river and removed any immediate or probable threat to the city, but it was decided to blow up the levee anyway. Two large parishes were sacrificed for the peace of mind of New Orleans businessmen. The city of New Orleans promised those affected that they would be fully reimbursed. They never were.

As always, Hoover was a tireless self-publicist. He travelled through the South in a private train, which included a carriage exclusively devoted to press operations. From this issued a stream of press releases mostly devoted to Hoover's vision and hard work. He also made sure that every Republican senator received a copy of a magazine article praising him. To any newspaper, however small, that questioned or criticized his efforts, he wrote a personal letter of rebuke. Sometimes these ran on for several pages.

Hoover boasted that no more than three people died in the flooding after he took control ('one of them an over-curious sightseer'), but in fact it was at least 150, and possibly many more. In the end, his efforts were far from an unqualified success. Relief funds were often wasted or misdirected. Emergency supplies were usually entrusted to the largest landowners to distribute to their tenants, and some owners unscrupulously charged tenants for the supplies or kept them to themselves. Reports of abuses were frequently brought to Hoover's attention, but he dismissed them all. The refugee camps themselves were not comfortable places and the food was often so poor and unwholesome that many of the residents came down with dietary diseases like pellagra. These were not matters that featured in Hoover's press releases.

To the wider world, however, the Mississippi flood merely consolidated Herbert Hoover's reputation as a colossus and made it almost a certainty that he would be the next Republican nominee for president. 'It is nearly inevitable,' he told a friend simply.

In the normal course of things, the Mississippi flood would not in itself have troubled Charles Lindbergh, but it happened to coincide with a broad band of turbulent weather that lay right across his flight path. A towering storm system darkened the skies over a huge area of the

Midwest and South-west and sent tornadoes spinning like demonic tops across eight states, from Texas to Illinois. In Poplar Bluff, Missouri, eighty people died and 350 were injured when a tornado tore through the business district. Elsewhere in Missouri, tornadoes claimed a dozen more lives, and many other deaths were reported in Texas, Arkansas, Kansas, Louisiana and Illinois. In St Louis, high winds caused extensive damage and killed one man ('a Negro', the *New York Times* noted solemnly) who was struck by falling debris. In Wyoming, three people caught in a sudden blizzard froze to death. Altogether the storm toll was put at 228 dead and 925 injured in two days.

In St Louis, on the morning of Lindbergh's arrival the winds eased but were replaced by heavy fog. Players at that day's baseball game between the St Louis Browns and New York Yankees at Sportsman's Park complained that they could not see ten feet ahead of them. Babe Ruth in any case saw well enough to hit a double and a home run, his eighth of the young season. No one yet suspected what kind of summer he was about to have. The Yankees won the game 4–2.

While a chill, damp fog lay over eastern Missouri, Chicago was suffering a scorching heatwave, while Colorado and the northern plains states lay buried beneath heavy late snows. Nebraska, bizarrely, experienced snow in several parts of the state while the south-western corner reported two sultry tornadoes. Never had weather been more unsettled and strange. Lindbergh seemed blissfully oblivious. If he had any trouble finding Lambert Field in the fog he never mentioned it. In fact, he said nothing at all of bad weather in any of his published accounts of those eventful days other than to note that he was glad of the storm system because it kept the other flyers in New York pinned down until he got there. That he was perhaps the only person between the two coasts bold enough to take to the air seems not to have occurred to him then or later.

In St Louis, Lindbergh showed off the new plane to the men who had paid for it, had a nap, wolfed down a plate of steak and four eggs at Louie's Café by the airfield, then took to the skies again, this time bound for New York. In reaching St Louis he had already notched up an impressive double achievement: he had become the first person to fly over the Rockies by night and he had set a record for the longest non-stop flight ever undertaken by an American pilot flying alone. Now, with the flight to New York, if all went to plan he would break the record for the quickest coast-to-coast flight as well. Remarkably, this was just at the time when dense fogs along the east coast grounded migrating birds and made the hunt for Nungesser and Coli futile. No airman in the eastern United States was going anywhere. Francesco de Pinedo, wishing to resume his stately progress around America in a replacement plane, tried for three days to fly to Philadelphia from New York, but was turned back each time by driving rain and low cloud.

Logically, the weather that was keeping aviators grounded in New York ought to have kept Lindbergh from getting through, but the normal rules of life appeared to have been suspended where he was concerned. For the time being at least, young Charles Lindbergh seemed to have acquired a curious immortality.

CHAPTER 4

To a foreign visitor arriving in America for the first time in 1927, the most striking thing was how staggeringly well off it was. Americans were the most comfortable people in the world. American homes shone with sleek appliances and consumer durables – refrigerators, radios, telephones, electric fans, electric razors – that would not become standard in other countries for a generation or more. Of the nation's 26.8 million households, 11 million had a phonograph, 10 million had a car, 17.5 million had a telephone. Every year America added more new phones (781,000 in 1926) than Britain possessed in total.

Forty-two per cent of all that was produced in the world was produced in the United States. America made 80 per cent of the world's movies and 85 per cent of its cars. Kansas alone had more cars than France. At a time when gold reserves were the basic marker of national wealth, America held half the world's supply, or as much as all the rest of the world put together. No country in history had ever been this well off, and it was getting wealthier daily at a pace that was positively dizzying. The stock market, already booming, would rise by a third in 1927 in what Herbert Hoover would later call 'an orgy of mad speculation', but in the spring and summer of 1927 neither he nor anyone else was worried yet.

The America that Charles Lindbergh crossed by air in May 1927 was, as you would expect, a rather different place from the America we find today. It was, for one thing, more roomy and self-evidently rural. With a population of just under 120 million, the United States had only about four people then for every ten it holds today. Half of those 120 million still lived on farms or in small towns, compared with just 15 per cent now, so the balance was much more in favour of the countryside.

Cities were, on the whole, agreeably compact: they had not yet acquired the radiating shock waves of suburban sprawl that we find today. Nor, by and large, did roads of any consequence emerge from them. In 1927, when people travelled or shipped goods, it was still almost exclusively by rail. Paved highways in most places were a rarity. Even the great, newly built Lincoln Highway – which proudly called itself the first transcontinental highway in the world – was continuously paved only from New York City to western Iowa. From there to San Francisco, only about half of it was. In Nevada, it was 'largely hypothetical', in the words of one contemporary, with not even roadside markers to indicate a notional existence. Other, shorter through routes like the Jefferson Highway and Dixie Highway were beginning to appear here and there, but these were enchanting novelties, not true harbingers. When people imagined the future of long-distance transportation it wasn't highways they thought of but aeroplanes and giant dirigibles cruising between city centres.

That was why the Orteig Prize was for an epic flight and not a road race. It was also why skyscrapers of the period began to sport pointed masts – so that airships could tie up to them. That this was patently inadvisable – imagine the *Hindenburg* crashing in flames on Times Square – seems not to have occurred to any architect. Even in routine dockings, airships often had to discharge quantities of ballast water for purposes of stability, and it is unlikely that passers-by below would have welcomed a regular downpour of aquatic bilge.

An alternative possibility for getting passengers into cities was the skyscraper aerodrome, with runways cantilevered outward from lofty rooftops or shared between buildings. One visionary architect came up with a plan to build a kind of giant table, with skyscrapers for the four legs and a four-acre landing platform perched across them. The *New York Times* for its part imagined a more personal approach. 'The helicopter and gyroscope will enable a man to land and start from a shelf outside his dwelling window,' it stated with hopeful conviction in an editorial on the coming future.

That none of this was in any respect achievable – in terms of engineering, architecture, aeronautics, financing, safety, building codes or any other consideration – seemed hardly to matter. This was an age that didn't like practical concerns to get in the way of its musings. A writer in the popular *Science and Invention* magazine confidently forecast that people of all ages would soon be travelling – and briskly – on motorized rollerskates, while Harvey W. Corbett, a prominent architect, predicted that skyscrapers would rise hundreds of storeys into the clouds and that people living on the upper levels would get their meals by radio, without explaining exactly how he imagined that would work. Rodman Wanamaker, the department store magnate and financier of Richard Byrd's flight, sponsored an exhibition in New York called 'The Titan City' that depicted a future world in which magnificent urban towers were connected by sleek aerial expressways while citizens were shot through glass tubes in pneumatic trains or glided regally from place to place on moving walkways. Whatever the future held, everyone agreed that it would be technologically advanced, American-led and thrilling.

Curiously, it was the present that people weren't so certain about. The First World War had left in its wake a world that nearly everyone thought shallow, corrupt and depraved – even those who were enjoying it for those very reasons. Prohibition was in its eighth year, and was a spectacular failure. It had created a world of gangsters and rattling tommy guns, and turned ordinary citizens into criminals. New York had more saloons now than it had had before Prohibition, and drinking remained so transparently prevalent that the mayor of Berlin on a visit reportedly asked Mayor Jimmy Walker when Prohibition was to begin. The Metropolitan Life Insurance Company reported in 1927 that more people were dying of alcohol-related causes now than at any time before Prohibition was introduced.

Moral decline was evident everywhere, even on the dance floor. The tango, shimmy and Charleston, with their insistent beats and flapping of limbs, had a hint of sexual frenzy that many an anxious elder found alarming. Worse was a popular dance called the Black Bottom, which involved hopping forward and backward and slapping the rump – an act of scandalous abandon focused on a body part that many would rather didn't exist at all. Even the hesitation waltz was deemed to contain some element of sultriness that made it tantamount to musical foreplay. Worst of all was jazz, which was widely held to be a springboard for drug-taking and promiscuity. 'Does Jazz Put the Sin in Syncopation?' asked an article in the *Ladies' Home Journal*. You bet it does was the answer. An editorial in the *New York American* called jazz 'a pathological, nerve-irritating, sex-exciting music'.

Many were dismayed to realize that America now had the highest divorce rate in the world after the Soviet Union. (To cash in on this, Nevada in 1927 slashed the residency requirement for divorce in the state to three months, and in so doing became the home of the 'quickie' divorce.)

Concern was greatest for young women, who seemed everywhere to have abandoned themselves to sordid habits. They smoked, drank, rouged their shining faces, bobbed their hair (which is to say cut it short and of even length all the way round), and clad themselves in silken dresses of breathtaking skimpiness. The amount of fabric in the average dress, it was calculated, fell from almost twenty yards before the war to a wispy seven after. The generic term of the day for women of lively and liberal disposition was 'flapper' – a word that originated in England in the late nineteenth century and originally signified a prostitute. (It was an offshoot of that other avian term for females, still in use in England today: 'bird'.)

The movies deftly caught, and often actively inflamed, the spirit of abandon that characterized the times. One film, according to its poster, offered its slavering audiences 'beautiful jazz babies, champagne baths, midnight revels, petting parties in the purple dawn, all ending in one terrific smashing climax that makes you gasp'. Another had 'neckers, petters, white kisses, red kisses, pleasure-mad daughters, sensation-craving mothers'. It didn't take a great deal of imagination to discern a direct-line connection between the wanton behaviour of the modern woman and the murderous instincts of a Ruth Snyder. It was often noted in newspaper accounts that the wicked Mrs Snyder before her downfall had been a great one for going to hot movies.

In desperation, lawmakers tried to legislate probity. In Oshkosh, Wisconsin, a local law made it an offence for dancing partners to gaze into each other's eyes. In Utah, the state legislature considered sending women to prison – not fining them, but imprisoning them – if their skirts showed more than three inches of leg above the ankle. In Seattle, a group called the Clean Books League even tried to get banned the travel books of the adventurer Richard Halliburton on the grounds that they 'excited to wander-lust'. Regulations of a moral nature were introduced all over the nation, and nearly everywhere were, like Prohibition itself, ignored. Among people of a conservative tempera-ment, it was a time of despair.

So when the *Spirit of St Louis* landed on Long Island and from it stepped a young man who seemed to represent everything that was modest and virtuous and good, a very large part of the nation stirred hopefully and took notice.

Up to this point Lindbergh had seemed 'a far-away and vague rival', as Clarence Chamberlin recalled later. Most people outside aviation had not even heard of him. But he now rapidly became the public favourite. As a *New York*

Times reporter observed just twenty-four hours after his arrival: 'Lindbergh has won the hearts of New Yorkers by his bashful smile, his indomitable pluck and his impetuous flight here from the Pacific.' Large crowds came to the airfields to see the person the papers were calling (to his extreme irritation) 'Lucky Lindy'. On the Sunday after his arrival, thirty thousand people – as many as would go to a Yankees game – turned up at Curtiss Field just in the hope of catching sight of the young aviator as he talked with his mechanics and worked on his plane. So many climbed on to the roof of a small paint shop next to the *Spirit of St Louis* hangar that the building collapsed under their weight. Luckily, no one was inside at the time and none of those who fell were seriously injured.

The two main airfields of Long Island, Roosevelt and its more diminutive neighbour Curtiss, didn't offer much in the way of romance. They stood in a dreary, semi-industrialized landscape of warehouses and low factories interspersed with market gardens and characterless housing developments. The airfields themselves were strictly utilitarian. Their hangars and service buildings were rough and unpainted. The parking areas were potholed and over-spread with brown puddles. After weeks of rain, the paths around the buildings were a shiny slick of mud.

Roosevelt was much the better of the two airfields,* thanks to money spent by Rodman Wanamaker on rolling and grading the runway since René Fonck's terrible crash

---

* The field was named after Quentin Roosevelt, son of Theodore Roosevelt, who had died in aerial combat in the First World War. Lindbergh had known him, at least slightly. They had been students at the same time at the Sidwell Friends School in Washington, though Roosevelt was five years older.

there eight months earlier. It was the only runway in New York long enough for an Atlantic flight, which could have been a problem since it was now leased exclusively to Wanamaker for Byrd's use,* but Byrd insisted that the other competitors be allowed to use it, too. To his immense credit, Byrd did everything he could to help his rivals. He freely shared his private weather reports, for instance. He was also one of the first to call on Lindbergh at his hangar at Curtiss Field and to wish him good luck. Then again, Byrd was by such a wide margin the front-runner and Lindbergh so obviously outclassed that Byrd could afford to be generous.

Despite the attention Lindbergh now received, most of the other aviators and crew didn't rate his chances highly. Bernt Balchen, a member of the Byrd team, recalled in his memoirs that Lindbergh was generally assumed to be out of his class. The president of the American Society for the Promotion of Aviation stated frankly that he didn't think Lindbergh, or indeed any of the pilots, stood a chance.

Compared with Byrd's operation, Lindbergh's was indeed arrestingly low-key. Byrd had a team of forty people – mechanics, telegraph operators, even kitchen staff to run a private mess hall. Lindbergh had no help at all lined up in New York. His backers in St Louis sent out a young man named George Stumpf, who had no relevant experience, in the vague hope that he might run errands or otherwise make himself useful. The Wright Corporation provided two mechanics to assist him with preparations (it

* In addition to Wanamaker, Byrd was supported by John D. Rockefeller, the National Geographic Society and, interestingly, Dwight Morrow, Charles Lindbergh's future father-in-law.

did this for all the teams using its engines, in its own interests) and also sent a PR man named Richard Blythe to help manage the press, but considered Lindbergh such a dark horse that it made the two of them share a room in the Garden City Hotel. Apart from this, Lindbergh was entirely on his own. Byrd's preparations were conservatively estimated to have cost $500,000. Lindbergh's total expenses – plane, fuel, food, lodging, everything – came to just $13,500.

Though Byrd was too well bred to betray his thoughts, he must have been appalled by what he saw when he called on Lindbergh. He was clearly just a boy. He had no relevant experience. His plane had no radio and a single engine – Byrd insisted on having three – and was built by a company no one had ever heard of. Lindbergh planned to carry no lifeboat and almost no back-up supplies. Above all, he proposed to go alone, which meant flying a difficult and unstable plane for a day and a half through storm and cloud and darkness while intricately balancing the flow of fuel through five tanks governed by fourteen valves, and navigating his way across a void without landmarks. When he needed to check his position or log a note, he would have to spread his work out on his lap and hold the stick between his knees; if it was night-time he would have to grip a small torch between his teeth. Taken together, these were jobs that would test a crew of three. Anyone who knew flying knew that this was more than any one person could do. It was madness.

Several newspapermen tried to talk Lindbergh out of his suicidal ambition, but to no avail.

'He won't listen to reason,' one complained to Balchen. 'He's just a stubborn squarehead.'

*   *   *

The atmosphere at the airfields, Lindbergh recalled years later in his autobiography *The Spirit of St Louis*, was decidedly tense. It was just over two weeks since Davis and Wooster had crashed fatally in Virginia and less than one week since Nungesser and Coli had gone missing. Myron Herrick, the American ambassador in Paris, had publicly announced that it would not be a good idea for any American airmen to fly to France for the time being. Now everyone was pinned down by bad weather anyway. It was all very frustrating.

Adding to Lindbergh's personal strain was a growing uneasiness with the press. Reporters persisted in asking him personal questions that had nothing to do with flying – did he have a sweetheart? Did he like dancing? – which he found embarrassing and intrusive, and photographers couldn't understand why he wouldn't let them take pictures of him relaxing or horsing around with the other flyers or mechanics. They were just trying to make him look normal, after all. At one point, two of them burst into his room at the Garden City Hotel, hoping to catch him shaving or reading or doing *some*thing that would suggest a kind of likeable boyish normality.

On 14 May, Charles's mother arrived from Detroit to wish him a safe journey. Reluctantly they posed for pictures, standing stiffly side by side like two people who had only just been introduced. Mrs Lindbergh declined all pleas to kiss or embrace her son, explaining that they came from 'an undemonstrative Nordic race', which in her case was wholly untrue. Instead, she patted her son lightly on the back and said, 'Good luck, Charles,' then added as an ominous afterthought: 'And goodbye.' The *Evening Graphic*, undeterred by their shyness, created a touching composograph for its readers in which Charles's and his mother's heads were pasted on to the bodies of more demonstrative models – though no art director could do anything about the strange, flat absence of emotion in mother's and son's eyes.

All three American competitors – Lindbergh in the *Spirit of St Louis*, Byrd with the *America*, Chamberlin and Acosta in Bellanca's *Columbia* – were reported as ready to go, so it was widely assumed that they would leave together the moment the weather cleared and that the Atlantic crossing would now be an exciting three-way race. In fact, unbeknown to Lindbergh and the rest of the world, things were not going well in the other two camps. Byrd seemed strangely reluctant to commit to the Paris flight. He endlessly tested and retested every system of the plane, to the mystification of his crew and the hair-rending exasperation of Tony Fokker, the plane's volatile designer. 'It seemed to me that every possible excuse for delay was seized on,' Fokker recalled in his autobiography four years later. 'I began to wonder whether Byrd really wanted to make the transatlantic flight.' To everyone's surprise, Byrd set the plane's formal dedication – with droning speeches and the plane draped in bunting – for Saturday 21 May, which meant that he couldn't go before the weekend even if the weather allowed.

In the *Columbia* camp, matters were even more unhappy, and all because of the odd and truculent nature of Charles A. Levine. The son of a scrap merchant, Levine had made his own fortune after the First World War by buying and selling surplus shell casings, which could be recycled for their brass. After developing an interest in aviation, he became known, all but inevitably, as 'the Flying Junkman'. By 1927 he claimed to be worth $5 million, though many who had seen his modest frame home in the Belle Harbor section of Rockaway, at the less genteel end of Long Island real estate, suspected that was an exaggeration.

Levine was bald, pugnacious, stockily built, and about five feet six inches tall. He dressed like a gangster in heavily pinstriped double-breasted suits and broad-brimmed hats. He had the quick mind and alert, roving gaze of a man always on the lookout for an opportunity. His smile was a grimace. He had recently celebrated his thirtieth birthday.

His two greatest personality faults were a pathological inability to be frank with anyone – Levine seemed some-times to be lying simply for the sake of it – and an equal difficulty in distinguishing legal activities from illegal ones. He had a fatal tendency to alienate and often cheat his business associates. In consequence he constantly ended up in court. It was legal problems that would prove his undoing now.

Levine's immediate difficulty was that he couldn't stand his chief pilot, Clarence Chamberlin. This was a rather odd sentiment since Chamberlin was a decent, amiable fellow and a first-rate flyer. He just lacked sparkle. The liveliest thing about him was his dress sense. He favoured snappy bowties and intensely patterned Argyle socks paired with capacious knickerbockers, but in all other respects he was almost painfully retiring.

Exasperated by Chamberlin's lack of dynamism, Levine openly manoeuvred to replace him as chief pilot. 'He wanted to eliminate me because I was not a "movie type" and would not film well after the big adventure,' Chamberlin recalled cheerfully in his autobiography.

Over the objections of Giuseppe Bellanca, who liked and admired Chamberlin very much, Levine chose Lloyd Bertaud, a burly, more outgoing type, to be chief pilot. Bertaud was unquestionably a good pilot and a fearless one. As a boy in California he had built his own glider and tested it – successfully, though none too prudently – by jumping off a high sea cliff. He was also a great publicity hound. His most inspired stunt was to get married while piloting a plane, a pastor crouched between him and his obliging bride. These impulses naturally endeared him to Levine.

So Bertaud now joined the *Columbia* team. Since Bert Acosta was also on the team, this meant that Levine had more pilots than he had space for in his aeroplane. Levine called Acosta and Chamberlin together and informed them that he hadn't made his mind up which of them would fly to Paris as Bertaud's co-pilot. He would decide with a toss of a coin on the morning of the flight. Acosta stared at him in disbelief for a long moment, then crossed the airfield and joined the Byrd team. Bertaud thereupon declared that he didn't want Chamberlin with him in any case, and endeavoured to have his own co-pilot appointed. Bellanca said he would not let his plane take off without Chamberlin aboard.

Giuseppe Bellanca was forty-one years old in 1927, which made him considerably senior to nearly everyone else involved in the Atlantic flights. Small (just five foot one), reserved and kindly, he had grown up in Sicily, the son of a flour-mill owner, and studied engineering at the Technical Institute in Milan, where he developed an interest in aviation. In 1911, Bellanca emigrated with his large family – parents and eight brothers and sisters – to Brooklyn. In the basement of their new house, he built a plane. His mother sewed the linen fabric; his father helped with the carpentry. He then took it to a field and taught himself to fly, taking short, cautious hops at first, then gradually increasing them in distance and duration until he was actually, properly airborne. Bellanca was a brilliant and innovative designer. His planes were among the first in the world to use air-cooled engines, to enclose the cockpit (for aerodynamic purposes, not the comfort of the occupants) and to incorporate streamlining into every possible aspect of the plane's exterior design. A strut on a Bellanca plane didn't just hold up the wing; it added lift or, at the very least, minimized drag. In consequence, Bellanca's plane was probably, for its size, the best in the world.

Unfortunately, Bellanca was a hopeless businessman and always struggled for funds. For a time, he designed for the Wright Corporation, but then Wright decided to get out of plane-building and concentrate on engines, so, to Bellanca's presumed horror, it sold his beloved plane to Charles Levine. Since the plane was the only Bellanca demonstrator model in existence, Bellanca the man had little choice but to go along with Bellanca the plane. And so began his brief, unhappy connection to Charles Levine.

All the parties on the Levine team now squabbled endlessly. Levine insisted that the plane should carry a radio, not for safety but so that the flyers could send reports to passing ships, which he could then sell profitably to newspapers. To make such contact easier, Levine wanted the *Columbia* to follow the principal shipping lanes rather than the great circle route (the shortest, most direct crossing), adding distance as well as danger to the enterprise. Bellanca, normally a mild man, responded furiously. A radio, he argued, would add weight that they could ill afford, presented a fire hazard, and had great potential to interfere with the plane's compasses. In any case, the men aboard the plane would be too busy flying it to write jolly accounts of their adventures for newspapers. On at least four occasions, Levine ordered the ground crew to install a radio, and on each occasion Bellanca had it taken out again – an operation that cost Levine $75 a time and left him in a sputtering rage.

Shortly before the planned day of departure, Levine made matters infinitely worse by presenting Bertaud and Chamberlin with contracts to sign. For weeks he had been promising to give them half of all earnings from the flight and to provide them with generous life insurance cover for the security of their wives should they lose their lives in the crossing attempt, but the document he now presented mentioned neither. Instead it declared that Levine would receive all monies earned and that for a period of one year following the flight they would cede to him total management of their lives. Levine alone would decide on endorsements, film roles, vaudeville tours and any other professional commitments. From these earnings, Levine would pay them each $150 a week, to which he would add unspecified 'bonuses' from time to time as seemed to him appropriate. When pressed about the insurance, Levine said he would consider it once Bertaud and Chamberlin had signed the contracts. Having just told Bertaud and Chamberlin that he was taking everything they earned, Levine informed reporters that 'every nickel of the prize money goes to the *Columbia*'s pilots'.

Bertaud, exasperated beyond forbearance at Levine's endless duplicity, found a lawyer named Clarence Nutt, who took out an injunction enjoining Levine from sending the plane anywhere until the matter of insurance and a fair contract was resolved. A court hearing was scheduled for 20 May – a date that would prove to be fateful for all concerned. In a demonstration that there was almost no limit to his unpredictability, Levine now said that he would pay Lindbergh $25,000 to accompany him to Paris. Lindbergh politely pointed out that his plane didn't have room for a passenger.

The upshot was that Lindbergh suddenly had the running all to himself, at least until the weekend, if only the weather would permit. He was beginning at last to win converts, too. After working with Lindbergh for a week, Edward Mulligan, one of the mechanics assigned to help him, rushed up to a colleague and, in a mixture of excitement and wonder, cried: 'I tell you, Joe, this boy is going to make it! He is!'

Chapter 5

THE WEATHER REMAINED terrible, not just in New York but everywhere. In Washington, DC, on 14 May, a tornado fifty feet across at the base touched down at Prospect Hill Cemetery and proceeded in an erratic fashion up Rhode Island Avenue, uprooting trees and causing consternation among onlookers before harmlessly dematerializing a minute or so after forming. Further west, unseasonably late blizzards caught much of the country by surprise. In Detroit, a Tigers–Yankees game was postponed because of snow – the latest snow-out of a major league baseball game ever recorded. Rains continued to pound the beleaguered central and lower Mississippi Valley.

In Chicago, Francesco de Pinedo, having resumed his tour of America, arrived more than five hours late from Memphis because of bad weather. His tour had become increasingly embarrassing to his hosts because his rallies were more and more overtly political and increasingly ended in violence, while Pinedo himself had a tendency to say strangely inappropriate things. 'I think New York is the best Fascist city in the whole world,' he declared generously but bewilderingly after meeting with Mayor Jimmy Walker. Two days later when Pinedo addressed a fascist rally at an Italian Legion post on Second Avenue, two thousand anti-fascist demonstrators marched on the hall. Bricks were thrown through windows, and most of those inside rushed outside and began fighting with the demonstrators. By the time police arrived in force a crowd estimated at ten thousand had gathered. Police restored order by wading through the crowd and clubbing people robustly with truncheons. Pinedo, meanwhile, continued giving his talk, seemingly unaware that he was addressing an almost entirely empty hall. The number of injured was not recorded.

Chicago was the last of Pinedo's forty-four stops in the United States before he headed back to Europe by way of Quebec and Newfoundland. His hope now was to steal a march on the Roosevelt Field aviators by getting across the Atlantic ahead of them. He couldn't qualify for the Orteig Prize because he needed to refuel in the Azores en route, but it would still be a glorious symbolic triumph for fascism if he were waiting at Le Bourget, fists on hips, to greet with an air of cheerful condescension the first American flyers to get there.

Happily there were no anti-fascist demonstrations in Chicago – though ironically Pinedo faced serious injury from the exuberant backslaps and crushing embraces of several hundred black-shirted supporters who greeted him at the dockside of the Chicago Yacht Club.

One of those waiting to welcome Pinedo at the official reception was Chicago's leading Italian-American business-man, Al Capone. Even in Chicago, the most corrupt city in America, it was a little striking to see the nation's most notorious hoodlum mingling with the mayor, the local head of the Coast Guard, and several judges and other civic dignitaries. It was the first time Capone had been invited to take part in an official ceremony in his adopted city – the first time any gangster had been invited into society. So it was a proud moment for Capone. In fact, though he had no idea of it yet, he was just one day away from the start of his downfall.

The person responsible for this unexpected turn of events was a slight, very remarkable 37-year-old woman named Mabel Walker Willebrandt. Until only a little more than a decade earlier, Willebrandt had been an anonymous housewife in California. But, growing bored with that life, she enrolled in night classes at the University of Southern California and in 1916 emerged with a law degree. For the next five years, she represented battered women and prostitutes – an unusually noble use of a law degree in the 1910s. (She also at some point shed Mr Willebrandt in a divorce.) She so distinguished herself that in 1921 she was brought to Washington and made assistant attorney general in the Harding administration. This made her the most senior woman in the federal government. She was given special responsibility for enforcing Prohibition and income tax laws. It was a wonderfully prescient, if inadvertent, combination of roles because it led her to hit on an ingenious way to tackle organized crime.

Until now, mobsters had seemed invincible. They couldn't be prosecuted for murder or other serious crimes because no one was ever brave enough to testify against them. It was almost impossible to connect them to their illicit businesses because they never put their names to contracts or other incriminating documents. Willebrandt, however, was struck by the thought that mobsters were always demonstrably rich and yet never filed an income tax return. She decided to go for them on those grounds. Prosecuting criminals for tax evasion is such a common ploy now that it is easy to overlook how brilliantly original – how completely, stunningly out of left field – the idea was when she first came up with it. Many judicial authorities thought it was completely insane.

The man she targeted, as a kind of specimen case, was a bootlegger in South Carolina named Manley Sullivan. Lawyers for Sullivan argued that criminals could not file tax returns without incriminating themselves, and that would be a breach of their Fifth Amendment rights. The lawyers also maintained that in claiming a share of the illegal profits the government would make itself an accessory to the original crime – a breach of its fiduciary responsibilities. The person most implacably opposed to Willebrandt's strategy was a federal appeals court judge named Martin Thomas Manton. 'It is hard to conceive of Congress ever having had in mind that the government be paid a part of the income, gains, or profits derived from successfully carrying on this crime,' he wrote. 'It is incredible to believe that it was intended that a bootlegger be dignified as a taxpayer for his illegal profit, so that the government may accept his money for governmental purposes, as it accepts the money of the honest merchant taxpayer.'

Despite Manton's objections and those of many others, the case went all the way to the Supreme Court. Formally known as 'United States vs Sullivan, 274 U.S. 259', it was scheduled to be decided by the court on 16

May 1927 – the day after Capone met Pinedo in Chicago. Mabel Walker Willebrandt would argue more than forty cases before the US Supreme Court, but none would have a more lasting effect than this one – if she won.

She did.

By a neat touch of irony – indeed, it would be hard to find a neater – the following decade the opinionated Judge Manton was successfully prosecuted by the Internal Revenue Service for non-payment of taxes after *he* was found guilty of pocketing $186,000 in bribes. He served seventeen months in a federal penitentiary.

Thanks to United States vs Sullivan, Al Capone's days were numbered, though neither he nor almost anyone else realized it yet. The *New York Times*, along with virtually all other papers in America, barely noted US vs Sullivan, reporting it in a small story on page thirty-one – just as it paid little attention to another landmark Supreme Court case that month, Buck vs Bell (about which much more anon). Instead, it gave far more prominence that day to a brief but lively return to the news of Ruth Snyder and Judd Gray, who on the morning of 16 May were transferred the thirty-five miles from their prison on Long Island to death row at Sing Sing in a scene of mayhem dazzlingly reminiscent of a Keystone Kops feature.

A crowd of ten thousand people – many standing on rooftops or fire escapes to get a better view – gathered outside the Queens County Jail to watch as a motorcade of fourteen cars, escorted by six police motorcycles with sidecars (each containing a policeman with a rifle), set off with America's two most popular murderers just after 10.30 in the morning. The convoy included prison officials, newspaper reporters and two aldermen, James Murtha and

Bernard Schwartz, who had nothing to do with the case but came along for the ride. 'They were accompanied by their wives and children, who seemed to enjoy the outing,' noted a *New York Times* correspondent.

From the jail, the procession drove at high speed (which in 1927 was about 40 miles an hour) over the Queensboro Bridge, then across Manhattan by way of Central Park, but it constantly got bogged down in traffic.

No place in the world was less hospitable to a speeding convoy than New York in the 1920s. It was the most congested city on earth. It contained more cars than the whole of Germany, but it also still had 50,000 horses. The combination of hurrying motorized vehicles, plodding carts and horses and lunging pedestrians made New York's streets wildly dangerous. Over a thousand people were killed in traffic accidents in New York in 1927 – four times the number that are killed in traffic accidents today. Taxi cabs alone were responsible for seventy-five deaths in Manhattan that year.

In an effort to improve things, traffic lights had been introduced to Manhattan three years earlier, but so far had little detectable effect. Elsewhere traffic improvements were being implemented where they could be, but in the short term these just added to the chaos. Along Park Avenue, the leafy central esplanade was in the process of having eighteen feet sliced off each side to add extra lanes between Forty-Sixth and Fifty-Seventh Streets, thus taking most of the park out of Park Avenue. Along the west side of Manhattan, noise and congestion were further aggravated by the construction of the Holland Tunnel, which would open that autumn. It was a wonder of the age – the longest underwater tunnel in the world – but the challenge of boring and ventilating a tube a mile and a half long a hundred feet beneath the earth was so formidable that the tunnel's designer and chief engineer, Clifford M. Holland, dropped dead from the stress before it was finished. He was only forty-one, but at least he had the consolation of having the tunnel named after him. His successor, Milton H. Freeman, keeled over just four months into the job himself, dead of a heart attack of his own, but received no commemoration. Thirteen other workers died in the course of construction. To most New Yorkers in the summer of 1927, however, the Holland Tunnel was just a mighty disruption to traffic.

So it was optimistic of the Snyder–Gray motorcade to hope that it could somehow clear a way through the chaotic streets. Worse, because it was so instantly recognizable, whenever the motorcade stopped or slowed, people crowded round to peer through the windows in the hopes of spying the murderers within, slowing its progress even more. News of the convoy's arrival on a street spread like wildfire. 'Occupants of street cars deserted their seats to rush out into the roadway,' noted the *Times* reporter in a tone of some amazement.

Matters actually worsened when the motorcade got moving. Many onlookers excitedly stepped into the road to try to get a better view, forcing the motorcycles to swerve dangerously. Several cars in the motorcade were involved in minor accidents, some repeatedly, often with each other, and the head of the motorcycle squadron, Sergeant William Cassidy, was thrown from his bike and into the side of the car carrying Ruth Snyder, causing her to shriek, but he suffered only minor injuries. Alderman Murtha's car overheated and failed to make it out of the city, to the presumed disappointment of his wife and children. At length, Snyder and Gray arrived at Sing Sing, where they vanished through the gates and off the nation's front pages. They would not be big news again until the following January when their execution was set.

Then came the most shocking story of the summer.

On the morning of 19 May, readers of the *New York Times* woke up to this headline:

MANIAC BLOWS UP SCHOOL,
KILLS 42, MOSTLY CHILDREN;
HAD PROTESTED HIGH TAXES

The maniac in question was one Andrew Kehoe, who until that day had been regarded by everyone who knew him in his home town of Bath, Michigan, as a sane and pleasant man. A graduate of Michigan State University, just down the road in Lansing, Kehoe farmed just outside town and was part-time treasurer of the local school board. He was so little suspected of anything untoward that a teacher from the school just the previous day had phoned and asked if they could hold a school picnic on his land. What the teacher didn't know at the time of the call was that Kehoe either had slaughtered or was just about to slaughter his poor wife. What is certain now is that Andrew Kehoe had become severely unhinged. A bank was about to foreclose on his farm, an act he blamed on local school taxes, and he was poised to respond in the most chilling manner imaginable.

In the early hours of 18 May, while the rest of Bath slept, Andrew Kehoe made repeated trips into the basement

121

of the school carrying boxes of dynamite and pyrotol, a military explosive. Altogether he stacked 500 pounds of explosives throughout the basement. Then he wired them all together and ran a master line out to his car, parked out front. The following morning children arrived at school as on any normal day. Bath's school educated children from every level, from kindergarten through twelfth grade. On this day, attendance was slightly reduced because it was graduation week and seniors had been given the day off, but otherwise the school was full.

At 9.40 a.m., a sudden and tremendous explosion blew apart the building's north wing, which housed the younger pupils. 'Witnesses say that Kehoe sat in his automobile in front of the school and gloated as he watched the bodies of the children hurled into the air by his diabolical plot,' the *New York Times* reported in horrified tones. Ninety children were trapped in the wreckage, many seriously injured.

As the whole town rushed to the scene, Kehoe tried to detonate a second cache of explosives in the boot of his car, but it failed to go off. Emory Huyck, the school superintendent, struggled with Kehoe to stop him from doing any more damage, but Kehoe managed to pull out a pistol and fire it into the boot, setting off another blast that killed him, Huyck and a bystander. Many others were injured. Altogether, forty-four people died that day: thirty-seven children and seven adults. Three families lost two children each. When firemen and policemen went through the building afterwards, they were astonished to find that several stacks of explosives under the building's other wings hadn't detonated. Had they done so, the death toll would have been in the hundreds.

By coincidence, just across the fields from Bath was Round Lake, site of a summer cottage where Al Capone was often to be found, particularly when he needed to lie low because of police investigations. Capone had spent the whole of the previous summer there. At the time of the school massacre, however, he was in Chicago, representing the Italian-American community for the visit of the aviator Francesco de Pinedo. Another celebrity familiar with the locality was Babe Ruth, who had been arrested the previous June just down the road in the town of Howell for fishing illegally before the start of the season.

After the massacre, it emerged that these may not have been Kehoe's first murders. Years earlier, he may very possibly have murdered his stepmother. This unfortunate woman, his father's second wife, died in hideous pain when an oil stove she was lighting exploded in her face, covering her in burning oil. Investigations showed that the stove had been tampered with. Andrew Kehoe, still just a boy, was the only person who could have done it, but nothing could be proved and no charges were brought.

The Bath massacre was the largest and most cold-blooded slaughter of children in the history of the United States, yet it was quickly forgotten. Within two days, the *New York Times* had almost completely stopped covering it. Instead, like nearly everyone else in the world, it became consumed with the story of a young man from Minnesota and his heroic flight to Paris. For the next six weeks, on every day but two the lead story in the *New York Times* was about aviation.

CHAPTER 6

O N THE LAST night of his life that he could move about freely in the world, like a normal person, Charles Lindbergh agreed to a suggestion by Richard Blythe, the Wright Corporation PR man, that they go into the city and attend a show.

It was a great year for play-going – the best ever on Broadway in terms of choice, if not quality. Two hundred and sixty-four productions opened that year, more than at any time before or since. Lindbergh and Blythe had about seventy-five plays, musicals and revues to choose among. They decided on *Rio Rita*, a musical comedy in two acts – a good choice, since not only was it a smash hit, but it was also in the lavish new Ziegfeld Theatre at Sixth Avenue and Fifty-Fourth Street, which was itself an attraction.

The theatre had opened in March and was an extravaganza of architectural opulence. Among much else, it boasted the largest oil painting in the world. Depicting great lovers in history, it was larger than the ceiling frescoes in the Sistine Chapel and more agreeable to contemplate, as a reporter for the *New Yorker* drily remarked, because you didn't have to lie on your back to enjoy it. The new theatre was so plush, many observers noted, that the seats were upholstered on the backs as well as the fronts.

The plot of *Rio Rita* was interestingly improbable. Set in Mexico and Texas, it involved an Irish-American singer named Rio Rita, a Texas Ranger travelling incognito while looking for a bandit named Kinkajou (who may or may not have been Rita's brother), a bigamous soap salesman named Chick Bean, and a character identified only as Montezuma's Daughter. These characters and some others of equal implausibility engaged in a series of amusing misunderstandings interrupted at intervals by songs that had little or nothing to do with the actions that preceded or followed. A cast of 131 and a full orchestra provided a great deal of happy noise and spectacle, if not always an abundance of sense.*

Plausibility, it seems, was not something that audiences insisted on in the 1920s. *Katy Did*, which had opened the previous week at Daly's 63rd Street Theatre, involved a waitress who, according to the plot summary, falls for 'a dishwasher and part-time bootlegger who turns out to be the exiled King of Suavia'. *Stigma*, by Dorothy Manley and Donald Duff, concerned a lonely professor's wife who falls for a handsome boarder (played by Duff), but loses her mind when she discovers that he has impregnated their black maid. *Spellbound*, by Walter Elwood, centred on a mother who poisons her two sons' coffee in the curious belief that it will discourage them from drinking alcohol, but with the unfortunate consequence that

---

* Casts in the 1920s could be enormous. A Max Reinhardt production of 1924, *The Miracle*, had a cast of 700.

one son is rendered paraplegic and the other left brain-damaged. The poor mother runs off in despair to do missionary work. Even by the forgiving standards of 1927, that play was so bad that it closed after three days.

It wasn't all froth and melodrama, however. Eugene O'Neill produced his longest and densest play in 1927, *Strange Interlude*, which took five hours to perform and gave audiences an expansive, not to say exhausting, look at insanity, abortion, heartbreak, illegitimacy and death. Audiences watched the first part of the play from 5.15 p.m. to 7 p.m., then had a break for dinner and returned at 8.30 for a further three and a half hours of punishing gloom.

In the event, Lindbergh's party (one or two others from the airfield had joined them) never got to the theatre that evening. As they arrived in Manhattan, Lindbergh decided to check the weather forecasts for one last time that day. A light rain was falling and the tops of the skyscrapers around him were lost in drifting murk, so the phone call was really a formality, but to his astonishment Lindbergh learned that conditions at sea were clearing and that reasonably good weather was expected. At once, they returned to Long Island to prepare for a morning flight.

They had much to do, including getting his plane towed from Curtiss Field to Roosevelt. Lindbergh fussed over the plane for a few hours, but late in the evening his mechanics ordered him to go back to the Garden City Hotel and get some sleep. There Lindbergh was met in the lobby by reporters who had learned of his planned departure and wanted information for the morning editions. They detained him for half an hour with their questions. By the time Lindbergh finally got to bed it was after midnight. He was just dropping off when the door

flew open and George Stumpf – who had been posted outside to see that no one disturbed him – came in. 'Slim,
what am I going to do when you're gone?' he asked
plaintively – a strange question since they had known each
other for only a week. Lindbergh spoke patiently to Stumpf
for a minute or two, then sent him away, but it was too late
and he was too keyed up. In the end, he got no sleep that
night.

Lindbergh returned to Roosevelt Field a little before
3 a.m. A light drizzle hung in the air, but the weather
reports promised clearer weather by morning. Fuelling the
plane took most of the night – it was a fussy process
because the fuel had to be filtered through cheesecloth to
remove any impurities – and all the systems had to be
checked. If Lindbergh was nervous, he gave no hint of it.
His manner was calm and cheerful throughout the final
preparations. He packed five ham and chicken sandwiches, though he would eat only one, when he was
already over France. He took two pints of water.

At some time after seven in the morning, Lindbergh
folded his lanky frame into the cockpit. The plane started up
with a throaty rumble and coughed out a cloud of blue
smoke before it settled into a rhythmic roar – intensely loud
but reassuringly steady. After a few moments Lindbergh gave
a nod and the plane began to creep forward.

After weeks of rain, the runway was soft and strewn
with puddles. The *Spirit of St Louis* moved as if rolling over
a mattress. Almost all the other airmen and crews had
arrived to watch. Fokker drove his big Lancia sedan, loaded
with fire extinguishers, to the far end of the runway. Just
beyond him, the spot where Fonck had crashed eight
months earlier still bore scorch marks.

Lindbergh's plane slowly gained speed, but seemed 'glued to the earth', as Fokker recalled later. The propeller had been set at an angle to provide maximum fuel efficiency in flight, but that meant a sacrifice in power at lift-off – and that deficiency was worryingly evident as the plane used up more and more runway without showing any sign of rising. Lindbergh in his cockpit had another concern to deal with. His lack of forward visibility, he now realized, made it impossible for him to be certain that he was moving in a completely straight line – something he very much needed to do. The plane had never been this loaded before – indeed, no Wright Whirlwind engine had ever tried to lift this much.

'Five hundred feet from the end, it still hugged the earth,' Fokker wrote in his memoirs. 'In front of him was a tractor; telephone wires bordered the field. My heart stood still.' As with Nungesser and Coli at Le Bourget, Lindbergh's plane rose tentatively and came back to earth with a clumsy bump, then rose and fell again. Finally, on the third try it lifted. It was, some spectators reported, as if Lindbergh had willed it into the air. Even Lindbergh viewed it as a kind of miracle – '5,000 pounds balanced on a blast of air', he wrote in *Spirit of St Louis*.

The plane rose so ponderously that it seemed to have little chance of clearing the telephone wires straight ahead – wires that Lindbergh could not himself see. He would learn of his failure from the sudden twang of snagged cables, followed an instant later by a crash no human could survive. Bernt Balchen, watching from halfway along the runway, was certain that Lindbergh could not make it, and cried out with relief when he just cleared the wires. He called it a masterly takeoff. Chamberlin declared: 'My heart was in my throat. It seemed impossible. It took guts.' Fokker predicted that Lindbergh would reach Europe, but would come nowhere near Paris because of the impossibility of navigating while flying solo. Byrd was especially gracious. 'His takeoff was the most skilful thing I have ever seen on the part of any aviator,' he told reporters. 'He is a wonderful boy.'

What most spectators remarked on afterwards was the silence. As the *Spirit of St Louis* took to the sky, there was no cheering – just an uneasy quiet at how close Lindbergh had come to those wires and how alone he now was in that small, fabric-covered plane. The time of takeoff was officially recorded as 7.52 a.m. The spectators watched until the plane was no longer visible, then quietly dispersed, in a contemplative frame of mind.

From Roosevelt Field, Lindbergh turned north, passing over the great estates of Long Island's North Shore, before heading out over the misty grey waters of Long Island Sound at Port Jefferson. Across the sound lay the Connecticut shore, thirty-five miles away. Perhaps nothing speaks more powerfully of the challenge that faced him than that that was more water than he had ever crossed by plane before.

Through most of that Friday Lindbergh's progress could be followed fairly closely. As the *Spirit of St Louis* sailed over Connecticut, Rhode Island and Massachusetts, reports came in more or less constantly confirming his position and that he seemed to be doing fine. By noon he was over Nova Scotia, and at mid-afternoon over Cape Breton Island. In Washington, Congress interrupted its proceedings for regular announcements of his progress. Everywhere people gathered outside newspaper offices for updates. In Detroit, Mrs Lindbergh taught chemistry at Cass Technical High as on any other day. She wanted to keep the flight out of her mind, but students and colleagues constantly brought her the latest news. Shortly after 6 p.m. eastern time Lindbergh passed over the last rocky extremity of North America on the Avalon Peninsula of Newfoundland and headed out over open ocean.

Now he would be out of touch completely for sixteen hours if all went well; for ever if it didn't.

At Yankee Stadium that night, an audience of 23,000 people attending a fight between Jack Sharkey and Jim Maloney bowed their heads in a minute of silent prayer before Sharkey beat Maloney senseless. All across America wherever people gathered, prayers were said. No one could do anything now but wait. For many the tension was too much. Ten thousand people called the *New York Times* asking for news even though everyone knew there couldn't be any.

In Paris the possibility of Lindbergh's arrival stirred little sense of anticipation at first. Myron Herrick, America's ambassador, had no idea at all when he awoke on Saturday 21 May what excitements the weekend had in store for him. He planned to spend that Saturday at the Stade Français at Saint-Cloud watching his fellow Americans Bill Tilden and Francis T. Hunter compete against Jean Borotra and Jacques Brugnon in Franco-American team matches, a kind of warm-up for the coming Davis Cup tournament.

A wealthy widower in his seventies, Herrick was a former governor of Ohio (Warren G. Harding had been his lieutenant governor), and now was a good and caring ambassador. He had matinee idol looks – silvery hair, excellent teeth, dapper moustache – and the kind of effort-less charm that wins hearts. He had made his wealth as a lawyer and banker in Cleveland. In Paris, he endeared himself to the locals with his warm manner and deep pockets. In two years he spent $400,000 of his own money on entertainments and improvements to the ambassador's residence.

The match at Saint-Cloud offered a welcome and very exciting diversion, for tennis was a big attraction in 1927 and Bill Tilden was the greatest – and most improbably great – tennis player of the age. For the last seven years he had utterly dominated the game. Yet, curiously, before that he had shown almost no special aptitude for the game at all.

Tilden grew up in a rich and distinguished family in Philadelphia – a cousin, Samuel Tilden, had been the Democratic Party nominee for president in 1876 – but his personal life was full of tragedy. All four of his siblings and both of his parents died before he reached adulthood. It was his older brother, Herbert Marmaduke, who had been the star player of the family. Tilden himself couldn't even make the tennis team at the University of Pennsylvania. But after his brother's death from pneumonia in 1915, Tilden decided to become a great player, and devoted him-self tirelessly, obsessively and without the help of a coach to improving his game. He hit balls against a wall over and over until he was flawless from every position on the court. When he emerged from his four years of intensive prepar-ation, he was not just the best player in the world, but the best who had ever lived.

Beginning at the advanced age of twenty-seven, he was

world number one for seven straight years and was not beaten in a significant tournament in the whole of that time. America under his leadership won the Davis Cup seven times in a row. He won seven US clay court titles and five US doubles championships. In 1924 he didn't lose a match, and in the summer of 1925, aged thirty-two, he reeled off fifty-seven consecutive winning games – a feat as rare as Babe Ruth hitting sixty homers or Joe DiMaggio hitting safely in fifty-six straight games.

On the court his grace was balletic. He didn't run so much as glide, and had an uncanny knack for being perfectly positioned for every return shot. It often looked as if the ball was following him around the court rather than he the ball. When serving, his favourite trick was to hold five balls in his hand, firing off four aces in a row and tossing the fifth ball aside as obviously unnecessary. His manner was arrogant and insufferable. He was widely hated by other players, but his skills on the court broadened tennis's appeal greatly.

Tilden's career almost ended before it began. In September 1920, he was playing for his first national singles title at Forest Hills before an audience of ten thousand when a plane carrying a pilot and photographer approached to take aerial pictures of the contest. As the plane neared the stadium, its engine sputtered and then cut out altogether. For several seconds, Tilden and his opponent, Bill Johnston, and all the people in the grand-stands watched in eerie silence as the plane, itself silent, headed straight for them. The plane just cleared the court and crashed in an open area a short distance beyond. The pilot and photographer were killed instantly. Tilden and Johnston looked uncertainly at the referee, who nodded for them to resume. Tilden served and won the point en route to winning the set and match 6–1, 1–6, 7–5, 5–7, 6–3. It was the start of a streak in which he did not lose a significant match for five years.

Tilden's unbroken run of achievement was made all the more remarkable by the fact that in the midst of it, in 1922, he suffered an injury that should by any reckoning have ended his career altogether. While playing in a tournament of absolutely no consequence in Bridgeton, New Jersey, he lunged for a ball and caught the middle finger of his racquet hand on the perimeter fence. The injury itself was trifling, but it became infected and two weeks later the top joint of the finger had to be amputated. Today the problem would be resolved with a course of antibiotics. In 1922 he was lucky not to lose his arm, or even his life. (Calvin Coolidge's son would die from a similar infection the following year.)

Tennis in the 1920s was a much more innocent pastime. In a thrilling men's singles final at Wimbledon in 1927 Henri Cochet beat 'the Bounding Basque' Jean Borotra with a dubious shot in which Cochet appeared to hit the ball twice, which should have cost him the point. The umpire asked him if that was in fact so, and Cochet, with a look of childlike innocence, replied, '*Mais non.*' So the point, match and championship were awarded to Cochet on the grounds that tennis was a gentleman's game and no gentleman would lie, even though it was pretty clear to all concerned that Cochet just had.

To win a major tournament in the 1920s, a player had to win five or six matches in as many days, so it was a highly taxing sport. Yet it was also an amateur one. Competitors didn't receive prize money and had to pay their own expenses, so tennis was a sport confined to the wealthy. Those who didn't fall into that category – and Tilden, his father dead, didn't quite – had to make money elsewhere. At the peak of his career, Tilden decided to become a Broadway impresario. He began to write, produce and award himself starring roles in plays that always lost a fortune. In 1926, he launched and starred in a production called *That Smith Boy*, which was such an embarrassment that the theatre owner asked him to close the show after two weeks even though Tilden was prepared to cover the costs. Subsequent plays did little better, and exhausted his savings. Remarkably, throughout this period he would often play in the US Open or Davis Cup tournament by day, then rush to the theatre to appear on stage by night.

Not surprisingly, age began to catch up with him. By the summer of 1927, he was still great but no longer invincible. The French now had four of the best players in the world – Cochet, Borotra, Brugnon and René Lacoste.

Tilden and Hunter played valiantly against Borotra and Brugnon at the Stade Français that Saturday, but the Frenchmen were too youthful and strong and won the match 4–6, 6–2, 6–2. A reporter for the Associated Press called it 'probably the greatest men's doubles match ever staged in France'. Herrick, alas, didn't get to see it all. Halfway through the third set he was handed a telegram informing him that Lindbergh had been sighted over Ireland and would be in Paris that evening. Herrick recalled later that he had not until that moment recognized the importance of Lindbergh's takeoff. Rodman Wanamaker had so inundated him with cablegrams that it had not actually occurred to him that someone other than

Byrd might get there first. He now left the stadium in a hurry. To him the prospect of Lindbergh's safe arrival in Paris was not good news, but a source of serious concern.

In 1927, Americans were not terribly popular in Europe and not popular at all in France. America's insistence on being repaid in full, with interest, the $10 billion it had lent to Europe during the war seemed a bit rich to the Europeans since all the money borrowed had been spent on American goods, so repaying it would mean that America profited twice from the same loans. That didn't seem to them quite fair, particularly as the European economies were uniformly wrecked while America's was booming. Many Americans failed to share this perspective. They took the view that a debt is a debt and must be honoured, and interpreted Europe's reluctance to pay as a shabby betrayal of trust. For those Americans of an isolationist bent – of whom our hero Charles Lindbergh would one day become the most strikingly outspoken – the situation offered powerful vindication of the belief that America should always avoid foreign entanglements. In a renewed spirit of isolationism, America increased its already high tariff barriers, making it nearly impossible for many European industries to trade their way back to prosperity.

The result of all this was quite a lot of anti-American sentiment, especially in France, where the struggling natives had to watch American tourists – many of them young, noisy and made obnoxious by wine, and no doubt sometimes also by nature – living like princes and whooping it up on their debased currencies. The number of francs to the dollar had almost tripled in the last year, making life a struggle for the natives and a frolic for visitors. On top of this, the French keenly felt the humiliating failure of Nungesser and Coli's mission; many were reluctant to give up the suspicion that American meteorologists had withheld crucial information from the Frenchmen. In consequence, American tour buses in Paris sometimes felt the thump of an angry stone, and American parties sometimes found it hard to get served in cafés. The atmosphere was unquestionably uneasy. Ambassador Herrick had every reason to urge caution. No one could begin to guess what would happen when the first American flew in.

What happened, remarkably enough, was that a hundred thousand people dropped whatever they were doing and went, entranced, to Le Bourget.

Charles Lindbergh's achievement in finding his way alone from Long Island to an airfield outside Paris deserves a moment's consideration. Maintaining your bearings by means of dead reckoning means taking close note of compass headings, speed of travel, time elapsed since the last calculation and any deviations from the prescribed route induced by drifting. Some measure of the difficulty is shown by the fact that the Byrd expedition the following month – despite having a dedicated navigator and radio operator, as well as pilot and co-pilot – missed their expected landfall by two hundred miles, were often only vaguely aware of where they were, and mistook a lighthouse on the Normandy coast for the lights of Paris. Lindbergh by contrast hit all his targets exactly – Nova Scotia, Newfoundland, the Dingle Peninsula in Ireland, Cap de la Hague in France, Le Bourget in Paris – and did so while making the calculations on his lap while flying an unstable plane. That achievement alone makes him unquestionably a candidate for the greatest pilot of his age, if not all ages. He was the only pilot that year to land where he said he would. All the other flights that summer – and there were many – either failed, made forced landings on water or came down without knowing where they were. He seemed to think that flying straight to Le Bourget was the most normal thing in the world. For him, in fact, it was.

As Lindbergh covered the last leg from Cherbourg into Paris he had no idea that he was about to experience fame on a scale and of an intensity unlike any experienced by any human before.

It never occurred to him that many people would be waiting for him. He wondered if anyone at the airfield would speak English and if he would be in trouble for not having a French visa. His plan was that first he would see to it that his plane was stowed securely, then he would cable his mother to give her the news that he had arrived. He supposed there would be one or two press interviews, assuming reporters worked that late in France. Then he would have to find a hotel somewhere. At some point he would also need to buy clothes and personal items because he hadn't packed anything at all – not even a toothbrush.

A more immediate problem confronting him was that his map didn't show Le Bourget. All he knew was that it was some seven miles north-east of the city and that it was big. After circling the Eiffel Tower, he headed in that direction, but the only possible site he could see was ringed with bright lights, as if it were some kind of industrial complex, with long tentacles of additional bright lights stretching out from it in all directions. This was nothing like the dozing airport he had expected to find. What he didn't realize was that the activity was all for him; the sinuous tentacles of light were the headlights of tens of thousands of cars all spontaneously drawn to Le Bourget and now caught in the greatest traffic jam in Parisian history. Cars and trams were abandoned all along the roads to the airport.

At 10.22 p.m. Paris time – precisely 33 hours, 30 minutes and 29.8 seconds after taking to the air, according to an official barograph that the National Aeronautic Association of America had bolted into the plane just before departure – the *Spirit of St Louis* touched down on the grassy spaciousness of Le Bourget. In that instant, a pulse of joy swept around the Earth. Within minutes the whole of America knew he was safe in Paris. Le Bourget was instantly a scene of exultant pandemonium as tens of thousands of people rushed across the airfield to Lindbergh's plane – 'a seething, howling mass of humanity . . . surging towards him from every direction of the compass', in the words of one onlooker. An eight-foot-high chain-link fence that surrounded the field was flattened, and several bicycles were crushed under the mass of charging feet. Among those in the rush were the dancer Isadora Duncan (who would die four months later in a freak accident, strangled when the long scarf she was wearing got caught in the wheel of a car) and Jean Borotra, who with Jacques Brugnon had beaten Bill Tilden and Francis T. Hunter at Saint-Cloud that day.

For Lindbergh, this was an entirely alarming circumstance, as he was trapped and in actual danger of being pulled to pieces. The throngs hauled him from his cockpit and began to carry him off like prize booty. 'I found myself lying in a prostrate position, up on top of the crowd, in the centre of an ocean of heads that extended as far out into the darkness as I could see,' he reported. 'It was like drowning in a human sea.' Someone yanked his leather flight helmet from his head and others, worryingly, began to pull at his clothes. Behind him, to his greater alarm, his beloved plane was being ruined by the swarms climbing over it. 'I heard the crack of wood behind me when someone leaned too heavily against a fairing strip. Then a second strip snapped, and a third, and there was the sound of tearing fabric.' Souvenir hunters, he realized, were going wild.

Somehow in the confusion he found himself on his feet and the crowd moving past him. Miraculously, in the poor light their focus switched to a hapless American bystander who bore a passing resemblance to Lindbergh, and they now carried him off, wriggling and protesting vehemently. A few minutes later, officials in the airport commandant's office were startled by the sound of breaking glass and the sight of the unfortunate victim being passed through the window to them. Wild-eyed and bedraggled, the new arrival was missing his coat, his belt, his necktie, one shoe and about half his shirt; a good deal of the rest of his clothing hung from him in shreds. He looked rather like the survivor of a mining disaster. He told the bemused officials that his name was Harry Wheeler and that he was a furrier from the Bronx. He had come to Paris to buy rabbit pelts, and had been drawn to Le Bourget by the same impulse that had attracted much of the rest of Paris. Now he just wanted to go home.

Lindbergh, meanwhile, was rescued by two French aviators who conducted him to the official reception area. There he met Myron Herrick and Herrick's son, Parmely, and daughter-in-law, Agnes. They gave Lindbergh a few minutes to catch his breath and assured him that his plane would be made safe. It took some hours for Lindbergh and the Herrick party to make their way through the congested streets to the ambassador's residence on the Avenue d'Iéna in central Paris. There Lindbergh declined the offer of a medical examination, but gratefully accepted a glass of milk and a little food, followed by a brief hot bath.

By now Lindbergh had been up for over sixty hours, but he agreed to meet with reporters who had collected outside the residence. Parmely Herrick showed them in. Though Lindbergh was clearly very tired, he chatted genially with them for several minutes. He told them that he had fought sleet and snow for a thousand miles; sometimes he flew as low as ten feet, sometimes as high as ten thousand. Then, in a pair of pyjamas borrowed from Parmely, he crawled into bed. It was 4.15 a.m.

The most famous man on earth closed his eyes and slept for ten hours.

CHAPTER 7

Iᴛ ᴡᴀꜱ ᴅᴀʏᴛɪᴍᴇ in America. The news of Lindbergh's arrival was known all over within minutes. Horns sounded, sirens blared, church bells rang. From end to end the nation erupted in the kind of jubilant cacophony made when wars end.

Newspapers struggled to find words adequate to Lindbergh's superlative achievement. The *New York Evening World* called it 'the greatest feat of a solitary man in the records of the human race'. Another called it 'the greatest event since the Resurrection'. According to the *North American Review*, the Earth reverberated with 'the long-waiting joy of humanity at the coming of the first citizen of the world, the first human being truly entitled to give his address as "The Earth," the first Ambassador-at-Large to Creation'. In terms of rhetoric and emotion, this was a Second Coming.

The *New York Times* gave Lindbergh's flight the whole of the first four pages of the paper even though there was little more to say than that he had made it. In the first four days after the flight American newspapers ran an estimated

250,000 stories, totalling 36 million words, on Lindbergh and his flight. Unsuspecting of just how much attention he would get, Lindbergh had subscribed to a newspaper-clipping service, with the articles to be sent to his mother, who discovered to her horror that a fleet of trucks was preparing to deliver several tons of newspaper articles by the end of the first week.

A kind of mania swept the nation. Proposals were put forward to exempt Lindbergh for life from paying taxes, to name a star or planet after him, to install him in the cabinet as head for life of a new aviation department, and to make 21 May a permanent national holiday. He was given a lifetime pass to all major league baseball games everywhere. Minnesota for a time considered a proposal to rename itself Lindberghia.

President Coolidge announced that 11 June would be Lindbergh Day in America – the highest tribute ever paid to a private citizen by the nation. The Post Office rushed out special airmail stamps – the first time a living person had been so honoured.

Parks were named after him, children were named after him, streets and mountains, hospital wards and zoo animals, rivers and high schools and bridges – all were named after him. In Chicago, plans were announced to erect a 1,328-foot-high commemorative Lindbergh Beacon with a beam that could be seen three hundred miles away.

More than 3.5 million letters were sent to Lindbergh – primarily from females, it was noted – along with 15,000 parcels containing gifts and mementoes. Many of his correspondents included return postage – about $100,000 worth altogether, it was estimated – in the patently deluded hope that he would find time to reply. Western

Union received so many messages that it had to assign thirty-eight employees full time to manage them all. One message from Minneapolis contained 15,000 words of text, 17,000 signatures and stretched 520 feet when unfurled. For the less imaginative, Western Union offered twenty pre-written forms of congratulatory message that people could choose from. Thousands did.

In Hollywood, a young cartoonist named Walt Disney was inspired to create an animated short feature called *Plane Crazy* featuring a mouse who was also a pilot. The mouse was initially called Oswald, but soon assumed a more lasting place in the nation's hearts as Mickey. Robert Ripley, author of the syndicated *Ripley's Believe It or Not* newspaper feature, received 200,000 furious letters and telegrams after he ungraciously pointed out that sixty-seven people had crossed the ocean by air before Lindbergh did. (Mostly in dirigibles. A later, more careful count showed that the number was actually closer to 120.)

At least 250 popular songs were written for Lindbergh and his flight. The most popular was called 'Lucky Lindy' – the term he hated – and was often played at dinners he attended, 'much to my embarrassment and annoyance', he later recorded. The 'Lindbergh Hop' became a popular dance – ironically, since the virginal Lindbergh had never danced with a girl.

Meanwhile, in Paris the delirium was no less intense. At Le Bourget on the morning after Lindbergh's arrival, cleaners gathered more than a ton of lost property, including six sets of dentures. Under Herrick's benign tutelage Lindbergh did everything right. Stepping on to the embassy balcony to greet the crowds after rising on his first full day in France, he waved a French flag, inducing delirious joy in the uncountable thousands who thronged the street below. Then he and Herrick visited Nungesser's widowed mother in her tiny sixth-floor flat on the Boulevard du Temple near the Place de la République. It was two weeks to the day since the disappearance of her son. Although the visit was not publicly announced, ten thousand people filled the street for Lindbergh's arrival. Also on that busy first day, Lindbergh called home on the new transatlantic telephone line, becoming one of the first private individuals to speak across the Atlantic as well as to fly it, and visited sick soldiers at Les Invalides.

In the days that followed, he went to the Élysée Palace to receive the Légion d'honneur from the president, Gaston Doumergue – the first time a French president had personally bestowed the nation's highest honour on an American – addressed the Chamber of Deputies, was fêted by the Aéro-Club de France, had a parade witnessed by up to a million people, and received the key to the city at the Hôtel de Ville. Whenever he spoke, it was with modesty and aplomb, and he never missed an opportunity to praise the accomplishments of French aviation or the kindness of the French generally. His achievement, he made clear, was merely a small part of a large collective effort. In weepy joy, France clasped Lindbergh to its bosom. They called him 'le boy'.

No foreign visitor to France had ever been so extravagantly honoured. The American flag was hoisted over the Quai d'Orsay, the Ministry of Foreign Affairs – the first time Old Glory had ever flown over that hallowed building. A striking feature of Lindbergh throughout this busy period was his appearance. Everything Lindbergh wore over the next few days was borrowed – and not too many people had clothes that would fit such a tall and lanky frame. Though reporters were too tactful or overawed to remark upon it, it was obvious that Lindbergh was going about Paris in jackets that fell short on his wrists and trousers that didn't reach his shoes.

Five days after his flight, crowds of a million people still lined the streets wherever he went. He smiled a good deal in those early days and waved whenever a crowd greeted him. That wouldn't last.

On Thursday 26 May Lindbergh went to Le Bourget to check on his plane. It had been heavily damaged by the happy crowds, but was now being painstakingly repaired. While he was at the airfield, Lindbergh borrowed a French Nieuport fighter plane and took it up for a spin. Although he had never flown a Nieuport before and could not be sure of its tolerances, he proceeded to execute a series of loops, rolls, corkscrews, barrel turns and other aerial acrobatics. French officials watched in something like stupefaction as the most esteemed and treasured human being on Earth swooped and rolled in the sky above them, pushing to its limits a plane he knew nothing about. With frantic gestures and much hopping, they implored him to cease these dangerous manoeuvres and return to earth. Eventually, good-naturedly, Lindbergh did. It was an arresting demonstration of the proposition that Lindbergh was very possibly both the best and luckiest pilot who ever lived.

Lindbergh's plan was to make a tour of Europe – he particularly wished to visit Sweden, land of his fathers – and then fly back to America. He was still undecided as to whether he would attempt a risky return crossing of the

Atlantic against the prevailing winds or whether he should continue east, flying home across Asia and the north Pacific. In fact, Herrick informed him, he would do neither. President Coolidge had dispatched a naval cruiser, the USS *Memphis*, to bring him home so that America could honour him in person and in style. The president wanted to get the ceremonies over with so that he could start a vacation trip to the Black Hills of South Dakota.

Lindbergh was allowed to make brief visits to Brussels and London to honour promises made earlier. Remarkably, he was permitted to fly himself.

More than 100,000 people were waiting for him at Croydon Aerodrome outside London – so many that the police couldn't keep the runway clear. Twice Lindbergh had to abort landings as the excited crowds surged forward on to the grass – a sight that must have been deeply unnerving to a pilot without any forward visibility. Then the car carrying Lindbergh was mobbed. The police were able to force it through the crowds only by getting Lindbergh to lie down under a coat and telling people that the car was carrying a seriously injured woman.

Eventually he made it to Buckingham Palace where the king famously startled Lindbergh by asking him how he had peed during the flight. Lindbergh explained, a touch awkwardly, that he had brought along a pail for the purpose.

George V, not to be deflected from a full understanding of this aspect of his flight, asked how many times Lindbergh had employed it.

Coming from the family he did, Lindbergh may never before in his life have discussed his evacuations with anyone, and now here he was doing it with the king of England.

'Twice,' he whispered hoarsely, looking as if he might faint.

'And where was that?' the king persisted.

'Once over Newfoundland and once over the open ocean.'

The king nodded thoughtfully, satisfied.

Three days later Lindbergh was in Cherbourg, boarding the USS *Memphis* for the trip home. He waved to the crowds and they cheered him in adoration. Many threw flowers. The French newspapers all wrote warm tributes and wished the young American bon voyage.

Then life in France returned to normal. Within a day or so, American tour buses were being thumped with stones again and visitors on the Champs-Élysées were finding it awfully hard to catch the waiter's eye. As it turned out, this was only a prelude. Before the summer was over, millions of French would hate America as they never had before, and it would actually be unsafe to be an American on French streets. The summer of 1927 would not only be the most joyous in years for America, but quite an ugly one, too.

JUNE
THE BABE

'He was bigger than the President. One time, coming north, we stopped at a little town in Illinois, a whistle stop. It was about ten o'clock at night and raining like hell. The train stopped for ten minutes to get water, or something. It couldn't have been a town of more than five thousand people, and by God, there were four thousand of them down there standing in the rain, just waiting to see the Babe.'

Richards Vidmer, *New York Times* sportswriter

Chapter 8

In the late nineteenth century, Baltimore was the sixth largest city in America (it has since slipped to twenty-first) and one of the roughest, and the roughest area of Baltimore was a district close to the Inner Harbor known without irony or affection as Pig Town.

It was here, on 6 February 1895, that George Herman Ruth was born into a household that was moderately impoverished, emotionally barren and seemingly doomed. Six of his eight siblings would die in childhood, and both his parents would follow while George was still young, his mother of tuberculosis, his father in a knife fight outside his own saloon. This was not a family that had a lot going for it.

The opening sentence of Ruth's autobiography is 'I was a bad kid,' which is no more than partly true. A few lines later he adds: 'I hardly knew my parents,' which is much closer to the mark. Ruth essentially raised himself through his earliest years. His parents weren't so much bad as distracted. His mother spent most of his childhood dying bleakly in a crowded apartment above the saloon. His father, deprived of a healthy partner, ran the business below single-handed – a job that consumed nearly all his waking hours. Perhaps nothing better reflects the detached and insubstantial nature of Ruth's family life than that he grew up not knowing his actual age. Until he saw his birth certificate for the first time when applying for a passport at the age of thirty-nine, he thought he was a year older than in fact he was. For his part, Ruth was not a terribly attentive son. In his autobiography he states that his mother died when he was thirteen. In fact, he was sixteen. He also got her maiden name wrong.

The saloon where Ruth grew up is long gone. By happy chance, the site today lies just beneath centre field in Camden Yards, the home of the Baltimore Orioles – not unfitting, since it was as a Baltimore Oriole that Ruth first played professional baseball and first got his nickname 'Babe'.

In the spring of 1902, while the infant Charles Lindbergh was gurgling in a plush bassinet in Minnesota, Babe's father took young George to the St Mary's Industrial School for Boys in Baltimore – a large, dark, forbidding edifice on Wilkens Avenue about three miles west of his old neighbourhood – and left him there. St Mary's was one of nearly thirty homes for orphaned or wayward children in Baltimore in 1900 – a reflection of the dire social conditions for many in the city at the time. This would be Ruth's home for most of the next twelve years.

St Mary's was an unusual institution – part orphanage, part reform school, part private academy. Of the 850 boys enrolled at any one time, about half were tuition-paying boarders. Parents from across America sent their boys to St Mary's, often as a last resort when other schools had failed them.

The school was run by the Xaverian Brothers, a Roman Catholic order whose members embraced piety and celibacy but not full priesthood, and the conditions were rigorously monastic. Pupils had no privacy. Everything they did – sleeping, showering, dining, studying – was done communally. Beds, desks, shower stalls, all were set out in long regimented ranks, as in some grim Victorian penitentiary. But St Mary's was not at all a bad place as these places go. The children were treated with dignity and even a kind of gruff affection, and they were rewarded for good behaviour with 25 cents of weekly pocket money. Boys at St Mary's received a sound basic education and were taught a vocation. Ruth trained to be a tailor and shirtmaker, and delighted years later in showing team-mates how skilfully he could turn a cuff or collar.

All the students had a history of behavioural problems, but the brothers attributed that to inadequacies of upbringing rather than any deficiency of character – a decidedly enlightened view for the time. They believed that any boy treated with decency, encouragement and respect would grow into a model citizen, and they were nearly always right. Ninety-five per cent of Xaverian boys went on to live normal, stable lives.

Ruth as a boy was a large, bumptious, pug-faced, happy-go-lucky, rather endearingly tragic figure. He was always much larger than his classmates – so much so that once when charity workers were handing out Christmas presents he was mistaken for an attendant and passed over. When the mistake was realized, George was given his own giant box of chocolates. Instead of hoarding them – and bear in mind that never in his life would he have had something this special to call his own – he immediately shared them all around. This was a kid who deserved a happier childhood. From 1912 to 1914 not a single person visited him.

The brothers at St Mary's were exceedingly devoted to baseball. The school fielded no fewer than forty-four teams, all fully equipped and with uniforms. No amount of money could have bought Ruth better preparation for a career in baseball. It was through baseball that Ruth 'met and learned to love the greatest man I've ever known' – Brother Matthias Boutilier. Of French stock from Cape Breton, Nova Scotia, Matthias was a gentle, kindly giant. He stood six feet six inches tall and weighed 250 pounds, but always spoke softly. He was a wonderful baseball player, too, as well as a gifted coach – and in Babe Ruth he had a youngster who was both more talented and hard-working than anyone he had ever come across. At eight, George was playing with twelve-year-olds; at twelve with sixteen-year-olds. By early adolescence he could play every position on the field better than anyone else at the school – even catcher, where he had to wear a right-handed mitt on the wrong hand because the school didn't own a left-handed mitt. As a batter, he was incomparable. By his teenage years, he stood six feet two inches tall, weighed nearly 200 pounds, and was immensely strong.

Hearing about an amazing kid at St Mary's, in 1914 a scout for the Baltimore Orioles, then a minor league team in the International League, came to have a look. When George came to the plate, the scout was surprised to see that the right fielder left his normal spot and trotted to a position much further out – so far out, in fact, that he stood on another playing field. Ruth still lofted the ball over his head. It was one of three long shots he hit that day. Surprisingly, the scout was not particularly captivated by Ruth's power. Hitting baseballs a great distance in 1914 was an interesting talent, but not one worth cultivating. It was pitching that the Orioles needed and it was as a pitcher that they signed him.

Thus it was in early March 1914 that George Herman Ruth, just turned nineteen, bade farewell to Brother Matthias and his St Mary's friends, boarded a train and headed south to Fayetteville, North Carolina, for his first spring training and a new life as a professional baseball player. It was the first time he had been on a train, first time he had been out of Maryland, first time he had seen small towns and open countryside, first time he had stayed in a hotel or ordered from a menu. He could not have been greener. He didn't even realize that the majors consisted of two leagues. The nickname his teammates gave him now, 'Babe' (on account of his innocence and youthfulness), could hardly have been apter. Ruth was in every sense but the physical one a little boy. With his first paycheque he bought himself a bicycle. In hotels, when there was nothing else to do, he rode the lifts for hours. His years of communal living had left him wholly innocent of modesty when naked or on the lavatory, and with virtually no sense of private property. His first roommate, Ernie Shore, was dismayed to discover weeks into the season that throughout that period Ruth had been sharing his toothbrush.

Almost at once Ruth displayed the outsized appetite for which he became famous. The notion of being able to order whatever he wanted in hotel dining rooms was a treat he never got over. He also quickly discovered sex. He had no shyness there either. A teammate named Larry Gardner recalled walking into a room and finding Ruth on the floor having sex with a prostitute. 'He was smoking a cigar and eating peanuts and this woman was working on him,' Gardner said in a tone of understandable wonder.

'When they let him out,' another teammate recalled, 'it was like turning a wild animal out of a cage.' Neither then nor later was Ruth terribly picky. Marshall Hunt of the *New York Daily News* once remarked of Ruth's women that generally they 'would really only appeal to a man who was just stepping out of a prison after serving a 15-year sentence'.

The Orioles in 1914 were a team in trouble. Their fans were deserting them in droves for the Baltimore Terrapins of the new (and short-lived) Federal League.* At one point the Orioles played before an audience of just seventeen people while the Terrapins entertained a full and roaring house across the street. Unable to meet their payroll, the Orioles began selling players. In July of his rookie season, Ruth found himself abruptly dealt to the Boston Red Sox. He hurried north and on the day of his arrival in Boston, 11 July, was sent out to pitch, which meant that the first major league game he ever saw was one he played in.† He scattered eight hits and won 4 to 3.

*A year before Ruth turned professional, a group of businessmen formed a new, rival league called the Federal League, and tempted some of the leading players from the American and National Leagues to jump to the new league by offering them better salaries. The Federal League ultimately failed, but for a time it seriously undermined the cosy status quo of major league baseball.

† A brief primer for those who don't know American baseball: at the top level, there are two leagues, the American League and the National League. Together these are known as the major leagues. This was where every serious baseball player wanted to end up, but

So, just four months after leaving St Mary's, without ever having lived independently in the outside world, Babe Ruth was a major league baseball player. During that summer, Ruth frequently ate breakfast at a coffee shop called Lander's. There he chatted to a pretty waitress named Helen Woodford. One day, if Ruth's own account is to be believed, he said to her: 'How about you and me getting married, hon?' After a few minutes' reflection, she accepted and they were wed in the autumn of 1914. Ruth was nineteen, she possibly no more than fifteen. It was not a hugely successful pairing. In his autobiography, Ruth got her name wrong.

From the perspective of our own age, it isn't easy to grasp just how central to American life – how culturally and emotionally dominant and unchallenged and saturating – baseball was in the time of Babe Ruth. It was the nation's joy and obsession. It was called 'the National Game', with capital letters. In sporting terms, it was all that much of America thought about for a good part of the year.

For big events like the World Series, newspapers in every major city erected giant scoreboards outside their offices, and these unfailingly attracted large crowds. In many cities, impresarios hired theatres or other grand spaces (Madison Square Garden, for instance) to provide paying audiences with simulated games. One version employed a large diagram of a baseball diamond, with coloured lights to show

most players began with lesser teams in the minor leagues (or 'minors') until they were good enough to advance to the top level. For Babe Ruth to go from the minor league Baltimore Orioles to the major league Boston Red Sox in his first season was highly unusual and a reflection of his skills.

balls, strikes and outs, bells for hits, and white footprints tracing a path around the base paths. An announcer on the stage would relate – and sometimes creatively embellish – developments on a distant playing field from fragmentary information supplied by ticker tape while the scoreboard lit up, clanged and traced footsteps in support. Another system used live boys, each representing a real player, who took up positions on a baseball field on the stage, where they pitched, batted and fielded an imaginary ball, and ran from base to base as distant reality required. As one observer marvelled, no crowds in ballparks were 'more loudly appreciative of every fine play than those millions jammed into the various halls or thronging the streets in front of newspaper offices'.

This was the happy and exciting world in which Babe Ruth found himself now. Considering all that he wrought with his bat, it is an extraordinary fact that Ruth spent nearly the first quarter of his career as a pitcher – and not just *a* pitcher, but one of the very best in baseball. In 1915, his first full season with the Red Sox, he won 18 games against 8 losses, the fourth best winning percentage in the league. He struck out 112 batters, gave up fewer hits per game than any other player in the league but one, and finished the year with an exceedingly respectable earned-run average of 2.44. The next year, he had a record of 23 wins and 12 losses, and led the league in earned-run average, shutouts, hits per game and opponents' batting average. He was third in number of wins, second in winning percentage and strikeouts, and fourth in number of complete games. His nine shutouts (that is, holding the opposing team scoreless) remains a record for a left-hander. In 1917, he again dominated or featured in nearly every pitching category and had a record of 24 wins and 13 losses. Almost incidentally, in the same period he began a run of twenty-nine and two thirds consecutive scoreless innings pitched in World Series play – a record that stood for forty-three years.

It is almost impossible to exaggerate how extraordinary this was. Boys straight out of school didn't just stroll into major league ballparks and start confounding experienced hitters like Ty Cobb and Shoeless Joe Jackson. Even the best young pitchers needed time to gain confidence and perspective. Walter Johnson in his first three years in the majors had a record of 32 wins and 48 losses. Christy Mathewson was 34 and 37. Ruth in the same period was 43 and 21. Altogether in his time as a pitcher Ruth had a win–loss record of 94–46 and an earned-run average (a basic statistical measure of a pitcher's potency) of just 2.28, a very impressive figure indeed. His winning percentage of .671 remains the seventh best of all time.

The problem was – and never before for any human had this been a problem – he was also a peerless hitter. In 1915, his first full season, Ruth hit four home runs in 92 at-bats.* That was just three fewer than Braggo Roth, the American League home run leader, who had more than four times as many plate appearances. In 1918, to take

* An at-bat is an important but slightly arcane concept in baseball. In rough terms, it is a record of the number of times a player has gone to the plate to bat in a given period. A player's batting average is his number of at-bats divided by the number of times he has reached base safely with a hit. The batting average is expressed as thousandths of a percentage. A batting average of .333 means that a batter has hit safely in one third of his recorded at-bats. A batting average of .300 is considered good and of .350 or better is sensational. Only a few times have players finished a season batting .400 or better.

advantage of his bat, the Red Sox began playing Ruth at first base or in the outfield when he wasn't pitching. Nineteen eighteen proved to be the worst year ever for home runs in major league baseball. The Senators as a team hit just 4 home runs that year. The Browns hit 5, the White Sox 8 and the Indians 9. Babe Ruth alone hit 11. The next year, despite pitching 133⅓ innings (including 12 complete games), Ruth hit 29 home runs, almost doubling the American League record set by Socks Seybold of the Philadelphia Athletics in 1902. In 111 games in the out-field he had 26 assists and just 2 errors. His fielding average of .996 was by a considerable margin the best in the league. That is a most astounding achievement – and it was, of course, only the beginning.

Modern baseball has a certain air of timelessness that is much cherished by its fans. A visitor from our age trans-ported to a major league ballpark of the 1920s would find himself, in most respects, in entirely familiar territory. The play on the field, the sounds of the crowd, the cries of the vendors would all be reassuringly familiar in ways that many other aspects of life in 1920s America would not. (The same visitor would struggle to start a car, make a phone call, tune a radio, even cross a busy street.) But even at the ballpark differences would soon become apparent.

For a start, games were generally a whole lot brisker. Traditionally, they started at 3 p.m. and rarely went much beyond five. (The ability to provide that day's baseball scores had a great deal to do with the popularity of evening newspapers.) Ninety-minute games were not uncommon, but sometimes they were even faster than that. On one notable occasion, on 26 September 1926 in

St Louis, the Browns beat the Yankees 6–1 in just 1 hour and 12 minutes in the first game of a doubleheader, then came back and won the second game 6–2 in 55 minutes. These were both full nine-inning games. Quite how they managed it is a wonder. The two teams banged out 25 hits between them in the first game and 20 in the second, so these were hardly classic pitchers' duels. There was just a lot less messing around.

Games were often a good deal wilder, too. Fights were common and sometimes involved fans as well as players. In 1924, a punch-up between Ruth and his great rival Ty Cobb in Detroit not only cleared both benches, but caused a riot in the stands. Seats were ripped out and thrown on the field, and at least a thousand spectators invaded the playing area. The game had to be abandoned. Players also didn't hesitate to go into the stands after fans who heckled them beyond forbearance. Ruth in 1920 vaulted into the stands to confront a man who had called him 'a big piece of cheese' – then retreated smartly when the man pulled a knife on him. Ty Cobb once went for a spectator who had been riding him all afternoon, and beat the man severely. When fans shouted at Cobb that the man was a war veteran who had no hands, Cobb cried, 'I don't care if he has no feet,' and kept pummelling until police arrived and pulled him off. Cobb was suspended for ten days for that. Ruth once punched an umpire in the jaw in an argument. He was fined $100 and suspended for ten days, too, and was very lucky to get away with that.

For players, life wasn't terribly glamorous. When a visiting team arrived in a city on a road trip, the players usually walked from the station to the hotel, and carried their own bags. They often played in dirty uniforms, particularly in Chicago where White Sox owner Charles Comiskey charged his players for doing their laundry.

The major leagues were more cosily compact, with just sixteen teams in ten cities, as compared with thirty in twenty-seven cities today. Boston, Chicago, St Louis and Philadelphia each had two major league teams; New York had three. St Louis was as far west as the major leagues went, Washington as far south.

Parks often had distinctive idiosyncrasies, which gave them a kind of interesting unpredictability. At the Polo Grounds, home field of the New York Giants, the outfield sloped so severely towards the fence that from the dugouts only the outfielders' heads and shoulders were visible, like ships sailing over a horizon. (Polo was never actually played there. The Polo Grounds were named after an earlier field near Central Park where polo was played.) At Griffith Stadium in Washington, the outfield wall zig-zagged crazily around five houses and an overhanging tree whose owners had refused to sell when the park was built, providing arresting angles for caroms and amusing confusion among visiting outfielders. In at least three ball-parks, including Yankee Stadium, flagpoles stood in fair territory in centre field, waiting to snag any centrefielder who forgot they were there. At Fenway Park in Boston, left fielders had to scramble up a steep bank to catch balls hit to the wall.

Perhaps the biggest shock to the visitor from today to a ballpark of the 1920s would be how sloppily maintained they were. Outfields were generally little better than cow pastures, and areas of heavy traffic such as base paths and around home plate were often ragged and bare, and grew more so as the season wore on. After rain, groundsmen sometimes spread petrol around the infield and set it alight to dry out the earth – hardly conducive to a fine, delicate tilth.

Safety features were almost entirely absent. Batting helmets did not exist. Outfield walls were unpadded. Gloves were so inflexible and primitive that a one-handed catch 'was apt to cause a sensation', as Marshall Smelser has noted. Bat racks had not yet become standard, so at most parks the players lined up their bats on the ground in front of the dugout, to the considerable peril of catchers or infielders going after foul pop-ups. Outfielders commonly left their gloves on the field, too, when their team went in to bat. There was, in short, a lot to fall over or crash into. People frequently did.

For fans, it was considerably harder to work out what was going on in the game. Throughout the 1920s no American ballpark had a public address system. Usually there was just a man with a megaphone who called out the names of batters and very little else. Unfamiliar players weren't easy to identify because uniforms had no numbers. Putting numbers on uniforms didn't start until 1929, when the Yankees and Indians introduced it. The Yankees then gave numbers to the starting players in the order they batted (more or less), which is why Ruth was number 3 and Gehrig 4. Scoreboards didn't list hits and errors, so spectators had to know themselves when a no-hitter or perfect game was in progress. Anyone keeping careful score at his seat would become a fount of information for those around him.

On the field, players were often a lot more casual about inflicting injuries on others. Ty Cobb, who was only a degree or two removed from clinical psychopathy, always slid into base with spikes raised in the sincere hope of drawing blood, but many other players were only fractionally more considerate of their fellows. Throwing at batters was a common strategy accepted by all. Burleigh Grimes of the Brooklyn Dodgers, who was famously bad-tempered, set a record of sorts by throwing at a batter before he had even stepped to the plate. Walter Johnson of the Washington Senators never intentionally threw at anyone, but he hit more than a few opponents by accident. He ended the career of a Lee Tannehill of the White Sox when he broke his arm so badly just above the wrist that Tannehill could never again grip a bat. Two weeks later Johnson shattered the jaw of a rookie named Jack Martin. (Johnson, an intensely decent man, always fell to pieces after hurting a player and usually had to be lifted from the game.) Ruth in his autobiography notes that he once tried to brush back a player named Max Flack, and accidentally hit him bang in the middle of the forehead. Flack fell like a collapsing tower, but survived. Ruth recounted the story merely as an example of the amusing things that happened on the field of play.

Fatalities would seem a reasonable expectation in such circumstances, but in fact only one player was ever killed during the course of play. It was in August 1920 and Babe Ruth was present when it happened. Late in the afternoon in poor light Yankees pitcher Carl Mays, who was known for being aggressive and was disliked by nearly everyone, including his own teammates, threw an inside pitch to an Indians player named Ray Chapman that Chapman never saw at all. Since balls were seldom replaced during a game they tended to grow dull and scuffed as the day wore on, a fact that pitchers often exploited to their advantage in fading light. Mays moreover had a submarine-style delivery, which made his pitches even harder to pick up. In any case, Chapman never saw it. The ball struck him on the side of the head at the temple with a sickening thud and with such force that it bounced straight back to Mays, who fielded it and threw it to the first baseman, thinking it had come off Chapman's bat. Then everyone realized the full horror of what had just happened. Chapman, gravely injured, dropped his bat and began walking in a dazed manner towards second base, evidently making for the club-house in centre field. After a few steps, his legs gave way and he collapsed. He was taken to St Lawrence Hospital and died the next day. He never regained consciousness.

Ruth said nothing of the incident in his autobiography other than that it provoked so much bad feeling among the Indians that Mays wasn't played against them again that year. Chapman remains the only major league ballplayer to have been mortally injured on the field of play.

The most dangerous part of the ballpark was actually the stands. In the worst incident in baseball history, in 1903 at Baker Bowl in Philadelphia, a wall at the back of the grandstand on which fans were perched gave way without warning and hundreds of people were pitched backwards on to the street thirty feet below. Twelve died and two hundred were injured, many seriously. Remarkably, an even worse catastrophe nearly happened at the same stadium in the spring of 1927, the week before Charles Lindbergh's flight to Paris. In the seventh inning of a game between the Philadelphia Phillies and St Louis Cardinals on 14 May, a sudden cloudburst – part of the same intractable storm system that was keeping the

Atlantic flyers pinned down on Long Island – prompted hundreds of fans in the bleachers to rush for shelter under the covered upper terrace of a double-deck grandstand along the first base line. In the previous inning, the Phillies had staged an eight-run rally, an event so rare in Philadelphia that the fans had reacted with joy, and it is thought that their exuberant stomping may have stressed the ageing structure beyond its frail limits. Now under the extra weight of several hundred people, the grandstand issued a long, plaintive moan and abruptly and spectacularly collapsed. Miraculously, no one was killed outright, though a fifty-year-old lithographer named Robert Haas was trampled to death in the panic that followed. Fifty people were injured seriously enough to require hospital treatment, but all but two were released within twenty-four hours. Never in American history had a sporting disaster been more spectacular and merciful at the same time.

A simple if not very noble reason lay behind years of slack maintenance at Baker Bowl and many other ageing ball-parks: economics. Baseball was a treasured institution but a poor investment. Its most elemental problem was that its games were played during the day when most people were at work. In many cities – Boston until 1929, Pittsburgh and Philadelphia until 1933 – Sunday baseball was not permitted either, so many teams had just one day a week, Saturday, when they could hope to draw a good crowd. Even the most successful teams often played before more empty seats than full ones. Yankee Stadium broke all attendance records with a crowd of over 70,000 (including a lot of standees) when it opened for the first time on

18 April 1923, but the next day just 12,500 people turned up. Altogether in the 1910s, average major league attendance was about 4,000. Ballparks were often pretty quiet places in Ruth's day.

Apart from a percentage on concessions and profits from exhibition games, teams had almost no source of income beyond ticket sales, and from these they had to fund a formidable range of costs – salaries, spring training, road trips, uniforms and equipment, clubhouse staff, a network of scouts and a home stadium. This last could be staggeringly expensive. In 1913, Charles Hercules Ebbets, owner of the Dodgers, spent $750,000 – as much as the cost of a big office building in Manhattan – building Ebbets Field in Brooklyn, then spent the rest of his life vainly trying to fill it. On the day that Lindbergh flew to Paris, for example, the Dodgers played before an audience of fewer than 4,000, which was fairly typical for them even in good years. Other teams like the St Louis Browns, which never *had* good years, sometimes had average attendances of about 1,500. It is a miracle that many teams held on as long as they did.

Surprisingly, the man who made more money out of baseball than almost anyone else was an enterprising Englishman named Harry Stevens, who came to America as a young man around the turn of the century, fell for baseball in a big way and hit on the best idea of his life – namely, that fans might enjoy a hot snack in the course of a game. He experimented with various combinations of hot sandwiches and found that sausages in a roll kept warm longer than anything else he tried. He secured the right to sell his 'red hots', as he rather generously called them, at the Polo Grounds and almost at once began doing brisk business. It was Stevens's products that the cartoonist Tad Dorgan called 'hot dogs', in jocular reference to their supposed principal constituent. Stevens loved the term, and by the 1920s hot dogs were indelibly associated with baseball games all across the nation, and Stevens had the concession operations at all three New York ballparks and others as far afield as Chicago. He was also rich in a way that most baseball club owners could only ever dream of being.

In desperation, team owners resorted to economies that often made them look ridiculous. Most ballparks, for instance, insisted on reclaiming foul balls hit into the stands. A few enlightened owners, like Barney Dreyfuss of the Pittsburgh Pirates, let fans keep balls as souvenirs, but others were ferocious in defending what they saw as an important property right. Matters came to a head in 1923 at – appropriately enough, it would seem – Baker Bowl in Philadelphia, when an eleven-year-old boy named Robert Cotter caught a foul ball and refused to give it back. When it was also discovered that he had no ticket but had sneaked in, the Phillies' management had young Cotter arrested and charged with theft. He spent a night in jail and was hauled before a judge the next day. The judge, to the delight of the city, ruled that it was entirely reasonable that a kid would want to keep a foul ball – particularly as Cotter had made a really good catch. After that, ballparks everywhere largely gave up trying to keep hold of foul balls.

The paradoxical upshot of all this was that baseball at the time Babe Ruth came into the game was immensely popular but dangerously uneconomic – and of no team was that more true than the New York Yankees. In 1914, the year Ruth joined the Red Sox, it became known in the baseball world that the Yankees were for sale if anyone wanted to buy them. They were not an enticing proposition. They didn't have a single player of real talent, generally finished near the bottom of the standings, attracted poor crowds and didn't even have a home ground. They played in the Giants' stadium, the Polo Grounds. Until recently they hadn't even had a fixed name, but were known variously and casually as the Highlanders, Hilltoppers and Americans.

The Yankees' owners, William S. Devery and Frank J. Farrell, asked John McGraw of the Giants to help them find a new owner. McGraw approached two men who had never met but were keen on baseball: a New York beer baron named Jacob Ruppert and a businessman from Ohio who rejoiced in the name of Tillinghast L'Hommedieu Huston. Huston sadly was not as exotic or even as interesting as his name might lead us to hope. Born in 1866, one year before Ruppert, he had grown up in a middle-class household in Cincinnati, trained as an engineer, and made a fortune helping to rebuild Cuba after the Spanish–American War. He liked to drink, was a bit of a slob, was always cheerful, and loved baseball. That was about all there was to him.

Ruppert, by contrast, was a more complex character. The scion of a wealthy brewing family, he grew up in a rambling mansion in the German-American enclave of Yorkville on the Upper East Side of Manhattan – the same neighbourhood that produced, in more modest circustances, Lou Gehrig and the Marx Brothers – close to the yeasty smell of the Ruppert Brewery, which was the biggest in the nation, occupying an enormous site between Ninetieth

169

and Ninety-Third Streets. It produced Knickerbocker, Ruppert and Ruppiner beers, which, not incidentally, sold very well at ballparks.

Jacob Ruppert was a rather odd and solitary man. He lived alone in his big family house, attended by five servants. He served four terms as a congressman, from 1899 to 1907, for the Democratic Party, but then seems to have lost interest in politics. He spoke with a German accent – he called Ruth 'Root', for instance – which was a little puzzling because he had lived his whole life in America, as indeed had his parents. He collected jade, books, ceramics, dogs, horses and art, and had what was called 'America's finest collection of small monkeys'. Though not adventurous himself, he was keen on exploration and in 1933 would sponsor an expedition by Richard Byrd to the Antarctic. Ruppert's most arresting peccadillo was that he kept a second home in Garrison, New York, where he maintained a shrine to his mother in the form of a room containing everything she would need if she came back to life. This may go some way towards explaining why he never married.

Wealth and a love of baseball were about all that Ruppert and Huston had in common. Despite these drawbacks, on the last day of 1914 Ruppert and Huston each paid $225,000 for a half-share of the Yankees – a staggering sum bearing in mind that Devery and Farrell had bought the team for $18,000 only a decade before. McGraw was elated – as well he might be. To any dispassionate observer, Ruppert and Huston were idiots.

As it turned out, they couldn't have come into baseball ownership at a worse time. One bad thing after another befell major league baseball in the following years. First, competition from the Federal League clobbered revenues. Attendance in American and National League parks dropped by a quarter during the two years of the Federal League's existence. Then America's entry into the First World War depressed attendance further. That was followed by the great Spanish flu epidemic of 1918, which killed millions across the world and left most people severely disinclined to gather in public places. At the same time, President Woodrow Wilson announced that the 1918 major league season would be reduced to 130 games as a gesture towards the war effort. Total attendance that year fell to just three million – a decline of 50 per cent from ten years earlier. Finally, in 1919, Congress brought in the Volstead Act, which declared that Prohibition would begin in January 1920. That would remove beer sales from ballparks, eliminating a crucial source of revenue.

Many teams barely clung on. No owner was in a more parlous state than the soon-to-be-notorious Harrison Herbert Frazee of the Boston Red Sox. Harry Frazee was really a theatrical impresario, but he loved baseball, too, and in 1916, with a partner named Hugh Ward, he bought the Red Sox – then the best team in the game. They paid $1 million, far more than they could afford. Very quickly Frazee and Ward found themselves struggling to meet loan repayments.

In the first week of January 1920, facing imminent default, Frazee did something that Red Sox fans spent the rest of the century obsessing over: he sold Babe Ruth to the Yankees for $100,000 in cash and a loan of $350,000. Although not so well noticed by history, but just as devastating to the team, Frazee offloaded sixteen other

171

players to the Yankees between 1918 and 1923. The Yankees even acquired his general manager, Ed Barrow. In a sense, the Red Sox franchise moved to New York. Frazee sold out altogether in 1923. Coincidentally, Huston would sell out to Ruppert in the same year.

Even more unnoticed by history was the timing of the Ruth deal. It is not at all a coincidence that the New York Yankees purchased Babe Ruth in the same month that Prohibition came into effect. Jacob Ruppert at the time of the Ruth sale was three weeks away from losing his brewery business. He urgently needed an alternative source of income. Now he was going to find out if it was actually possible to get rich from owning a baseball team, and he was going to do it by staking nearly everything on the most brilliant, headstrong, undisciplined, lovable, thrillingly original, ornery son of a bitch that ever put on a baseball uniform.

It would be quite a ride.

CHAPTER 9

BEFORE BABE RUTH changed everything, a home run in baseball was a pretty rare event. John Franklin Baker of the Philadelphia Athletics became known to posterity as 'Home Run' Baker not because he banged out lots of home runs, but because in the 1911 World Series he hit crucial homers in two successive games. The rest of the time Baker didn't hit many home runs at all – just two all season in 1910, for instance. Even so, he was one of the game's pre-eminent sluggers, and the name 'Home Run' Baker didn't seem silly to anyone.

In baseball's deadball era, as the period before 1920 is commonly known, teams didn't look for rocket-like hits and big rallies, but manufactured runs 'scientifically', by slapping out singles and moving runners along by any means possible – through bunts and walks and other patiently incremental strategies. Some teams actually practised getting hit by pitches. Scores tended to be low but close.

There was a good reason for this. Hitting a baseball is hard, and in many ways it was harder in Babe Ruth's day than it is now. A baseball thrown at 90 miles an hour hits the catcher's mitt four-tenths of a second after it leaves the pitcher's hand, which clearly does not allow much time for reflection on the batter's part. Moreover, in order to get his bat to the plate to meet the ball's arrival, the batter must start his swing at 0.2 seconds when the ball is still only halfway there. If the pitch is a curve, nearly all its deviation will still be to come. Half of it will occur just in the last fifteen feet. If the pitch is some other sort – a fast ball, change-up or cutter, say – the ball will arrive at a fractionally different instant and at a different height. Because of friction, the ball will also lose about five miles an hour of speed during the course of its short journey from the pitcher's hand. In Babe Ruth's day, pitchers had an additional advantage in that the mound they stood on was fifteen inches high instead of the modern ten. That makes a difference, too.

So the batter, in this preposterously fractional part of a fraction that is allotted to him for decision-making, must weigh all these variables, calculate the place and moment that the ball will cross the plate and make sure that his bat is there to meet it. The slightest miscalculation, which is what the pitcher is counting on, will result in a foul ball or pop-up or some other form of routine failure. To slap out a single is hard enough – that is why even the very best hitters fail nearly seven times out of ten – but to hit the ball with power requires confident and irreversible commitment.

It was this that Babe Ruth did as no man ever had before. Ruth used a mighty club of a bat – it weighed 54 ounces – and gripped it at the very end, around the knob, which enhanced the whip-like motion of his swing. The result was a combination of power and timing so focused and potent that it generated 8,000 pounds of force (scientists actually measured it in a lab) and, in the space of one thousandth of a second – the duration of contact – through the miracle of physics it converted the sizzling zip of an incoming 90 mph baseball into an outgoing spheroid launched cloudward at 110 mph.

The result was like something fired from a gun. It was hypnotic and rare – and now here was a man who could do it pretty regularly. Babe Ruth's home runs were not merely more frequent, they were more majestic. No one had ever seen balls travel so loftily and far.

'During batting practice all the Cleveland players stopped what they were doing just to watch him hit,' Willis Hudlin, a pitcher for the Indians at the time, recalled more than seventy years later for *Sports Illustrated*. 'He's the only guy the players ever did that for.'

No player had ever brought this kind of excitement to the game. When Ruth came to the plate, the whole ball-park fell silent. 'Even the peanut vendors paused in their shouting, and turned to watch,' noted one observer. With Ruth at bat, as Marshall Smelser put it in a 1993 biography, the game became a contest 'between two men instead of eighteen'.

In 1920, his first year with the Yankees, Ruth hit 54 home runs – more than any other *team* in the major leagues. He batted .376 and led the league in ten batting categories. It was almost impossible to imagine anyone ever having a better year – or, come to that, a more timely one. Baseball in 1920 was about to be sent reeling by its greatest scandal, the throwing of the 1919 World Series by the Chicago 'Black Sox', a game-fixing scam by a group of White Sox players which, when exposed, wholly undermined people's faith in the game. Ruth's colossal swatting was the greatest distraction in sporting history. He didn't just transform the game, he very probably saved it.

In 1921, impossibly, Ruth had an even better year than in 1920. He hit 59 home runs – a number so high as to be beyond the reach of any meaningful adjective – and scored more runs, had more extra base hits, and racked up more total bases than any player ever had before. He led the league in runs batted in and bases on balls, and had the third highest batting average at .378, just behind Harry Heilmann and Ty Cobb. Ruth also stole seventeen bases and led the Yankees to their first league championship. This was the best season that any player had ever had.

Curiously, it wasn't just Babe Ruth who was hitting home runs in volume as the 1920s began. Suddenly balls were flying out of parks all over the place. From 1918 to 1922, American League home runs traced an unexpectedly impressive trajectory, as a simple summary shows:

$$1918 - \ 96$$
$$1919 - 240$$
$$1920 - 369$$
$$1921 - 477$$
$$1922 - 525$$

For the major leagues as a whole, the total number of home runs went from 235 in 1918 to over a thousand in 1922 – a quadrupling in just four years, a wholly unprecedented level of change. So what happened? Well, quite a lot actually.

First, in the wake of the Ray Chapman killing, umpires were instructed to keep a decent ball in play at all times.

No more would pitchers be allowed to turn the ball brown with dirt and tobacco juice, making it all but invisible in late innings. The major leagues also banned what was loosely known as the spitball. The application of spit (or grease, tobacco juice, Vaseline or any of at least two dozen other globulous additives) to the side of the ball induced an imbalance that caused the ball to wobble and dip in abrupt and unpredictable ways, rather as a modern knuckleball does, but with the difference that spitballs could be thrown hard.

Every spitball pitcher had his own favourite substance. Eddie Cicotte of the Chicago White Sox used paraffin wax to great effect, though how he did so without poisoning himself over the course of nine innings was something of a wonder. Home teams on the receiving end of doctored balls sometimes tried to discourage opposing pitchers by painting that day's game balls with mustard oil, tincture of capsicum or some other fiery surprise, which at least provided the home players with the possibility of amusement, if not more hittable pitches.

After the 1919 season it was decided to ban the spitball for everyone except seventeen pitchers whose careers were dependent on it. They would be allowed to retain the pitch until their own retirements. The last legal spitballer was Burleigh Grimes, who retired in 1934. Babe Ruth, for one, believed that without the banning of doctored balls no batter could risk the big swings necessary to hit home runs.

The most important change of all, however, was that the ball itself became livelier – though when exactly, why exactly and by how much are questions that are surprisingly difficult to answer.

The quest to produce a sturdier, more resilient baseball was a longstanding one. Ben Shibe, co-owner of the Philadelphia Athletics and a manufacturer of sporting goods, who had begun his colourful career in the leather-goods industry and so knew his way around stitched products, for years devoted much of his spare time to trying to make better baseballs. In 1909 he invented the cork-centred ball. Cork centres were lighter than rubber centres, which meant that the balls required more twine, wound tighter, to obtain their regulation weight and circumference. Shibe's new ball, nearly everyone agreed, was notably livelier. Hits seemed sharper, particularly in the later innings of games when balls normally grew spongy. Then some time after the war – when precisely is another curiously vague matter – Shibe's company, A. J. Reach, began to import a superior grade of wool from Australia, which was even springier and could be wound tighter still around its feather-light cork. The result was what was commonly known as the 'rabbit ball' because of its liveliness.

Interestingly, Reach strenuously denied that the new ball was livelier, and produced results from the US Bureau of Standards showing that the ball was neither more nor less bouncy than those that preceded it. Most players didn't agree, however. 'There was a great difference between the ball that was in use when I broke in and the rabbit ball that was handed us a few seasons ago,' Walter Johnson told a reporter in the summer of 1927. 'This ball travels with much more speed than the old one when hit.'

Although home run numbers grew generally, no one came close to matching Ruth's totals. In 1920, when Ruth hit 54 homers, no other player hit even 20. In 1921, his 59 homers were 11 more than the next two best hitters combined. By July 1921, in only his second year as a full-time batter, Ruth had already hit 139 home runs, more than any person had hit in a career before. 'So compelling is his presence at the plate, so picturesque and showy and deliciously melodramatic his every move and appearance that he is, from the point of the onlooker, a success even when he is a failure,' wrote one observer. Even his pop-ups (that is, a ball hit in the air and caught for an out) were sensational and were often hoisted so high that he had comfortably rounded second base before the ball dropped into an infielder's glove.

In Babe Ruth's first year in New York, the Yankees' attendance more than doubled to 1,289,000 even though they finished third. The Giants had never attracted a million fans in a year. The Yankees now never attracted fewer. John McGraw was so offended by Ruth's assault on the principles of 'scientific' baseball, and so envious of the Yankees' success, that he ordered them to leave the Polo Grounds and find a new home. In 1922, Jacob Ruppert began building Yankee Stadium – the greatest ballpark ever seen to that time. He placed it on a plot of land carefully chosen to be within sight of McGraw's Polo Grounds. When finished, the stadium cost $2.5 million and was 50 per cent bigger than any previous ballpark. From the day of its opening it was known as 'The House That Ruth Built'.

Babe Ruth became celebrated as no sports figure ever had before. Everything about him, said the writer Paul Gallico, seemed larger than life – 'his frame, his enormous head surmounted by blue-black curly hair, his great blob of a nose spattered generously over his face'. He wasn't good-looking, but he was irresistibly charismatic. As his friend and teammate Waite Hoyt put it: 'He was one of a kind. If he had never played ball, if you had never heard of him and passed him on Broadway, you'd turn around and look.'

Ruth's rise to fame could not have been more impeccably timed. It coincided precisely with the birth of tabloid newspapers, newsreel films, fan magazines and radio – all vital cogs in the new celebrity culture – and his arrival in New York brought him into the throbbing heart of the media world. Newspapers began running a daily column entitled 'What Babe Ruth Did Today'. When Babe Ruth had a bunion trimmed, it received national coverage. Interest in him went way beyond the sports pages, however. He featured on the covers of dozens of magazines that had nothing to do with baseball, from *Hardware Age* to *Popular Science*. The *Literary Digest* ran an admiring profile, as did the *New Yorker* soon after it began publication. No ballplayer had ever attracted this kind of attention in the wider world before.

He came to be regarded as a kind of god. In 1921, a team of professors at Columbia University hooked him up to wires and something called a Hipp chronoscope, subjected him to a battery of physical and mental tests, and pronounced him 'one man in a million' for his reflexes, eyesight, hearing and 'nervous stability'. He even scored 10 per cent above normal for intelligence – a fact that he boasted of with particular pride to anyone who would listen.

People loved him – that's genuinely not too strong a word – and not without reason. He was kind and generous, especially to children, and endearingly unpretentious.

Introduced to President Coolidge on a sweltering day at Griffith Stadium in Washington, Ruth wiped his face with a handkerchief and said, 'Hot as hell, ain't it, Prez?' At a party he referred to the holders as 'the hostess and hoster'. But at the same time, he commanded a certain wit. Once when a traffic cop shouted at him, 'Hey, this is a one-way street', Ruth yelled back, 'I'm only driving one way!' The sportswriter Red Smith became convinced that Ruth possessed a first-rate brain – one that combined shrewdness with simplicity, and innocence with penetrating perception. 'It was, in its special way, a great mind,' he insisted.

Those who knew him well weren't so sure, for Ruth's brain had wondrous gaps. He could never remember names, for instance. When Waite Hoyt, his closest friend, left the team for the Detroit Tigers after eleven years as Ruth's teammate, Ruth's parting words to him were: 'Take care of yourself, Walter.' He was equally hopeless at learning lines. Once for a national radio broadcast he was coached again and again to say: 'As the Duke of Wellington once said, the Battle of Waterloo was won on the playing fields of Eton.' When it came time to recite the line, Ruth proudly blurted: 'As Duke Ellington once said, the Battle of Waterloo was won on the playing fields of Elkton.'

His extravagance was legendary. On one road trip, he wore twenty-two silk shirts in three days, then gave them all to the chambermaid upon departing. In Cuba, he lost $26,000 on a single horse race, and $65,000 in a few days. 'It has been necessary for his employers to have him followed by detectives to protect him from himself as well as from confidence men, blackmailers, racetrack touts and bookmakers, gamblers and scheming young ladies,' noted the *New Yorker* in 1926. Despite his wealth, often he didn't have the cash to pay his income tax bills, including in 1927 when Ruppert made him the highest paid baseball player in history. Over the course of his career, by his own estimation, he lost or wasted well over a quarter of a million dollars.

His teammates did what they could to help him, taking it in turns to go through his mail to alert him to anything important. 'Ruth had 24 secretaries,' Hoyt once observed. Doc Woods, the team trainer, once found $6,000 worth of cheques in mail that Ruth had discarded. Woods also commonly faked Ruth's signature on baseballs and photographs, and reportedly forged some 10,000 signatures in one year.

His appetites for sex and food, both seemingly bound-less, were a source of perennial wonder. Marshall Hunt, sports editor of the *New York Daily News*, told how on road trips they would drive out into the country looking for restaurants that did chicken dinners. 'What Babe really wanted,' Hunt said, 'was a good chicken-dinner-and-daughter combination, and it worked out that way more often than you would think'.

His indiscretions often led to complications. Fred Lieb (the *New York Evening Telegram* sportswriter who first called Yankee Stadium the House that Ruth Built) once watched as Ruth was chased through a train in Shreveport, Louisiana, by a woman (reputedly the wife of a state legislator) armed with a knife. Ruth escaped only by jump-ing off the train and then back on again just as it was departing. On another occasion he was chased 'near naked' out of a hotel by an aggrieved husband with a gun. When someone asked his Yankee teammate Ping Bodie what it was like to room with Ruth, Bodie replied, 'I don't know. I room with his suitcase.'

As the 1920s progressed, Ruth increasingly stayed at superior hotels to the rest of the team, at his own expense. There he would hold court to anyone who cared to drop by. Waite Hoyt once counted 250 visitors to his suite over the course of an evening. Ruth seldom knew who any of the visitors were. At a party in his rooms at the Book Cadillac Hotel in Detroit, Ruth famously stood on a chair and shouted, 'Any woman who doesn't want to fuck can leave now.'

If sex was unavailable, he just ate. Marshall Hunt swore he once watched Ruth down eighteen hot dogs at a sitting. Several witnesses reported seeing him order a dinner that consisted of double helpings of everything – two porterhouse steaks, two mountains of fried potatoes, two salads, two slabs of apple pie with ice cream – then come back six hours later and consume the same meal again; in between he ate eight hot dogs and drank six bottles of pop. 'Lord, he ate too much,' Harry Hooper, a teammate, told Lawrence Ritter in *The Glory of Their Times*. Over the course of his career, it was calculated that Ruth had gained and lost two and a half tons.

On the whole, he got away with his wayward lifestyle, but when he faltered, he faltered spectacularly. In 1922, he had a dreadful year. He was suspended on five separate occasions for various behavioural breaches and altogether missed about a third of the season. He squabbled endlessly with his manager, the long-suffering Miller Huggins. Once when Huggins criticized Ruth and his teammate Bob Meusel for their lack of discipline and output, Ruth carried the diminutive Huggins to the rear platform of the observation car and dangled him upside down over the rails until he withdrew his complaint. After Huggins's death, one of his sisters claimed that Ruth had taken five years off his life.

In the winter of 1922, at what was supposed to be a testimonial dinner, Jimmy Walker, soon to be mayor of New York – and a man who knew a thing or two about high living – publicly castigated Ruth, calling him 'a great athlete, but also a great fool'. Ruth, he said, had let everybody down by his loutish behaviour during the season. 'Worst of all, worst of all,' Walker went on:

> you have let down the kids of America. Everywhere in America, on every vacant lot where kids play baseball, and in the hospitals too, where crippled children dream of movement forever denied their thin and warped little bodies, they think of you, their hero. They look up to you, worship you. And then what happens? You carouse and abuse your great body . . . The kids have seen their idol shattered and their dreams broken.

Ruth by this point was sobbing piteously – but worse was still to come. As he left the dinner that evening he was served a summons on behalf of one Dolores Dixon of Brooklyn, charging him with being the father of her unborn child. Ruth was in the embarrassing position of not being able to recall whether he had slept with the woman or not. In the end, it appeared that he had not. 'Dolores Dixon' turned out to be a fictitious name and the woman in question was unable to supply dates or places that tallied with Ruth's known movements. The suit was dropped, but not until Ruth had been made to look exceedingly foolish.

In 1925 everything went wrong again. He arrived at spring training 40 pounds overweight, and struggled to regain his form. In early April, as the Yankees were playing a series of exhibition games on the way home from spring training, Ruth began to feel unwell. By the time the team reached Asheville, he was feverish and barely coherent. Once outside the train, he collapsed. As he was obviously in no state to play in an exhibition match, Miller Huggins, the manager, told him to continue on to New York. At Grand Central Station he collapsed again and went into convulsions. He was rushed to St Vincent's Hospital.

Rumours circulated that Ruth had eaten too many hot dogs. The episode became known as 'the bellyache heard round the world'. The hospital was curiously vague about Ruth's condition and treatment, which led others to suppose that he was being treated for syphilis or some other venereal embarrassment. It now seems evident that whatever ailed Ruth, it was seriously acute and almost certainly gastric. Ruth was in bed for a month and weak enough to need a wheelchair for several days beyond that. Altogether he spent almost seven weeks in the hospital. When he did return to the Yankees, he was sporting a fresh abdominal scar and was a ghost of his former self: he had lost 76 pounds during his illness, and was now a trim but feeble 180 pounds, compared with the 256-pound tub of joviality he had been less than two months earlier. His legs were especially thin. He looked, said one observer, like 'a bag of oats on two toothpicks'.

But almost at once he returned to his former habits and within a month was becoming an overweight glutton again. On a road trip in August, the Yankees played appallingly and Ruth contributed very little. More than once he fought with teammates. In St Louis after Ruth stayed out all night, Huggins fined him $5,000 – a huge sum, double some players' annual salaries – and suspended him indefinitely. Ruth fumed and ranted, but eventually grew contrite and was reinstated to the line-up. He hit 10 home runs and batted a very respectable .345 in his last twenty-nine games and didn't cause anyone any trouble at all, but by that time it was too late. The Yankees finished the season in next to last place with a record of just 69 wins against 85 losses and attendance down by 700,000.

In 1926, as so often with Ruth, he rebounded. He went through an intensive six-week fitness regime, shed 40 pounds of doughy fat, and took almost nine inches off his waistline. He had a good season, too: he hit 47 home runs, batted .372 and drove in 146 runs. Above all, he behaved himself, by and large. But in the World Series against the Cardinals, Ruth ended the year with an astoundingly ill-judged play. With two outs in the ninth and the Yankees trailing by one run, Ruth walked and then – to everyone's astonishment – tried to steal second base. He was thrown out by ten feet, ending the game and giving the Cardinals the World Series. 'I guess I did something rash,' Ruth conceded. It was, by nearly everyone's estimation, one of the most foolish plays ever made in a World Series and it undid nearly all the good that he had achieved during the season.

So at the start of 1927, Babe Ruth was in need of redemption again. That, however, wouldn't be easy now. He was nearly thirty-two years old and suffered from low blood pressure, chronic indigestion and occasional shortness of breath. This was not a man in his prime. It seemed highly unlikely that he would have a good year. In fact, and amazingly, he was about to have rather more than that. He was about to have a year that no one who knew baseball would ever forget.

Chapter 10

In the summer of 1927 whenever Babe Ruth was missing from his usual haunts he could often be found in a cinema somewhere, sitting in a middle seat near the front, his broad face a picture of pride and delight as he watched a six-reel film called *Babe Comes Home* starring himself and the Swedish actress Anna Q. Nilsson.

Shot in twenty-two days the previous January at the First National studios in Burbank, California, the film was by all accounts dreadful. No copy of it survives, so exactly what the plot consisted of is uncertain, but it was said to have been loosely modelled on Babe Ruth's own life, except of course that in the movie he didn't eat like a glutton, swear profanely or have sex on the floor at frequent intervals. The movie was not in any case a success. The big hit of the season was a steamy offering called *Don Juan* in which Hollywood heart-throb John Barrymore managed to plant no fewer than 143 kisses on compliant females – so many that hardly anyone later remembered that the movie was even more memorable for containing a soundtrack. Although *Don Juan* offered only recorded music and not speech – and hence was not a 'talkie' – it still preceded *The Jazz Singer* as a sound picture by several months.

In Manhattan, an even greater hit was not a feature film but a Fox Movietone newsreel, showing exclusively at the new Roxy Theatre, of Charles Lindbergh's departure for Paris from Roosevelt Field. This, too, had a novel element of sound. Loudspeakers were set up in the theatre wings and a technician with good timing played a separate soundtrack so that the engine's initial sputters and final triumphant roar matched the images on the screen. It wasn't the most high-tech performance even for the age, but it brought six thousand patrons to their feet every time it was played.

Against this, *Babe Comes Home* was pretty tame stuff. It was also notably unlucky in its timing for it was released on 22 May, the day after Lindbergh's arrival in Paris, when the world was fully caught up in the joyous mania of that achievement. But the movie was sufficiently bad that it probably wouldn't have found a following anyway. All this was a particular shame for Ms Nilsson, who is forgotten now but was once so popular that she received 30,000 fan letters a week. In 1925, she was seriously injured in a fall from a horse, and spent a year immobilized while convalescing. *Babe Comes Home* was intended to be her comeback movie, but it died quietly, unmourned by anyone but its male lead.

Also easing his way into obscurity by this time was the increasingly hapless and marginalized Francesco de Pinedo. Pinedo and his two loyal crewmen had managed to get to Newfoundland ahead of Lindbergh, but then were pinned down by rough seas – one of the common and inescapable drawbacks of seaplanes. Lindbergh had actually flown straight over them on 20 May. Pinedo was able to get away three days later, but engine troubles brought him down in the sea 360 miles short of the Azores and he had to be towed into the port of Fayal by a passing Portuguese fishing boat. By the time his arrival was reported, Lindbergh was the world's hero, and nobody was interested in an Italian who reached his destination at the end of a tow rope.

Still Pinedo pressed on, but the final stages of his journey became small paragraphs tacked on to other aviation stories. On 11 June, he reached Lisbon. On 15 June, a small report in the *New York Times* noted that while flying to Barcelona Pinedo had been forced down by bad weather near Madrid and had had to complete his journey by train. When at last he made it back to the Bay of Ostia, near Rome, the wider world hardly noticed.

With Lindbergh at sea and out of touch but for a daily ghostwritten (or at least ghost-assisted) dispatch to the *New York Times*, which was nearly always agonizingly dull, the world craved some fresh excitement. Happily, things were beginning to stir again at Roosevelt Field. After Lindbergh's successful flight, no one was sure what would become of the two remaining teams – whether they would just pack up and go away or try flights of their own. Charles Levine, the injunction against him lifted, now abruptly made clear that he still intended his plane to fly.

Early on the morning of 4 June, the *Columbia* was wheeled on to the grassy runway and Clarence Chamberlin, dressed in a leather jacket, knickerbocker breeches and patterned stockings that could be seen from half a mile away, emerged from the hangar, waved to the crowd and climbed alone into the cockpit. Levine's belief seemed to be that if he couldn't get to Europe sooner than Lindbergh, he could at least get there more strangely. Nearly everything about the production was a little odd. For one thing, he and Chamberlin refused to say where the plane was headed. Nor would either say why Chamberlin was unaccompanied when the cockpit had a second seat for a navigator and co-pilot.

Then something even more unexpected happened. As Chamberlin brought the plane round to its takeoff position, he slowed for a moment and a bald, stocky man in a business suit bolted from the sidelines and climbed hurriedly on board. To everyone's astonishment, it was Charles Levine.

Levine's wife, in evident confusion, cried out in dismay: 'Oh-h-h! He's not going? He's not going!' When she saw that indeed he was going, she swooned and fell into the arms of the man standing behind her. Clarence Chamberlin later confided to a reporter, however, that Mrs Levine had actually known all along that her husband was going, so the theatrics, it appears, were for the sake of the press.

Minutes later, the *Columbia* was airborne, and the second flight of the summer to Europe was under way – though where exactly it was bound not even the two men aboard knew. Their tentative plan was to try for Berlin, but in truth they would be happy to land almost anywhere.

Levine quickly proved himself almost totally useless. He had no navigational skills at all and in the one moment that Chamberlin let him try to fly he almost immediately put the plane in a dangerous spin. His only real contribution was to reach for things behind the seat and help keep Chamberlin awake. Quickly they realized that navigating a route to Europe was not as easy as Lindbergh had made it look. By the time they reached Newport, Rhode Island, barely an hour into the flight, they were four miles off course and their earth inductor compass was not working. They were never quite sure where they were at any point after that. Luckily Europe was a big target and Chamberlin was the world's most laid-back pilot. It was just a question of going in the right direction, he insisted.

Chamberlin was about to become – albeit briefly and somewhat tepidly – nearly as famous as Lindbergh. Thirty-three years old in the summer of 1927, he came from Denison, Iowa, a town much like Lindbergh's Little Falls one state to the north, though slightly more in the mainstream as it was on the Lincoln Highway. Chamberlin's father ran a jewellery store and repair shop, so the family was comfortable. Growing up in Denison at the same time was a girl named Donna Mullenger, who would later become famous as the actress Donna Reed. Today people in Denison remember her with great fondness. Hardly anyone remembers Clarence Chamberlin.

Chamberlin's mother was English and, for reasons unknown, when Clarence was about ten she moved back to England, taking Clarence with her. Chamberlin's autobiography is wondrously unrevealing on all aspects of his private life – he doesn't even disclose his wife's first name; she is simply 'Mrs Chamberlin' throughout – and he says nothing of his English interlude other than that he hated it. After about a year, they returned to Denison and family life resumed as before.

After high school, Clarence attended Iowa State College, as it then was, and acquired a degree in engineering. He learned to fly while serving with the Signal Corps during the First World War. He became a flight instructor and never saw battle – indeed, never left America. Like most pilots, after the war Chamberlin took whatever work he could find. For a time he was an aerial photographer. Several well-known photographs of important events as seen from the air, including Yankee Stadium on its grand opening in 1923, were taken by Chamberlin. Like Lindbergh, he had also crashed a lot of planes – about ten, by his own estimation – and was involved in a fatal crash in an air race in 1925 when a passenger riding with him was killed. Chamberlin didn't actually know the passenger – it was just a young man who asked if he could go along for the ride. Oddly, Chamberlin seems never to have bothered to learn his identity. In his autobiography, Chamberlin merely records that he himself was knocked unconscious in the crash and learned afterwards 'that my companion had been killed'. Chamberlin was seriously injured and was told by doctors that he probably wouldn't walk again, but clearly he proved them wrong. He was, if nothing else, fearless.

Early on the morning of 5 June, passengers on the Cunard liner *Mauretania*, bound for New York from Cherbourg, were startled to see an aeroplane drop out of the sky and circle the ship just above deck level. The plane was recognized at once as the *Columbia*. Most of the passengers – who by chance included Raymond Orteig, returning to America from his summer home in France to present Lindbergh with the Orteig Prize the following week –

assumed the visit of the *Columbia* was a kind of salute. The two men aboard waved in a friendly manner. In fact, Chamberlin was trying to find out where he was. He was looking for the ship's name, to check against a list of sailing times in a copy of the *New York Times* he was carrying. Knowing how long the ship had been at sea would give him an idea of how much ocean he still had to cross. As it happened, he only just missed dropping down on the *Memphis* and being able to exchange waves with a presumably bemused Charles Lindbergh. Using the *Mauretania*'s wake as a kind of pointer, Chamberlin adjusted his course, rose back into the clouds and carried on towards Europe.

That was the last anyone heard of him or Levine for many hours, but on the morning of 6 June, after nearly two days in the air, they came down in a field somewhere in north-eastern Germany. Remarkably, neither Chamberlin nor Levine had thought to pack any maps of Europe, so they had no clear idea where they were. They had been in the air for nearly forty-three hours and had flown 3,905 miles, breaking both Lindbergh's distance and duration records by considerable margins. The first person to greet them was a farmer's wife who was furious at the damage their plane had done to her cereal crop. Among others to turn up was – by rather extraordinary good luck – an aeroplane mechanic who was home visiting his mother. He spoke good English and informed them that they were at Mansfeld, near Eisleben, 110 miles from Berlin and heading the wrong way. The mechanic knew how to order a delivery of aviation fuel – something that would have been entirely beyond them otherwise – but when the tanker arrived its nozzle proved too big for the plane, so fuel had to be transferred laboriously via a long-spouted tea kettle borrowed from the farmer's wife, who had presumably calmed down a little.

When at last the plane was refuelled and the adventurers were pointed in the right direction, they took off again. Soon, however, they were lost once more. Chamberlin and Levine spent the morning flying around blindly and bickering over where they were before running out of fuel a second time and making another forced landing. This time they discovered that they had gone some distance past Berlin and were in a small town called Cottbus, almost at the Polish border.*

Too tired to continue, they retired to Cottbus's best and only hotel and fell into bed. When they awoke, they found that they were national heroes in Germany and that a fleet of military planes had arrived to conduct them to the capital. The following morning, under a guiding escort, the two men flew the last leg to Tempelhof airfield in Berlin. More than 150,000 people were waiting to greet them. An additional 20,000, misled by rumour, turned up at Warsaw Airport and were sent away disappointed.

Germany gave the two flyers a reception as jubilant and welcoming as Lindbergh's had been in Paris. No humans would attract larger and more enthusiastic crowds in Germany until the rise of Adolf Hitler. America grew nearly as excited as when Lindbergh had landed. For three days, the *Times* in New York gave the two heroes its maximum headline – three decks across eight columns – and covered their every thought and movement in exhaustive detail. The general public was excited, too. When Levine's

* Coincidentally, just down the road from Kamenz, home town of Bruno Hauptmann, the kidnapper of Lindbergh's baby in 1932.

and Chamberlin's wives travelled to Hoboken Pier to catch a ship to Germany, six thousand people turned up to see them off – at one o'clock in the morning.

Soon, however, the celebrations took on a slightly strained air. President Coolidge sent congratulations from America – but only to Chamberlin. His pointed snub was widely interpreted as anti-Semitic. The Jewish newspaper *The Day* observed from Manhattan: 'Two men left New York; two men risked their lives; two men have shown heroism and created a record even greater than Lindbergh's. Two men left; two men arrived, Americans both. But the President of the United States congratulates only one, and by strange coincidence the one whom the President has not found worthy of being mentioned by name is named Levine . . .'

Lindbergh, in his daily dispatches to the *New York Times* from aboard the *Memphis*, also praised Chamberlin generously without once mentioning Levine, though this almost certainly was more out of bitterness at the way Levine had treated him over the Bellanca deal than because of any active anti-Jewish sentiment.

The Germans, too, seemed a little uncomfortable with Levine. A restaurant in Berlin started offering roast beef à la Chamberlin with Cottbus potatoes, and a brewery sought permission to issue a Chamberlin beer, but again without mention of Levine.

Levine for his part did almost nothing to ingratiate himself with the people of Germany. He visited no hospitals, called on no widows, offered no praise to German aviators. He didn't even have anything good to say about Lindbergh, attributing his success to favourable weather rather than skilful flying. 'Lindbergh was lucky and we were not,' Levine told reporters. 'If we had one-tenth of Lindbergh's luck, we would have done much better.' To the acute embarrassment of the German and American authorities alike, a German businessman, Dr Julius Puppe, whom Levine had cheated out of $5,000 in a deal in America, now came forward with a writ and tried to have his plane seized. Chamberlin was amiable, but had nothing to say, and gave the impression of having not a thought in his head when not in the air, which was perhaps not far from the actuality.

The world quickly realized that it didn't particularly like Charles Levine and was never going to get anything interesting out of Clarence Chamberlin, so its attention turned elsewhere.

Lindbergh, though far away at sea and steaming home slowly, managed to raise a frisson of excitement with the news that he had come close to being swept overboard from the *Memphis* three days out from Cherbourg. The headline in the *New York Times* read:

LINDBERGH IN PERIL
AS WAVE TRAPS HIM
ON CRUISER'S BOW

The world's most beloved hero, it turned out, had gone for a stroll after dinner in rough seas, and was standing in the bow when a sudden succession of big waves crashed over the deck from the side, isolating him from the rest of the ship. Lindbergh had to hold tight to a lifeline to keep from being knocked off his feet and possibly swept overboard. B. F. Mahoney, the owner of Ryan Airlines, was also present, but safely on the other side of the crashing waves. Lindbergh waited ten minutes or so for the waves to ease, then strode smartly back to safety. 'It was an exciting experience,' he related afterwards. It was not, however, a good omen for any nervous crew, of whom there were almost certainly many. This USS *Memphis* was a recent replacement for an earlier USS *Memphis* which was sunk by a mysterious rogue wave in the Caribbean in 1916, with the loss of some forty lives. It would not have escaped many of the sailors that 'Memphis' was something of a cursed name.

With Lindbergh temporarily unavailable, what America needed was some kind of sublimely pointless distraction, and a man named Shipwreck Kelly stood ready to provide it. At 11 a.m. on 7 June, Kelly clambered to the top of a fifty-foot flagpole on the roof of the St Francis Hotel in Newark, New Jersey, and sat there. That was all he did, for days on end, but people were enchanted and streamed to Newark to watch.

Kelly had grown up in Hell's Kitchen, Manhattan's toughest district, in just about the grimmest circumstances possible. Seven months before he was born, his father, a rigger on construction sites, had plunged to his death when an assistant accidentally pulled the wrong lever on a derrick he was working on. Kelly's mother, heartbroken and bereft of a breadwinner, then died in childbirth. Kelly was adopted by the assistant and thus raised by the man who had accidentally but carelessly killed his own father. Kelly ran off to sea at thirteen and spent most of the next fifteen years as a sailor. He got his nickname, according to *Time* magazine, by surviving the sinking of the *Titanic* in

1912, but that seems to have been just a bit of inventive whimsy by a *Time* reporter. In fact, it came because he briefly tried to make a career as a boxer under the name Sailor Kelly, but he was beaten so often – he lost eleven bouts in a row – that he became known as the Shipwrecked Sailor. According to Kelly himself, he survived five other shipwrecks, two aeroplane crashes, three car crashes and a train wreck, all without a scratch, during a busy career as a steeplejack, aeroplane stunt performer and 'human fly' (which is to say, someone who climbs buildings for publicity purposes) before taking up flag-pole-sitting in 1924. By 1927, he had pretty much made the business his own.

Kelly would reside for days or weeks on a tiny perch – a padded disc about the size of a bar-stool seat – attached to a flagpole on the top of a tall building. The most devoted admirers paid 25 cents to go on to the hotel rooftop, where they could see Kelly at comparatively close range and even engage him in conversation. The rest crowded the streets below, causing traffic jams and even trampling flower beds and breaking down fences through their force of numbers. Food, shaving implements, cigarettes and other vital items were conveyed to Kelly by rope. To sleep without tumbling off, he would lock his ankles around the pole and jam his thumbs into two small holes drilled into the side of the seat. Normally he dozed for no more than about twenty minutes so that he didn't fall into a deep and forgetful slumber. Periodically, to please the crowds and relieve stiffening muscles, he would stand up on his precarious platform – an action that took considerable agility and not a little courage, especially if the wind was blowing. During the whole of his time aloft, he didn't leave the perch. No record appears to indicate how he dealt with bodily functions. For two days beforehand and throughout the sitting he took no solid food – just milk, broth and coffee – which may partly answer the obvious question. He smoked four packs of cigarettes a day. Otherwise he just sat. He billed himself as 'The Luckiest Fool Alive'.

Newark proved to be more or less the summit of Shipwreck Kelly's brief career. He sat on many more flagpoles – once for up to forty-nine days – through blizzards, lightning storms and other meteorological perils, but gradually the world lost interest in him and flagpole work dried up. Kelly dropped from sight and didn't appear again until August 1941, when he was briefly jailed for drunken driving in Connecticut. He died of a heart attack on a New York street in 1952, by which time he was living in poverty. At his death, he was carrying a scrapbook of newspaper clippings of his old exploits. His age was given variously as fifty-nine to sixty-seven years old.

Even now, in 1927 in Newark, newspaper interest in Kelly dwindled after the first few days since there was never anything to report other than that he was still up there. By the time he came down and kissed his bride of six months, exactly twelve days and twelve hours after ascending, the public was little moved and the press barely noticed.

Besides, a much, much bigger story had captured everyone's attention. Charles Lindbergh was home.

Chapter 11

THE MORE FAMOUS her son became, the more evident it grew that Evangeline Lodge Lindbergh was a little odd. Invited east for Charles's homecoming, she ignored an invitation to stay with President and Mrs Coolidge, and instead quietly checked into a Baltimore hotel.

Since White House officials had no idea what had become of Mrs Lindbergh, they were naturally alarmed. It would hardly do to lose the mother of the nation's greatest hero on the eve of his return. Luckily, a newspaper article disclosed her whereabouts and officials were able to send a car to bring her, however reluctantly, back to Washington.

The Coolidges were not living in the White House at this time. They had been moved out in March – the president, it was said, all but wriggling in indignation – so that urgent repairs could be made to the roof and third floor. They resided instead in what was being called the 'temporary White House', a mansion at 15 Dupont Circle lent to them by one Cissy Patterson, a member of the *Chicago Tribune–New York Daily News* newspaper clan.

One other house guest was present when Mrs Lindbergh arrived – 'a gnomelike little man of fifty-four', the increasingly ubiquitous Dwight Morrow. Mrs Lindbergh seemed to enjoy and relax in Morrow's company – he was famously gracious – which was just as well because in under two years they would be bound by the marriage of her son to his daughter.

Morrow had become almost absurdly rich as a banker with J. P. Morgan & Co. The Morrow family had a house with thirty-two servants in Englewood, New Jersey, and that was mostly just for weekends. During the week they lived in a grand apartment in Manhattan. Stories of Morrow's absent-mindedness were legion and reported with relish in such places as the New Yorker's Talk of the Town section. The most oft-repeated Morrow story concerned the time he climbed into his bath while still dressed. On another occasion, he was reported to have used a visitor's bald head to knock the ashes from his pipe. Once a friend encountered Morrow at Grand Central Station looking perplexed and feeling helplessly in his pockets. 'Lost your ticket?' asked the friend. 'No, worse than that,' Morrow replied disconsolately. 'I can't remember where I was going.'

His celebrated inability to keep himself satisfactorily dressed led Morgan Bank to post an attendant in the men's room whose exclusive role was to make sure Morrow always returned to the world in a presentable state. In fact, in all these instances Morrow was not so much absent-minded as incapacitated by drink. He was, it appears, a hopeless souse. Yet his mind was so sharp that even the most copious infusions of alcohol couldn't truly dull it. He was for years one of J. P. Morgan & Co.'s most trusted senior partners. Both Yale and the University of Chicago wanted him for their president.

Morrow and Coolidge had been friends since they were classmates at Amherst. Morrow seems to have been one of the few people of that era who thought that Calvin Coolidge had the makings of greatness. In 1920, he formed a committee to promote Coolidge, who was then governor of Massachusetts, for president. In the event, the Republican Party chose the more charismatic Warren G. Harding, but Coolidge's selection as vice-president was in large part thanks to Morrow's efforts behind the scenes. Coolidge proved remarkably ungrateful. When Harding died and Coolidge succeeded him three years later, it was widely expected that Morrow would be appointed to the cabinet as secretary of state or of the Treasury. But no call came. Not until 1925 did Coolidge give him any post at all – and that was a slightly demeaning one as head of the commission appointed to bring some order and discipline to America's chaotic aviation business.

Now he was being invited to become ambassador to Mexico – another dubious proposition since Mexico was in the throes of revolution and in a strongly anti-American frame of mind. Bandits roamed the country, often killing foreigners. Morrow accepted anyway.

The morning of 11 June – Charles Lindbergh Day – dawned hot and clear. As the USS *Memphis* steamed towards its berth at the Washington Navy Yard, it was accompanied by four naval destroyers, eighty-eight aeroplanes, two giant dirigibles (one of them the *Los Angeles*, whose last official duty had been to look for Nungesser and Coli on the lonely North Atlantic) and fleets of private boats whose sheer numbers and slapdash manoeuvrings added an element of mayhem and near misses to the proceedings. Onshore a festive atmosphere reigned with bands playing merry airs and a large crowd waiting in happy expectation. Mrs Lindbergh was present, too, but was unaccompanied by the president, to the surprise of many. In fact, Calvin Coolidge was not always terribly comfortable in a nautical setting. Recently he had been sent to review the American fleet from the bridge of the presidential yacht, the *Mayflower*, at nearby Hampton Roads, but got seasick even though the ship wasn't moving, and refused to wear the naval uniform provided – a breach of protocol and an insult to the navy. He went below after just twenty minutes and completed his review from a reclining position while looking bleakly out of a porthole. For Lindbergh's arrival he decided to wait in the city.

Mrs Lindbergh was piped aboard and met Charles privately in the captain's quarters, then the two of them stepped out on to the deck. Charles, dressed in a blue suit, looked rested and refreshed after a week at sea. The crowd issued an adoring roar at Lindbergh's appearance and he was given a twenty-one-gun salute of cannon fire – a tribute normally accorded to heads of state. Across the city, factory whistles sounded and church bells rang.

Through the happy din a radio broadcaster named Graham McNamee kept up a steady patter. McNamee was himself making history. His broadcast was being carried by fifty stations across the nation by the new National Broadcasting Company, America's (and indeed the world's) first radio network. Twelve thousand miles of AT&T telephone cables were pressed into service to give

America its first coast-to-coast broadcast. It was believed that virtually every radio set in the nation was tuned in. No person in history had spoken to so many people at one time as Graham McNamee did now.

McNamee's position as America's most trusted voice was entirely an accident. A Minnesotan like Lindbergh, he had moved to New York as a young man to pursue a career as a singer in both light and serious opera. In 1923, while walking along lower Broadway, he passed the offices of radio station WEAF. Knowing that radio stations some-times aired recitals, he asked if there was any chance of an audition. The station manager, Samuel L. Ross, thought McNamee had the perfect voice for radio – warm and clear – so he hired him on the spot to introduce programmes, read news bulletins and occasionally sing. That autumn WEAF had the rights to broadcast the World Series between the Yankees and Giants – the first time the Series had been broadcast to a mass audience. W. O. McGeehan of the *Tribune* was employed to provide play by play and McNamee was sent along to assist him. McGeehan had no talent for broadcasting. He spoke in a flat tone and made no effort to fill the dead space between plays. During the fourth inning of the third game, he told McNamee he didn't want to do it any more and left. McNamee had no choice but to take over, which was something of a challenge since he knew very little about professional baseball.

He was, however, a born broadcaster. McNamee described the crowds, the weather, the air of excitement that was rippling through the park. He picked out celebrities. He made the listeners feel present and welcome, like old friends. People loved his broadcasts even if he didn't always entirely grasp what was happening on the field. Ring Lardner wrote on one occasion: 'I don't know which game to write about, the one I saw today or the one I heard Graham McNamee announce as I sat next to him at the Polo Grounds.' Soon McNamee's was the best-known voice in America, and not just for World Series games but for every kind of important gathering – championship prize fights, political conventions, Rose Bowls and the arrival home of Charles Lindbergh.

Lindbergh Day in Washington was in many ways the day that radio came of age. It takes some effort of imagination to appreciate how novel radio was in the 1920s. It was the wonder of the age. By the time of Lindbergh's flight, one third of all the money America spent on furniture was spent on radios. Stations sprouted everywhere. In a single year, 1922, the number of American radio stations went from 28 to 570. Anyone could start one. Nushawg Poultry Farm in New Lebanon, Ohio, had its own station. So did many department stores, banks, hardware stores, churches, newspapers, utilities and schools. Production at even the larger stations tended to be more than slightly amateurish. When Norman Brokenshire, a broadcaster for WHN in New York, found himself with a long lull to fill and nothing more to say, he announced: 'Ladies and gentlemen, we bring you the sounds of New York City,' and thrust the microphone out of the window.

Not everyone was captivated by the new technology. Many believed that all the invisible energy flying through the air must be dangerous. One widespread belief was that birds found dead on the ground were there because they had been struck by radio waves. But on the whole people were enchanted. The ability to sit in one's own living room and listen to a live event in some distant place was approximately as miraculous as teleportation. When an advertiser wrote, 'Radio Leaps the Barriers of Time and Distance!' it was as much an expression of wonder as of fact. For many, the broadcast of Lindbergh's arrival was nearly as notable and exciting as the arrival itself.

'Here comes the boy!' McNamee cried now as Lindbergh appeared on the deck of the *Memphis*. 'He stands quiet, unassuming . . . He looks very serious and *awfully* nice. A darn nice boy!' An estimated thirty million enraptured listeners hung on his every word that day. What none of them could see were the tears of joy running down McNamee's cheeks.

Among the welcoming shore party were the secretaries of the navy and of war, and a phalanx of naval officials, including Commander Richard E. Byrd, dressed in dazzling whites and still strangely and conspicuously earthbound. People were wondering if he was ever going to leave for Europe. It was not a matter he and Lindbergh could discuss now, for Lindbergh was hustled into an open-top Pierce-Arrow with his mother to proceed under cavalry escort to the Washington Monument.

No one knows how many people lined the streets of Washington that day, but it was universally agreed that it was the largest gathering the capital had ever seen. As his motorcade proceeded towards the Mall, Lindbergh waved occasionally, but mostly stared opaquely at the crowds. Many of those lining the streets wept as he passed – 'they knew not just why', reported the writer and explorer Fitzhugh Green (who was also to be editor of Lindbergh's book *We*). At the Washington Monument, a sea of heads covered the entire visible landscape and young boys filled the nearby trees like Christmas ornaments. At the foot of the monument stood a canopied platform on which President Coolidge and all the members of the cabinet but one were gathered. The lone missing figure was Herbert Hoover. He was stuck in Gulfport, Mississippi, still dealing with the Mississippi flood, which was as bad as ever but almost completely forgotten now by those who weren't directly affected by it. Even Hoover's tireless PR operatives couldn't keep it on the front pages with Lindbergh in the country.

When at last Lindbergh reached the speaking platform, he nodded to those present and accepted the cheers of the crowd. President Coolidge made a short speech of welcome, pinned a Distinguished Flying Cross on his lapel, and with a gesture invited Lindbergh to speak. Lindbergh leaned into the microphone, for it was set a little low for him, expressed pleasure at being present, said a very few words of thanks, and stepped back. A moment of eerie stillness followed as it dawned on the watching throngs, most of whom had been standing in the hot sun for hours, that they were in the presence of two of the most taciturn men in America and that this ceremony was over. But then, recovering their sense of occasion, the people burst into riotous applause and 'clapped until their hands were numb'. Many wept here, too.

And then began Charles Lindbergh's new life as a public figure. From now on, his every waking moment would be an endless round of banquets, speeches and shaking hands. In just over thirty-six hours in Washington, Colonel Lindbergh (as he now was) would attend three banquets, make several (short) speeches, visit sick soldiers at Walter Reed Hospital, lay a wreath at the Tomb of the Unknown Soldier and visit the Capitol. Everywhere he went people lined the streets to cheer him as he passed. It was a touching display of adulation, but it was only the faintest prelude to what awaited him in New York.

In the 1920s America became a high-rise nation. By 1927, the country boasted some 5,000 tall buildings – most of the world's stock. Even Beaumont, Texas, had six buildings of ten storeys or higher, which was more than Paris, London, Berlin or any other European city. J. L. Hudson of Detroit in 1927 opened the world's tallest department store at more than twenty storeys, and Cleveland saw the topping out of the fifty-two-storey Union Terminal Building, the second tallest building in the world. Los Angeles instituted strict limits on building heights – which is partly why LA sprawls so today – but still allowed the City Hall to rise to twenty-eight storeys in violation of its own ordinances. It was as if the country couldn't stop itself from building ever upwards.

As buildings grew taller, the number of workers pouring into city centres grew and grew. Boston by 1927 had 825,000 people a day coming into its downtown – or more than the entire population of the city. Pittsburgh absorbed 355,000 workers every day, Los Angeles and San Francisco 500,000 each, Chicago and Philadelphia over 750,000 apiece; and New York, superlative in everything, took in a whopping daily load of three million.

In 1927, New York had just overtaken London as the world's largest city, and it was easily the most cosmopolitan. A quarter of its eight million residents had been born abroad; it had more foreign-born residents than

Philadelphia had people. Native-born Americans were flocking to it, too. Two hundred thousand southern blacks had moved to New York since the end of the First World War, and now the Mississippi flood was sending tens of thousands more.

As well as being the headquarters of many of America's principal service industries – banking, stockbroking, publishing, advertising, most of the arts – New York was still also the nation's largest industrial centre.* It was home to 30,000 factories. One tenth of all that America produced originated in the city. More than 40 per cent of the nation's overseas trade went through the Port of New York, as did the overwhelming share of international passenger traffic. As many as 12,000 passengers sailed from piers on the west side of Manhattan every day, and something of the order of 25,000 went to see them off. Such was the density of people around the docks that traffic was gridlocked daily for blocks around from 8 a.m. to 1 p.m.

Every four years the city grew by the equivalent of a Boston or St Louis. Developers couldn't keep up. At one point in 1926, more than a thousand new office buildings were being constructed or rebuilt. To try to reduce the crowding, the City of New York enacted tough new ordinances, restricting tall buildings to big lots and forcing architects to design them with setbacks to allow more air to flow between them and more light to reach the ground. The unintended effect of this was actually to accelerate the

* New York's Woolworth Building, 792 feet high, built in 1913, was still the tallest in the world. The Chrysler Building and Empire State Building, which would both overtake the Woolworth, would not be built until 1930 and 1931 respectively.

pace of growth, since big lots required giant structures if they were to offer an economic return. It also encouraged skyscrapers to march northwards up Manhattan. By 1927, New York had half the nation's skyscrapers, and half of those were now in midtown. The canyon-like streets and spiky skyline that we associate with New York are largely a 1920s phenomenon.

Many of the new buildings added enormously to pressure on the city's stretched infrastructure. When the colossal Graybar Building, the world's largest office building, opened in early 1927 at 420 Lexington Avenue, it brought 12,000 office workers to one site. A single block in Manhattan now could easily contain 50,000 people. All this high-rise density made New York the most breathtakingly packed and challenging city in the world in which to live and move about, but it also provided the most exhilarating and perfect backdrop for a ticker-tape parade, and it was now about to have the biggest one ever seen.

On Monday 13 June, Charles Lindbergh flew himself in a borrowed navy aeroplane to Mitchel Field on Long Island, where he was immediately transferred to a waiting amphibious plane for the short trip onward to the city. He could not possibly be prepared – no human could – for what awaited him. What he saw now as he came into New York Harbor was perhaps the most extraordinary sight ever accorded an individual: an entire city, the greatest in the world, standing ready to receive him.

The harbour was a mosaic of boats; beyond, from the bottom of Manhattan to Central Park, people thronged every street and filled every rooftop and office window. No one can possibly say how many people witnessed the parade. Most estimates put the number at between four and five million. It may well have been the biggest crowd ever assembled anywhere to pay tribute to a single person.

Lindbergh was met in the harbour by the mayoral yacht (a gift to the city from Rodman Wanamaker) for the transfer to the Battery and the beginning of his parade. A buffet lunch had been laid on, but it turned out that the newspapermen and photographers who had got there first had eaten every bit of it, so Lindbergh had to face the festivities on an empty stomach.

An estimated 300,000 people were waiting for him at Battery Park, where he climbed into an open-topped Packard and perched on the back seat beside Mayor Jimmy Walker, who was dressed, a little anachronistically, in a top hat. Lindbergh, as always, stayed bare-headed. They proceeded up Broadway through a blizzard of ticker tape and drifting confetti so dense that at times Lindbergh and Walker were all but invisible to those lining the route. The scale of the occasion was without precedent. After the armistice parade in 1918, street sweepers cleared 155 tons of debris. For the Lindbergh parade, it was 1,800 tons. Some spectators in their excitement emptied whole wastebaskets out of their office windows, without always considering whether they might contain heavy objects. Among the items collected the next day were phone books and business directories and other bulky detritus that had been dropped or joyously flung from lofty windows and miraculously hurt no one.

One person standing anonymously among the onlookers was a young woman named Gertrude Ederle, who may have qualified as the most forgotten person in America. The daughter of German immigrants – her father owned a butcher's shop on Amsterdam Avenue – Ederle was the finest swimmer America had ever produced, of either sex. In a single day in 1922 she broke six national records. She was also as strong as an ox and capable of swimming vast distances. In August 1926, she not only became the first woman to swim the English Channel, but did it faster than any man ever had. This feat so impressed and excited her fellow Americans that she, too, was given a great ticker-tape parade and was for a while so famous that crowds followed her everywhere.

At the height of her brief celebrity, Ederle received commercial offers worth $900,000, but her manager believed she was worth more than that and wouldn't let her sign any of them. Unfortunately, the world simultaneously noticed that when out of the water Trudie Ederle was not terribly interesting or attractive. She was a little stocky and not over-blessed with charisma. She was also very hard of hearing, which made her seem irritable and impatient during press interviews. Just after her arrival home, another woman, a Danish-born American named Mille Gade, swam the Channel, too, which made Ederle's achievement suddenly seem slightly ordinary. The world speedily lost interest in Gertrude Ederle, and indeed in Channel swimming generally. In the end, Ederle made just $19,793 in personal-appearance fees. By the time of Lindbergh's parade she was earning $50 a week as a swimming instructor and was able to walk through the city without attracting notice. When she was mentioned at all it was as an example of the fate that no doubt awaited Charles Lindbergh.

With stops at City Hall, St Patrick's Cathedral and Central Park, the parade took most of the afternoon. It was the start of four days of intense activity for Lindbergh – more speeches, receptions, honours and parades – as well as a belated trip to see *Rio Rita* at the new Ziegfeld Theatre. For the duration of their visit, Lindbergh and his mother had been lent the use of a large apartment at 270 Park Avenue owned by none other than Harry Frazee, the man who sold Babe Ruth to the Yankees. By coincidence, Frazee's building had also been well known to Charles Nungesser. His beloved Consuelo Hatmaker had resided there when Nungesser was courting her. It was at Frazee's apartment that Mrs Lindbergh reluctantly agreed to meet the press in an informal press conference. Her performance was a masterclass in how not to answer questions.

'What do you think your son will do next?' one of the reporters asked her.

Mrs Lindbergh said she had no idea.

'Did he bring you any souvenirs from Paris?' asked another.

'No.'

'Would you ever like to fly the Atlantic with your son?'

'He hasn't asked me.'

'What are your plans for the next few days?'

'They are in the hands of the organizing committee.'

And so it went for half an hour until the reporters were out of questions and there were just long, awkward silences. When an assistant stepped in to end the conference, Mrs Lindbergh breathed an audible sigh of relief. 'I've already said too much,' she confided.

There was no getting away from the fact that both the Lindberghs were a little odd, and that the two together were more than a little odd. On the evening of his parade, Charles and his mother, accompanied by Mayor Walker, were driven to the Long Island estate of a multimillionaire named Clarence H. Mackay for a banquet to be followed by dancing. Shortly after dinner, it was noticed that Lindbergh was no longer present. A panicky Mackay instituted a search of the estate, unable to imagine what had become of his prize guest. It turned out that Lindbergh and his mother had departed for Manhattan without saying thank you or goodbye to their host, the governor, the mayor or any of the other five hundred guests. They evidently hadn't told the mayor that they were leaving him without a ride either.

For three days Lindbergh stories completely filled the front page of the *New York Times* and most of several pages beyond. On the day of his parade, Lindbergh stories occupied the first sixteen pages of the paper. Such was the intensity of interest in everything to do with Lindbergh that when Mrs Lindbergh went to Pennsylvania Station on 15 June to catch a train back to the Midwest, 500 policemen had to link arms to hold back the crowds.

Lindbergh was now the most valuable human commodity on the planet, and he was bombarded with lucrative proposals – to make movies, write books and newspaper columns, advertise products of every description, appear in vaudeville productions, travel the world giving lectures. According to his own recollections, he was offered $500,000 and a percentage of the profits to star in a film based on his life story, and $50,000 to endorse a popular brand of cigarettes. Another company offered him $1 million if he would find and marry the girl of his dreams and allow the whole process to be immortalized on film. Senior figures in Washington urged him to enter politics. 'I was advised,' Lindbergh wrote later, 'that if I would enter a political career, there was a good chance that I could eventually become president.'

So many parties tried to cash in on Lindbergh's name without his approval or knowledge that he had to hire a detective agency to track down the worst of them. The *New York Times* cited the example of an entrepreneur in Cleveland who found a man named Charles Lindberg, a railway mechanic who knew nothing of aviation, and made him the nominal head of a company called the Lindberg Aeronautics Corporation with plans to sell $100 million in stock certificates to a gullible and admiring public.

The biggest event of Lindbergh's week – of anyone's week – was a dinner given for him by the City of New York at the Hotel Commodore. The *New York Times* put the number of guests at 3,700 – all male since no women were invited. It was the biggest dinner ever given in the city. All the papers enjoyed listing the great quantities of food and crockery involved – 300 gallons of green turtle soup, 2,000 pounds of fish, 1,500 pounds of Virginia ham, 6,000 pounds of chicken, 125 gallons of peas, 15,000 bread rolls, 2,000 heads of lettuce, 100 gallons of coffee, 800 quarts of ice cream, 12,000 pieces of cake, 300 pounds of butter, 36,000 cups and plates, 50,000 pieces of silver – though it may also be noted that only rarely did the numbers entirely agree from one publication to the next. Dinner was scheduled to start at seven, but because of the confusion of such a mass of people all searching for the right chairs, it was nine o'clock before everyone was seated and serving could begin. The speeches didn't start until eleven o'clock – three hours late.

The increasingly surreal and draining nature of Lindbergh's life was demonstrated on the evening of 15 June. After a full day of speeches and receptions, he finally got to a performance of *Rio Rita*, but the audience was so ecstatic to see him that police had to be called in to calm them and the play started more than an hour late. It was nowhere near finished when Lindbergh had to leave to attend a benefit evening for Nungesser and Coli at the new Roxy Theatre. There he sat politely for an hour, before slipping out of a side door and being driven to Mitchel Field, where he pulled on a flying suit over his tuxedo and took off for Washington.

In Washington, he carefully went over the repairs done to the *Spirit of St Louis*, climbed into the familiar cockpit and returned with it to New York. At seven thirty in the morning he landed at Mitchel Field, content that he was at last reunited with his beloved ship. After a quick shower and a change of clothes back at the Frazee apartment, he resumed his public engagements on no sleep.

As it turned out, the plans for Lindbergh on that day were wildly and unrealistically ambitious. He was sent on a long parade through Brooklyn, which included a speech to 200,000 people in Prospect Park, followed by a formal luncheon with a branch of the Knights of Columbus. Then he was to go to Yankee Stadium to meet the Yankees and watch them play the St Louis Browns before speeding back into Manhattan for the presentation of the Orteig Prize at the Hotel Brevoort, followed by yet another formal dinner.

At Yankee Stadium, three sections of box seats had been freshly painted to receive Lindbergh and his party, and 20,000 fans turned out to cheer him. Babe Ruth had promised to hit a home run in his honour, but at game time the great aviator was nowhere to be seen. The teams and spectators waited nearly half an hour for Lindbergh to get there, but when word arrived that he was still in Manhattan the umpires started the game without him.

Baseball seasons unwind slowly and at this stage of proceedings no one had any inkling that this season would prove unusually productive for Ruth or any other Yankees. Just before the season started, Ruth himself told a reporter that he didn't expect ever to break his 1921 home run record. 'To do that, you've got to start early, and the pitchers have got to pitch to you,' he said. 'I don't start early, and the pitchers haven't really pitched to me in four seasons.' As if to prove his point, he left the first game complaining of dizziness and failed to hit with vigour through the first month of the season. By 21 May, the day Lindbergh landed in Paris, Ruth had hit just 9 home runs in thirty-two games.

Then two things happened. *Babe Comes Home* went on general release and Ruth suddenly came to life. Goodness knows exactly how the movie galvanized him, but its release coincided neatly and peculiarly with his hitting a lot of home runs – 5 in two days, for one of which, in Philadelphia, the ball was hit so far that it left the park and cleared a two-storey house across the street. By 7 June, Ruth's total had jumped to 18 – a much more respectable and promising number. Two days later against Chicago at Yankee Stadium, Ruth stole home plate – something that thirty-two-year-old men with paunches didn't normally do. The season was suddenly getting interesting.

True to his word, Ruth hit a home run for Lindbergh on Lindbergh Day. It came in the bottom of the first against Tom Zachary, who would yield a rather more momentous home run to Ruth at the end of the season. Lou Gehrig followed Ruth to the plate and hammered a home run to almost exactly the same spot. Lindbergh, alas, never arrived to see either. 'I'd been saving that homer for him, and then he doesn't show up,' Ruth said afterwards. 'I guess he thinks this is a twilight league.'

Lindbergh, through no fault of his own, simply couldn't get there. Delayed at every turn by people wanting to speak to him, shake his hand, have a moment of his time, he didn't reach Yankee Stadium until well after 5 p.m. when the game was nearly finished, at which point it was decided that he didn't have time to go in anyway, so his motorcade turned round and went back to town for him to collect the Orteig Prize from Raymond Orteig at the Hotel Brevoort in Greenwich Village. There, as everywhere, he was met by a mob and had to be bundled into the building through a sea of straining hands.

Lindbergh was beginning to look distinctly shell-shocked. The historian Hendrik Willem Van Loon met him in the midst of all this and reported with genuine concern: 'Never have I seen anyone as hopelessly tired, as courageously tired, as that boy whose brain was still doing a duty which the rest of his body could no longer follow up. Another three days of this and the reflected-glory hounds will chase him to his death.' In fact, Lindbergh had much more than three days of it to get through, and it would only get worse.

He must at least have been glad to meet Raymond Orteig, for Orteig was a delightful and likeable man with a knack for putting people at their ease. He had started life humbly as a shepherd boy in the French Pyrenees, but in 1882, aged just twelve, he had followed an uncle to

America. There, he taught himself English, got a job as a hotel waiter, and worked his way up the ladder of opportunity until he was first the maître d', then the manager and finally the owner of two of Manhattan's smartest hotels, the Lafayette and Brevoort, both in Greenwich Village. For Orteig, Lindbergh was a saviour. The Orteig Prize, offered in a moment of impetuous magnanimity, had become something of a nightmare for the Frenchman. Six men had lost their lives trying to win the prize, and until Lindbergh's triumph it had seemed likely that that number would just keep rising. Critics had begun to observe that Orteig, however well-meaning, was a murderer – a thought that was understandably painful for him to bear.

So it was with relief and pleasure that he handed Lindbergh his cheque – though he must also have felt a stab of unease at parting with such a hefty sum, for $25,000 was a great deal of money in 1927 and rather more than he could comfortably afford.

The unfortunate fact of the matter was that Orteig was slowly going out of business, and he was being killed by the same thing that was killing lots of other people, sometimes all too literally: Prohibition.

Chapter 12

Some time on the night of 23 June 1927, Wilson B. Hickox, aged forty-three, a wealthy businessman from Cleveland, Ohio (and, coincidentally, a neighbour of the US ambassador to France, Myron Herrick, in the suburb of Cleveland Heights), returned from an evening out in New York City and poured himself a nightcap in his room in the Roosevelt Hotel.

Shortly thereafter, Mr Hickox began to feel some peculiar and unpleasant sensations – a tightening of the throat and chest, a kind of bitter pain spreading through his body. We may reasonably imagine the glass slipping from his hand and Mr Hickox rising with difficulty and stumbling towards the door to summon help as his symptoms swiftly worsened. One by one his body systems were collapsing into paralysis as the toxic effects of strychnine swept through him. Mr Hickox never made it to the door but died slowly and wretchedly on the floor of his room, bewildered, frightened, and unable to move a muscle.

What was most notable about Mr Hickox's death was

not that he had been poisoned but that it was his own government that had killed him. The 1920s was in many ways the most strange and wondrous decade in American history, and nothing made it more so than Prohibition. It was easily the most extreme, ill-judged, costly and ignored experiment in social engineering ever conducted by an otherwise rational nation. At a stroke it shut down the fifth largest industry in America. It took some $2 billion a year out of the hands of legitimate interests and put it in the hands of murderous thugs. It made criminals of honest people and actually led to an increase in the amount of drinking in the country.

Nothing, however, was stranger than that it became the avowed policy of the United States government to poison a random assortment of citizens in an attempt to keep the rest of them sober. Mr Hickox was unusual only in that well-off people generally weren't the victims since they were careful to get their booze from reliable suppliers. That was why people like Al Capone did so well out of Prohibition: they didn't kill their customers.

Mr Hickox died because of a problem that hadn't been fully thought through when Prohibition was introduced – namely, that alcohol is used for all kinds of things besides drinking. It was (and in many cases remains) an essential ingredient in paint thinners, antifreezes, lotions and antiseptics, embalming fluid and much more. Thus it was necessary to allow its continued production for legitimate purposes. Inevitably, some of that still-legal alcohol (actually a great deal: 60 million gallons a year, by one estimate) was diverted into the bootleg trade. To render industrial alcohol disagreeable for drinking, the government took to 'denaturing' it by dosing it with poisons such as strychnine and mercury which had the power to blind, cripple or kill those who drank it. Denatured alcohol became 'America's new national beverage', in the cheerful words of one Prohibition official.

Figures vary wildly on just how many people died wretchedly from drinking denatured alcohol. Root and De Rochemont in their authoritative *Eating in America* report that 11,700 people died in 1927 alone from imbibing drink poisoned by the government. Other sources put the number much lower. However small or large the total, it is surely the most bizarrely sinister episode in American history that officialdom was prepared to deliver to its own citizens an agonizing death for engaging in an act that had until recently been an accepted part of civilized life, was still legal nearly everywhere else in the world and was patently harmless in moderation.

Almost everything about Prohibition was either inept or farcical. The Treasury was charged with enforcing the new laws, but it wholly lacked the necessary qualifications, funding or zeal for the job. Starved of resources by Congress, the Prohibition Department hired just 1,520 agents,* and gave them the impossible task of trying to stop the production and consumption of alcohol among 100 million citizens (or about 75,000 people per agent) within an area of 3.5 million square miles while simultaneously protecting 18,700 miles of coastline and border from smugglers. The federal government expected the states to take up the slack and enforce the laws, but the states were almost everywhere severely disinclined to

---

* The force was later increased slightly, but at no point exceeded 2,300 agents.

do so. By 1927, the average state was spending eight times more on enforcing fish and game laws than it spent on Prohibition.

The economic cost to the nation was enormous. The federal government lost $500 million a year in liquor taxes – nearly a tenth of national income. At state level the pain was often even greater. New York before Prohibition relied on liquor taxes for half its income. It is little wonder that states were reluctant to find the money in their reduced budgets to prosecute a law that was impoverishing them.

Speakeasies proliferated wildly. One block in midtown Manhattan was found to contain thirty-two places where one could get a drink. Liquor was so freely available, and often so little hidden, that Prohibition seemed sometimes barely to exist. In Chicago, where some 20,000 saloons remained in business, in some neighbourhoods bars operated openly and didn't pretend to be anything else. In New York, the number of drinking establishments was put at 32,000, double the pre-Prohibition total.

And of course the stuff that was sold in these new establishments was entirely unregulated. In Chicago, a municipal chemist tipped some bootlegged whisky down a sink and watched in astonishment as it sizzlingly ate through the porcelain. Curious to know what exactly *was* in bootlegged whisky, the *New York Telegram* employed a chemist to test 341 samples brought from city speakeasies. Among the ingredients he isolated were kerosene, nicotine, benzene, benzol, formaldehyde, iodine, sulphuric acid and soap. About one in six samples, he found, posed a serious threat to health.

A reasonable question is how all this came to be. The answer resided, to an exceptional degree, in a mousy-looking little man with a neat moustache and pince-nez spectacles named Wayne B. Wheeler. Despite his manifestly unthreatening appearance, Wheeler was for a time the most feared and powerful man in America, and – unless you believe that people should die in agony for having a drink – possibly the most misguidedly evil as well.

Wayne Bidwell Wheeler was born in 1869 and grew up on a farm in eastern Ohio. There one day he was carelessly speared in the leg with a pitchfork by an inebriated farm employee. Though he seems not to have been otherwise directly inconvenienced by insobriety, Wheeler developed an almost evangelical zeal to drive drinking out of American life.

After qualifying as a lawyer, he became superintendent of the Anti-Saloon League in Ohio and there quickly showed a flair for political manipulation. In 1905 he took on the popular governor of Ohio, a man who had been elected two years earlier by the widest margin in that state's history and was often mentioned as a future presidential candidate – but who, unfortunately, did not support the ASL's wish to make Ohio dry. The man in question was Myron T. Herrick, who was about to learn that it never paid to oppose Wayne B. Wheeler. A master propagandist, Wheeler never deviated from a single purpose, which was to drive from office any politician who didn't whole-heartedly support Prohibition, and he would use any means necessary to get his way. Often he employed private eyes to dig up dirt on politicians who failed to support him with sufficient enthusiasm, and viewed blackmail as an entirely legitimate means to achieve his desired ends.

Nothing mattered to him but making America dry. Where other temperance groups involved themselves in all kinds of side issues – tobacco, short skirts, jazz, even post office policy and government ownership of utilities – Wheeler never strayed from his single monotonous message: that drinking was responsible for poverty, broken marriages, lost earnings and all the other evils of modern society.

By opposing Wheeler's call for state prohibition, Myron Herrick made himself look out of touch and lacking in compassion. He was overwhelmingly defeated, and never held elective office again. Instead, the rising star of Ohio politics became Herrick's spectacularly undistinguished lieutenant governor, Warren G. Harding. Across America, politicians quickly learned either to support Wheeler and the Anti-Saloon League or to give up any hope of being re-elected.

Under 'Wheelerism', as the ASL's strategy became known, much of America was dry long before Prohibition was enacted. By 1917, twenty-seven states were completely dry and several more were preponderantly dry. It was possible to travel across much of the country – from Texas to the Dakotas, from Utah to the eastern seaboard – without passing through a single area where a drink could be had. Only in a few scattered outposts, mostly cities and industrial areas where immigrants congregated in large, thirsty numbers, was it still legally possible to get a drink. These, however, were the places where drinking was most stubbornly ingrained and where the ASL stood little chance of changing local or state laws. But then Wheeler got what was for him a lucky break: the First World War.

*   *   *

226

When the First World War broke out, most Americans were content for it to remain a distant, European conflict. But then Germany made some tactical blunders that wholly changed sentiment. First, it began bombing civilian targets. We have grown inured to wars that target civilians, but in the 1910s killing innocent people by intent was widely seen as a barbarity. When the Germans began, as a kind of experiment, sending a plane to Paris each afternoon about five o'clock to drop a single bomb on the city, President Woodrow Wilson was so incensed that he sent a personal letter of protest to the German authorities.

Then, worse, Germany announced that it would target passenger ships at sea. In May 1915, a U-boat torpedoed the passenger liner *Lusitania* as it sailed in neutral waters off the Irish coast near Kinsale. The ship sank in just eighteen minutes, taking with it 1,200 people. A third of the victims were women and children; 128 of the dead were Americans whose country was not even at war. Outrage was immediate, but Germany made matters infinitely worse by declaring – almost unbelievably – a national holiday to celebrate the slaughter. Dr Bernhard Dernburg, head of the German Red Cross in the United States, said that those aboard the *Lusitania* got no more than they deserved. He was expelled from America and was lucky to get away with his life.

Others did not fare so well. A German man in St Louis, who was believed to have spoken ill of his adopted country, was set upon by a mob, dragged through the streets tied up in an American flag and lynched. A jury subsequently found the mob leaders not guilty on the grounds that it had been a 'patriotic murder'. German businesses were boycotted or had bricks hurled through their windows. People with German names frequently decided for safety's sake to change them to something less obviously Teutonic. One such was Albert Schneider, who became better known the following decade as the murder victim Albert Snyder. Restaurants stopped serving German food or gave it non-German names; sauerkraut famously became 'liberty cabbage'. Some communities made it illegal to play music by German composers. Iowa, to be on the safe side, outlawed conversations in *any* language other than English in schools, at church, or even over the telephone. When people protested that they would have to give up church services in their own languages, Governor William L. Harding responded: 'There is no use in anyone wasting his time praying in other languages than English. God is listening only to the English tongue.'

It escaped no one's attention that American breweries were nearly all owned by men of German extraction and presumed German sympathies. Temperance advocates seized on this to make beer-drinking seem an all but treasonous act. 'We are fighting three enemies – Germany, Austria and Drink,' asserted Kellogg's, the cornflakes company, in a patriotic ad that ran just after America joined the war. In point of fact, the claim had substance. The National German–American Alliance, an organization largely funded by the breweries, turned out not only to have lobbied against Prohibition, but also, and more deviously, on behalf of Kaiser Wilhelm. It was not a combination that won it many friends.

The rise in anti-German sentiment gave a huge boost to the temperance movement. The Eighteenth Amendment, banning the production and consumption of alcohol, swept towards ratification, guided expertly through one state legislature after another by a freshly energized ASL. On 16 January 1919, Nebraska became the thirty-sixth state to ratify, giving the three-quarters majority necessary for the law to be enacted and to go into effect one year later.

Though the Eighteenth Amendment made Prohibition a legal reality by outlawing intoxicating drinks, it didn't define how it would work or even indicate what was or was not an intoxicant. That required an additional piece of legislation, known as the Volstead Act, to deal with the details. The act was named after Andrew J. Volstead, a Minnesotan like Lindbergh, whose principal distinguishing feature was a spectacular moustache that hung from his upper lip like a bearskin rug. Though a non-drinker himself, Volstead was no zealot and would never have sought a national ban on alcohol. His name became attached to the legislation simply because he was chairman of the House Judiciary Committee, and therefore required to draft it. Although Volstead's name rang through the decade, he himself was thrown out by the electorate at the next election, and he returned to his home town of Granite Falls, Minnesota, where he quietly practised law and listed his principal hobby as reading the Congressional Record. Wayne Wheeler always claimed that he really designed and wrote the legislation, an assertion heatedly disputed by Volstead, though why either would want credit for the act is a reasonable question because it proved to be a strikingly ill-constructed bill.

The Volstead Act was introduced to Congress on 19 May 1919. Its intentions, stated succinctly in a preamble, didn't seem too alarming: 'To prohibit intoxicating beverages, and to regulate the manufacture, production,

229

use, and sale of high-proof spirits for other than beverage purposes, and to insure an ample supply of alcohol and promote its use in scientific research and in the development of fuel, dye and other lawful industries.' The phrasing may have been a little ungainly, but the sentiment didn't seem too threatening. It was only in the fine print that the world discovered that the Volstead Act defined intoxicating liquor as anything with an alcoholic content greater than one half of 1 per cent – about the same level as sauerkraut. Many of those who had supported the Prohibition amendment had assumed that beer and unfortified wines would be spared. It was only now that it began to dawn on people just how sweeping – how dismayingly total – Prohibition was going to be.

That was perhaps the most remarkable feature of all in the introduction of Prohibition to America – that it took so many people by surprise. As Frederick Lewis Allen wrote in *Only Yesterday*: 'The country accepted it not only willingly, but almost absent-mindedly.'

Prohibition was so flawed, and in so many ways, that even many of those who supported it in principle were appalled by how it developed in practice. For a start, it brought an entirely new level of danger to American life. The national murder rate went up by almost a third after Prohibition was introduced. Being a Prohibition agent was dangerous – in the first two and a half years of Prohibition thirty agents were killed on the job – but just being in the vicinity of agents was often dangerous, too, for they frequently proved to be trigger-happy. In Chicago alone, Prohibition agents gunned down twenty-three innocent civilians in just over a decade.

Despite the hazards, Prohibition agents were paid less than garbage men, which all but invited corruption. A common ruse was for agents to confiscate liquor, then immediately sell it back to the original owners. Bribery was routine. The average speakeasy paid out about $400 a month to police and city officials, which worked out at about $150 million a year in bribes in New York City alone. In short, a lot of people made a lot of money from Prohibition.

The temptations of corruption extended far beyond American shores. Canada, under pressure from the United States, made it all but impossible for its brewers and distillers to sell their products to Americans, but smugglers, ever resourceful, found an alternative in the form of the little-known territory of St Pierre and Miquelon, just off the southern tip of Newfoundland. Through an accident of history, these 'two dots of gorse and granite' in the North Atlantic had belonged to France since 1763, so were outside American and Canadian jurisdiction. Overnight, St Pierre and Miquelon became the world's greatest importer of alcoholic beverages. It brought in three million bottles of champagne, making it France's biggest overseas market, along with vast quantities of brandy, Armagnac, Calvados and other spirituous refreshments.

When asked by American authorities to explain how 4,000 people had developed such a sudden attachment to alcohol, the governor replied, with Gallic aplomb, that he was unaware of any significant rise in alcohol imports and hadn't noticed the two dozen large new warehouses that had sprung up around the main port at St Pierre, but promised to look into the matter. Subsequently, he confirmed to the Americans that there was indeed a little wine on St Pierre and Miquelon now, but it was all bound for the Bahamas, where drinking was legal. It was apparently just resting in St Pierre.

Prohibition bred great volumes of hypocrisy, too. In the summer of 1926, Colonel Ned Green, Prohibition administrator for northern California, was suspended after it emerged that he held cocktail parties in the Prohibition administration offices in San Francisco. 'I should have been suspended long ago,' he amiably told reporters.

Even when the government seized illicit liquor, it didn't look after it terribly vigilantly. In Chicago, in the summer of 1920, 134,000 gallons of whisky – 670,000 bottles – vanished from a warehouse where it was being stored following seizure. The nightwatchmen in charge professed – not altogether convincingly, it must be said – that they had not noticed anything amiss at any point in their recent shifts. Nationally, records showed that of 50 million gallons of whisky held in government warehouses at the start of Prohibition, two thirds was missing at the end of Prohibition in 1933.

Prohibition laws were nearly impossible to enforce in any case because they were so riddled with loopholes. Doctors could legally prescribe whisky for their patients and did so with such enthusiasm that by the late 1920s they were earning $40 million a year from the practice. In most cases, according to the *New Yorker*, the doctors simply handed out blank prescription slips. (In the week that Lindbergh flew to Paris, US Prohibition Commissioner James M. Doran authorized the production of an additional three million gallons of whisky for medicine. When it was suggested that that was a lot of whisky for such a narrow purpose, a Treasury official replied that stocks were rapidly depleted 'from evaporation'.)

Religious groups were allowed to stock alcoholic beverages for sacramental purposes, and that market proved remarkably robust, too. One wine grower in California offered fourteen types of communion wines, including port and sherry, suggesting that perhaps not all were intended to be wholly holy, as it were. In California the amount of land given over to growing grapes actually soared in the first five years of Prohibition from 100,000 acres to nearly 700,000, and that wasn't because people were suddenly eating a lot of raisins. It was because no wine was being imported, so there was a surge in demand for domestic grapes to satisfy a booming market.

Although it was illegal to produce wine for private consumption, vineyard owners could send out packets of grape concentrate, which could be turned into wine at home. In case anyone missed the point, the packets came with warnings in large type that read: 'Caution: Will Ferment and Turn Into Wine Within 60 Days'. Unfortunately for lovers of fine wine, grape growers grubbed up most of their existing vines and put in grapes that provided bulk but not quality. It would take California vineyards a generation to recover.

The loss of liquor sales hit many restaurants hard. In New York the casualties included Shanley's, Rector's, Sherry's and Browne's Chop House – all beloved institutions. Delmonico's, the most venerable of all, held out until 1923 before finally throwing in the towel just short of its hundredth birthday. For the most part, drinking was driven to speakeasies (a term that originated in the United States as far back as 1889, when it described any

233

place that sold booze illegally), which made up in imaginative naming for what they generally lacked in elegance. Among the better known spots were the Hyena Club, the Furnace, the Ha! Ha!, the Eugenic Club, the Sawdust Inn and Club Pansy. For those who liked music with their drinks, Harlem was the place to go. There people flocked to the Bamboo Inn, Lenox Club, Clam House, Smalls' Paradise, Tillie's Chicken Shack, the Cotton Club and the memorably named Drool Inn, among many others. Sunday night was the biggest night. Patrons could experience some of the best and most original music performed by a galaxy of talents – Duke Ellington, Cab Calloway, Fats Waller, Eubie Blake, Bessie Smith, Bill Basie (he would later become Count Basie), Louis Armstrong and plenty more. In many Harlem clubs only whites were admitted. The only blacks in the house were waiters and entertainers. The cover charges in the most popular clubs could be as much as $20 – close to a week's wages for an average working person – and a couple of rounds of drinks could easily add as much again.

Attempts at enforcement were sporadic at best, but occasionally some authority or other would get serious about it. In March 1925, Emory Buckner, a successful lawyer, became Prohibition enforcer in New York and hit upon a new strategy that for a time struck a chill into the hearts of drinking people and those who supplied them.

Buckner inaugurated a policy of padlocking any premises found to be in violation of the Volstead Act. The law allowed him to shut such premises for a year without going to court. So now, instead of arresting a few hapless and expendable waiters and bartenders, as generally had been the case before, it was possible to hit the owners themselves where it most hurt, on their balance sheets. Buckner announced plans to shut down a thousand establishments in New York, and he started with the most famous and visible places like the El Fay club run by Texas Guinan, and Owney Madden's Silver Slipper. This was a direct attack on the city's more sophisticated drinkers, and they reacted with something approaching panic.

Happily for the clubs, the crisis proved to be temporary. Prohibition was much too lucrative to be easily defeated. At least one club used the padlocking as a cover; it left its front entrance sealed and welcomed customers back through a more humble entrance at the rear. Others simply moved to new premises with different names, so that the El Fay Club became successively the Del Fay Club, Fay's Follies, Club Intime, Club Abbey, the Salon Royal and the Three Hundred Club – though generally they were all known as Texas Guinan's after their celebrated proprietress. Guinan was a slightly larger-than-life character. Originally from Waco, she was forty-three years old in 1927 and of a fair size, with platinum hair and a great toothy smile. It was her habit to insult her customers, especially if they weren't spending freely, and she was much loved for it. Her catchphrase was 'Hello, sucker.' Most of her clubs were small and packed. The girl dancers were frequently all but naked and often appallingly youthful. Ruby Keeler started at Tex Guinan's when she was just fourteen and left three years later to marry Al Jolson – who was, like many another, smitten with her trim figure and slight but fetching lisp. Another Guinan dancer, Ruby Stevens, became better known later as Barbara Stanwyck.

Guinan acted as master of ceremonies. She loved her girls, but didn't take their talents too seriously. 'Now this little gal isn't much of a singer,' she would say. 'She learned singing by a correspondence course, and she missed a coupla lessons, but she's the nicest little gal in the whole show, so I want ya to give her a big hand.' ('Giving a big hand' was said to be another Guinan coinage.) So celebrated did Guinan become for being padlocked that the Shubert brothers starred her in a Broadway revue called *Padlocks of 1927.*

Since clubs might be shut down at any moment, the minimum amount of money was spent on comforts and decor. Customers didn't seem to mind as long as they could get a decent drink. For more public and rooted places like hotels, the options were far fewer. The bar in the Knickerbocker Hotel (reputed birthplace of the dry martini) took in $4,000 a day before Prohibition, a sum not easily replaced. Without its bar takings, the Knickerbocker went under. So, too, did the Manhattan Hotel, where the manhattan cocktail was first created. Some hotels tried to survive by offering what were known as 'set-ups' – ice, seltzer, Angostura bitters and so on – to which the customer could add his own alcohol, but that hardly compensated for all the lost liquor business. Others continued selling alcohol discreetly in the hope that it would somehow escape official notice. Sooner or later they were nearly always disappointed.

In March 1926, Buckner padlocked the dining room of the Brevoort Hotel for six months. That meant that it lost not only all its liquor revenue, but also its luncheon and dinner business. It couldn't even serve its guests breakfast, so many clients abandoned it altogether. Eventually, Raymond Orteig succumbed and closed the Brevoort.

Buckner's padlocking policy caught on and was employed all over the country, including on a redwood tree in California in which was found an illegal still (though this sounds suspiciously like a publicity stunt). Altogether, in 1925, the peak year, authorities padlocked some 4,700 premises across America.

Interestingly, Buckner didn't actually believe in Prohibition, and admitted that he enforced it because it was the law and not out of any moral conviction. 'I am not very much interested in it, except as a legal problem,' he explained. He made no secret of the fact that he had often imbibed drink himself (though not since being appointed district attorney). The whole thing was a terrible mistake, in his view. 'It has brought about a vicious criminal situation, with its offshoots of perjury, murders, the moral poisoning of public officials, assaults, thefts and all manner of interrelated lawbreaking. All the good which the law may produce is worthless compared to the chain of serious crimes which it is producing every day.'

Nearly everyone recognized Prohibition as a colossal failure, and yet the nation persevered with it for thirteen years. A poem in Franklin Pierce Adams's popular newspaper column 'The Conning Tower' in the *New York World* perfectly caught the official attitude:

> *Prohibition is an awful flop.*
> *We like it.*
> *It can't stop what it's meant to stop.*
> *We like it.*
> *It's left a trail of graft and slime,*
> *It's filled our land with vice and crime,*
> *It don't prohibit worth a dime,*
> *Nevertheless, we're for it.*

It was in fact because Prohibition wasn't working very well that Wheeler and his supporters insisted that the government poison industrial alcohol. Other denaturants such as soap or detergents would have worked just as well in making drinks unpalatable, but hardcore drys weren't satisfied with that. Wheeler sincerely believed that people who drank poisoned alcohol got what they deserved. It was, in his view, 'deliberate suicide'. The Reverend John Roach Straton, last seen here hoping for the speedy execution of Ruth Snyder, was even more unyielding. When he learned that the governor and attorney general of Indiana had both given small doses of whisky to desperately ill loved ones on doctor's orders, Straton declared: 'They should have permitted the members of their family to die, and have died themselves, rather than violate their oaths of office.'

In June 1927, Prohibition seemed set to endure for ever. In fact, it was about to reach a turning point. Though there was no sign of it quite yet, for Wayne Wheeler the summer of 1927 would prove to be both the worst summer of his life and the last one.

CHAPTER 13

AFTER PRESENTING CHARLES Lindbergh with his Distinguished Flying Cross in Washington on 11 June, Calvin Coolidge didn't hang around. As soon as he could decently get away, he went with Mrs Coolidge to Union Station, where a special train was waiting to take them and a small army of reporters and presidential staff – some seventy-five people in all, along with two collies and a pet raccoon named Rebecca – to South Dakota for a long summer vacation. Coolidge suffered from chronic indigestion and asthma, which left him eager to flee muggy Washington for clean western air. It was the first time that the White House had decamped to such a distant spot.

In effect, the seat of government of the United States for the next three months would be Rapid City High School. The Coolidges themselves, however, were to be based thirty-two miles away at a residence called the State Game Lodge at the foot of Mount Harney in Custer State Park. 'State Game Lodge' sounds rather grand, but the Coolidges' accommodation was in fact just a sitting room and bedroom, with a bathroom down the hall. They didn't mind in the least. It was a simpler age.

President Coolidge delighted in seeing himself in newsreels. Because he did not reach the game lodge until after dusk, the next morning he had the whole presidential party – now grown to some two hundred people with the addition of local officials and support staff – reload every bag and suitcase into cars, drive two hundred yards down the road and re-enact the presidential arrival as the cameras recorded the fictitiously historic moment.

For the state of South Dakota, the president's presence was a very big deal. It desperately wanted to be perceived as an attractive destination for tourists. The thought occurred to someone that if the president was seen to be enjoying himself fishing in the state's sparkling waters then other anglers might be tempted to travel there as well. To make sure the exercise was a success, two thousand full-grown trout were sent from the state trout hatchery at Spearfish. These trout – all large, sluggish and hand-fed from birth – were secretly confined to a pool of water outside the Coolidge residence by submerged nets strung strategically between the banks. To his hosts' dismay Coolidge declared that he had no interest in fishing. Eventually he was persuaded to give it a try. Dressed in a business suit, he dipped a baited rod in the water. Instantly the starving fish erupted in a silvery frenzy around the hook and a moment later Coolidge lifted a wriggling prize from the water. He beamed from ear to ear and could barely be coaxed away from the stream after that. He and Mrs Coolidge dined proudly on his caught trout daily even though they were, by all accounts, almost inedible. Coolidge didn't like dealing with worms, however, and had his Secret

Ruth Snyder (**above**), housewife, and her adulterous lover, Judd Gray (**right**), a corset salesman. Their inept 'sash weight murder' of her husband Albert Snyder was the tabloid sensation of 1927; they were convicted in a lurid trial and sentenced to death.

Charles Lindbergh instantly became the most famous person on the planet when he landed his plane, the *Spirit of St Louis*, at Le Bourget airfield in Paris on 21 May 1927. But as this typical deadpan expression suggests, the experience of fame brought him little joy.

Main picture: Lindbergh's appearance on the Washington mall on 11 June 1927 attracted the largest crowd in the city's history to date. Virtually every radio in America coast-to-coast was tuned in to the broadcast event.

Below: A less than jubilant Lindbergh (*left*) with the obviously ecstatic British aviator Sir Alan Cobham (*centre*) and the American ambassador Myron Herrick greet the crowd outside the French Aéro-Club in Paris.

Bottom left: Wherever he landed, Lindbergh attracted a huge crowd. Here his plane is dangerously mobbed at Croydon Aerodome in Surrey.

Bottom right: His ticker-tape parade up Broadway attracted an enraptured crowd of between four and five million on 13 June 1927. Eighteen hundred tons of debris had to be cleaned up afterwards.

The famed (and vainglorious) explorer Richard Byrd (*second from left*) with his crew (*from the left*) Bert Acosta, George Noville and Bernt Balchen in front of their huge trimotor plane, the *America*. They took off from Roosevelt Field for Paris on 29 June . . .

. . . but 43 hours later were forced to ditch the plane in the waters off Ver-sur-Mer, France (**above**). All survived.

Left: Among other intrepid aviators attempting to cross the Atlantic that summer were the French aces Charles Nungesser (*left*) and François Coli. They took off from Paris in *L'Oiseau Blanc* on 8 May for New York City and were never seen again.

Above: Clarence Chamberlin (*right*), the pilot of the *Columbia*, and its owner, the businessman and publicity hound Charles Levine (*second from right*), landed in a field near Eisleben, Germany, after a remarkable (if crooked) flight of 3,905 miles and 43 hours' duration. Their reception in Berlin, when they finally arrived on 8 June, rivalled that of Lindbergh in Paris.

Left: Francesco de Pinedo (*left*), the barnstorming aviator and hero of fascist Italy, with the Italian ambassador in Washington, DC, on 20 April 1927. He crossed the Atlantic flying westward in a seaplane (although not non-stop) and then toured America on a victory lap that stirred up great political controversy.

Right: The titanically talented slugger Babe Ruth. As a teammate later recalled, 'God, we liked that big son of a bitch. He was a constant source of joy.'

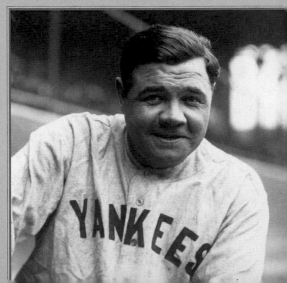

Above: The instrument of Ruth's greatness was his heavy bat, of 54 ounces, which he used to clobber more homers than any baseball player – any team – had ever hit before.

Right: Lou Gehrig and Babe Ruth posing for a photo in Bushwick, Brooklyn. The two home run rivals on the Yankees were unlikely friends, despite vast differences in temperament and habits. For a while in summer 1927 it seemed as if Gehrig would emerge the home run champion.

The Great Mississippi Flood: after weeks of torrential rain, 500 miles of the river flooded from Illinois to New Orleans, putting an area the size of Scotland under water.

Above left: President Calvin Coolidge appointed Herbert Hoover (*left*), whom he referred to derisively as 'Wonder Boy', to manage the relief efforts for the human calamity of the flood – a task he performed ably and with a notable absence of warmth.

Left: On 18 May in Bath, Michigan, the maniac Andrew Kehoe, protesting about high taxes on his farm, killed his wife and blew up the local elementary school with 500 pounds of dynamite. Thirty-seven children and seven adults died that day – still the largest and most cold-blooded slaughter of children in American history.

Above: Nan Britton, the mistress of Warren G. Harding, and the child she had by him. Her sizzlingly tell-all memoir of their affair, including multiple trysts in a White House cupboard, created a sensation.

Right: Calvin Coolidge fled his none-too-taxing job as President of the United States (four hours a day, tops) for a three-month extended vacation in the Black Hills of South Dakota. Here he is with his wife, in his full cowboy regalia, a get-up he wore that summer on every possible occasion.

(*From left*:) Hjalmar Schacht, head of the German Reichsbank; Benjamin Strong, governor of the Federal Reserve Bank of New York; Sir Montagu Norman, governor of the Bank of England; Charles Rist, deputy governor of the Banque de France. At a secret meeting on a Long Island estate in June 1927 these four lords of finance made a fateful decision to lower interest rates. This action further inflated the stock market bubble and led indirectly to the disastrous crash of 1929.

Above: Wayne B. Wheeler, fanatical head of the Anti-Saloon League and the single most forceful advocate behind the insane social experiment that was Prohibition. In order to prevent industrial alcohol being used as a beverage, Wheelerites insisted that it be 'denatured' (**right**) and thus rendered poisonous. Those who drank it and died, they reckoned, simply got what they deserved.

Left: Dwight Morrow, a J. P. Morgan banker, US Ambassador to Mexico, pioneer in the development of the American aviation industry and eventual father-in-law of Charles Lindbergh.

Service men bait his fish hook for him. Apart from the worms, he was immensely happy.

While the Coolidges enjoyed themselves in the Black Hills, Charles Lindbergh continued, with ever-decreasing enthusiasm, to receive the adulation of the American people. Alva Johnston, writing in the *New York Times* from St Louis, was struck by how unmoved Lindbergh appeared to be by the parade and other festivities laid on for him there. 'Colonel Lindbergh never indicated by expression or gesture that he understood that the demonstration was for him,' Johnston wrote. 'He did not smile or wave. Nothing moved him to admit that the glittering spectacle and the deafening uproar was a personal tribute.' The following day Lindbergh delighted a crowd of 100,000 in Forest Park with aerial acrobatics, but underwent an abrupt mood change upon landing. 'The holiday spirit deserted him when he touched earth again,' Johnston reported. 'As soon as he left his own element, the stern and rather gloomy demeanor returned. He is not quite at his ease on land.'

Things got worse. From St Louis, Lindbergh flew to Dayton, Ohio, to visit Orville Wright, co-inventor of the aeroplane with his late brother Wilbur. Thrilled city officials hastily organized a parade and reception, and were dismayed when Lindbergh refused to take part in either on the grounds that this was a private visit. When disappointed townspeople learned that Lindbergh had declined their tribute, many of them marched on Wright's home and demanded to see their hero. When Lindbergh still refused to appear, the crowd grew restive and threatened to do actual damage to Wright's house. Only then did Lindbergh, beseeched by Wright for the sake of his property, step on to a balcony and briefly wave to the crowd.

Reporters found Lindbergh close to sullen when he returned to New York via Mitchel Field on 24 June. 'Colonel Lindbergh appeared much more tired than when he left New York a week ago. He did not smile once,' wrote another *Times* reporter. As Lindbergh was about to climb into an automobile for the drive into Manhattan, a pretty girl rushed up and asked if she could shake his hand. Lindbergh's reaction surprised everybody. 'He looked at her severely and said: "No shaking hands," and drew his arm away swiftly,' wrote the *Times* reporter. The girl was clearly crushed, and Lindbergh embarrassed, but he seemed powerless to behave in a more relaxed and thoughtful way.

The world, however, refused to see him as anything other than a warm-hearted hero, and the press soon stopped noting his curiously flat aspect and lack of enthusiasm for those who adored him, and resumed depicting him as the obliging hero the world wished him to be.

While Lindbergh was breaking hearts at Mitchel Field, Commander Richard Byrd was continuing to mystify the flying fraternity at Roosevelt. A special earthen ramp about six feet high and fifty feet long had been erected at the starting point for takeoff to help the *America* get airborne. Three times the plane was hauled to the top of its takeoff ramp, and three times Byrd gravely scanned the sky and ordered a postponement. The delays 'began to look something more than ridiculous', fumed Fokker.

With Floyd Bennett permanently lost to the team, Byrd appointed Bert Acosta as chief pilot. A tanned and rakish-looking fellow of exotic Mexican-Amerindian lineage, Acosta was a celebrated ladies' man. 'His Latin allure and his low "come-hither" voice wrought havoc among the fair,' wrote one admiring biographer. 'In the movies he might have been another Valentino.' Acosta was also one of the world's most daring stunt pilots. His speciality was to pluck a handkerchief from the ground with a wingtip. Not surprisingly, these skills would prove somewhat irrelevant on an ocean crossing.

To assist Acosta, Byrd selected the Norwegian Bernt Balchen as co-pilot – though Balchen was listed only as mechanic and relief pilot because Rodman Wanamaker wanted to keep the enterprise all-American. Balchen was only allowed to come at all after agreeing to apply for US citizenship. Byrd, in a press conference, said that Balchen was primarily a passenger, though he might also be allowed to do a little navigating when Byrd was busy with other duties. In fact, Balchen did nearly all the flying.

On an early test flight with Acosta, Balchen got a glimpse of the problems the team faced. As the *America* flew into cloud, Acosta grew tense and flustered. Within minutes he had put the plane into a dangerous spin. Balchen grabbed the controls, which Acosta yielded gratefully. 'I'm strictly a fair-weather boy,' Acosta told him, blushing. 'If there's any thick stuff I stay on the ground.' Acosta, it turned out, had no idea how to fly on instruments. The only reason that Byrd's flight made it to France was that Balchen was willing to fly most of the way without demanding any of the credit or glory.

The fourth member of the crew was the most anonymous. George Noville, the radio operator, was retiring, bespectacled, and all but invisible to history. He was the son of a wealthy hat manufacturer from Cleveland (who was important enough to merit an obituary in the *New York Times*, something his son never got). If Noville made any impression on his fellow flyers, none bothered to record it. He barely appears in Byrd's and Balchen's auto-biographies, is entirely missing from all others and left no account of his own.

As for Byrd himself, he was a remarkable human being, but not at all an easy one to figure. A born adventurer, he made his first trip around the world at the age of just twelve after persuading his parents – who were evidently seriously indulgent – to let him travel alone to the Philippines to visit a family friend and then to con-tinue home the long way round. He was nearly fourteen by the time he completed his circumnavigation.

Byrd was smart, handsome, reasonably brave and unquestionably generous, but he was also almost patho-logically vain, pompous and self-serving. Every word he ever wrote about himself made him seem valorous, calm and wise. He was also, and above all, very possibly a great liar.

On 9 May 1926 – almost exactly one year before Nungesser and Coli disappeared – Byrd and Floyd Bennett made a celebrated flight from Spitsbergen, in the Arctic Ocean, to the North Pole and back in 15½ hours, just beating a rival flight in an airship by the Norwegian explorer Roald Amundsen (and piloted by Umberto Nobile, another Italian fascist airman). Byrd's polar flight was considered a feat for the ages. Byrd was promoted to commander and lavishly treated to parades and medals upon his return home. People named children after him. Streets were named after him. One overexcited admirer penned a biography of his dog Igloo.

From the outset, however, doubts were privately voiced about Byrd's achievement. Knowledgeable observers couldn't see how Byrd and Bennett could have made the round trip in 15½ hours. Balchen had flown the same plane extensively and had never got the cruising speed above 65 knots (74.8 mph). Byrd's flight to the Pole required a cruising speed nearly a third faster. Moreover, for the polar flight Byrd's plane had been fitted with enormous skis for snow landings, which added substantial drag to the craft and knocked perhaps five miles an hour off its speed. When Balchen mentioned to Bennett that he couldn't understand how they had made it to the North Pole and back in such a short time, Bennett replied, 'We didn't.' He confided to Balchen that the plane had developed an oil leak soon after taking off, and that they had flown back and forth for fourteen hours without ever losing sight of Spitsbergen.

Rumours that Byrd had at the very least exaggerated his achievement persisted for years, and suspicions were darkened by his family's long refusal to let scholars examine his papers. It wasn't until 1996, after Byrd's archive was purchased by Ohio State University for its new Byrd Polar Research Center, that his log of the flight became available for examination. The log showed heavy erasures where Byrd had done his calculations of distance travelled, suggesting to many that he had falsified the data. A more generous interpretation would be that he had made a mistake in his first calculation and started over. No one can absolutely say, but according to Alex Spencer of the National Air and Space Museum in Washington, it is now generally believed among experts that Byrd and Bennett never reached the Pole.

What is certain is that when Balchen's autobiography was published in 1959, two years after Byrd's death, it aired some of the doubts about Byrd's claims. Byrd's family volubly protested. Under pressure, Balchen's publishers agreed to cut several passages and to withdraw from sale the first four thousand copies of the book. The Byrd family wasn't fully placated, however. Balchen by this time was an American citizen and a respected member of the United States Air Force, but Senator Harry Byrd, the explorer's brother, reportedly blocked Balchen's promotion to brigadier general and had him quietly relieved of duties. Balchen passed the rest of his career sitting in the Pentagon library reading.

Just as people were wondering if Byrd would ever take off for Europe, he decided to make the flight. In the early hours of 29 June, the *America* was rolled to the top of its takeoff ramp in readiness for a dawn departure. This would be the first big plane to attempt a takeoff for an Atlantic flight since Fonck's crashed in flames, and it was even more perilously overloaded. The radio equipment alone weighed 800 pounds. Byrd packed for every possible contingency. He even brought along a kite, which he thought could act as both an antenna for the radio and as a sail to pull the plane through the water in the event of a forced landing. He also packed two lifeboats, three weeks' worth of rations, a bag of airmail letters and a 'consecrated' American flag as a gift to the people of France. At the last minute, in slight panic, Byrd decided to slim down the load. He removed two cans of petrol, a flask of hot tea and four pairs of moccasins, and took the mudguards off the plane wheels, which clearly can't have made much difference, but happily that didn't matter. After an excruci-atingly laboured takeoff, the plane lumbered into the air, cleared the wires at the runway's end and was on its way to Europe.

Byrd's stated aim was not to be the first to fly to Paris – loftily, he pointed out that he had not even entered for the Orteig Prize – but to demonstrate that the world was ready for safe, regular, multi-person flights over the Atlantic. What he proved was that such flights were indeed just about possible so long as those aboard didn't mind crash-landing in water considerably short of their destin-ation. Had it been his avowed purpose to show just how wonderful a pilot Charles Lindbergh was in comparison with nearly everyone else, Byrd could hardly have done better.

Despite all the preparations, almost nothing in the flight went according to plan. A crawl space had been inserted under the main fuel tank in the middle of the plane so that the crew could move between the front and back, but no one had thought to test it while fully kitted out in cold-weather gear. Byrd got stuck and spent ten minutes trapped with no one able to hear his calls above the engines' roar. Noville, getting cramp in his confined space, stretched his leg to relieve it and inadvertently put his foot through some wires, knocking out the radio and rendering himself pointless. Somewhere over the Atlantic, Balchen asked Acosta to take the wheel for a minute while he felt under his seat for a packet of sandwiches. In that short interval, Acosta put the plane in a spiral so severe that its airspeed rose to 140 mph, just short of the speed at which the wings would be torn off. Balchen had to wrestle the plane back to stability. 'You'd better handle it from now on,' Acosta told him quietly, and Balchen flew virtually all the rest of the way. According to *Time* magazine, Byrd was so seized with anxiety at one point that he struck Acosta across the head with a torch. They were supposed to make landfall at Bray Head, Ireland, but in fact missed Ireland altogether and hit Europe at Brest, in France, more than two hundred miles from where they expected to be.

None of these things are mentioned in *Skyward*, Byrd's account of the journey published the following year. This made it sound as if he and his crew had completed one of the most heroic undertakings in the history of human endeavour. 'Hour after hour . . . it was utterly impossible to navigate,' Byrd wrote. 'We could not tell which way the winds were blowing, which way we were drifting, or what sort of land or water was below us.' In grave conclusion he added: 'I sincerely hope no other flyers ever have that experience.' All this rather overlooked the fact that Charles Lindbergh had flown the same route five weeks earlier, completely alone, in similar conditions, had landed where and when he said he would, and had never once complained about any of it.

In a separate account written for *National Geographic* in autumn 1927, Byrd made it sound as if he had intentionally sought out bad weather. 'I had determined not to wait for such conditions [i.e., good ones], because I felt that the transatlantic plane of the future could not wait for *ideal* conditions,' he wrote. 'Moreover, we probably could gain more scientific and practical knowledge if we met some adverse weather.' The result, he said, was 'the toughest air battle I believe that has ever taken place'. He went on: 'I did not convey my apprehension to my shipmates. They had enough upon them already. It was a terrific strain. Only an aviator knows what it means to be 18 hours without seeing the ground or water beneath. I doubt whether any other plane has ever flown blindly for half that time.'

All this stands in interesting contrast with an account Balchen wrote for the *New York Times* just after the flight: 'We had a good plane. Our motors never gave us any trouble. Not once during the whole flight did I have to crawl out on the wings to wipe the engine . . . So far as this flight across the ocean is concerned, it was one of the dullest and most monotonous I have ever been on.' In his own book, Balchen described their night in the air as one of 'beautiful starlight' all the way. That was one of the statements that the Byrd family later made him excise.

Upon reaching the French coast at Brest, Byrd instructed Balchen to follow the coastline towards Le Havre rather than head overland to Paris – a strangely deviant route. As Balchen noted later, a railway line beneath them traced a straight route to Paris, but Byrd insisted that they follow the coast to the mouth of the Seine and then follow that – a move that added two hours to the journey and ensured that they arrived after the bad weather.

As with Lindbergh, a crowd of thousands waited at Le Bourget, but as midnight came and went, and the rain continued, most gave up and went home. Among those in attendance were Chamberlin and Levine, who had flown into Paris that day as part of a tour of European capitals.

Byrd wrote: 'All the French aviators waiting for us at Le Bourget agreed that not only should we not have been able to land on account of the very thick weather but that we should have surely killed people had we attempted it.' This rather jars with Chamberlin's account. 'There was only a light drizzle of rain,' he recalled. 'The clouds were low but not too low for the ship to have come in safely if she had sighted the glow of Paris through the fog and been able to come down.' Byrd said in his book that his plane was clearly heard by those on the ground. Chamberlin said they never heard a thing.

'My big job now was to try not to kill anyone beneath us and to save my shipmates,' Byrd went on, turning a manifest failure into a selfless act of heroism. 'The only thing to do was to turn back to water.' He ordered the plane to return to the Normandy coast.

By the time they got there, their fuel was all but spent. In the darkness it was too risky to land in a field, so they elected to ditch in the sea. Balchen made a perfect landing about two hundred yards off the village of Ver-sur-Mer, and the four men waded ashore at a spot that would become more famous, seventeen years later, as one of the landing beaches for British forces during the D-Day invasions. The landing sheared off the wheels and landing gear, but the plane remained intact.

Of the landing Byrd wrote: 'I felt myself entirely responsible for the lives of my shipmates. I don't believe they thought there was much chance of getting down safely, but still they faced it gallantly . . . to the last they calmly obeyed orders. Balchen happened to be at the wheel.' This was breathtakingly disingenuous. In fact, Balchen had been flying for hours and very probably saved all their lives with his skilful landing.

The ridiculousness was not over yet. All four members of the crew were suffering from engine deafness and couldn't hear each other. Acosta, according to nearly all accounts, had broken his collarbone, though he later said he didn't feel any pain at the time. The others entirely escaped injury. They straggled ashore and almost immediately encountered a youth on a bicycle on the coast road, but he fled at the sight of four strange men entering France from the sea. Dripping and cold, they went from house to house, but could not make anyone understand who they were. Noville, still unable to hear, unnerved villagers by shouting at them in poor French. At length they came to a lighthouse on a hilltop about half a mile inland from the beach. Marianne Lescop, daughter of the lighthouse keeper, recalled later that the family had already been woken once by the droning of the plane – an unusual sound in Ver-sur-Mer – and had looked out of the windows but seen nothing in the dark. 'About three o'clock,' she went on, 'we were woken again by hammering on the door. Father saw four figures down below. One of them shouted, in French, "Airmen America!" Four exhausted men came in. They'd knocked in vain at many other doors. They were queerly dressed, soaking wet, ragged, covered in mud. We were rather suspicious . . .'

Monsieur Lescop and his family brought the flyers in, and gave them blankets and hot drinks. They listened in astonishment to Noville's account of their flight, but they couldn't report *America*'s arrival to the world because the town had no telephone or telegraph service between 6 p.m. and 8 a.m. By the time Byrd and his men managed to return to the beach and check their plane, it was daylight and they found that the locals had dragged it on to dry land. Less helpfully, the same locals were now plundering it, as they might a shipwreck. Six men were staggering up the beach under the weight of one of the large motors. Byrd prevailed upon them to bring the motor back, but other parts of the plane were permanently missing, including a forty-foot strip of fabric bearing the plane's name: '*AMERICA*'. The missing strip was later reported to be hanging on the wall of the casino in Deauville. The plane was never reassembled. All that remains of it today are a few tattered bits of fabric in a glass display case in a museum in Ver-sur-Mer. The forty-foot strip appears to have vanished permanently.

Despite their blunderings, the reception the Byrd team received in Paris when they finally got there (by train, the following day) was no less rapturous than that accorded Lindbergh. 'Never have I seen anything like the wild hysteria of Paris,' Balchen wrote in his memoirs. 'Around the railroad station when we arrived the streets were blocked with crowds and they swarmed over the car and broke the windows and almost tipped it over.' Women bruised them with kisses. Such was the crush that Acosta's collarbone may in fact have been broken by the jostling crowds. It was then in any case that he first noticed pain. The car that was supposed to take them to the Hotel Continental wouldn't start, so the mob pushed them there, shouting joyously as they went. 'Women jumped on the running board and threw their arms around us and kissed us until our faces were daubed with red,' Balchen went on. 'Gendarmes flung up their arms in despair at controlling the traffic, and elbowed their way through the crowds to the car and begged for autographs themselves.'

In America, the excitement was almost as great as it had been for Lindbergh and much more than for Chamberlin and Levine. Newspapers persisted in putting a positive spin on every aspect of the flight. The fact that Byrd's plane was in the air for forty-three hours – almost

25 per cent more air time than Lindbergh required – was treated as heroic in itself and not a reflection of their failure to reach their destination by a direct route. Byrd told the *New York Times*: 'We are nearly as all right as four men could be who went through such a strain as we did through those forty hours.' He admitted frankly that for much of the flight they did not know where they were – a confession that would be eliminated from his book of the trip the following year.

Because of his superior rank, the official reception for Byrd was even grander than Lindbergh's had been. On his second day, Byrd visited Les Invalides. There a paralysed aviator named Captain Legendre was so inspired by Byrd's presence that he rose from his chair and, for the first time in nine years, walked. Hand in hand, he and Byrd moved towards the tomb of Napoleon, a sight that made grown men weep.

America, it seemed, had become a land of gods.

July
THE PRESIDENT

'I've never liked that man from the day Grace married him, and the fact he's become President of the United States makes no difference.'

Lemira Barrett Goodhue, mother-in-law of

Calvin Coolidge

Chapter 14

FOR WARREN G. HARDING, the summer of 1927 was not a good one, which was perhaps a little surprising since he had been dead for nearly four years by then. Few people have undergone a more rapid and comprehensively negative reappraisal than America's twenty-ninth president. When he died suddenly in San Francisco on 2 August 1923, of an apparent cerebral haemorrhage (though some said it was heart failure and others ptomaine poisoning), he was widely liked and admired. He had been elected in 1920 with the largest majority in modern times. An estimated three million people turned out to watch the funeral train that carried him back to Washington. The *New York Times* called it 'the most remarkable demonstration in American history of affection, respect, and reverence'. In fact, at the time of his death President Harding was on the brink of being exposed as a scoundrel and a fool.

Three years earlier hardly anyone outside Congress had even heard of him. He was simply the junior senator from Ohio. By background and temperament he was a small-town newspaper proprietor, and that was about as far as his talents should have carried him. His nomination for president was one of the great astonishments of the age. It came about only because delegates to the 1920 Republican Party convention in Chicago grew hopelessly deadlocked over a slate of poor candidates and, after four days of indecision in the midst of a merciless heatwave, settled on the worst one on offer. Harding's only obvious qualification for higher office was his handsome bearing. 'He looked,' one contemporary observed, 'like a President ought to look.' In nearly every other respect – intelligence, character, enterprise – he fell considerably short of mediocre. His crassness in private could be startling. The *New York Times* reporter Richards Vidmer confided to a friend that he once saw Harding rise from his chair in the middle of a conversation and casually urinate into a White House fireplace. For his running mate, the party selected a person nearly as obscure and even more unpromising (though at least rather more refined): Calvin Coolidge.

Harding's administration was the most breezily slack in modern times. Although he made a few irreproachable appointments – Herbert Hoover at Commerce, Henry C. Wallace at Agriculture, Charles Evans Hughes at the State Department – for many posts he selected people he simply liked without considering whether they were qualified or not. His choice for head of the Federal Reserve Board was Daniel R. Crissinger, a friend and neighbour from Marion, Ohio, whose previous highest professional achievement was to be a director of the Marion Steam Shovel Company. For chief military adviser, Harding chose Ora Baldinger, who had formerly been the family newsboy. Harding gave his sister a senior position in the US Public Health Service and made her husband superintendent of federal prisons; previously the couple had been Seventh Day Adventist missionaries in Burma.

The most extraordinary appointee of all was Charles Forbes, whom Harding had befriended on a trip to Hawaii and about whom he knew almost nothing. Appointed to the role of head of the Veterans' Bureau, Forbes managed in two years to lose, steal or misappropriate $200 million. Other Harding appointees wrought similar financial havoc at the Justice, Interior and Naval departments and at a department left over from the First World War called the Office of the Alien Property Custodian. The interior secretary, Albert Fall, corruptly sold oil leases to two slick (as it were) oil men in return for $400,000 in 'loans'. One of the leases was at a place near Casper, Wyoming, formally called US Naval Oil Reserve Number Three but popularly known as Teapot Dome, and that became the name of the scandal. The total cost to the country of all the various acts of incompetence and malfeasance in the Harding administration has been put at $2 billion – a sum that goes some way beyond stupendous, particularly bearing in mind that Harding's presidency lasted just twenty-nine months.

Harding's death was so well timed, in terms of escaping scandals, that it was widely rumoured that his wife had poisoned him for the sake of his reputation. Her behaviour following his death was certainly curious: she immediately began destroying all his papers and wouldn't allow a death mask to be made. In addition, she stoutly refused to give permission for an autopsy, which is why the cause of his death has always been uncertain. All that can be said is that the president had been unwell ever since arriving in California from Alaska, where he had been on vacation. He seemed, however, to be rallying when at 7.35 p.m. on 2 August 1923, while in conversation with his wife in their room in the Palace Hotel, he shuddered and stopped talking. A moment later he was dead.

On the night he became president, Calvin Coolidge was at his boyhood home in Vermont visiting his father. It was after midnight in the east, and he and his wife were fast asleep when news of Harding's passing was brought to the Coolidge home from the nearby general store, the only place in town with a telephone.

By the light of a kerosene lamp – the Coolidge house did not have electricity or plumbing; rural homes still very often didn't – Coolidge's father, a notary public, swore his son in as president. As presidents go, Calvin Coolidge was not a magnificent specimen. He was slight of build and terse of manner. His face was pinched and inclined to scowl; he looked, in the well-chosen words of Alice Roosevelt Longworth, as if he had been 'weaned on a pickle'. Where Warren G. Harding had charm but no brains, Coolidge had brains but little charm. He was the least affable, gregarious, metaphorically embraceable president of modern times. Yet America came to adore him. Though he would spend the 1920s doing as little as possible – that was essentially his declared policy as president – he set the mood in the nation in a way few other presidents have. If the 1920s was the age of anyone, it was the Age of Coolidge.

Calvin Coolidge was born on the Fourth of July 1872 in Plymouth Notch, a scattered hamlet of two dozen or so people in a lofty cleft of the Green Mountains of central

Vermont. The Notch, as it was known, commanded a lonely valley about a dozen miles from Ludlow, the nearest outlet to the wider world. 'The scene was one of much natural beauty, of which I think the inhabitants had little realization,' Coolidge wrote in later life. His birthplace was the general store and post office that his father ran, though the family later moved to a larger house across the road – the house where Coolidge was sleeping on the night he learned he was president.

The Coolidges were reasonably well off. His father also owned the blacksmith's and a small farm, from which he produced maple syrup and cheese. But the family also had its share of suffering. Calvin's mother died from tuberculosis when Calvin was just twelve, an event that touched him deeply. He recorded the event simply but rather movingly in his autobiography:

> When she knew that her end was near she called us children to her bedside, where we knelt down to receive her final parting blessing. In an hour she was gone. It was her thirty-ninth birthday. I was twelve years old. We laid her away in the blustering snows of March. The greatest grief that can come to a boy came to me. Life was never to be the same again.

That was no exaggeration. Forty years later in the White House, according to Coolidge's Secret Service agent, Colonel E. W. Starling, Coolidge 'communed with her, talked with her, and took every problem to her'. Coolidge also lost his only sibling, his beloved sister Abbie. Five years after his mother's death, almost to the day, she died from a ruptured appendix.

In autumn 1891, Coolidge entered Amherst, then a small college of 350 or so students, in central Massachusetts. He was a conspicuous oddity. His hair was iron red and his face a splodge of freckles. He was painfully shy, and failed to find a single fraternity that wished to have him as a member – a level of rejection that was more or less without precedent. Only the kindly Dwight Morrow befriended him. With all others he was almost completely silent. 'Often hardly a word would pass his lips for days at a time, except such as were absolutely necessary to keep him supplied with food and to report his presence in the classroom,' the writer and advertising man Bruce Barton, also an Amherst alumnus, wrote years later in a recollection.

Coolidge did eventually warm up a little and even gained admission to a fraternity, but socializing was never his strong suit. Instead he worked hard and graduated with honours. After Amherst, he crossed the Connecticut River to nearby Northampton and there studied law in the offices of Hammond and Field, whose partners were also Amherst men. In 1899, he impetuously ran for a seat on the city council and was elected. It was the beginning of a long political career. In 1905, he married (over the strident objections of her mother, who thought him weedy) a teacher of the deaf, Grace Goodhue, a fellow Vermonter whom he met in Northampton and who was as outgoing as he was retiring. Grace was a great support and did all the talking for both of them in social situations. He doted on her and called her 'Mamma'.

With Grace at his side, Coolidge began his long climb up the political ladder. First he became mayor of Northampton; then a member of the Massachusetts legislature, the General Court; then lieutenant governor; and finally, in 1918, governor. In all positions, he distinguished himself by his diligence, thrift and parsimony of speech, attributes that endeared him to New Englanders. His personal frugality was legendary. In 1906, he moved with Grace into a modest rented duplex on Massasoit Street in Northampton and remained in modest rented premises for the rest of his life.

In 1919 Boston had a celebrated police strike. The city's policemen were paid barely $20 a week, and from that they had to buy their own uniforms, so their grievances were real, but their actions alienated public opinion and left Boston at the mercy of lawless elements. For two days, mobs roamed the streets, robbing and intimidating innocent citizens, and looters had a field day. When city authorities failed to assert control, Coolidge, as governor, stepped in. With an unwonted show of forcefulness he called out the State Guard, dismissed the strikers and hired a new force. 'There is no right to strike against the public safety by anybody, anywhere, any time,' he declared – the only occasion in his life, as far as can be told, that he uttered a ringing statement. His action made him a national figure and propelled him on to the nomination for vice-president on the Harding ticket the following year.

As vice-president, it is fair to say, he made little impression on anyone, even within the administration. Theodore Roosevelt, Jr, assistant secretary of the navy, said he sat through innumerable cabinet meetings that Coolidge attended and couldn't remember him ever once uttering a word.

When the nation awoke in August 1923 to find that

Harding was dead and the obscure Coolidge was president, most were dumbfounded. Some had stronger feelings. Oswald Garrison Villard, editor of the *Nation*, wrote: 'I doubt if it [the presidency] has ever fallen into the hands of a man so cold, so narrow, so reactionary, so uninspiring, so unenlightened, or who has done less to earn it than Calvin Coolidge.' Yet most people found themselves quickly warming to Coolidge, almost in spite of himself. The nation grew fond of his peculiarities and often exaggerated them in anecdote. His most celebrated trait was his taciturnity. An oft-told story, which has never been verified, is that a woman sitting next to him at dinner gushed: 'Mr President, my friend bet me that I wouldn't be able to get you to say three words tonight.'

'You lose,' the president supposedly responded.

Beyond doubt, however, is that the President and Mrs Coolidge once sat through nine innings of a Washington Senators baseball game without speaking except for once when Coolidge asked her the time and she replied, 'Four twenty-four.' On another occasion, a woman sitting beside him at an official dinner, hoping to spark a conversation, asked if he didn't get tired of having to endure so many such dinners. Coolidge shrugged and said, 'Gotta eat somewhere,' and returned to his meal. He was known, not surprisingly, as Silent Cal.

In some settings, however, Coolidge could be much more forthcoming – 'almost garrulous', in the words of one biographer. Twice a week he held private press conferences in which he met with correspondents and spoke freely and sometimes even animatedly, though his comments were all off the record and all questions had to be submitted in advance to his private secretary, a man with a name that sounded like a W. C. Fields snake-oil salesman: C. Bascom Slemp.

His private eccentricities were even greater than his public ones. According to Arthur M. Schlesinger, Jr, while having breakfast he liked to have his valet rub his head with Vaseline. He was so hypochondriacal that he often stopped in his work to take his own pulse. He had the White House physician examine him every day whether he felt unwell or not. Those who worked closely with him learned to be wary of a streak of 'pure cussedness', to quote his long-suffering aide Wilson Brown, with which he rather joyously made many people's lives hell. Once, on a trip to Florida, the secretary of state, Frank B. Kellogg, asked Brown to find out what clothes he should wear for a parade through Palm Beach later that day. Kellogg was too frightened of Coolidge's temper to ask the president himself, so Brown went to the executive quarters for him. Brown later wrote:

> I found Mrs Coolidge knitting tranquilly while the President hid behind a newspaper. When I told him that Mr Kellogg had asked whether the delegates should wear top hats and tail coats for the drive through the city, or straw hats and summer clothes, he answered without looking up from his paper, 'That's his hunt.'
>
> 'Now, Calvin,' Mrs Coolidge said, 'that's no message to send to the Secretary of State.'
>
> Mr Coolidge angrily lowered his paper, glared at me and said, 'What do you think I should wear?'
>
> I advised straw hat and summer clothes.
>
> He snapped, 'Tell Kellogg to wear a top hat.'

No one has ever more successfully made a virtue out of inertia than Calvin Coolidge as president. He did nothing he didn't absolutely have to do, but rather engaged in a 'grim, determined, alert inactivity', as political commentator Walter Lippmann put it. He declined even to endorse National Education Week in 1927 on the grounds that it wasn't necessary for the president to do so. In recent years a revisionist view has emerged that Coolidge was in reality cannier and livelier than history has portrayed him. Well, perhaps. What can certainly be said is that he presided over a booming economy and did nothing at all to get in the way of it.

Calculated indolence could not be called a good policy exactly, but for most of his term it wasn't a bad one either. With the markets constantly on the rise, he didn't need to do anything except keep out of the way. Under Coolidge's benign watch, Wall Street rose by more than two and a half times in value. The success of the economy not surprisingly did wonders for Coolidge's popularity. As the newspaperman Henry L. Stoddard wrote in 1927, 'He inspires a deep, nation-wide confidence that all will go well with the country while he is in the White House.' It became known as 'Coolidge prosperity', as if it were his personal gift to the nation.

Coolidge was also morally impeccable and honest to his bootlaces – qualities that came to seem all the more valiant and noble as the scandals of the Harding administration spilled out. Teapot Dome and the other Harding transgressions occupied great amounts of congressional and court time throughout the rest of the decade and were still rattling on in the summer of 1927. On 6 July, Albert Fall, the interior secretary, and oil man Edward L. Doheny were finally ordered to stand trial in Washington, DC, on bribery charges – charges that both had been fighting since just after Harding expired.

In the event, Doheny was acquitted. His partner Harry Sinclair, also on trial for corruption in 1927, would have got off scot-free too but foolishly hired twelve detectives from the William Burns Agency and had each tail a juror to see if any could be bribed, blackmailed or otherwise influenced. Sinclair was acquitted of the corruption charges but jailed for six and a half months for the attempted jury-tampering. He was also given three months for contempt for refusing to answer the questions of a Senate committee investigating the oil lease scandals. For those who like to think that cheats never prosper, Sinclair is a painful contradiction. After his short prison spell, he turned Sinclair Oil into one of the country's largest oil companies, made a fortune supplying chemicals to the military in the Second World War, became part owner of the St Louis Browns baseball team, and, in the admiring words of the *American Dictionary of National Biography*, became 'one of the most respected business leaders in the United States'. His companies were worth $700 million when he died in 1956.

Secretary of the navy Edwin Denby, who was also implicated in the Teapot Dome scandal, was forced to resign from the Cabinet but never charged with anything. Fall was eventually found guilty of corruption and sent to jail for nine months, the first time a Cabinet secretary had been convicted of a felony. Also jailed was Colonel Thomas W. Miller, who had accepted bribes while in the position of alien property custodian. Harry M. Daugherty, attorney general, had to resign over alleged kickbacks. He probably should have gone to jail but was acquitted at a trial in 1927. Daugherty's close associate Jess Smith was found dead of a gunshot wound, which was ruled a suicide, but others publicly suggested it was murder.

Charles Forbes, who had lost $200 million at the Veterans' Bureau, an unknown quantity of which ended up in his own pocket, was fined $10,000 and given a two-year prison term. In the summer of 1927 he was in Leavenworth, but he would be released in November having served just one year and eight months.

In his autobiography, Coolidge was wonderfully coy about all this. He didn't mention Teapot Dome at all and had merely this to say about Harding's last days:

> I do not know what had impaired his health. I do know that the weight of the Presidency is very heavy. Later it was disclosed that he had discovered that some whom he had trusted had betrayed him, and he had been forced to call them to account. It is known that this discovery was a very heavy grief to him, perhaps more than he could bear. I never saw him again. In June he started for Alaska and – eternity.

Although Harding was not personally implicated in any of the corruption – his only crime was to be a complete fool – his reputation was ruined. By the summer of 1927, it seemed as if it could sink no lower. Then it sank lower.

In July, an attractive young woman of his intimate acquaintance named Nan Britton produced an eye-poppingly juicy book called *The President's Daughter*. The story was unedifying but irresistible. As a schoolgirl in

Marion, Ohio, Miss Britton had formed a crush on her father's handsome friend, the stately Mr Harding, proprietor of the *Marion Star*. Harding was thirty-one years Britton's senior and was in any case engaged in a hot affair with his wife's best friend – he truly was a bit of a dog – so a crush was as far as things ever seemed likely to go.

But then Miss Britton did something that Warren Harding always found hard to resist: she grew into womanhood. Meeting again some time later, Harding was moved and smitten. Miss Britton was only too willing. They embarked on a passionate affair. Harding was now a successful politician, and Miss Britton often accompanied him on the campaign trail, generally posing as his niece. On 22 October 1919, she gave birth to a daughter, Elizabeth Ann, in Asbury Park, New Jersey. Britton was twenty-three, he was fifty-four. Harding did the decent thing and supported Britton with regular payments of $100 or $150. He also continued relations with Britton as his political career blossomed, but he never saw the child. With his sudden death the payments to Britton ceased. When Harding's family refused to extend any additional support, she decided to reveal all in a book.

No mainstream publisher would touch it, so Britton set up a special imprint, the Elizabeth Ann Guild, to produce it. Even then, Britton alleged, she received anonymous threats, her phone lines were cut and a truck carrying the printing plates for the book was torched. When *The President's Daughter* came out in July 1927, Harding's reputation had already reached what seemed an unsurpassable nadir, but now the reading public rushed to find out what an unprincipled rascal he was.

The best-thumbed passages in every household were

those dealing with their trysts in the White House. Miss Britton did not want for candour. She recorded how the president, consumed with lust, bundled her into

> the one place where, he said, he thought we might share kisses in safety. This was a small closet in the ante-room, evidently a place for hats and coats, but entirely empty most of the times we used it, for we repaired there many times in the course of my visits to the White House, and in the darkness of a space not more than five feet square the President of the United States and his sweetheart made love.

They also convened in apartments that Harding borrowed from pals.

Britton's book was a combination of wild improbabilities (that Harding wrote her love letters up to sixty pages long) and indubitably accurate descriptions of the interior of the White House (particularly when seen from floor level).

It was so scandalous that few publications reviewed it. Many bookstores provided it to customers only on request. Many others would not sell it at all. Even so, the book sold 50,000 copies in its first six months at $5 a copy, at a time when $5 was a lot of money. (Half a day's pay for Lindbergh as an airmail pilot, for instance.) One of the few publications to review it – though not until it had been out for three months – was the *New Yorker*. There, Dorothy Parker called it 'the most amazing work that has yet found its way into these jittering hands . . . For when Miss Britton gets around to revealing, Lord, how she does reveal.'

All this could not have come at a worse time for the

memory of Warren Harding. A memorial in the shape of a mighty rotunda had been erected in Harding's home town, and dedication was set for 4 July. As a sitting president of the same party, Calvin Coolidge was required by tradition and etiquette to perform the dedication, but with so much unsavoury scandal swirling about he refused to go. In consequence, the dedication was postponed more or less indefinitely – a serious humiliation for the Harding family. (Eventually, in 1931, it was dedicated by Herbert Hoover, who would go, it was said, to the opening of a drawer.)

Instead Coolidge celebrated 4 July – which also happened to be his fifty-fifth birthday – by remaining in South Dakota, where he was having the time of his life. In recognition of all the publicity he was generating with his trip, the state of South Dakota presented him on his birthday with a cowboy outfit and horse. Named Kit, the horse was charitably described as 'spirited'. It was in fact all but unbroken. The president, who was by no means a horseman, was prudently kept well away from it. Instead his delighted attention was focused on his other main present – a cowboy outfit consisting of a ten-gallon hat, bright red shirt, capacious blue neckerchief, chaps, boots and spurs. Coolidge retired to put it all on and emerged clankingly, and a little clumsily, in the full regalia a few minutes later. He looked ridiculous but very proud, and posed happily for photographers, who could not believe their luck. 'Here was one of the great comic scenes in American history,' wrote Robert Benchley in the *New Yorker* that week.

Coolidge loved that outfit and wore it for the rest of the summer whenever he could. According to lodge staff, he often changed into it in the evening after his more formal day's duties were done, and for a few hours ceased to be the most important man in America and instead was just a happy cowpoke.

CHAPTER 15

WHILE PRESIDENT COOLIDGE amused himself as a cowboy in the Black Hills, across the country, and far beyond his present range of interests, four international bankers were quietly laying the groundwork for the collapse of the stock market and the Great Depression that followed. That wasn't their intention or expectation, of course, but that was the effect of it.

The men in question were: Benjamin Strong, governor of the Federal Reserve Bank of New York; Sir Montagu Norman, governor of the Bank of England; Hjalmar Schacht, head of the Reichsbank in Germany; and Charles Rist, deputy governor of the Banque de France. For men of such importance, they were a rather odd quartet. One was dying, one was strange, one was a future Nazi, and one was quite normal but of little consequence in the present circumstances.

They gathered at the Long Island estate of Ogden Livingston Mills, a rich Republican who had recently been beaten (indeed, heartily clobbered) by Al Smith in the race for governorship of New York. As a kind of consolation prize, Mills had been made undersecretary of the treasury in Washington. He would eventually succeed Andrew Mellon as treasury secretary – ironically, just in time to deal with the mess now being set in motion by his well-meaning but misguided house guests.

The bankers must have felt quite at home, for Mills's vast and blocky mansion looked more like a central bank than a comfortable residence. Surrounded by formal gardens, it occupied a prime spot on the 'Gold Coast', a privileged stretch of north-western Long Island where some six hundred great estates commanded the rolling hills and deeply indented coastline of Nassau and western Suffolk counties. Nearly all of America's wealthiest families – the Vanderbilts, DuPonts, Astors, Whitneys, Morgans, Hearsts, Fricks – had weekend places there. Some of these homes were immensely grand. Otto Kahn, a banker, had a castle with 170 rooms, including a dining room that could seat 200. The grounds included an eighteen-hole golf course and private zoo. Feeling his backdrop lacked grandeur, Kahn had his own small mountain built. Other Gold Coast owners bought and razed entire villages to improve their views and at least one had a public highway gated to stop common people from wandering on to the beach at the foot of his grounds.

The Mills estate was only about ten miles from Roosevelt Field and more or less directly on the flight path of all the recent Atlantic flights. Commander Byrd and his team had flown over in the *America* just two days before the bankers arrived. News of Byrd's splashdown at Ver-sur-Mer and triumphal reception in Paris devoured all the main news space in the papers for days, which pleased the bankers because it helped to distract attention from them. They relished secrecy.

The host of the meeting was Benjamin Strong. Fifty-five years old, he was a tall, handsome man, but one whose life was 'packed with secret sorrows and ill health', to quote the financial historian John Brooks. In the summer of 1927 he wore the tired and slightly haunted look of a man who has been fighting a long, losing battle with a fatal condition. His was tuberculosis.

Strong's personal and professional lives made a poignant contrast. Born in 1872 into a genteel but financially diminished old upstate New York family, he could not afford college and so instead went to work in banking in Manhattan. Thanks to his personable manner and natural authority, he climbed steadily through the ranks, but his ascent was considerably accelerated after 1898 when he moved with his wife and young family to Englewood, New Jersey, and became friends with several rising stars at J. P. Morgan & Co., notably Henry Davison, Thomas Lamont and (later) Dwight Morrow. With the benefit of his new contacts, Strong became a director of the Bankers' Trust Company, then president, and finally was made head of the New York Federal Reserve Bank at the time of its founding in 1913.

His personal life, alas, did not achieve a parallel happiness. His wife, who suffered from chronic depression, killed herself in 1905, leaving him with four young children, one of whom died of scarlet fever the following year. Two years later, Strong remarried, but that marriage was not a success either: his second wife left him in 1916 and moved to California with two further children he had had with her. At the same time, he was diagnosed with tuberculosis, and needed to spend extended periods convalescing in the clear air of Colorado. While there, he formed a relationship with a young woman, a fellow sufferer of TB, who killed herself horribly by drinking boot polish. This was not a man for whom life was a succession of joyous events. In the summer of 1927, he had just returned to work after six months' leave of absence.

At least he had the companionship of his best friend, Montagu Norman of the Bank of England. Strong and Norman were so close that they frequently holidayed together, usually in Maine or the South of France. Norman made a rather odd friend, but an even odder head of a central bank. Of a fragile and nervous disposition, he was 'a strange and lonely man' who was 'intensely neurotic and almost impossible to please', in the words of two of his many biographers. He sported what *Time* magazine in 1927 called 'a superbly pugnacious goatee' and had an affection for broad-brimmed hats and flowing capes that made him look like a cross between a Middle European spy and a second-rate stage conjuror. He was fiercely anti-Semitic, which was slightly unexpected because his own roots, it was said, led back to Sephardic Jews from southern Europe.

Among his many eccentricities, he always travelled in disguise, even when there was no plausible reason for doing so. Usually he adopted the name 'Professor Clarence Skinner', to the occasional consternation of the real Professor Clarence Skinner. He was much given to extravagant nervous breakdowns. Whenever he was feeling 'seedy', as he called it, he would take to his bed for days or even weeks. He didn't work at all from 1911 to 1913 after the Swiss psychiatrist Carl Jung diagnosed him, arrestingly and erroneously, as suffering from final-stage syphilis and gave him just months to live. It is more likely that he was at least mildly bi-polar. When in ebullient mood, his confidence was boundless. 'I don't have *reasons*,' he once corrected a friend. 'I have instincts.'

Norman lived alone (but attended by seven servants) in a rambling house in Holland Park in west London; Herbert Hoover was a near neighbour for several years. He almost never gave interviews or made speeches and he rarely socialized. His house had a music room in which he sometimes held small concerts for himself alone. He came from a family of considerable accomplishment. His brother became chairman of the BBC. His father was a partner in Martin's Bank, then one of the biggest in Britain, and both his grandfathers had been directors of the Bank of England, one of them later serving as governor.

Norman himself showed no particular promise as a young man. He worked capably enough in the family bank, but took long periods off for travel and nervous collapses. During his longest stretch of healthfulness, he spent four years with a merchant bank in New York. During the Boer War he enlisted as a captain in the British Army and, to the presumed astonishment of everyone who knew him, served so gallantly that he was awarded the Distinguished Service Order, the highest honour available to an officer (but then collapsed, predictably, in ill health). In 1915, at the advanced age of forty-four, Norman joined the Bank of England, and so impressed people with his fierce intellect and command of detail that within five years he was governor.

It would be safe to say that the Bank of England has never had a more erratic leader. Often, when feeling low, he took abrupt and lengthy leaves of absence – once for three months to South Africa – without explanation or farewell, leaving his subordinates to conduct the bank's affairs as they supposed he would were he there. At other times he vanished with his mother to Switzerland or France to attend one of the many clinics run by a small but charismatic Frenchman named Émile Coué. A pharmacist in Nancy, Coué became enormously popular in the 1920s through inventing a method of self-improvement that he called autosuggestion. Coué's system, which he explained in a slim best-selling book called *Self Mastery Through Conscious Autosuggestion*, was based on the simple idea of thinking of oneself in exclusively positive terms and of repeating over and over the simple mantra 'Every day in every way I am getting better and better.'*

Coué's book was just ninety-two pages long and the larger part of that was taken up with testimonials from his admiring clients. Followers of Coué's technique – who eventually numbered in the millions – credited the great man with curing almost any malady you could name: Bright's disease, sinusitis, neurasthenia, brain tumours, even nymphomania and club foot. One ecstatic client professed to have overcome a lifelong difficulty in digesting strawberries. Another joyously renounced kleptomania. By the mid-1920s, Coué had clinics all over Europe and North America.

Unfortunately, in the summer of 1926 the little Frenchman dropped dead of a heart attack, which rather

---

* In fact, the mantra as Coué gave it in his book was 'Every day in every *respect* I am getting better and better.' It was Coué's clients in America who autosuggested their way to the snappier version.

underscored the point that positive thinking, however diligently applied, could take one only so far. The movement lost its momentum and Norman returned to a state of chronic hypochondria, where he seemed more comfortable anyway. When not practising Couéism, Norman was also a committed dabbler in spiritualism and the occult. He once claimed to a colleague that he could walk through walls. Perversely, all this merely enhanced his reputation for financial wizardry.

The third member of the group was Hjalmar Horace Greeley Schacht, president of Germany's Reichsbank, who owed his memorable name to the fact that his father had resided for some years in America as a young man and had there developed an admiration for the crusading newspaperman Horace Greeley. Hjalmar Schacht later became a slavish supporter of Adolf Hitler (even going so far as to adopt a comical postage-stamp moustache in the Hitlerian mode) and minister of economics under the Nazis. In the words of one observer, 'Dr Schacht conferred legitimacy on Hitler's thugs.'

In 1927, he was a national hero, credited with bringing Germany through its greatest economic crisis. Four years earlier, in January 1923, the French, exasperated with Germany's failure to keep up with reparation payments, had seized the Ruhr, Germany's industrial heartland. The result was dizzying hyperinflation. The mark, which had traded at about four to the dollar before the war, now shot up to 600,000 to the dollar. By summer, the exchange rate was 630 *billion* marks to the dollar and inflation was so rampant that prices were doubling daily, sometimes hourly. People needed wheelbarrows or prams to carry enough paper money to conduct even the simplest transactions. Sending a letter cost 10 billion marks. A streetcar ride that had cost 1 mark in 1914 now cost 15 billion. Pensions became worthless. People found that savings carefully built up over a lifetime now wouldn't buy a cup of coffee. Eventually, at the peak of the madness, prices rose to 1,422,900,000,000 times their levels of ten years earlier.

In the last week of November 1923, Germany replaced the valueless reichsmark with a new currency, the renten-mark. Miraculously, the move had the desired effect and inflation sank back to more manageable, less hysterical levels. By a rather extraordinary coincidence, on the very day that the change was effected, Rudolf Havenstein, head of the Reichsbank, collapsed and died. His successor was Hjalmar Schacht. Because Schacht's arrival was so exquis-itely timely, he received all the credit for restoring stability to the German economy, and was hailed for evermore as a financial genius.

A second, later consequence of the French seizure of the Ruhr and all the disruption and bitterness that followed was the rise to power of Adolf Hitler. Some histo-rians have maintained that the Nazis could not have risen as they did without the legitimacy Schacht conferred upon them and the financial mastery he brought with him. After the Second World War, Schacht was tried at Nuremberg. In his defence, Schacht claimed that he had been against the persecution of Jews and had never joined the Nazi Party. He believed in stripping Jews of their rights, but not in killing them, which by the standards of the day made him almost an enlightened figure in Germany. He was acquitted and lived on until 1970. He and Norman also got along well. For the meeting on Long Island, they sailed to America together, under assumed names, aboard the *Mauretania*.

The fourth member of the gathering was Charles Rist, a Swiss-born economist and former professor of law at the Sorbonne who was deputy governor of the Banque de France. The governor, Émile Moreau, spoke no English, so sent Rist in his place. Bald and grave, Rist was eminently respectable, but very much the outsider at the meeting. He had joined the Banque de France only the previous year, so was not well known to the other three.

Each man naturally brought to the gathering a measure of national mood, self-interest and prejudice. France was having a terrible year. Its citizens were feeling poor and hard done by; the disappearance of Nungesser and Coli had been a bitter psychological blow. On an official level, the Banque de France was suspicious of Norman, believing that he would sell out the rest of Europe in an instant if it meant preserving London's status as a global financial centre. Britain, for its part, had just emerged from a costly general strike, and was pained and bewildered by its inability to regain its former supremacy in the world. Norman was personally furious with the French for engineering a quiet but insistent run on British gold reserves, and to show his displeasure was for the time being refusing to address any Frenchman in French. Germany was simply exhausted. Not only had it been landed with crippling reparation payments, but it had also been deprived of much of its capacity to earn foreign exchange. The allied powers had seized a good deal of its shipping, for instance. A fact largely forgotten now is that many of the great ocean liners of the 1920s were actually German ships under new names. Cunard's *Berengaria*, a vessel so splendid that Cunard made it its flagship, had originally been the German *Imperator*. The White Star Line's *Majestic* had been the *Bismarck*. The American *Leviathan*, on which Commander Byrd and his team were about to sail home, had earlier sailed proudly as the *Vaterland*.

America, in stark contrast to its European cousins, found itself in the unusual position of doing, if anything, too well. Its economy seemed unstoppable. Inflation was zero and had been for four years. Economic growth was averaging 3.3 per cent a year. The latest figures from the Treasury Department, released the day before the bankers assembled on Long Island, showed that for the fiscal year just completed the United States had enjoyed a record budget surplus of $630 million and had trimmed $1 billion off the national debt. It simply wasn't possible for an economy to do better.

In the stock market, people were making fortunes with no apparent effort at all. F. Scott Fitzgerald in *My Lost City* noted in amazement that his barber had retired after making $500,000 – nearly 400 times the average annual wage – on a single timely investment. For many, playing the market became almost an addiction. Warren Harding did so while president. (He wasn't supposed to.) When he died, he was $180,000 in debt to his broker. For many like Harding, the great attraction was that you didn't need money to take part. You could buy on margin – purchasing, say, $100 worth of shares for a down payment of $10, with the balance borrowed from your broker. He in turn borrowed from his bank. From the bankers' point of view, the arrangement could not have been more pleasing.

Banks borrowed from the Federal Reserve at 4 or 5 per cent and lent it on to brokers at 10 or 12 per cent. They were, as one writer put it, 'in the position of being handsomely paid simply for existing'.

As long as shares kept rising, the system worked fine, and for much of the 1920s that is exactly what shares did. It was clear to anyone who cared to look, however, that there was little correspondence between the prices of many shares and the values of the companies they supported. While national output (as measured by GDP) rose by 60 per cent in the decade, stocks went up by 400 per cent. Since most of these inflated rises had nothing to do with any underlying profits or productivity, all that kept them so giddily buoyant was the willingness of fresh buyers to bid the prices ever higher.

What most small investors didn't realize was that things were often stacked against them. Many of the most respected business leaders in the country took part in syndicates in which share prices were shamelessly manipulated for the sake of a large, quick gain at the expense of innocent investors. One such, reported by the financial writer John Brooks in his classic *Once in Golconda*, involved such luminaries as Walter J. Chrysler of the Chrysler Corporation; Percy Rockefeller, nephew of John D. Rockefeller; John Jakob Raskob, national chairman of the Democratic Party; and Lizette Sarnoff, wife of David Sarnoff, head of the Radio Corporation of America (RCA). A broker working for them bought large blocks of RCA stock at selected intervals. This had the effect of driving the price from 90 to 109. The rise attracted other investors. The broker then cashed in the syndicate's holding and the members shared a profit of nearly $5 million for less than a month's work. With the syndicate's money withdrawn, the shares sank back to 87, leaving other, underinformed investors nursing huge losses. There was nothing to be proud of in any of this, but nothing illegal either. Raskob made most of his fortune through such pools. So, too, did Joseph Kennedy, father of President John F. Kennedy.

In 1929, Raskob gave an interview to the *Ladies' Home Journal* that ran under the headline 'Everybody Ought to Be Rich' in which he insisted that anyone could get rich by playing the stock market. In fact, he had by then cashed in most of his shares in anticipation of the fall to come. Hypocrisy was not a condition many people recognized in the 1920s.

Borrowing funded not just a booming stock market but all of life. Thanks to a brilliant new financial invention, Americans could suddenly have things they had never expected to have – and they could have them right now. It was called the instalment plan, and it changed more than the way Americans shopped: it changed the way they thought.

The idea was simplicity itself. Say a radio cost $100. The customer bought it for $110 by paying $10 down and $10 a month for ten months – and thus had the pleasure of a radio immediately for an additional cost of just $10. The retailer sold the contract to a finance company for $83 which, with the $10 down payment, gave the retailer $93 in hand. At the end of the ten months, the finance company gave the retailer $10 more as a fee for collecting the monthly payments. The upshot is that at the end of the payment period the retailer earned $103, the finance company made $7 on an investment of $83 and the customer owned outright a treasure that previously he could only have dreamed of. As Louis Hyman notes in his history of consumer credit in America, *Debtor Nation*, the system was so slick that it left everybody happy. Customers buying vacuum cleaners through the Republic Finance Company paid interest of just $1.05 a month for five months, which seemed hardly anything, and yet it gave RFC and its shareholders a return of 62 per cent on their money. On such happy mathematics was a new world built.

'Buy now, pay later' proved such an irresistible concept that soon people were using it to purchase all kinds of things – clothing, furniture, household appliances, bathtubs, kitchen cabinets and above all cars. Instalment buying filled American homes with gleaming products and its roads with cars. It made America the consumer paradise it has remained ever since.

All this left America in a peculiar position. It was by far the most economically dynamic of the four nations at the summer conference on Long Island, but also the least experienced. Its own central bank, the Federal Reserve, was just thirteen years old, and so cumbersome in structure as to be almost incapable of decisive action anyway. A portion of the responsibility for the Fed's odd and hobbled nature lay, interestingly, with the father of America's most celebrated young aviator. As a member of the House of Representatives Committee on Banking and Industry, C. A. Lindbergh had helped to design the Fed. Like many rural Midwesterners, the senior Lindbergh felt a bitter antipathy towards eastern bankers – he would have been appalled to know that his son would marry the daughter of a Morgan partner – and wanted the new

Federal Reserve Bank's powers diffused widely rather than invested in a single east coast establishment. For that reason, he and his congressional colleagues decided not to have a single central bank, as in other countries, but to create a network of twelve independent regional banks, to be loosely overseen by a Federal Reserve Board in Washington.

It was – and remains still – a strange concoction. Although the twelve regional banks collectively form a single central bank and act on behalf of the government, they are at the same time private, individual, profit-making concerns owned by shareholders. Their principal function, from the government's point of view, is to control the money supply, which they do by adjusting the discount rate – the rate of interest at which reserve banks lend to commercial banks. The discount rate is the foundation rate against which all other bank rates are calibrated.

The twelve scattered outposts of the Federal Reserve were in principle each of equal importance, but in practice the New York Fed under Benjamin Strong was by far the dominant player. As Allan H. Meltzer said of Strong in his history of the Federal Reserve: 'He regarded the twelve reserve banks as eleven too many.' Under Strong, the New York Fed exploited its many advantages, notably that it was larger than any of the other reserve banks and conveniently located in America's financial capital. The Federal Reserve Board in Washington was still largely in the hands of fiscal incompetents thanks to the inept and careless appointments of President Harding. Crucially, Strong won for the New York Fed the right to be the exclusive agent for the United States in dealings with other countries. It became, in short, the de facto central bank –

more or less exactly what Congressman C. A. Lindbergh had been determined to avoid.

For five days, the four bankers met under a cloak of secrecy. They issued no public comments. Indeed, they wouldn't even confirm that they *were* meeting – rather extraordinary, considering that they were making decisions that would determine the direction of world finances for years to come. What exactly they discussed isn't known because no minutes were kept, but the problems that lay before them largely came down to a single issue: gold.

The international banking system remained almost obsessively devoted to the venerable but rather creaky mechanism known as the gold standard. A gold standard is an appealingly simple concept. Under it, any paper money in circulation is supported by gold reserves. When America was on the gold standard, a $10 bill could be exchanged for $10 of gold, and vice versa. It was gold, in other words, that gave value to the otherwise worthless slips of paper known as money. A gold standard had certain limitations – most obviously, the amount of money in circulation was limited by the amount of gold that had been discovered – but it had many compensating attractions that endeared it to bankers. It made inflation almost impossible since governments couldn't just print money. It kept the management of exchange rates out of the hands of politicians with their narrow, short-term interests. It promoted price stability and, by and large, kept the heavy wheels of international trade turning. Above all, a gold standard had a huge psychological importance. It worked. It had worked for a long time. It was what was known.

The problem was it wasn't working very well now. Half

of all the gold in the world was in the United States, mostly behind a ninety-ton steel door in a five-storey vault deep beneath the Federal Reserve Bank of New York in lower Manhattan. This was not actually a terrifically good thing. It might seem like a great idea to have all the gold, but in fact that would mean that other countries couldn't buy any more of your products because they would have no gold of their own to pay for them. In the interests of trade and a healthy global economy, gold should circulate. Instead, it was accumulating – steadily, relentlessly, in a country that was already better off than all the countries of Europe put together.

Prudence, not to mention simple decency, dictated that America should help its European friends. It was in America's interest to keep international trade rolling along. So Strong decreed that the Federal Reserve would cut its discount rate from 4 per cent to 3.5 per cent, to encourage holders of gold to move their savings to Europe where they would enjoy higher returns. That in turn would bolster European reserves, help stabilize European currencies and boost trade overall. Strong gambled that the American economy could absorb the stimulus of a small rate cut without going crazy. It would prove to be a spectacular miscalculation.

The four bankers concluded their meeting on 7 July and immediately travelled to Washington to inform selected members of the Federal Reserve Board of their decision. It was breathtakingly audacious of Strong to presume to instruct the Federal Reserve on how to conduct itself, and four of the reserve banks – in Chicago, San Francisco, Minneapolis and Philadelphia – refused to go along, partly in petulance no doubt, but also in the legitimate belief that it was madness to encourage more borrowing with market values so high already. But the Federal Reserve Board, in an unprecedented action, over-ruled the disobedient banks and instructed them to fall into line.

The cut in interest rates had an explosive effect – 'the spark that lit the forest fire', in the words of the writer and economist Liaquat Ahamed. The result was the Great Market Bubble of 1928. Over the next year, stocks would more than double from already irrational heights, and the volume of brokers' loans to investors would rise by more than $1 billion to a tottering and unsound $4.5 billion – all fuelled by the patently deluded belief that stocks could keep on rising for ever.

For the moment, however, few outside the banking system saw any cause for worry. Among politicians, only Herbert Hoover was immediately exercised – and he was furious. He called Strong 'a mental annex to Europe' (and would later accuse him of 'crimes worse than murder') and wrote to the Federal Reserve Board predicting that the rash cut in interest rates could well precipitate a depression. Separately, he urged Coolidge to do something to reverse the action. Coolidge declined in the belief that the market was doing fine – his trusted treasury secretary, Andrew Mellon, had recently assured the world: 'The stock market seems to be going on in very orderly fashion, and I see no evidence of over-speculation' – and anyway, the Federal Reserve was an independent body whose judgements were not his to overrule. And so, as usual, he did nothing, and instead returned to the happy business of catching trout. The Great Depression would be for someone else to deal with.

Chapter 16

A<small>T LAST THE NATION</small> was warming up and drying out. In New York, the temperature rose towards 80 degrees as the long Fourth of July weekend began. The first heatwave of summer was under way.

Heat transformed city life. It created an air of shared misery, and sparked conversations between strangers. For once everyone had something to talk about. Life became communal in ways that the world has mostly forgotten. People sat on stoops. Barbers brought chairs outside and shaved their customers beneath a shady tree or awning. Windows everywhere were lifted wide – in offices, apartments, hotels, libraries, hospitals, schools – so all the noises of the city drifted through wherever you were. The ocean roar of distant traffic, the cries of children at play, an argument in the next building – all these and a million other sounds played over you as you worked or read or tried fitfully to sleep. Today we go indoors to escape the commotion of the city. In the 1920s, much of it came inside with you.

Because the Fourth of July fell on a Monday, many

workers enjoyed a three-day weekend, a marvellous novelty at a time when most people were still getting used to the idea of having *any* kind of weekend. The average working week in America had fallen from sixty hours at the start of the decade to forty-eight hours now, so there was much more leisure time to be had, but the prospect of a three-day break was still rare enough to be thrilling. Nearly everyone seemed determined to try to make the most of it. By Friday all trains were packed and Pullman reservations were sold out for days ahead. Two million people were forecast to enter or leave New York during the 4 July break, the *Times* reported. The Pennsylvania Railroad laid on an extra 235 trains to help move the throngs, and the New York, New Haven & Hartford Railroad promised to make similar efforts for those heading north to Cape Cod and Maine.

Closer to home, Coney Island reported a million visitors on 3 July, the highest number ever recorded there, and the beaches of the Rockaways and Staten Island absorbed perhaps half a million more – though oddly, officials reported, Staten Island's own residents were mostly boarding ferries for New Jersey, where Asbury Park, Long Beach and Atlantic City all said they had larger crowds than they had ever seen before. At Atlantic City, the Boardwalk was solid with people from early morning to late at night on Saturday, Sunday and Monday.

Those who couldn't get out of the city did what they could to stay cool. Many went to picture houses that were pleasantly air-conditioned – though 'air-conditioned' as a word didn't quite exist yet. It would make its first recorded appearance, in the Reno, Nevada, *Evening Gazette*, the following month. For the moment, buildings that were artificially freshened were air-cooled, not air-conditioned.

For the more thrifty, open-sided trolleys ran on Broadway, and for a nickel people could ride them for as long as they liked. Hundreds did. At night, many people lugged mattresses on to fire escapes or rooftops and slept there. Large numbers went to Central Park with blankets and pillows and camped beneath the stars. The playwright Arthur Miller, then an eleven-year-old boy growing up on 110th Street, years later recalled the surreal experience of walking through an open-air dormitory: 'With a couple of other kids, I would go across to the Park and walk among the hundreds of people, singles and families, who slept on the grass, beside their big alarm clocks, which set up a mild cacophony of the seconds passing, one clock's ticks syncopating with another's. Babies cried in the darkness, men's deep voices murmured, and a woman let out an occasional high laugh by the lake.'

Those who couldn't sleep often went for long walks, or for drives if they had a car. On the night of 3 July, ten people from a boarding house in South Orange, New Jersey – six adults and four children – packed into a car and went out for a drive 'just to cool off', in the words of the car's owner, James De Cicco. One of the passengers, Mrs Catherine Damiano, was just learning to drive and asked if she could take the wheel to practise. De Cicco readily yielded it to her. Unfortunately Mrs Damiano stalled the car on railway tracks just as a train from the Pennsylvania Railroad – one of those being hurried to the city to help shift all the extra travellers – barrelled through. The train struck the car at 40 miles an hour. Mrs Damiano and all four of her children were killed instantly. Two other adults also perished. Two more were seriously injured. Only Mr De Cicco managed to jump clear. The seven deaths were thought to be the most ever in a one-car accident. Mrs Damiano's unfortunate husband, who had a night job and didn't know that his wife and children had gone out, learned the next morning that he had lost his entire family.

All this, it is worth noting, was with the night-time temperature in the seventies. Before the month was out, both temperature and humidity would climb to far more punishing heights over much of the country, and many more would die.

The warm weather and holiday spirits brought huge crowds to Yankee Stadium on Monday for a Fourth of July doubleheader between the Yankees and the Washington Senators. Seventy-four thousand people – more than had ever attended a regular season baseball game anywhere – packed into the stadium, and thousands more had to be turned away.

The weeks of bad weather that had caused so many flight postponements at Roosevelt Field wrought similar havoc with baseball schedules that summer. The Yankees played eighteen doubleheaders in 1927 – four in six days in June alone – but none would be more important than this Fourth of July meeting.* The Yankees had hit their stride in June, going 21 and 6 for the month and opening up a lead of 9½ games over the rest of the league, but now the Senators were heating up, too. They were hitting the ball well – five of their starting line-up were batting over

* A doubleheader is two games played on one day (usually because an earlier game was rained out).

293

.300 – and had just won ten straight to move into second place ahead of the White Sox. They arrived in New York in buoyant mood, confident that the series could be a turning point in their season. It was – but in the wrong direction.

The Yankees killed them. In the most humblingly lopsided doubleheader defeat ever meted out, New York won 12 to 1 and 21 to 1. The Yankees hit as if at batting practice, smacking nine two-base hits, four three-base hits and five home runs – 37 hits and 69 total bases in all. The team batting average for the day was .468. Every Yankee batter but one, pitchers included, got at least one hit, and six had four or more. Even the light-hitting, seldom used rookie Julie Wera, who played in only forty-three games in two short seasons in the major leagues, hit a two-run home run – the only one of his career. ('Julie', incidentally, was short for Julian.) The only player who didn't hit was pitcher Wilcy Moore, who was widely held to be the worst hitter in baseball, but he pitched nine complete innings and allowed the opponents to score just one run. This followed a similarly assured performance by George Pipgras, who gave up one run on nine hits in a complete game in the opener – but who also rapped out two hits as a batter.

'Never have pennant challengers been so completely shot to pieces,' observed the *New York World*. 'I wish the season was over,' said the Senators' first baseman, Joe Judge. In fact, in any meaningful sense it was. The Yankees extended their lead to 11½ games with the two victories. They would beat the Senators again the next day and in six of their seven remaining games after that. No team would come close to threatening the Yankees again.

All this was quite unexpected. Nearly everyone forecast the Philadelphia Athletics to win the American League pennant in 1927. The Yankees, all agreed, were past their best. Ruth, for a start, was thirty-two years old and demonstrably paunchy, and the pitching staff was even older. Dutch Ruether and Herb Pennock were both thirty-three. Bob Shawkey and Urban Shocker were thirty-six. The average age of the team was over twenty-eight. Only five of the players on the roster had been born in the twentieth century. Shocker was in such bad shape that he would actually die before the end of the next season.

Yet the 1927 Yankees would prove to be one of the greatest teams of all time – possibly the very greatest. Seven members (counting manager Miller Huggins) would be voted into the Baseball Hall of Fame, an extraordinary proportion for one team. Rarely has a group of players had such depth.

It is generally futile and foolish to compare athletic performances across decades, but what can be said is that when such rash assessments have been ventured the baseball team most often selected as the best ever is the '27 Yankees. It is certainly fair to say that they were an exceptional bunch, both as players and as people. Among the more memorable were:

Waite Hoyt, right-handed pitcher. Called 'Schoolboy' because he'd come to the big leagues when he was just seventeen, he was now in his tenth season in the majors and he was having one of his best ever years. He would finish the season with a record of 22 and 7, and would be at or near the top of the league in five categories for pitching.

Hoyt's private life was no less memorable. He was the

son of a well-known vaudeville performer, and was a talented singer and performer in his own right – good enough to have made a living on the stage had he chosen to. Hoyt's father-in-law owned a funeral parlour in New Jersey, and Hoyt often helped him out by fetching bodies from morgues in Manhattan and bringing them back to New Jersey to be prepared for burial. Sometimes, it appears, he would leave a cadaver in his car at Yankee Stadium during a game, then complete the delivery afterwards. Hoyt himself was studying in the off season to be a mortician.

Urban Shocker, also a pitcher, had been born Urbain Jacques Shockor to a French-Canadian family living in Cleveland. He was something of a drunkard, but then many ballplayers in those days were. He had a permanent crook in one of the fingers of his throwing hand, owing to an injury in his younger years, which gave him an unusual grip and greatly improved his slow curve ball. He was also one of the seventeen pitchers allowed to continue throwing a spitball after 1919. He was the third highest salaried player on the team, after Ruth and Pennock, at $13,500.

Shocker pitched thirteen years in the major leagues and never had a losing season. In 1927 he had a record of 18 wins and 6 losses. He had the second best winning percentage in the league, second fewest walks per batter faced, and third best earned-run average. What is truly extraordinary about all this is that he was dying as he did it. Shocker lived with a heart condition so severe that he had to sleep sitting up. (Some books say standing up, but that seems unlikely.) Photographs of him from 1927 show an ashen figure looking at least ten years more than his age. By the early autumn, he would be too ill to keep his place in the starting rotation. Within a year he would be dead.

Herb Pennock, pitcher, came from a wealthy Quaker family in Philadelphia and was known to his teammates as the Squire of Kennett Square. In the off season he hunted foxes, bred chrysanthemums and collected antiques. A left-hander, he spent twenty-two years in baseball, but by 1927 he was coming to the end of his career. After a game, he was often so sore that he couldn't raise his arm to comb his own hair. In 1927, Pennock was the second highest paid player on the team with a salary of $17,500. He was later elected to the Hall of Fame.

Wilcy Moore, pitcher, was the most cheerfully improbable member of the team. A rookie, he was at least thirty years old, though possibly considerably older. No one knew and he wouldn't say. A farm boy from Hollis, Oklahoma, he had been a journeyman pitcher in the minor leagues for years, but in 1925 he broke his wrist and that somehow changed his delivery for the better. Although he occasion-ally started (as on the Fourth of July), he served mostly as the team 'fireman' – a relief pitcher who came in and closed down the opposition with men on base and the situation precarious. The team called him Doc because he specialized 'in treating ailing ballgames', as one reporter put it. In 1927 he had an incomparably good year – the only one he would ever have.

Tony Lazzeri, second baseman and shortstop. (A short-stop is a fielder who stands between second and third base.) Although 1927 was only his second season, he was already considered possibly the best middle infielder in the majors. Though he weighed only 165 pounds, Lazzeri was a formidable slugger. He hit 60 home runs and had 222 runs batted in for Salt Lake City in the minor Pacific Coast League in 1925 before breaking into the majors with the Yankees in 1926.

Lazzeri was a particular hero to Italian-Americans. It is a little surprising to think of Italians as rarities in professional baseball, but in 1927 they were. Italians were associated in the popular mind either with gangsters like Al Capone or anarchists like Sacco and Vanzetti, so an Italian who did well at the most American of sports was treated with almost godlike reverence in the Italian community. Lazzeri's great secret was that he had epilepsy – this at a time when epileptics were still frequently detained in institutions – but in fourteen years in the majors he never had a seizure on the field. He was also a future Hall of Famer.

Bob Meusel, left fielder. Known as 'Silent Bob', he often went days without speaking and was aloof even with his own teammates. He never acknowledged the cheers of the fans and seemed impervious to both praise and criticism. Meusel had a career year in 1927, batting .337 with 174 hits and 103 runs batted in. He and Ruth got along very well, largely because Meusel liked to party. He just partied in silence.

Earle Combs, centre fielder, was quiet and amiable. He had been a country schoolteacher in Kentucky before he came to professional baseball. He didn't smoke, drink or swear, and spent much time reading the Bible. He was probably the best-liked player on the team, both among players and sportswriters. He was a solid and dependable centre fielder and one of the best lead-off hitters of all time. In 1927 he would have the best season of his career. His 231 hits set a Yankees record. He was one of those elected to the Hall of Fame.

Benny Bengough, reserve catcher. Though not much of a player – he appeared in just thirty-one games – Bengough was one of the most popular members of the team. He had been born in Liverpool, England, but grew up in Niagara Falls, New York, and had studied to be a priest before deciding instead to be a ballplayer. Bengough was completely bald. He went to bed one night with hair and woke up the next day with none. As a joke he would often pretend to run his fingers through his hair. Ruth in particular was very fond of him.

Also worthy of note was Eddie Bennett, the team batboy. Bennett was a hunchback, and the players rubbed his hump for luck before games. Bennett had an almost uncanny reputation for bringing teams good fortune. He was batboy for the White Sox in 1919 when they won the pennant. Then he moved across to the Dodgers in 1920, and they won a pennant, too. In 1921 he came to the Yankees just at the time they started their dynasty, and won their own first pennant. By 1927, he was one of the most valued figures in baseball. Some accounts suggest that he was as much a kind of bench coach as a batboy.

Finally, and above all, came Ruth and Gehrig, the most formidable double act baseball has ever produced. Lou

Gehrig was doing something no human had ever done before: he was hitting home runs as well as Babe Ruth did. Together in 1927 they would hit a quarter of all home runs in the American League.

On the face of it, Lou Gehrig possessed every quality a hero could require. He was gracious and good-looking, with a winning smile, deep blue eyes and a dimpled chin, was immensely talented, and had a physique that seemed to be hewn from granite. But he suffered from an almost total absence of personality and a crippling shyness, especially around women. At the age of twenty-three, he had never had a girlfriend and still lived at home. He claimed once in a magazine interview that he smoked sometimes and liked to drink a little beer, but hardly anyone ever saw actual evidence of that. Feeling sorry for him, his teammates Benny Bengough and Mark Koenig once had him up to their apartment so he could meet some girls. Gehrig arrived in a good suit, neatly pressed by his mother, and sat mutely on the sofa, too terrified to speak. He didn't utter a word the whole evening.

Like Lindbergh, Gehrig was not a great mixer, but whereas Lindbergh was happily self-contained, Gehrig was almost unnaturally solitary. He would often go to an amusement park and ride the roller coaster alone for hours. He paid little attention to his appearance, and was notable for refusing to wear a coat or other outerwear; even in the most frigid weather he walked about in shirtsleeves. He hated to make a fuss, which is why Jacob Ruppert was able to pay him no more than he paid many reserve players. Gehrig always accepted whatever salary Ruppert offered him, so Ruppert always offered a poor one.

Gehrig was a native New Yorker, born in 1903 to poor

German immigrant parents in Yorkville. At his birth, according to some accounts, he weighed a whopping fourteen pounds. (His mother was a block of a woman.) Gehrig grew up speaking German. His father rarely worked and was probably an alcoholic. Mrs Gehrig had three other children, but all died in infancy, so Lou grew up not just as an only child but as the only surviving child, which made his mother even more clinging and fretful.

Gehrig was extraordinarily devoted to his mother. Where other ballplayers took their wives to spring training, Gehrig took his mother. On road trips, he wrote to her daily. Before departure, they would kiss and hug for ten minutes, to the acute discomfort of teammates nearby. On an exhibition tour of Japan, Gehrig spent nearly all of his free time, and much of the money he earned, buying gifts for his mother.

Gehrig was powerfully built from childhood and was a natural athlete. By the time he got to Commerce High School, he could hit a baseball harder and further than any high-school player any New York City coach had ever seen. In 1920 Commerce was invited to Chicago to play the best high-school team there, Lane Tech, at Cubs Park. In the ninth inning, with the bases loaded, Gehrig hit a home run that flew over the back wall of the park and bounced into Sheffield Avenue – a feat that would have been astounding in a major leaguer. Gehrig was seventeen years old.

That autumn he enrolled at Columbia, where his mother worked as a cleaner and cook at the Sigma Nu fraternity house. Not the most outstanding of scholars, Gehrig flunked introductory German even though it was his first tongue. He flunked English as well. He did pass trigonometry, however. His patchy performance almost certainly owed more to a demanding schedule than to any mental shortcomings. Each day he had to rise at dawn and hurry to the dining hall to clear tables for two and a half hours. Then he spent the day in classes. That was followed by baseball or football practice, depending on the season. After a shower and a quick dinner, he returned to the dining hall to clear tables and wash dishes until late.

In 1923, he signed with the Yankees and two years later became a regular member of the team. On 1 June 1925, he pinch-hit for a player named Wally Pipp, then did not miss another game for fourteen years until May 1939, a total of 2,130 consecutive games – a continuity record that stood for sixty-four years.*

Ty Cobb of the Detroit Tigers, the most unstable man in baseball, decided from their first meeting that he disliked Gehrig intensely – for his meekness and lack of wit, and above all for his fixation with slugging. He never passed Gehrig without insulting him. If Gehrig was on base near him, Cobb crept as close as he could and rode him mercilessly. 'Keep your foot on the bag, Wiener Schnitzel. Go on back there, you thick-headed Dutch bum,' he would call. When Gehrig was playing first base, Cobb would keep up a string of insults from the bench. Eventually, Gehrig could take no more and charged into the Tigers' dugout to get him. As Cobb prudently found someone bigger to stand behind, Gehrig smacked his head against a supporting stanchion and fell down senseless. Cobb was so impressed that he never insulted him again.

* A pinch-hitter is someone who is sent in to bat for another, usually for some strategic reason.

Now, in his third year in the majors, it was becoming evident that Gehrig might very well be having the best year that any player had ever had. There was even every likelihood that he would beat Ruth's home run record of 59. In the last twenty-one games – which is to say, since about the day that Lindbergh had failed to turn up at Yankee Stadium – Ruth had hit 5 home runs, a more or less normal pace for him. Gehrig in the same period had hit 14, including 3 in one game at Fenway Park in Boston – something that no one had ever done before. Gehrig's pace in those twenty-one games would, if sustained, produce over 100 home runs in a full season.

In the Fourth of July doubleheader against Washington, Gehrig hit 2 more, including a grand slam. At the end of the day, he had 28 home runs to Ruth's 26. No one had ever pushed Ruth like this before. The baseball world was about to experience its first great home-run race, and the excitement this would generate was almost uncontainable.

Remarkably, despite the rivalry and the fact that their personalities could not be more different, Ruth and Gehrig were the best of friends. Gehrig often had Ruth to his home, where Babe enjoyed Mrs Gehrig's hearty cooking and, according to several biographies, speaking German. (In fact, according to Ruth's own sister, Babe spoke no German at all.) 'I came to love that big Dutchman like a brother,' Ruth recalled, with every appearance of sincerity, in his autobiography. Ruth was as excited as any fan by Gehrig's success, while Gehrig for his part was happy just to be allowed to play in the same ballpark as Ruth. He was especially touched by Ruth's generosity of spirit. 'It would be almost impossible to feel envy for a man who is as unselfish as Ruth,' he told reporters.

That warmth wouldn't last, alas. By the 1930s, Gehrig would hate Ruth about as passionately as it was possible to hate a person. The fact that Ruth reportedly had by that point slept with Gehrig's wife would seem, not surprisingly, to have had something to do with it.

Out west, the good weather was the best possible news, for the waters of the Mississippi were at last receding, if slowly. One and a half million acres were still under water as July began, but the worst was over and Herbert Hoover was finally able to leave the day-to-day running of relief efforts to others.

For Hoover, the Mississippi flood was a personal triumph. He was especially proud that the federal government had provided no financial assistance at all. All the money for relief efforts came in the form of donations from private citizens and organizations like the Red Cross and Rockefeller Foundation. 'But those were days,' Hoover noted with a certain misty fondness in his memoirs thirty years later, 'when citizens expected to take care of one another in time of disaster and it had not occurred to them that the Federal Government should do it.' In fact, the support provided for those trying to get back on their feet was hopelessly inadequate. Hoover helped to push through the creation of a $13 million loan fund to help flood victims, which sounds reasonably generous, but in fact worked out at just $20 per victim, and was, for all that, only a loan, hardly a useful sum to even the poorest person who had lost everything.

The great Mississippi flood of 1927 had two lasting legacies. First, it accelerated the movement of blacks out of the South in what is known as the Great Migration.

Between 1920 and 1930, 1.3 million southern blacks moved north in the hopes of finding better-paying jobs and more personal liberty. The movement transformed the face of America in a decade. Before the Great Migration, only 10 per cent of blacks lived outside the South. After the Great Migration, half did.

The other important effect of the Mississippi flood was that it forced the federal government to accept that certain matters are too big for states to handle alone. For all Hoover's proud reminiscence of how relief efforts were entirely private, it was widely recognized that government could not stand by when disaster struck. In 1928, Calvin Coolidge reluctantly signed into law the Flood Control Act, which appropriated $325 million to try to avert future disasters. It was, in the view of many, the birth of Big Government in America. Coolidge hated the idea and refused to have any kind of ceremony to celebrate the passing of the act. Instead, he signed the bill in private, then went to lunch.

Meanwhile, back in the flood zone not quite everyone was benefiting from the receding waters. In Morgan City, Louisiana, Mrs Ada B. Le Boeuf, wife of a prominent local businessman, had a good deal of explaining to do when the body of her husband, bearing obvious gunshot wounds, was found bloated and glistening on a newly exposed mudbank nine days after she reported him missing. Under questioning, Mrs Le Boeuf confessed that she had formed an attachment to another prominent Morgan City citizen, Dr Thomas E. Dreher, who was a doctor and surgeon and, not incidentally, her husband's best friend. The devious Dreher had invited Le Boeuf out for a day's fishing, shot him, weighted the body and dumped it overboard.

Nineteen twenty-seven was a memorable year for foolish murders, and this was certainly one of those, for it seems not to have occurred to Dr Dreher that it's never a good idea to dump a body in floodwaters because the waters will eventually go away whereas the body may not. Dr Dreher and Mrs Le Boeuf were tried, convicted and hanged side by side.

For Charles Lindbergh, July did not start at all well. Although he had nobly resisted the crasser commercial blandishments waved before him, he did agree to two money-making propositions and it was now time to make good on those. One was to undertake a three-month tour of America in the *Spirit of St Louis*. The idea was to visit every one of the forty-eight states, partly to satisfy the national craving to see him in the flesh but also to help promote aviation. The Daniel Guggenheim Fund for the Promotion of Aeronautics would pay him $2,500 a week during the trip, a generous sum. The tour details would be arranged by Herbert Hoover's ubiquitous Department of Commerce. The tour was scheduled to start on 20 July.

At the same time, Lindbergh contracted with the publisher G. P. Putnam's Sons to produce a quick auto-biography. Putnam appointed a ghostwriter, Carlyle MacDonald of the *New York Times*, who came up with a first draft, but Lindbergh couldn't stand his folksy tone and insisted on writing the book himself – a matter of alarm to his publishers since he had only about three weeks to do it, and that included time off for a trip to Canada to attend that country's diamond jubilee celebrations as a guest of the prime minister.

The Canada trip proved tragically eventful. On the

Fourth of July, while the rest of America was celebrating, Lindbergh flew to Selfridge Field in Michigan where a squadron of military planes was waiting to escort him onwards to Ottawa. The plan in Ottawa was for Lindbergh to land first while the others circled above. Unfortunately, two of the escort planes clipped wings and one went into a nosedive. Lieutenant J. Thad Johnson jumped free of the crashing plane but lacked the height to get his parachute open. He struck the earth with a sickening thud close to where Lindbergh had just landed, and died instantly. The incident rather spoiled the day for many people, but Lindbergh accepted it calmly. In his world, death was an occupational hazard.

Immediately after Ottawa, Lindbergh returned to Long Island and moved into Falaise, a French-style chateau on the Guggenheim family estate at Sands Point on the Gold Coast, a dozen miles from the Mills property where Benjamin Strong and his fellow bankers were concurrently holding their talks. The Guggenheims' end of the Gold Coast was fractionally more bohemian than the rest and was popular with people from Broadway and the arts. Florenz Ziegfeld, Ed Wynn, Leslie Howard, P. G. Wodehouse, Eddie Cantor, George M. Cohan and, for a time, Scott and Zelda Fitzgerald all had homes there, as did a few more louche types, like the mobster Arnold Rothstein. This was the world of *The Great Gatsby*, published two years earlier. Sands Point, where the Guggenheims clustered in three substantial houses, was the wealthy East Egg of the novel.

Working in a bedroom overlooking the sea, Lindbergh scribbled out his life story, using Carlyle MacDonald's draft as a guide. In a little under three weeks he completed a manuscript of about 40,000 words – an impressive achievement in terms of output if not literary merit. The book, called *We*, was coolly received by critics. Lindbergh devoted just eighteen lines to his childhood and seven pages to his historic flight. The rest was mostly about barnstorming and delivering airmail. As one reviewer drily observed, 'as an author Lindbergh is the world's foremost aviator'. The buying public didn't care. *We* was published on 27 July and went straight to the top of the bestseller list. It sold 190,000 copies in its first two months. People couldn't get enough of anything Lindbergh did.

And now the attention that he so little enjoyed was not only about to get much worse, but at times quite dangerous.

CHAPTER 17

FOR A MAN who changed the world, Henry Ford travelled in very small circles. He resided his whole life within a dozen miles of his birthplace, a farm at Dearborn, just outside Detroit. He saw little of the wider world and cared even less for it.

He was defiantly narrow-minded, barely educated, and at least close to functionally illiterate. His beliefs were powerful but consistently dubious, and made him seem, in the words of the *New Yorker*, 'mildly unbalanced'. He did not like bankers, doctors, liquor, tobacco, idleness of any sort, pasteurized milk, Wall Street, overweight people, war, books or reading, J. P. Morgan & Co., capital punishment, tall buildings, college graduates, Roman Catholics or Jews. Especially he didn't like Jews. Once he hired a Hebraic scholar to translate the Talmud in a manner designed to make Jewish people appear shifty and avaricious.

His ignorance was a frequent source of wonder. He believed that the earth could not support the weight placed on it by skyscrapers and that eventually cities would collapse in on themselves, as in some kind of biblical apocalypse. Engineers explained to him that a large sky-scraper typically weighed about 60,000 tons while the rock and earth excavated for the foundations would weigh more like 100,000 tons, so that skyscrapers actually reduced the burden on the earth beneath them, but Ford was unpersuaded. He seldom let facts or logic challenge the certainty of his instincts.

The limits of his knowledge were most memorably exposed in 1919 when he sued the *Chicago Tribune* for libel for calling him an 'ignorant idealist' and an 'anarchist'.* For eight days, lawyers for the *Tribune* entertained the nation by punting through the shallow waters of Ford's mind. Asked to identify the notorious traitor Benedict Arnold, Ford replied: 'I have heard the name.'

'Who was he?' pressed the lawyer.

'I have forgotten just who he is,' Ford answered. 'He is a writer, I think.'

Ford, it transpired, did not know much of anything. He could not say when the American Revolution was fought ('In 1812, I think; I'm not quite sure') or what the issues were that provoked it. Questioned about politics, he conceded that he didn't follow matters closely and had voted only once in his life. That was just after his twenty-

---

* The background to the case was complicated. In 1916, the Mexican revolutionary Pancho Villa led a raid that killed seventeen Americans in New Mexico. This inflamed American sentiment against Mexico and led President Woodrow Wilson to dispatch National Guardsmen to the border. Henry Ford reportedly declared that he would not pay the wages of any employees called up and sent to New Mexico, causing the *Tribune* to criticize him and leading to the libel suit. In fact, it appears that Ford never made the assertion that provoked the libel.

first birthday when, he said, he had voted for James Garfield. An alert lawyer pointed out that Garfield was in fact assassinated three years before Ford reached voting age.

And so it went on, day after day. The world was so delighted and enthralled with Ford's ignorance that one enterprising man sold hastily printed copies of Ford's testimony for 25 cents each day outside the courthouse, and bought a house with the profits. (Eventually the jury found in Ford's favour, but the jurors – twelve stolid Michigan farmers who clearly believed they had better things to do with their time – awarded him damages of just 6 cents. The *Tribune* never paid.)

Whether Ford was stupid or just inattentive has fuelled debate among historians and other commentators for nearly a century. John Kenneth Galbraith had no doubt about the matter. Ford's life and career, he maintained, were 'marked by obtuseness and stupidity and, in consequence, by a congeries of terrible errors'. Allan Nevins and Frank Ernest Hill in a generally sympathetic biography of 1957 called him 'an ignoramus outside his chosen field [but] an ignoramus of sense and integrity'. That was about as warm a tribute as Henry Ford received from those who knew him well or considered him carefully. He was not, in short, a terribly bright or reflective human being.

Yet against this must be set his extraordinary achievement. When Henry Ford built his first Model T, Americans had some 2,200 makes of cars to choose from. Every one of those cars was in some sense a toy, a plaything for the well-to-do. Ford changed the automobile into a universal appliance, an affordable device practical for all, and that difference in philosophy made him unimaginably successful and changed the world. Within just over a decade Ford had more than fifty factories on six continents, employed 200,000 people, produced half the world's cars, and was the most successful industrialist in history, worth perhaps as much as $2 billion, by one estimate. By perfecting mass production and making the automobile an object within financial reach of the average working man, he wholly transformed the course and rhythm of modern life. We live in a world largely shaped by Henry Ford. But in the summer of 1927, Henry Ford's part of that world was beginning to look a little rocky.

Henry Ford was born in July 1863, the same month as the Battle of Gettysburg, and lived into the atomic age, dying in 1947 just short of his eighty-fourth birthday. His earliest conviction was that he didn't want to be a farmer, for 'there was too much work on the place'. For the first half of his long life, he was little more than an accomplished mechanic. After leaving school at sixteen, he worked in various machine and engine shops in Detroit, eventually becoming chief engineer of the Edison Illuminating Company. In the 1890s, he quit that to pursue a fixation with building the best possible motor car. According to Morris Markey, writing in the *New Yorker*, Ford was at a car race one day when a French driver crashed and was mortally injured. While others rushed to the stricken driver, Ford rushed to the car, which had survived better than he thought possible. Taking a hunk of chassis away with him, he discovered it was made of vanadium steel, a strong but lightweight material. Vanadium steel became the foundation metal for every car he made henceforth. However true or not that story is, it is certainly the case that Ford didn't rush into production until he had worked out every detail of manufacture and composition. He was forty years old before he founded the Ford Motor Company in 1903 and forty-five when he produced his first Model T.*

The Model T, like Ford himself, was an unlikely candidate for greatness. It was almost wilfully rudimentary. For years the car had no speedometer and no fuel gauge. Drivers who wanted to know how much petrol they had in the tank had to stop the car, get out and tip back the driver's seat to check a dipstick located on the chassis floor. Determining the oil level was even trickier. The owner, or some other compliant soul, had to slide under the chassis, open two petcocks with pliers and judge from how fast the oil ran out how much and how urgently more was needed. For gears, the car employed something called a planetary transmission, which was famously idiosyncratic. It took much practice to master the two forward gears and one reverse gear. The headlights, run off a magneto, were uselessly dim at low speeds and burned so hot at high speeds that they were inclined to explode. The front and rear tyres were of different sizes, a needless quirk that required every owner to carry two sets of spares. Electric starters didn't become standard until 1926, years after nearly all other manufacturers included them as a matter of routine.

Yet the Model T inspired great affection. It was the source of many loving jokes. In one, a farmer whose tin house roof had been mangled in a tornado sent it to the

---

* The Model T was preceded by eight other models: A, B, C, F, N, R, S and K, in that order. If there was a logic to that sequence, Ford failed to explain it in his memoir, My Life and Work.

Ford factory hoping they could advise him how to restore it. The message came back: 'Your car is one of the worst wrecks we have ever seen, but we should be able to fix it.' For all its faults, the Model T was practically indestructible, easily repaired, strong enough to pull itself through mud and snow, and built high enough to clear ruts at a time when most rural roads were unpaved. It was also admirably adaptable. Many farmers modified their Model Ts to plough fields, saw lumber, pump water, bore holes or otherwise perform useful tasks.

One central characteristic of the Model T that is now generally forgotten is that it was the first car of consequence to put the driver's seat on the left-hand side. Previously nearly all manufacturers placed the driver on the outer, kerb-side of the car so that an alighting driver could step out on to a grassy verge or dry pavement rather than into the mud of an unpaved road. Ford reasoned that this convenience might be better appreciated by the lady of the house, and so arranged seating for her benefit. The arrangement also gave the driver a better view down the road, and made it easier for passing drivers to stop and have a conversation out of facing windows. Ford was no great thinker, but he did understand human nature. Such, in any case, was the popularity of Ford's seating plan for the Model T that it soon became the standard adopted by all cars.

The Model T was an immediate success. In its first full year, Ford produced 10,607 cars, more than any manufacturer had ever made before, and still couldn't meet demand. Production doubled annually (more or less) until by 1913–14 it was producing nearly 250,000 cars a year and by 1920–21 over 1.25 million.

The most persistent belief about the Model T, that you

could have it in any colour so long as it was black, was only ever partly true. Early versions of the car came in a small range of colours, but the colours depended on which model one bought. Runabouts were grey, touring cars red and town cars green. Black, notably, was not available at all. It became the exclusive colour in 1914 simply because black enamel was the only colour that would dry fast enough to suit Henry Ford's assembly line methods, and that lasted only until 1924, when blue, green and red were made available.

One thing above all accounted for Ford's competitive edge: the moving assembly line. The process was perfected bit by bit between 1906 and 1914, not so much as a progressive, systematic plan, but more as a series of desperate expedients to try to keep up with demand. The basic idea of the assembly line – or 'progressive assembling', as it was at first known – came from the movement of animal carcasses through the slaughterhouses of Chicago, which, as has often been noted, was actually a kind of 'disassembly line'. Other companies used assembly line techniques – it was how Westinghouse made air brakes – but no other manufacturer embraced the system as comprehensively and obsessively as Ford. Workers in Ford plants were not permitted to talk, hum, whistle, sit, lean, pause for reflection or otherwise behave in a non-robotic fashion while working, and were given just one thirty-minute break per shift in which to go to the lavatory, have lunch or attend to any other personal needs. Everything was arranged for the benefit of the production line.

Henry Ford was always happy to take credit for the invention of the assembly line process, but it seems he may have been generous to himself. 'Henry Ford had no ideas on mass production,' Ford's colleague Charles Sorensen once recalled. 'Far from it; he just grew into it like the rest of us.'

Thanks to the slickness of operations, the time it took to produce a Ford car fell from twelve hours in 1908 (which was already good going) to just one hour and a half after 1913 when the company's Highland Park factory opened. At the peak of production, a new car, truck or tractor rolled off a Ford assembly line somewhere in America every ten seconds. By 1913, the company had sales of nearly $100 million and profits of $27 million. With the greater efficiencies costs fell, too – from $850 in 1908 to $500 in 1913 and down to $390 in 1914 before finally settling at an almost preposterously reasonable $260 by 1927.

In 1914, Ford introduced an eight-hour day, forty-hour week and doubled average salaries to $5 a day in what is often presented as an act of revolutionary magnanimity. In fact, it was necessitated by the costly waste of high employee turnover – a breathtaking 370 per cent in 1913. At the same time, Ford established its notorious Sociological Department, employing some two hundred investigators who were empowered to look into every aspect of employees' private lives – their diet, hygiene, religion, personal finances, recreational habits and morals. Ford's workforce was full of immigrants – in some periods as many as two thirds of his employees were from abroad – and Ford genuinely wished to help them live healthier, more satisfying lives, so his sociological meddling was by no means entirely a bad thing. However, there was almost nothing Henry Ford did that didn't have some bad in it somewhere, and the Sociological Department certainly had a totalitarian tinge. Ford employees could be ordered to clean their houses, tidy their yards, sleep in American-style beds, increase their savings, modify their sexual behaviour, and otherwise abandon any practice that a Ford inspector deemed 'derogatory to good physical manhood or moral character'. Foreign-born workers who wished to advance within the company were required to take citizenship and language classes.

Ford also, it must be said, employed a great many disabled people – including (in 1919) one man who had no hands, four who had no legs or feet, four who were blind, thirty-seven who were deaf and sixty who had epilepsy (at a time when epileptics were scorned). He also employed between 400 and 600 ex-convicts. Ford also hired black men, though he nearly always gave them the hottest, dirtiest and most exhausting jobs. (Black women in 1927 were never hired.)

Who deserves the credit for Ford's success has been a matter of dispute since that success began. Many have suggested that the real brains of the operation was James Couzens, Ford's Canadian-born partner. Couzens had started his working life as a clerk in a coal yard, but joined Ford early on and showed an extraordinary flair for business. Couzens set up and managed Ford's finances, sales, distribution network and advertising. Henry Ford attended almost exclusively to production. By this view, Henry Ford gave the company a name and an ethos, but Couzens made it a global colossus.

Ford and Couzens constantly squabbled, sometimes bitterly, and success only made matters worse. Ford began to resent Couzens's $150,000 salary, particularly after he worked out that it added 50 cents to the cost of every car they built. He didn't think Couzens was worth it and essentially drove him to leave. Couzens sold out in 1915 and went into politics, eventually becoming a US senator for Michigan where he made himself famous by attacking Andrew Mellon for favouring the rich (an irony appreciated by many, since Couzens was believed to be the wealthiest man in Congress).

Couzens's departure was a source of immediate worry for many. 'There was something of a feeling that while Ford was a great mechanic he wasn't much of a business-man,' a Ford insider named E. G. Pipp wrote in 1926, 'and there were fears of what would happen to the company if Couzens left.' What happened in fact isn't certain. Without Couzens, Ford carried on much as before. Though it did go into a gradual decline, it is impossible to say to what extent that was a reflection of Couzens's departure. What can be said is that all the real innovations at Ford happened when Couzens was there and none of lasting consequence happened after – at least not until the summer of 1927, and those were by no means unalloyed successes.

By the late 1920s, one American in six owned a car – which was getting close to a rate of one per family – and many people were finding the automobile an essential part of life. The sociologists Robert and Helen Lynd, in their classic study of middle America, *Middletown*, published in 1929, found to their surprise that more people in the anonymous town of the title (which in fact was Muncie, Indiana) had cars than bathtubs. Asked why, one woman replied simply: 'Because we can't go to town in a bathtub.'

Unfortunately, and increasingly, the cars Americans loved were not Fords. Other makers were producing cars of superior quality and value. General Motors supplied as standard such devices as speedometers and shock absorbers that Ford was slow to supply at all. GM more-over produced a range of cars to fit every pocket, from Chevrolets at the basic end to Cadillacs at the top. (Cadillac was such an exclusive division that it maintained a showroom in Manhattan where, as its ads boasted, 'Sales are neither made nor discussed.' Visitors could admiringly inspect the latest models, but had to go elsewhere for the sordid business of making a purchase.)

Under the enterprising leadership of Alfred Sloan, Jr, General Motors constantly restyled and refined its cars, adding new colours and features to stimulate interest and excitement. By the late 1920s GM was well on its way to perfecting the annual model change, a practice that was essentially needless but magnificently effective as a marketing tool. Also racing up from behind was the new Chrysler Corporation, which was formed out of the old Maxwell Motor Company and named after Walter Chrysler, its dynamic head. By the late 1920s Chrysler was doing so extraordinarily well that he could afford to build a splendid monument to himself: the fabled seventy-seven-storey Chrysler Building, which upon completion was the world's tallest building. (Not for long, however. Eleven months later it was superseded by the Empire State Building.)

All this combined to make Ford look increasingly old-fashioned and flat-footed. Ford's last really good year was 1923. Between then and the end of 1926, total production at the company went down by 400,000. During the same period production went up by an almost equal amount at Chevrolet – a division that had been developed by William Knudsen, a brilliant former Ford engineer who had been driven into the arms of General Motors by Henry's autocratic methods.

Remarkably, while this was happening Henry Ford increasingly occupied himself with other, less urgent matters. He pursued a fixation with finding industrial uses for agricultural products. He was particularly taken with what he saw as the infinite adaptability of the soybean. He wore suits woven from soy fibres and built experimental cars made almost exclusively with soy plastics and other materials. (The car never went into production because it never could be made not to stink.) He fed guests dinners that consisted primarily of soybean products – 'pineapple rings with soybean cheese, soybean bread with soybean butter, apple pie with soy crust, roasted soybean coffee, and soymilk ice cream', in the words of his biographer Greg Grandin. Ford so admired the head of his soybean research division, Edsel Ruddiman, that he named his only child after him.

To promote his personal beliefs he bought a dying weekly newspaper, the *Dearborn Independent*, and turned it into a general-interest magazine. The *Independent* became famous for the dullness of its features and the waywardness of its views. It was produced from some surplus factory space, prompting one wag to call it 'the best weekly ever turned out by a tractor plant'. Ford interfered with it extensively. One of his ideas was to bring assembly line methods to its production. Instead of assigning each article to an individual writer, as on a conventional publication, he wanted the articles to proceed along a kind of editorial assembly line where a team of specialists would each make a specific contribution and then pass the article on. One writer would supply the facts, another the humour, a third the moral instruction and so on. Ford was persuaded to drop that idea, but tinkered enough in other areas to ensure that the *Independent* was always terrible. He lost hundreds of thousands of dollars a year on the magazine, and would have lost still more had he not forced his dealers to take copies to sell on to their customers – though it was a rare customer who was eager to read long articles like 'Famous Frenchmen I Have Met' by A. M. Somerville Story (a writer about as obscure then as now) or 'The American Merchant Marine Must Be Built by Business Enterprise and *Not* by Government Subsidy' by W. C. Cowling, a Ford executive.

Regularly, and more notoriously, the *Independent* ran strident attacks on the world's Jews. It accused them of manipulating stock markets, working for the overthrow of Christianity, using Hollywood as a propaganda tool for Jewish interests, promoting jazz ('moron music', as the *Independent* called it) to the masses for nefarious purposes, encouraging the wearing of short skirts and rolled stockings, and fixing the 1919 World Series, among much else. Accuracy was not its strong suit. In a 1921 article entitled 'How Jews Degraded Baseball', it pilloried Harry Frazee of the Red Sox on the assumption that he was a Jew. In fact, Frazee was Presbyterian.

The bulk of these essays were gathered together in a volume called *The International Jew*, which was greatly admired in Nazi Germany, where it was reprinted no fewer than twenty-nine times. Henry Ford had the additional distinction of being the only American mentioned favourably in *Mein Kampf*, Adolf Hitler's memoir of 1925. Hitler, it was said, kept a framed photo of Ford on his wall.

Ford's anti-Semitism seems to have been of a type peculiarly his own. For one thing, it appears not to have been personal. So far as can be told, he had nothing against Jews as individuals. He happily put the design of his factories in the hands of Albert Kahn, a Jewish émigré, with whom he had a good relationship for thirty-five years. When Rabbi Leo Franklin, an old friend and neighbour, broke with Ford over some of the accusations contained in the *Independent*, Ford was genuinely mystified. 'What's wrong, Dr Franklin?' he enquired sincerely. 'Has anything come between us?'

Ford's antagonism was instead based on the conviction that a shadowy cabal of Jews was trying to take over the world. The source of these beliefs was a mystery to all. 'I am sure that if Mr Ford were put on the witness stand, he could not tell to save his life just when and how he got started against the Jews,' remarked Edwin Pipp, first editor of the *Independent*, who soon quit the magazine rather than print the kind of essays Ford wanted.

Ironically, it was a personal attack that got Ford in trouble now. In the course of its rantings, the *Independent* libelled a lawyer named Aaron Sapiro by claiming that he was a member of 'a band of Jew bankers, lawyers, advertising agencies and produce buyers' who had cheated American farmers as part of a conspiracy to take control of the American wheat market. Sapiro sued for defamation, demanding $1 million in damages. The case would cast a shadow over Ford for much of the first half of 1927.

Ford was scheduled to give testimony in the trial on 1 April, but the day before his appearance he was involved in a strange accident. According to Ford's own account to police, he was driving home from work when two men in

322

a Studebaker forced him from the road. Ford bounced out of control down a steep embankment and crashed into a tree on the bank of the Rouge River. The tree very possibly saved his life, for the river was dangerously swollen from recent heavy rains – the same rains that were causing the Mississippi floods further south. Ford arrived home on foot, dazed and bleeding, with a deep gash over one eye and another serious cut on the top of his head. The two men in the Studebaker were never found.

A widespread presumption was that Ford had faked the crash to avoid having to testify the next day, but the severity of his injuries seemed to belie that. An alternative theory was that Ford, who was a notoriously exasperating motorist to be stuck behind – he drove slowly and in the middle of the road – had been overtaken by a frustrated driver and was accidentally bumped off the road or swerved off in startlement. Whatever the cause, the effect was to stop the libel case from proceeding as planned.

A new trial was scheduled, but Ford decided not to fight. Instead, after lengthy reflection, he issued a seemingly heartfelt letter apologizing to Sapiro personally (and enclosing a cheque for $140,000 to cover his costs) and to Jews generally, and promised never to attack either again. The letter was dated 30 June, but made public on 8 July.

In the letter, Ford claimed that he had been unaware of the terrible things that the *Independent* had been saying about Jews. 'Had I appreciated even the general nature, to say nothing of the details, of these utterances, I would have forbidden their circulation without a moment's hesitation,' he declared in language that was patently not his own. 'I have been greatly shocked as a result of my study of the files of *The Dearborn Independent* and of the pamphlets entitled "The International Jew". All this was a little rich, as many of the charges made against the Jews had been contained in a column signed by Ford or in interviews that he had given to other publications. Joseph Palma, a Ford official who was closely involved with drafting the letter, confided afterwards that Henry Ford had never in fact read his own letter of apology and was only loosely acquainted with its contents.

At all events, the *Independent* ceased its vituperative attacks. With the paper's circulation falling, Ford halved the cover price to a nickel, but still no one bought it, so in late 1927 he closed it. In eight years, it had cost him nearly $5 million.

Ford remained true to his word and never publicly criticized Jews again. That isn't to say that he necessarily abandoned his beliefs, however. Just over a decade later, on his seventy-fifth birthday, he accepted one of Nazi Germany's highest civilian honours – the Grand Cross of the German Eagle – which came garlanded with praise from Adolf Hitler. Only one other prominent American of the period was so admired and honoured by the Nazis (or so openly admired them in return): Charles Lindbergh.

But in 1927 all that lay in the future. For now, with the Sapiro affair out of the way, Henry Ford could turn his attention to some other, more pressing matters. One was a mad scheme to grow rubber in South America. The other was trying to save his business.

CHAPTER 18

IN 1871, A twenty-five-year-old English adventurer named Henry Wickham moved to the steamy far north of Brazil, just below the equator, with his large extended family – wife, mother, brother, sister, sister's fiancé, brother's fiancée and brother's fiancée's mother – and two or three other prospective adventurers who signed on as help. This unlikely group settled at Santarém, at the confluence of the Amazon and Tapajós rivers, with high hopes of becoming rich as planters. The experience proved disastrous. Their crops repeatedly failed and tropical fevers carried off three members of the group in the second year and two more in the third. By 1875, only Wickham and his wife remained. The other survivors had gone back to England.

In an attempt to salvage something from the experience, Wickham travelled upriver and into the jungle, and laboriously collected 70,000 seeds of the Brazilian rubber tree *Hevea brasiliensis*. Rubber was becoming a valued product in the world and had brought great wealth to Manaus, Pará and other Amazonian ports. Brazil controlled

– and jealously guarded – most of the world's output, so Wickham's seed-collecting had to be done furtively and involved a certain measure of personal risk. He brought the seeds back to England, and sold them for a good price to the Royal Botanic Gardens at Kew.

With the money thus made, Wickham went to Queensland, in Australia, to start a tobacco plantation. That failed. Then he went to Central America, to British Honduras, to grow bananas. That venture failed, too. Nothing if not resilient, Wickham recrossed the Pacific to British New Guinea (now Papua New Guinea), took out a twenty-five-year lease on land in the Conflict Islands, and set about collecting sponges, cultivating oysters and producing copra from coconuts. At last he achieved modest success, but the isolation was more than his wife could bear. She decamped to Bermuda and never saw him again.

In the meantime, the rubber seeds Wickham had brought back to England were doing spectacularly well.* Kew sent them to several British colonies and found that they thrived in the rich soils and humid conditions of the tropical Far East – did better, in fact, than in their native jungles. In Brazil, hevea occurred in densities of only three or four trees per hectare, so workers had to cover lots of ground to tap meaningful supplies of latex. In Singapore, Malaya and Sumatra, however, hevea formed luxuriant groves. It had no natural enemies in Asia, so no insects or fungal blights disturbed its growth and the trees rose majestically to heights of one hundred feet. Brazil could

---

* Wickham returned to England around 1910 to find himself a national hero. He was given a life annuity by the British Rubber Growers' Association and knighted by the king.

not compete. Where once it had a virtual monopoly on the world's high-quality rubber, by the 1920s it produced less than 3 per cent.

Roughly four fifths of all that rubber was consumed in the United States, mostly by the automobile industry. (Tyres on early cars needed replacing every 2,000 or 3,000 miles on average, so demand was constant and high.) In the early 1920s when reports circulated that Britain intended to introduce a hefty rubber levy as a way of paying off its war debts, America's Commerce Department under the tireless watch of Herbert Hoover responded with a crash programme to see if there was not some way America could escape its foreign dependence, either by producing its own rubber or inventing a synthetic substitute. Nothing, however, worked. Rubber trees didn't do well anywhere in America and not even Thomas Edison could come up with an artificial version that would work half as well.

Henry Ford took this as a personal challenge. He hated being dependent on suppliers who might raise prices or otherwise take advantage of him, so he always did all in his power to control all the elements of his supply chains. To that end, he owned iron ore and coal mines, forests and lumber mills, the Detroit, Toledo & Iron-town Railroad, and a fleet of ships. When he decided to make his own windshields he became at a stroke the second largest manufacturer of glass in the world. Ford owned 400,000 acres of forests in upper Michigan. At the Ford lumber mills, it was the proud boast that they used every bit of the tree but the shade. Bark, sawdust, sap – all were put to commercial use. (One Ford product still with us from this process is the Kingsford charcoal briquette.) He could not bear the thought of having to stop production because some foreign despot or business cabal was denying him access to some needed product – and by the 1920s he was the single biggest user of rubber on earth. Thus it was in the summer of 1927 that Henry Ford embarked on the most ambitious and ultimately foolish venture of his long life: Fordlandia.

His plan was to build a model American community in the jungles of Brazil and from it run the greatest rubber-producing estate in the world. The Brazilians were so desperate to rejuvenate their moribund rubber industry that they were happy to give Ford almost anything he asked. They sold him two and a half million acres of rain-forest – an area approximately the size of Connecticut – for the knockdown price of $125,000, and excused him for fifty years from paying import duties on materials brought in or export duties on latex sold abroad. He was given per-mission to build his own airports, schools, banks, hospitals and private railways. Essentially Ford was allowed to set up an autonomous state within Brazil. The company was even given permission to dam the Rio Tapajós if that would make it more comfortable and productive.

To supervise and execute this immense project, Ford dispatched a 37-year-old junior manager named Willis Blakeley. Blakeley's instructions were precise and vastly beyond his capabilities. He was to build a complete town with a central square, business district, hospital, cinema, ballroom, golf course and other useful and fulfilling municipal enterprises. Surrounding this were to be residential neighbourhoods of white shingled cottages, each with a neat lawn, flower beds and vegetable gardens.

Artists' illustrations, which the Ford company helpfully provided, showed a tranquil and idyllic community complete with paved streets and Ford cars, in defiance of the obvious fact that there would be nowhere beyond the very modest confines of the town for them to go. Henry Ford considered almost every detail of the undertaking. The clocks would be set to Michigan time and Prohibition would be observed, even though it was not the law of Brazil. Whatever the cost, Fordlandia would be dedicated to American laws, culture and values – an outpost of Protestant ideals in the middle of a hot, godless jungle.

Beyond and around the town would lie the greatest agricultural operation on the planet. Blakeley was not just to plant and nurture forests of towering rubber trees, but also to find industrial uses for all the other fruits of the jungle. Fordlandia would produce paints, fertilizers, medicines and other useful compounds from the leaves and bark and gummy resins of its dense and prolific plant life.

Blakeley had no skills or experience that would allow him to achieve any of this. He was little more than an uneducated thug. Long before he got his first sight of the land he was to manage, he was already proving himself an embarrassment to civilized values. Settling temporarily in the port city of Belém, six days downriver from the site of Fordlandia, he took a suite in the Hotel Grande overlooking the main plaza. There he horrified the locals by walking around naked and making love to his wife with the shutters open in full view of citizens out for their evening constitutionals. He was frequently drunk, generally boastful and always obnoxious. He alienated most of the officials who could help him as well as the business people on whom he would be dependent for supplies.

Using American and Brazilian overseers, Blakeley hired 3,000 labourers to clear the jungle and build the camp, but little went well once work began. Clearing the jungle was a nightmare. Saw blades designed for the soft-wood forests of Michigan spun uselessly against iron-hard Brazilian hardwoods. In the dry season the water level in the Tapajós could fall by as much as forty feet, and for much of the year it was too shallow for boatloads of equipment to reach the plantation. Such equipment as did arrive frequently proved to be useless or at least premature. One crate sent from Detroit contained ice-making machines. Another consignment included a narrow-gauge steam locomotive and several hundred feet of track. Blakeley failed to build adequate storehouses, so supplies spoiled on the riverbanks. Bags of cement absorbed moisture from the air and became hard as rock. Machines and tools rusted and grew unusable. Anything that was remotely portable was pilfered.

Blakeley found moreover that local growers, fearful of his competition, would not sell him seedlings, so his stock had to be imported from the Far East. Although the seeds he brought in were descended from seeds native to Amazonia – Wickham, as it happened, had collected just across the river from the Ford estate – they struggled to thrive when planted on newly cleared land. Blakeley failed to appreciate that hevea was a jungle tree and needed protection from the scorching sun. It had evolved to grow in isolation, so lacked the resistance needed in crowded conditions. When planted together, the trees became magnets for leafhoppers, caterpillars, red mites, whiteflies and other ravenous insects which overwhelmed the trees with devastating effect.

The clearing of great swathes of landscape also exposed to direct sunlight streams that had formerly been heavily shaded. Now algae bloomed as never before, causing snail populations to explode. The snails hosted tiny parasitic worms that harboured schistosomiasis, a horrible disease that leaves its victims chronically prostrate with abdominal pain, high fever, fatigue and diarrhoea. Schistosomiasis had been unknown in the region before Ford came along; after Fordlandia, it was endemic. Malaria, yellow fever, elephantiasis and hookworm were rife as well.

Agonizing discomfort could come from almost anywhere. The river teemed with a little fish, the candiru, or toothpick fish, which would swim into any available human orifice (most notoriously the penis), then extend prickly, backward-facing spines, making it impossible to dislodge. On land, maggots from the botfly *Dermatobia hominis* burrowed into the skin and hatched eggs; victims knew of an infestation when they could see something wriggling just under their skin or when sores erupted and newborn maggots spilled out.

Beyond the camp boundaries, vipers and jaguars lurked in the undergrowth. The natives were universally hostile. By coincidence, this was the area where the British explorer Percy Fawcett had famously vanished two years earlier with his son and another young Englishman while searching for the mythical lost city of Z. Fawcett had developed a theory – more a fixation really – that a great civilization of pale-skinned people had once existed deep in the rainforests and had left behind a magnificent city that awaited rediscovery. He called the city Z for no reason that he ever explained. He had no evidence for its existence; he was driven purely by intuition. Fawcett may have been slightly mad, but he was an experienced explorer. He had been making expeditions through Amazonia since 1906, so he knew his way around. That he and his two companions vanished without trace was something of a testament to how tough conditions were in this part of the world.

One theory was that Fawcett and his companions had been confused with the members of another party of adventurers led by the American Alexander Hamilton Rice, who had been exploring the area at about the same time (to Fawcett's extreme irritation). Rice was fabulously rich thanks to marriage to a wealthy widow, Eleanor Widener (who endowed the Widener Library at Harvard). His wife's money allowed Rice to fund enormous expeditions with all the latest gadgetry. The expedition of 1925 even included an aeroplane – one of the first archaeological expeditions to do so. Rice used the plane for aerial survey-ing but also stocked it with bombs to drop on any jungle natives he found difficult or obstreperous. This naturally left them disinclined to look favourably on any white people who stumbled into their midst, which may explain poor Fawcett's unfortunate end.

Considering that he had three thousand workers at his disposal, Blakeley's achievements were slight. A small section of road was graded and paved. A clinic and dining hall were built. Accommodation was provided, though it was mostly rough and substandard. Superior houses for American managers were sent in kit form from America, but these had been designed by architects in Michigan and showed a complete lack of understanding of jungle conditions. All were provided with heat-retaining metal roofs instead of the traditional thatch, which made them like ovens. No one at Fordlandia was ever comfortable.

Blakeley, having proved largely incompetent, was replaced by Einar Oxholm, a Norwegian sea captain who was described by one impartial observer as a big man with a small mind. Like Blakeley, Oxholm knew nothing about botany, agronomy, the tropics, rubber or anything else that would help him to run a large agricultural operation in the jungle. He was a better human being than Blakeley, but not a more competent one and merely extended the run of ineffectual management.

During Oxholm's unhappy time there, four of his own children died from fevers. Oxholm's maid went bathing in the river one evening and emerged in wide-eyed shock with an arm missing. A caiman had bitten it off. The unfortunate woman bled to death.

Morale, never good, plunged further under Oxholm. Workers were deeply disenchanted over pay and conditions and mystified by the American foods like oatmeal and Jell-O that they were served in the dining hall (though mercifully Ford did not insist on his workers following his soybean diet). Wages were a particularly sore point. Most estate employees had assumed that they would be paid $5 a day, as Ford workers in America were. Instead, they found their pay was 35 cents a day, and from those meagre wages money was deducted for food whether it was eaten or not. The limitations placed on personal freedom – in particular strictures against drinking – were also much resented, especially when the plantation managers could be seen enjoying cocktails on their verandas of an evening.

The upshot is that the employees one night cracked and rioted, running through the camp with machetes, belaying pins and other dangerous implements. Many of the managers had to escape by boat or flee into the jungle until things calmed down.

Eventually, Ford appointed a Scottish-born manager named Archibald Johnston, who was intelligent and able and made many belated improvements. Shops and a school, better housing and a clean water supply were all provided. He and his estate managers even managed to get 700,000 rubber trees growing, but only at the cost of keeping them constantly fumigated against insects and diseases. Even so, workers had to be sent out to pick caterpillars off the trees by hand. The costs were out of all proportion to any possible profits. At the same time, the onset of the Great Depression meant that demand and prices both slumped; then in the Second World War artificial rubber was developed. In 1945, after nearly twenty years of failed efforts, Ford gave up on its Amazonian dream and essentially gave back its jungle estates to the Brazilian government. Many estate employees didn't know the Americans were pulling out until the day they departed. In an ultimate irony, the land was eventually taken over by the American company Cargill and today produces great quantities of soybeans, the agricultural product that Henry Ford esteemed above all others.

If things were going badly for Ford in Amazonia, in Detroit they were doing even worse. For years, Ford's son and heir, Edsel, had argued that the Model T should be retired and replaced with something more stylish, but his father more or less reflexively dismissed almost everything Edsel ever said. Indeed, Henry devoted much of his life to humiliating his son. Although he had appointed Edsel president of the company in 1919, when Edsel was just twenty-five years old, Henry routinely belittled his son in front of others or countermanded his orders. Once when Edsel had a new set of coke ovens built at the River Rouge factory, Henry waited until the work was finished and then ordered them taken down.

But now with sales plummeting Henry had to acknowledge, if not exactly admit, that the Model T had had its day. On 26 May, while the world was in the grip of Lindbergh mania, the Ford Motor Company produced what it claimed was its fifteen-millionth Model T (in fact, it was at least number 15,348,781, if not more – no one really knew), and immediately stopped production in order to build an entirely new car. For an indefinite period, the world's largest car manufacturer would have no new products to sell. Sixty thousand Ford employees in Detroit were immediately thrown out of work. Tens of thousands more at assembly plants across America and throughout the world were similarly idled. Most would be out of work for at least six months, many considerably longer. The shutdown was hard on Ford's long-suffering dealers as well, particularly those with city showrooms with high rents. Many never fully recovered.

Work on the new car was done in the utmost secrecy. Not even the name was revealed. Many guessed that it would be called the Edison after Henry Ford's close friend and hero. Only a few within the company knew that it was to be called the Model A. Rumours abounded as to what was going on within the plant. Henry Ford was said to be living in the factory, sleeping on a camp bed in his office or in one of the workshops. (He wasn't.) The amount of work involved in producing a new car from scratch was daunting, to say the least. It was almost certainly the biggest industrial retooling ever undertaken anywhere, before or since. The new car would contain 5,580 separate components, nearly all of them brand new, so all had to be designed afresh – and not just the parts themselves, but also several thousand new machines to make the parts. Some of these were enormous. Two power presses stood almost three storeys high and weighed 240 tons each.

Remarkably, the company did almost all of the design and retooling without expert guidance, for Henry Ford hated experts and refused to employ them. As he put it in his 1924 book *My Life and Work*: 'I never employ an expert in full bloom. If ever I wanted to kill opposition by unfair means I would endow the opposition with experts.' Later he added: 'We have most unfortunately found it necessary to get rid of a man as soon as he thinks himself an expert – because no one ever considers himself expert if he really knows his job.'

In consequence, Ford had no one on the payroll with advanced engineering or design engineering skills. The company didn't even have a proving ground, but tested its cars on public highways, to the dismay of the police. Ford's chief tester, Ray Dahlinger, was a man of very few words. He offered only two terse verdicts on any car: it was either 'damn good' or 'no damn good'. 'You could never get any details from him as to what was wrong or what needed improvement,' sighed one engineer. The company did have a stylish research lab, designed by Kahn, but Henry Ford

refused to invest in precision instruments or other useful
tools. Much of the space was given over to his experiments
with soybeans and other foods.

Ford's refusal to employ experts was what doomed
Fordlandia and now it threatened to doom the Model A.
For years, the Model T had been criticized for having unreliable brakes. Many states were beginning to require
annual safety inspections, and there were fears within Ford
that Model Ts wouldn't pass the examinations. Germany
was reportedly considering banning the Model T outright
because of concerns over the brakes' safety. For that reason,
Lawrence Sheldrick, Ford's top engineer, made sure new,
safer brakes were designed for the new Model A. Henry
Ford bitterly resented the idea of outsiders telling him
how to make his products, and for some time through the
summer refused on principle to let the safer brakes be
incorporated into the new car, slowing progress further.

As Charles E. Sorensen, a long-suffering Ford
executive, later noted, no rational business person would
have stopped production of the Model T without having a
replacement model designed and ready to go into production. Putting the new car together on the fly, Sorensen
calculated, added between $100 million and $200 million
to the cost of the changeover. The additional costs of
Henry Ford's intransigence were beyond computation.

On 26 July, four days before Henry Ford's sixty-fourth
birthday, General Motors declared first half earnings of
$129 million. No manufacturer had ever made that much
money in six months before – and that was on sales made
before the Ford shutdown. Now with Ford making no cars
at all, his competitors had the marketplace all to themselves. How well, or even whether, Ford could recover from

such an extended shutdown was a question many within the industry were beginning to ask.

The rest of the world was beside itself with curiosity to know what Henry Ford would come up with as a replacement for the Model T. What the world didn't know was that many within Ford were just as curious to have that question answered themselves.

CHAPTER 19

BEFORE THE 1920s, Florida was known for citrus fruits and turpentine and not much else. A few rich people went there for the winter, but hardly anyone else considered the state a destination. But then the wider mass of Americans discovered the attractiveness of Florida's climate and the pleasantness of its beaches, and it suddenly became desirable. In 1925, Florida repealed income and inheritance taxes, which made it even more attractive. People swarmed into the state in huge numbers and began an intense and increasingly irrational property boom.

A plot of land in Miami that had been worth $800 before the boom now sold for $150,000. Property deeds sometimes changed hands two or even three times in a day as frantic buyers tried to trade their way to ever greater wealth. Some eager buyers bought plots of land under water on the hopeful understanding that they would soon become prized beachfront through the miracle of landfill. (And in some cases, it must be said, that actually happened.) The *Miami Herald* carried so many property ads that one Sunday edition ran to 504 pages.

One of those drawn to Florida was Yankees owner Jacob Ruppert. Ruppert bought ten thousand acres on Tampa Bay with plans to build a resort community, modestly called Ruppert Beach, on a scale to rival Coral Gables or Palm Beach. As part of the process, he moved spring training to nearby St Petersburg in 1925. Conditions were a little rough at first. At one practice, Babe Ruth was unable to take his place in the field until a groundsman chased an alligator back into the swamp beyond the (unfenced) right field boundary. Ruppert gave the development a catchy slogan – 'Where Every Breath Brings Added Health and Every Moment Pleasure' – and the promise that this would be the finest investment opportunity on the Gulf Coast. In the spring of 1926, Ruppert Beach was advertising building plots as being available from $5,000 – 'at the moment'.

Then disaster struck. On 18 and 19 September 1926, a massive hurricane, the first of notable proportions in twenty years, crashed into Florida, laying waste to Miami Beach and much else beyond. Four hundred and fifteen people were killed. Eighteen thousand were made homeless. The bottom dropped out of the property market all over Florida, even where the storm didn't hit. Carl Fisher, a businessman from Indiana who had more or less started the boom, saw his net worth fall from $500 million to less than $50,000. Also hit hard was Jacob Ruppert. When the storm passed, he was left with nothing but 'ten thousand acres of alligators and seagulls', according to one contemporary observer. Ruppert Beach was never built.

In consequence of the hurricane, Ruppert entered

1927 in a fiscally cautious frame of mind and with heightened respect for the unparalleled earning power of America's newest sporting infatuation: boxing.

To a surprising extent, boxing was a 1920s phenomenon. Although people had been smacking each other around in rings for over two hundred years, prize-fighting in the 1920s acquired three things it had never had before: respectability, mass appeal and Jack Dempsey. Together they made it a sumptuously lucrative pastime. It was this that stirred the interest of men like Jacob Ruppert.

The rise of modern boxing could be assigned any number of starting points, but a reasonable place to begin is with Jess Willard. Willard was a giant Kansas ploughboy, and would permanently have remained so except that a boxing promoter spotted him throwing 500-pound bales around as if they were scatter cushions and encouraged him to take up fighting. This was in about 1910. At six feet six inches and 225 pounds, Willard was certainly built for the game. He proved to be a terrifyingly powerful puncher. In his fifth bout, against a promising young fighter named Joe Young, he hit the poor youth so hard that the blow drove a piece of Young's jaw up into his brain and killed him. Willard scythed his way through a number of opponents, then became heavyweight champion of the world by knocking out the great – but conspicuously black and recklessly outspoken – Jack Johnson in twenty-six rounds in Havana.

Willard's victory provided a crucial, if not laudable, milestone for boxing: it gave it a white heavyweight champion, a shamefully necessary prerequisite for it to become a popular mainstream sport. Before this time, boxing was virtually the only sport in America – indeed, pretty much the only activity – in which blacks could compete with whites on equal terms. It is an ironic point from a modern perspective, but part of the reason boxing was considered unwholesome and insupportably raffish before about 1920 was that it *wasn't* racist. And a big part of converting it into a respectable entertainment in the 1920s was making sure that it was, like all other major sports, dominated by white people. No black fighter would get a crack at the heavyweight title for a generation.

With only white boxers to fight, Willard began to look invincible. Then he met Jack Dempsey. Their fight, on the Fourth of July 1919 in Toledo, Ohio, attracted enormous attention. Dempsey was a hot young boxer from out of the west. Willard had actually killed a man in the ring. This was a combination the public could not resist.

Toledo was chosen not because it was a popular place for boxing, but because it was a legal one, and in 1919 there were not so many of those. In most places – New York State, most notably – boxing was banned altogether or so ringed around with restrictions as to make it ridiculous. Prize fights, where they were allowed at all, had to be advertised as 'sparring exhibitions' or 'illustrated lectures on pugilism', with the participants sometimes described as 'professors'. Because the matches were only exhibitions, it was forbidden for one participant to knock out another or for a panel of judges to declare one man the winner. In consequence, prize-fighting remained a marginal sport and fights were held in (no disrespect to Toledo intended) marginal places.

Toledo didn't have a stadium sufficient to hold a crowd of 90,000 so one was built, to be used just once, then torn down. To keep gatecrashers out, Tex Rickard, the promoter, had it constructed with a single entrance and exit. Had fire broken out the consequences would have been unimaginable, but at least they had the wisdom to ban smoking for the duration of the contest.

Willard entered the fight supremely confident. Dempsey was scrawny-looking for a heavyweight, slender and wiry rather than bulgingly muscled. Willard was a full head taller and sixty pounds heavier. 'This will be one of the easiest bouts I've ever had,' he assured reporters, adding with a dash of bigoted loftiness that was distasteful even then, 'I am better today than when I restored the championship to the white race.' As a demonstration of his confidence, he demanded to be indemnified in case he killed the challenger.

This proved to be something of a misjudgement. Dempsey may have been scrawny, but he was built of iron – hitting him, it was said, was like hitting a tree – and he attacked with startling ferocity, flying at his opponents like a loosened pit bull and pummelling them with merciless intensity. He had just won twelve fights in a row, nine with knockouts in the first round, one in just fourteen seconds. He was an unbelievably destructive fighter, and he proved it now.

Dempsey charged from his corner and smashed Willard's jaw so hard that he broke it in thirteen places, then followed up with a hook that sprayed six of his teeth across the canvas. Dempsey floored him seven times in the first round, then pounded away at him for two rounds more, cracking his cheekbone and at least two ribs. Dazed and disheartened, Willard failed to rise for the fourth round. For the rest of his life Willard insisted that the tape under Dempsey's gloves had been coated with concrete. It appears that it merely felt that way.

Dempsey's purse for his title fight against Willard was $27,500. Within two years, he would be fighting for purses of nearly $1 million, and the whole world would be his audience. Boxing had just changed for ever.

Damon Runyon dubbed him 'the Manassa Mauler', but the name was no more than partly correct. Dempsey didn't maul, but struck with deadly, repetitious precision, and Manassa, a small agricultural community in southern Colorado near the New Mexico border, was his home for just the first ten years of his life. After that he grew up all over – in Denver and smaller towns in Colorado, Utah and West Virginia – as his alcoholic and ne'er-do-well father drifted hazily from job to job.

He was born William Harrison Dempsey – his family called him Harry – in June 1895 (four months after Babe Ruth), into a clan that was unusually mongrel: part Cherokee, part Jewish, part Scots-Irish. Dempsey was the ninth of thirteen children, and the family was poor but close – a fact that would weigh heavily on him in the summer of 1927. As a youth he made a living by entering bars and challenging anyone in the place to fight him for a kitty collected from the other patrons. It made him awfully tough. From there it was only a short step to boxing for a living. He began to fight professionally in 1914, using the name 'Kid Blackie'. Along the way, he picked up a wife, Maxine Cates, a saloon-bar piano player and occasional prostitute fifteen years his senior. The marriage, not altogether surprisingly, didn't last. They separated after just a few months. (She would die horribly in a fire in a brothel in Juarez, Mexico, in 1924.)

As a fighter, Dempsey was instinctively brutal. 'In the

ring he seemed to enjoy hurting other people,' writes his biographer Roger Kahn. Once, in a bad mood, he knocked out every one of his sparring partners. When the writer Paul Gallico, then sports editor of the *New York Daily News*, accepted an assignment to spar a little with Dempsey, to demonstrate what it was like to face the champ, Dempsey hit him hard enough to kill him. Gallico didn't remember a thing, but reported afterwards that he felt like a building had fallen on him. The sportswriter Grantland Rice, who was present, wrote: 'At the end, the head of young Mr Gallico was attached to his body by a shred. We only hope he is not asked next to cover an electrocution.' Al Jolson, in a similar spirit, took a playful swing at Dempsey for photographers. Dempsey smacked Jolson so hard it split open his chin.

Yet the instant a fight was over, Dempsey would often bound forward and solicitously help to his feet the person he had just made horizontal. Although he looked every inch a villain with his prison haircut and steely gaze, in private Dempsey was a pleasant, rather shy, surprisingly thoughtful and articulate individual.

Nothing about Dempsey's fight against Willard in Toledo did more to excite entrepreneurial spirits than the knowledge that Tex Rickard had spent $100,000 on a temporary arena and still made a fortune on the undertaking. The crowd of 90,000 was the biggest ever to attend a sporting event anywhere on the planet – and in Toledo, Ohio, for goodness' sake. Boxing was clearly too lucrative to be left to marginal cities in the distant west, especially when existing venues like Yankee Stadium and the Polo Grounds stood unused for 250 days or more a year. Almost at once, New York State Senator (and soon-to-be New York

City Mayor) Jimmy Walker shepherded a bill through the legislature making boxing fully legal in New York. Other states quickly followed.

Boxing still faced a great deal of opposition in some quarters, however. Many people were horrified by its violence and brutality. Others fretted that it was an incitement to gambling. The Reverend John Roach Straton saw a worrisome threat to morals in allowing members of the weaker sex to gaze upon 'two practically naked men, battering and bruising each other and struggling in sweat and blood for mere animal mastery'.

In fact, as it turned out, that was very much what women wanted, and the person they most keenly wished to see glistening and lightly clad was the French boxer Georges Carpentier. He was, by universal female consent, an eyeful. 'Michelangelo would have fainted for joy at the beauty of his profile,' wrote one smitten female observer, and her comments were echoed in ladies' magazines across the land. Women simply adored him. When Gene Tunney beat Carpentier in a later fight, a distraught blonde leapt into the ring and tried to scratch his eyes out.

Carpentier was not a great fighter, and occasionally resorted to a helpful fix. This didn't always work out quite as planned. In 1922 in Paris, a Senegalese fighter known as Battling Siki agreed, for a generous consideration, to take a fall against Carpentier. Unfortunately, Siki forgot his commitment and instead knocked out the dumbfounded Frenchman in the sixth round. For Siki it was the high point of a mostly disappointing life. He never won another important match, and in 1925 was shot dead for no apparent reason on a Manhattan street. The murderer was never caught.

Carpentier landed a fight with Dempsey based almost entirely on three considerations: that he looked strong, made the ladies swoon and was a war hero. (He had been a decorated aviator in the First World War, in which capacity he became great pals with Charles Nungesser.) The fight attracted unprecedented levels of public interest. Reporters came from across the world. The *New York American* hired George Bernard Shaw to comment. H. L. Mencken, in an essay, expressed his satisfaction that it was a fight between white men.

Carpentier claimed to have developed a secret punch that would catch Dempsey by surprise. Damon Runyon suggested that he would be better off practising taking ten-second naps since that was mostly what he would be doing during the fight. Before the bout, Rickard beseeched Dempsey: 'Don't kill the son of a bitch, Jack.' Rickard wasn't concerned about Carpentier's well-being, but about what a death would do to boxing just as it was getting lucrative and respectable. 'The best people in the world are here today,' he said. 'If you kill him, all this will be ruined. Boxing will be dead.'

It did not take long for Carpentier to discover how out-classed he was. Dempsey broke his nose with his first punch. Soon afterwards, Carpentier hit Dempsey in the face with the hardest punch he could throw. Dempsey barely blinked. Carpentier broke his thumb in two places. Dempsey took just four rounds to demolish the Frenchman and leave him unconscious on his back in the middle of the ring. From beginning to end, the fight lasted twenty-seven minutes. The gate was $1,626,580 – a fourfold increase from the Dempsey–Willard fight of just two years earlier.

The problem for Dempsey now became an absence of

opponents rash enough or worthy enough to climb into the ring with him. Boxing might well have lost its momentum had it not been for the timely arrival on American soil of an Argentinian giant named Luis Angel Firpo – 'the Wild Bull of the Pampas', as he was extravagantly but accurately dubbed. A poor youth from Buenos Aires, Firpo arrived in America in 1922 carrying a cardboard suitcase that held one spare shirt collar, a pair of boxing trunks and nothing else.

He was not a stylish fighter – 'he punches like a man throwing rocks' is how one observer put it – but he was huge and powerful, and he now proceeded to club to the canvas one opponent after another. By the time he met Dempsey at the Polo Grounds in September 1923, he had won twelve fights in a row – nine by knockout. Like Dempsey, he was a fighter who was prepared to stand in one place and slug it out. The world couldn't wait to see what Dempsey would make of him. What followed was perhaps the most exciting four minutes of slugging ever seen in the ring.

Firpo brought a gasp to 80,000 pairs of lips by dropping Dempsey to one knee with his very first punch. Dempsey responded furiously and knocked down Firpo seven times in the first round, but Firpo got up each time swinging. After the seventh knockdown, Firpo reached back and caught Dempsey with a right hook so ferocious that it knocked the champ through the ropes and clear out of the ring. Dempsey fell into the crowd at ringside, and was pushed back by many sets of eager hands – 'so many that it looked like he was getting a back massage', Firpo recalled later. Among the enthusiastic pushers was Babe Ruth, beaming all over. Dempsey should have been disqualified for receiving assistance, but the referee let the fight continue.

In the first minute of the next round, Dempsey hit Firpo in the head with two mighty blows and Firpo slumped to the canvas not to rise again. Most reporters declared it the most exciting fight they had ever seen. Grantland Rice thought it the most exciting fight there had ever been.

And then Dempsey stopped boxing. Fights were mooted and even negotiated, but in every instance came to nought. From September 1923 to September 1926, Dempsey didn't fight at all. Instead, he settled in Los Angeles, acted in a couple of movies, had his nose fixed, married a minor movie star named Estelle Taylor (and slept with several others), and became pals with Charlie Chaplin and Douglas Fairbanks.

Dempsey's brother Johnny, who nurtured dreams of being a Hollywood star himself, was in Los Angeles already and had formed friendships of his own with several well-known figures, in particular a matinee idol named Wallace Reid, then one of the biggest box office draws in movies. Reid had the wholesome good looks of the boy every mother wants her daughter to marry, but in private life he was secretly and deeply addicted to narcotics. From Reid Johnny Dempsey learned the dangerous pleasures of cocaine and heroin. Reid died from the cumulative effects of dissipation in 1923 at the age of just thirty-one, but not before he had made Johnny Dempsey an addict, too. The young Dempsey's drug problems and deteriorating mental state would be a prolonged and painful distraction for his brother Jack.

In 1926, Philadelphia held a world's fair, called the Sesquicentennial Exposition, to mark the 150th anniversary of the Declaration of Independence. The enterprise was a fiasco from the start. The site chosen was marshy and difficult to build on. The vision for the fair was grand, but the funding meagre. The state of Pennsylvania declined to contribute anything to the costs.

Construction efforts fell so far behind that hardly any exhibits were finished when the fair opened on 31 May 1926. President Coolidge declined to attend and sent his secretary of state, Frank B. Kellogg, and omnipresent commerce secretary, Herbert Hoover. The park that greeted them was embarrassingly incomplete. An eighty-foot-high Liberty Bell, the exposition centrepiece, was still shrouded in scaffolding. Work hadn't even started on the New York State pavilion. The tardiest exhibition of all was Argentina's, which was dedicated on 30 October, just in time for the exposition's closing.

It rained almost all summer and into the autumn, depressing crowds in every sense of the word. The exposition had just one successful event. On the evening of 23 September, in a stadium otherwise rarely used, Jack Dempsey squared off against an up-and-coming young boxer named Gene Tunney in Dempsey's first fight in almost exactly three years.

After Dempsey's long layoff, interest in the fight was huge. One reporter, with just a hint of excess, called it 'the greatest battle since the Silurian Age'. The paid attendance was 120,000, but it is believed that as many as 135,000 packed in. Tunney was an intelligent boxer but a light hitter, and it was widely agreed that he would be overwhelmed by Dempsey's power. In fact, Tunney fought a brilliant and perfect fight, jabbing sharply, then wheeling away from Dempsey's killer right hand. Dempsey stalked him all night, while Tunney stung him repeatedly with sharp but wearing jabs. The effect was cumulatively formidable. By the seventh round, Dempsey's face was a swollen mess. One of his eyes was sealed shut and the other wasn't far behind. He chased Tunney all night, but managed to land just one good punch. Tunney won easily on points.

When the bruised and puffy-faced Dempsey arrived home afterwards, his horrified wife asked what had happened. 'Honey, I forgot to duck,' Dempsey famously replied.

Dempsey's defeat caused near universal dismay, but set the scene for the biggest rematch in boxing history. A small round of qualifying bouts was arranged as a way of maximizing excitement while milking the situation for every cent it would yield. The first qualifying bout was between Jack Sharkey and Jim Maloney. (This was the fight, mentioned on p. 130, at which 23,000 people paused to pray for Charles Lindbergh, who was at that moment alone over the Atlantic.) The winner of that fight – which in the event was Sharkey, easily – would then face a grand qualifying match against the ageing but formidable Jack Dempsey on 22 July. The venue for both qualifying bouts was Yankee Stadium – a matter that naturally warmed the heart of Jacob Ruppert.

So as July dawned on America – in the week that Richard Byrd and his team splashed down off the coast of France, that New York suffered its first heatwave, that Calvin Coolidge celebrated his fifty-fifth birthday by donning cowboy apparel, that Charles Lindbergh took off for Ottawa, that Henry Ford's minions prepared his apology to Jews, and that the world's leading central bankers assembled in secret conclave on Long Island – the story that preoccupied the nation was how fit and eager Jack Dempsey was. Scores of reporters filed daily reports from his training camp at Saratoga Lake, New York, suggesting that he was looking menacing and resolute and that his punches had a snap to them not seen in years.

Then came terrible news. On 2 July, a police car arrived at Dempsey's camp to inform him of a family tragedy. Dempsey's brother Johnny had gone increasingly off the rails in recent months, so much so that his young wife, Edna, had fled to the east with their infant child. Johnny Dempsey had tracked them to a boarding house in Schenectady, just twenty miles from his brother's training camp, and there he had shot and killed Edna, then turned the gun on himself. He didn't harm their child.

Jack Dempsey was devastated. The police drove him to Schenectady to identify the bodies. Then Dempsey returned to his camp, retired to his cabin and would not respond to knocking, leaving everyone to wonder what would become of the fight. To universal relief, after two days of seclusion Dempsey emerged from his cabin and grimly resumed training.

In Paris, Commander Byrd's crew, their formal commitments dealt with, celebrated their last night in the city a little more colourfully than Lindbergh ever had. Bert Acosta – or 'sleek, swart Bert Acosta', as *Time* magazine called him – took George Noville to some of the seamier night spots of Montmartre for an evening of jazz and cheerful abandon. Bernt Balchen was taken out for a drunken Viking evening by a group of Scandinavians based in Paris. Byrd declined to join either party and instead had an early night.

Levine and Chamberlin were in Paris at the same time, but seem to have been somewhat excluded from the celebrations. Levine, belatedly realizing the importance of public relations, abruptly gave 100,000 francs, or $4,000, to the Aéro-Club de France to build a clubhouse at Le Bourget. He also called on Madame Nungesser, who was now getting more than a little creepy in her stout refusal to accept that her son was gone for ever and not afloat on the North Atlantic, surviving comfortably on fish that he and Coli hauled gleaming from the sea while awaiting rescue from a passing ship.

Levine proposed to the other Atlantic flyers that they fly home together in their two planes, but the invitation was declined, partly because the Byrd plane was a wreck (it would never fly again), partly because a westward flight against the prevailing winds was insanely risky, and partly because no one wanted to be that close to Levine. Chamberlin decided that he had had enough of Europe (and probably Levine) and would sail home with the Byrd team on the SS *Leviathan* in a few days. Levine had promised Chamberlin $25,000 for his part in their adventure, but in the end paid him much less than half that.

A week after landing in French waters, the Byrd party travelled back to Normandy, to Le Touquet, where they had dinner with the Prince of Wales, then proceeded on to Cherbourg to board their ship home. Their sailing was given a giant three-deck headline and 5,000 words of coverage in the *New York Times*, as if it was in itself an act of heroism.

Then things went eerily quiet aviationwise. With Byrd and his team at sea, Lindbergh locked away on Long Island writing *We*, and Levine talking mostly nonsense, there was nothing aeronautical left to write about. On 12 July, for the first time in six weeks, no aviation story led the front page of the *Times*. At the bottom of page one, however, was a small story so curious as to be worth mentioning.

The previous day in Canada, according to an Associated Press report, a plane doing aerial survey work for the Canadian government had taken off from an airfield near Lake Manitoba. The plane carried a pilot, photographer and surveyor. The weather was good. Several witnesses reported that the plane climbed to about 2,000 feet in a normal manner, but then, as it emerged from a cloudbank and as onlookers watched in bewildered horror, the three occupants left the plane one after another and plunged to their deaths. What caused them to jump or fall is a question to which no plausible answer could ever be supplied.

The main news by mid-July was of a new and more brutal heatwave that was settling over much of the nation. In New York on 13 July, the temperature rose to 91 degrees at four in the afternoon, and broke 100 degrees elsewhere. By Saturday 16 July, the number of deaths in the city attributed to the heat was twenty-three and throughout the east it was at least sixty. In New York City, half a dozen of the victims drowned while trying to cool off. One lucky survivor was an eight-year-old boy named Leo Brzozowsky who was found floating in an inner tube five miles out in lower New York Bay. He had been in the water for at least five hours and was roughly halfway between Staten Island and Keansburg, New Jersey, when he was rescued by a passing motorboat. The boy was fully dressed – he was even wearing shoes – and was unable to explain why he had gone into the water fully clothed or how he had got so far from shore. Doctors said he was exhausted but would make a full recovery.

On 16 July, a torrential afternoon downpour cooled things off but brought chaos, too. Lightning knocked out power in several neighbourhoods and killed a couple sheltering beneath a tree on Staten Island and a policeman on a street corner in Brooklyn. Trains to and from Coney Island were stalled by flooded tracks and short-circuited electrical systems just as several hundred thousand people were trying to get home from the beaches. The rain caused much flash flooding. In Brooklyn, a 27-year-old man managed the unusual feat of drowning in his basement when six feet of water flooded in.

The worst heat-related disaster of the summer was not on the east coast, but on Lake Michigan at Chicago when some seventy-five people, mostly women and children, crowded on to a commercial pleasure launch for a trip on the lake in the hope of catching a breeze. As the boat cruised just offshore, a squall blew up. The passengers merrily raced to the sheltered side of the craft to escape the driving rain, but this unbalanced the boat and it capsized. Twenty-seven people drowned. Among those who rushed to the rescue was Johnny Weissmuller, not yet famous as Hollywood's Tarzan but celebrated for having won three gold medals in swimming at the 1924 Olympic Games in Paris. Weissmuller happened to be on the beach at the time of the capsizing and reportedly recovered a number of bodies, both living and dead.

* * *

The *Leviathan* arrived in New York in rain and fog on 18

July. Byrd and his crew, accompanied by Clarence Chamberlin, were transferred to the mayoral yacht, the *Macom*, where they were surprised to find waiting for them, rather secretly, Charles Lindbergh. Byrd was clearly touched that Lindbergh had come to greet them, but also no doubt relieved that Lindbergh declined to join them for the afternoon on the grounds that this was their day and he didn't wish to be a distraction. Lindbergh was surely glad to let someone else have the world's attention for a day.

As it was, the celebrations that followed were a little muted by Lindbergh standards, though this owed at least as much to the sodden weather as to jaded public sentiment. Byrd and his men, accompanied by Chamberlin, were placed in open-topped cars for a parade up Broadway. Unfortunately, the heavens opened in a clattering torrent just as they set off, driving many thousands of onlookers to scatter for cover and leaving Byrd and his men as drenched as if they had swum ashore. At City Hall a big viewing platform had been erected for a presentation ceremony, but about a hundred of the chairs were conspicuously empty, and about half the crowd melted away during the speeches as the rain continued to fall heavily.

A thought on many people's minds was whether the rain would ease for the Dempsey–Sharkey fight. Happily, it did. Though the air was thundery, the rain held off and the fighters and spectators enjoyed a comparatively cool, dry evening on 20 July. Eighty-five thousand people turned out at Yankee Stadium (more than had ever attended a baseball game, but then for a boxing match thousands of extra seats could be put on the playing field – and never mind that many in them couldn't see very much) – and the gate of $1,250,000 was a record for a non-title fight. Among those attending were Mayor Jimmy Walker, Franklin Delano Roosevelt, the cowboy star Tom Mix, the publisher Bernarr Macfadden and the Maharajah of Ratlam (or very possibly someone who fooled the world into thinking he was a maharajah). Two people who went almost entirely unnoticed in the crowd were Richard Byrd and Clarence Chamberlin.

Sharkey was the six-to-five favourite, based largely on the consideration that he was twenty-five years old and on the rise while Dempsey was thirty-two and all but retired. Sharkey was from Boston, the son of Lithuanian immigrants who had endowed him with magnificent strength and a name that no one could spell. It was variously rendered in official records as Zuhauskay, Zuhauskas, Coccoskey and Cukochsay before Sharkey chose his nom de ring as more sleekly American-sounding. He took 'Jack' from his greatest hero – Jack Dempsey.

The fight was disappointingly restrained. Dempsey was much less aggressive than of old. Sharkey dealt with his cautious attacks easily, and led comfortably through the first six rounds. In the seventh, however, Sharkey did the most brainless thing a boxer can do. Frustrated by Dempsey's repeated low blows, he turned to the referee to complain and Dempsey tagged him on the chin, knocking him out cold. Photographs show Sharkey dropped on the canvas like a discarded overcoat. Dempsey was declared the winner. He would now meet Gene Tunney in a rematch on 22 September in Chicago. It would be the biggest fight in history, and the most controversial.

An ecstatic Jacob Ruppert announced plans to increase

the seating capacity at Yankee Stadium by extending the decks down the left-field line, which would let him accommodate 90,000 spectators at boxing matches. This news was greeted with a certain cynicism among newsmen, who pointed out that many spectators were already so distantly seated that it had been like watching a bout through an inverted telescope. As one reporter put it only semi-wryly, at the conclusion of the fight hundreds of fans rushed from the stadium and 'bought late extras to find out what had happened'.

The next day Sharkey was rushed to hospital with severe internal bleeding. Happily, he made a full recovery, but it was a striking reminder that Dempsey, even in restrained mode, still hit with mighty force.

On the afternoon following the Dempsey–Sharkey bout, Charles Lindbergh, now embarked on his national tour, arrived in Boston in an unusually perky fashion. Coming in to land at the recently opened Boston Airport (on the site of the present Logan Airport), he raced across Boston Harbor just above the waterline, then at the last possible instant shot straight up into the sky to the point where it looked as if his plane must surely stall, then nonchalantly rolled to one side in a graceful arc and made a pinpoint landing, coming to a halt just before the doors of the hangar set aside for his arrival – all this in a plane with no brakes or forward visibility. The delighted roar of the crowd could be heard on Boston Common, three miles away.

The centre of Boston was a mass of people – 'the greatest throng that has ever gathered in this city to greet any man or body of men', in the words of one commentator.

Though the crowd was good-natured, it was so vast and rolling as to be essentially beyond control. When the Lindbergh motorcade arrived at the Common, the mass instinctively surged forward for a better view. Such was the momentum, reported the correspondent for the *New York Times*, that 'those nearest the middle were lifted bodily from their feet by the human pressure . . . Many women and children fainted and were saved from serious injury because the very weight of others round them prevented them from falling to the ground and being trampled under foot.'

Two soldiers and a policeman who tried to go to the aid of a woman who had fainted were themselves carried away, as if on a great tide. Others struggled not to be pushed under the wheels of the cautiously advancing motorcade. It was a wonder that many weren't crushed or asphyxiated. As it was, one man died of a heart attack and over a hundred were injured seriously enough to need treatment at field stations that had been set up around the Common. Fourteen people required hospitalization, and nearly everyone, according to the *Times* correspondent, 'returned home with bruised bodies and torn clothing'.

None of this would get better as the tour proceeded. Jostled, pounded on the back, tearfully adored, Charles Lindbergh was beginning to realize that this was not a passing thing. This was now his life.

It must have seemed as if nothing could eclipse the intensity of interest in him, but in fact something was about to, at least temporarily. In a prison nearby – close enough that those inside could clearly hear the cheers that greeted Lindbergh's arrival – two mild-mannered Italian anarchists sat on death row awaiting execution for murders that millions of people across the planet were certain they did not commit.

Their names were Nicola Sacco and Bartolomeo Vanzetti, and because of them the world was about to light up once more.

AUGUST
THE ANARCHISTS

'I never know, never heard, even read in history anything so cruel as this court.'

Nicola Sacco on being sentenced to death

Chapter 20

JUST AFTER 3 P.M. on a mild, sunny afternoon in April
1920, two employees of the Slater & Morrill Shoe
Company in South Braintree, Massachusetts, set off along
a dusty, sloping road from the company's offices on
Railroad Avenue to a separate factory building about two
hundred yards away on Pearl Street. Frederick Parmenter
was a payroll clerk, Alessandro Berardelli was his guard.
They were carrying $15,776.51 in cash in two metal boxes,
the week's wages for five hundred employees. Their route
took them past another shoe factory, Rice and Hutchins,
which occupied a five-storey building hard by the road,
giving it a dark and looming air.

As Parmenter and Berardelli passed the Rice and
Hutchins factory, two men who had been loitering nearby
stepped forward and demanded the cash boxes. Before
Berardelli could respond, one of the robbers shot him
three times. Berardelli sank to his knees and fell forward
on to his hands, head hanging. He coughed up blood and
struggled to breathe. The gunman then turned to
Parmenter, who was looking on aghast, and shot him.

Stunned and gravely wounded, Parmenter dropped the cash box and staggered into the road in a reflexive attempt to get away. One of the robbers – it is not clear from witness accounts which it was, or even whether a third gunman now appeared – followed Parmenter into the road and calmly dropped him with a single shot in the back. A gunman – again, witnesses could not agree which – turned to the crouching Berardelli and fired two shots into him from above, killing him.

A blue car containing two or possibly three other men screeched up, collected the robbers and cash boxes, and sped off across the tracks of the New York, New Haven & Hartford Railroad, firing at onlookers as it went. The entire incident lasted no more than a minute. It is testament to how swift and shocking the robbery was that witnesses could not agree even roughly on how many gunmen they saw or which did the shooting.

No one would ever have guessed that this cold-blooded but fairly commonplace killing on a back lane of South Braintree would capture the world's attention, but what happened there that day made it the most conse-quential crime scene on earth in the 1920s. Today little remains from that afternoon. The factory buildings are long gone, as are the cafés and small businesses that stood scattered along the street. Braintree is no longer a factory town but a pleasant suburb, twelve miles south of Boston. Pearl Street is a busy thoroughfare with turning lanes and traffic lights on gantries above the road. Where Parmenter and Berardelli fell is the site of a neighbourhood shopping centre, Pearl Plaza, anchored by a Shaw's supermarket and Office Max supplies store. Beside a railway bridge that wasn't there in 1927 is a small memorial to the two victims of the crime, erected in 2010 on the ninetieth anniversary of the robbery.

Berardelli died at the scene. He was forty-five years old and, like the two men eventually convicted of his killing, from Italy. He had worked for Slater & Morrill for about a year, and left a wife and two children. Parmenter died at Quincy City Hospital the next morning. A devoted church-goer who was popular with his workmates, he also left a wife and two children. That is about all that is known of the two victims.

The getaway car, a stolen Buick, was found abandoned at a place called Manley Woods two days later. Police at that time were looking for the perpetrators of a similar, botched hold-up in nearby Bridgewater the previous Christmas Eve. Chief Michael E. Stewart of the Bridgewater Police Department decided, for reasons unattached to evidence, that the culprits in both cases were Italian anarchists. He discovered that a man of radical sympathies named Ferruccio Coacci lived near where the getaway car was found and for that reason made him the chief suspect. As the *New Yorker* archly noted some time later, Stewart concluded 'that after a hold-up and murder, the murderer would naturally abandon the car practically in his own front yard'.

Although Stewart was indeed the chief of police for Bridgewater, the title suggests a scale of operations that considerably exceeded the reality. Stewart's 'force' was a single part-time assistant. Stewart himself had no training in investigating murders and almost no experience of serious crimes. That is no doubt why he investigated with such enthusiasm. This was the chance of a lifetime for him.

Coacci was quickly eliminated as a suspect: he had gone back to Italy. Living in the house now was a man named Mario Buda, and Stewart, in his dogged way, transferred his suspicions to him. On learning that Buda had a car in for repairs in the Elm Square Garage in West Bridgewater, Stewart left strict instructions with the proprietor to phone him the moment Buda called for it.

One evening three weeks later that call came. The garage owner told Stewart that Buda and three other men had just come for the car, but had left directly because it wasn't ready – Buda and one man on a motorcycle with a sidecar, the other two on foot. The two on foot were thought to be travelling to Brockton by streetcar, so Stewart alerted the police there. When the streetcar reached Brockton, a policeman boarded it, surveyed the few passengers and detained two uneasy-looking Italian men: Bart Vanzetti and Nicola Sacco. They were found to be carrying loaded pistols and a good deal of ammunition, some of it for guns other than the kinds they carried. They also possessed anarchist literature.

For Chief Stewart that was enough. Though neither man had been arrested for anything before and though Stewart had no evidence to suggest that either had been anywhere near South Braintree at the time of the murders, he had them charged.

It was not a good time to be either a radical or an alien in America, and a positively dangerous time to be both. America was in the grip of something known as the Great Red Scare. In 1917 and 1918 Congress had enacted two startlingly restrictive laws, an Espionage Act and a Sedition Act. Together these provided severe penalties for anyone found guilty of displaying almost any kind of disrespect to the American government, including its symbols – the flag, military uniforms, historic documents or anything else in which was deemed to repose the glory and dignity of the United States of America – and these were imposed with a harsh and punitive zeal. 'Citizens were imprisoned for criticizing the Red Cross at their own dinner tables,' one commentator noted. A clergyman in Vermont was given a fifteen-year jail term for handing out half a dozen pacifist leaflets. In Indiana, a jury took just two minutes to acquit a man who had shot an immigrant for speaking ill of America.

Crazily, it became riskier to say disloyal things than to do them. A person who refused to obey the draft law could be imprisoned for one year, but a person who urged others to disobey the draft law could be imprisoned for twenty years. More than a thousand citizens were jailed under the terms of the Espionage Act in its first fifteen months. It was hard to know what could get you in trouble. A filmmaker named Robert Goldstein was imprisoned for showing the British in a bad light in a movie about the American War of Independence. The judge allowed that such a depiction would be 'permissible or even commendable' in ordinary times, but 'in this hour of national emergency' Goldstein enjoyed 'no right to subvert the purposes and destiny of the nation'. For insulting a foreign army from 150 years earlier, Goldstein was sentenced to twelve years in prison.

Though the espionage and sedition laws were intended only as wartime measures, matters actually worsened with peace. The return home of two million job-seeking soldiers and the simultaneous dismantling of the wartime economy gave America a severe recession. Racial tensions erupted into riots in two dozen cities where blacks had moved in search of better jobs. In Chicago, where the black population had doubled in a decade, a black youth who fell asleep on a raft on Lake Michigan and drifted on to a white beach was stoned to death by a white crowd, provoking two weeks of bitter rioting in which thirty-eight people were killed and whole neighbourhoods razed.

At the same time much of the nation was rocked by industrial unrest. Longshoremen, clothworkers, cigar makers, construction workers, steel workers, telephone operators, elevated rail and subway workers, coal miners and even Broadway actors all walked off their jobs. At one point in 1919 two million people were out on strike.

Foreign agitators and radical organizations like the Industrial Workers of the World (or Wobblies, as the members were known for reasons that have never been determined) were widely blamed for the troubles. In Boston and Cleveland, the police helped citizens beat up May Day paraders, then the police in Boston went out on strike themselves (the event that propelled Calvin Coolidge to national prominence). In Washington state, Wesley Everest, an IWW employee, was hauled into the street by a mob, which beat him and cut off his genitals. As he begged to be put out of his misery, his tormentors took him to a city bridge, dangled him over the side on a rope, then shot him. His death was ruled a suicide. No charges were brought.

At the height of the tumult, someone – a disgruntled alien, it was presumed – began sending bombs. In Atlanta, a maid in the home of Senator Thomas R. Hardwick, head of the Senate Immigration Committee, had just taken delivery of a small brown package and was carrying it to the kitchen when it exploded, blowing off her hands. The next day a New York postal employee read about the bombing and realized that the description of the parcel exactly matched sixteen parcels he had put aside at a sorting office for insufficient postage. He rushed back to work and found the packages still there. All were addressed to prominent public figures – John D. Rockefeller, J. P. Morgan, Attorney General A. Mitchell Palmer, Judge Kenesaw Mountain Landis, the Chief Justice of the Supreme Court and several governors and congressmen. All bore return address labels to Gimbel Brothers department store at Thirty-Second and Broadway in Manhattan. It was subsequently discovered that several other packages had already been posted. In one bizarre incident, a package was returned to Gimbel Brothers for insufficient postage. A Gimbel's clerk opened the package, examined the odd contents – bottle of acid, timer, explosives – then packed it all up again, added the necessary postage and mailed it on. Altogether thirty-six bombs were found. Apart from the unfortunate maid, no one else was injured and no arrests were made.

But that was not the end of it. Just over a month later, on a balmy evening in a quiet, well-to-do neighbourhood of Washington, DC, Attorney General A. Mitchell Palmer and his wife were preparing to retire in their house at 2132 R Street NW when they heard a thump downstairs – 'as if something had been thrown against the front door', Palmer related afterwards. A moment later the night was rent by a tremendous explosion, which blew out the front of the Palmer house and left every room exposed, like a doll's house. People in neighbouring houses were thrown from their beds. Windows were broken for blocks around.

Stumbling through the smoke and dust, the Palmers – both miraculously unhurt – went downstairs and stepped out on to an eerie scene of devastation. Blast debris was everywhere – hanging from trees, littering the street, strewn across lawns and rooftops. Much of it was still smoking. Scattered about in an unintentionally festive manner were anarchist leaflets.

One of the first people on the scene was Assistant Secretary of the Navy Franklin Delano Roosevelt, who lived almost directly opposite. He had just parked and gone in after an evening out. The bomber had probably waited in the shadows for him to go, then proceeded to deposit the bomb. Had Roosevelt arrived a minute later, he might well have been killed and America would have a different history. Roosevelt found Mr and Mrs Palmer whitened with plaster dust and wandering in shock. The attorney general was speaking, distractedly, in the pronouns of his Quaker childhood, addressing his neighbours as 'thee' and 'thou'.

It was clear that the bomber had been blown to pieces by his own device. Alice Longworth, Roosevelt's cousin, who was also present, reported that 'it was difficult to avoid stepping on bloody chunks of human being'. One of the bomber's legs was on a doorstep across the street. The other was fifty feet away. A big section of torso, with clothing still attached, was found dangling from the cornice of a house on a neighbouring street. Another indeterminate chunk of flesh and cartilage had crashed through a window of a house across the way and landed at the foot of the bed of Helmer Byrn, Minister Plenipotentiary of

Norway. Most of the scalp was found two blocks away on S Street. To reach that point – both distant and uphill – the top of the bomber's head must have been launched on a trajectory 100 feet high and 250 feet long. It was a big bomb.

So many body parts were lying about that officials at first thought there had been two bombers, or perhaps one bomber and an unidentified, innocent passer-by. Clearly the bomb had gone off prematurely. The presumption was that the bomber had tripped as he was about to set it on the Palmers' steps.

Before the night was out newswires were clicking with reports that bombs of similar destructive magnitude had gone off in seven other localities – Boston, New York, Philadelphia, Pittsburgh, Cleveland, Paterson, New Jersey, and Newtonville, Massachusetts. Only one other person was killed – a nightwatchman in New York – but the knowledge that terrorists could mount coordinated violence on such a scale left many Americans distinctly unnerved. The bombs elsewhere were in some cases wholly mysterious, possibly because they had been delivered to the wrong houses. In Philadelphia, one of the bombs blew apart the house of a jeweller who had no connection to government or politics. Another severely damaged a Catholic church. Why the bombers targeted a Catholic church was never established.

Thanks largely to the fact that the Washington bomber had been wearing a distinctive polka-dot tie, detectives were able to identify him as Carlo Valdinoci. This was a big loss to the anarchist movement. Though just twenty-four, Valdinoci had become a legend in the underground. Federal agents had recently tracked him to a house in West

Virginia, but he had escaped just ahead of them, adding to his reputation for cunning and invincibility. Valdinoci had been on the run since 1917 after an infamous bombing in Youngstown, Ohio. That bomb had not gone off as planned either. In fact, it had not gone off at all, so the police, in an act of unimaginable foolishness, took it to the station house and placed it on a table in the main operations room in order to examine it closely. As they tinkered with it, it exploded, killing ten policemen and a woman who had come to report a robbery. The bombers were never caught and the case was never solved. Radical cases rarely were.

The bombings had a wondrous effect on the mind of A. Mitchell Palmer. A lantern-jawed Democrat from Pennsylvania, he had been attorney general for just three months, but had already been the target of two bombs – a 'Gimbel's' bomb that never reached him and now this one that most assuredly did. This left him powerfully inclined to listen to a young adviser in the Justice Department who had developed a private theory that America's immigrant subversives, in league with international communists, were planning a coup. The young man's name was J. Edgar Hoover, and he convinced Palmer that the plotters existed in vast numbers and were planning an imminent strike.

Hoover, who had only just graduated from law school, was put in charge of a hitherto inconsequential corner of the Alien Registration Section known as the Radical Division. He assembled an index file containing more than 200,000 names of individuals and organizations, all neatly cross-referenced. Forty translators were taken on to pore over radical publications, of which the tireless quantifier Hoover counted more than six hundred.

Palmer had high hopes of being his party's presidential nominee in 1920. Dealing decisively with radical elements became his strategy for showing what a muscular individual he was. In a series of apocalyptic speeches, he warned that the flames of revolution were sweeping across the country, 'licking the altars of the churches, leaping into the belfry of the school bell, crawling into the sacred corners of American homes, seeking to replace marriage vows with libertine laws, burning up the foundations of society'. Palmer claimed that some five million communists and fellow travellers were planning the overthrow of America. With his thrusting jaw and tough rhetoric, Palmer became known to his admirers as 'the Fighting Quaker'. He had just launched what was quickly dubbed the Great Red Scare.

Eagerly encouraged by J. Edgar Hoover, Palmer prepared a series of raids on radical gathering spots. The first were held on 7 November 1919 – the second anniversary of the Russian Revolution – and mostly involved federal agents and police in twelve cities storming selected clubs and cafés, smashing furniture and arresting everyone in sight. In New York, police raided the Union of Russian Workers, beating anyone who protested or even questioned what they were doing. The union was merely a social club, where members could go to play chess or take classes to improve their English; it had never had any connection to radical affairs. In Hartford, Connecticut, police arrested a large number of suspects – the exact number is uncertain – then arrested anyone who came to ask after them. In Detroit, an entire orchestra and all the patrons of a particular restaurant were among eight hundred detainees who were held for up to a week in a windowless corridor without adequate water, toilets or space to lie down. Eventually all were released without charge.

Palmer was so pleased with the publicity his raids generated and the fear they instilled that he ordered a second, larger set of raids in the new year. This time some 6,000 to 10,000 people (accounts vary widely) were arrested in at least seventy-eight cities in twenty-three states. Again, there was much needless destruction of property, arrests without warrants and beating of innocent people.

The Great Red Scare proved to be not so scary after all. In total, the authorities seized just three pistols and no explosives. No evidence of a national conspiracy was uncovered. The failure to catch any bombers or unearth any trace of planned insurrection ended Palmer's political prospects. At the Democratic convention in 1920, the delegates selected James M. Cox, governor of Ohio, to run against another Ohioan, Warren G. Harding. Although the Palmer raids didn't achieve anything, they had a powerful effect on national sentiment, which is almost certainly why Chief Stewart of Bridgewater decided, without benefit of evidence, that the murderers on his patch were foreign anarchists. And it is why Sacco and Vanzetti never really stood a chance.

Between 1905 and 1914, 10 million people, mostly from southern and eastern Europe, poured into the United States – a country that had only 83 million people to begin with. The numbers of immigrants changed the face of urban America utterly. By 1910, immigrants and the children of immigrants made up almost three quarters of the populations of New York, Chicago, Detroit, Cleveland and Boston.

Sacco and Vanzetti were among 130,000 Italians who arrived in 1908 alone. Sacco, from Torremaggiore in south-eastern Italy, was just sixteen years old on arrival. Vanzetti, who came from Piedmont, in the more prosperous north and not far from France, was three years older. Neither would ever see his homeland again. Though both settled in New England, they would not meet until 1917.

Sacco was small, lithe and handsome – 'clean cut as a Roman coin', in the words of one contemporary. Descriptions make him sound rather like the young Al Pacino – small, good-looking, quiet-spoken. He didn't drink or gamble. He got a job in a shoe factory and soon was a skilled craftsman on good wages. Four years after his arrival in America he married and started a family. At the time of his arrest he was thirty years old and a good, hard-working family man. He didn't seem an obvious candidate for anarchy.

Vanzetti was a different matter. Though he had trained as a pastry chef – a respectable profession – in Italy, in America he worked as a common labourer on the lowest wages, almost as if he were seeking out privation to prove a point about the evils of capitalism. He was frequently unemployed, always hard up and occasionally near starvation. In the spring of 1919, however, his economic circumstances and, it would seem, his entrepreneurial spirit took a sudden turn for the better when he bought a fish cart, complete with knives, weighing scales and a bell for attracting custom, and became a mobile fish vendor in Plymouth, Massachusetts. At the time of his arrest, he was thirty-three years old and doing rather well.

Vanzetti was an intellectual by nature. He read a great

deal and lived quietly and soberly. He never had a girl-friend. He had a melancholy air and a sad, gentle smile. His eyes had 'a tenderness that haunted one', one friend recalled. His most conspicuous attribute, after 1917, was a vast, drooping moustache. Although his manner was affable and even sweet-natured, he was a bitter foe of the state. 'Vanzetti was anarchism personified,' one associate said.

Vanzetti and Sacco were not especially great friends. They lived thirty miles apart – Sacco in Stoughton, near Bridgewater, and Vanzetti in Plymouth – and had known each other for less than three years when they became eternally yoked by the payroll murders in South Braintree.

Arrested and taken in for questioning, they didn't do at all well. They were unable to explain why they needed to be so extravagantly armed for a visit to a car repair shop. They claimed not to know Buda or the other man, and said they knew no one with a motorcycle – lies that were easily disproved. They denied that they were anarchists, and offered inconsistent and unpersuasive explanations for what had brought them to West Bridgewater. The suspicion has always been that they were there to move illicit materials – possibly explosives, possibly anarchist literature – and didn't wish to incriminate themselves.

Buda and the fourth man, subsequently identified as Riccardo Orciani, were arrested and brought in for questioning but released: Orciani because he could prove he was at work at the time of both robberies and Buda, who was very short and stocky, because he did not fit any of the witness descriptions. By default, therefore, Sacco and Vanzetti became the chief and only suspects, even though neither had a criminal record or links to any criminal gangs. All that the police had against them was that they were armed and untruthful when arrested.

Nearly all the evidence pointed away from them. They were the mildest of men. Nothing in their natures suggested the least capacity for violence. They had never even been known to raise their voices. No evidence of any kind, such as fingerprints on the stolen car, placed them at the scene of the crime.

Three witnesses, shown photographs, identified one of the gunmen as Anthony Palmisano – but Palmisano, it turned out, had been in prison in Buffalo since the previous January. At least two witnesses said that the principal gunman had a pencil-thin moustache, whereas Sacco had none and Vanzetti was famous for the luxuriant, drooping shag that all but covered his mouth. When Sacco and Vanzetti were paraded before witnesses they were not presented as part of a line-up, as procedures required, but shown individually to the witnesses, to whom it was made clear that these were the prime suspects. Even so, the woman who would be one of the chief witnesses at the subsequent trial failed to identify Sacco or Vanzetti when standing right in front of them.

No one at first saw their arrest as a big story. A reporter from New York sent to Massachusetts to look into the case reported back to his editor: 'There's nothing in it – just a couple of wops in a jam.' In Boston the big story in the spring of 1920 was how the Red Sox would do in their first season without Babe Ruth.

Vanzetti, to his astonishment, was charged not just with the Braintree crime, but also with an earlier one, at the L. Q. White Shoe Company factory in Bridgewater on

Christmas Eve 1919. Sacco was not charged because he was able to produce a time card showing he was at work that day. Vanzetti was not short of alibis himself. Thirty witnesses testified that they had seen, talked to or conducted business with him from his fish cart in Plymouth that day. Eels are a traditional Christmas dish for many Italians, so people remembered buying eels from him on the day before Christmas. Such evidence as was brought against Vanzetti was hardly the most persuasive. A witness, aged fourteen, when asked how he knew one of the robbers was a foreigner, replied: 'I could tell by the way he ran.'

The jury convicted him anyway, evidently discounting all the witness testimony on his behalf in the belief that 'all the wops stick together', as Vanzetti himself remarked bitterly afterwards. Had a Protestant minister or school principal testified in Vanzetti's favour, he would probably have been cleared, but unfortunately such people didn't buy eels on Christmas Eve.

A quotation often attributed to Judge Webster Thayer at the Vanzetti trial was: 'This man, although he may not actually have committed the crime attributed to him, is nevertheless morally culpable, because [his] ideals are cognate with crime.' It has been quoted many times, but in fact the statement is not in the trial transcript and no evidence exists that Thayer ever said such a thing. It was clear, however, that he had little sympathy for anarchists. He sentenced Vanzetti to twelve to fifteen years in prison – an unusually stiff sentence for a man with no criminal record. To many observers this was clearly a travesty, and the second trial would make matters far worse.

* * *

For Italian immigrants of the early twentieth century, America often came as a shock. As the historians Leonard Dinnerstein and David M. Reimers have observed, most 'were unprepared for the coolness with which so many Americans received them'. Often they found themselves excluded from employment and educational opportunities because of their nationality. Restrictive covenants kept them from moving into certain neighbourhoods. Italians who settled in the Deep South were sometimes made to attend black schools. At first, it was by no means clear that they would be allowed to use white drinking fountains and lavatories.

Other immigrant groups – Greeks, Turks, Poles, Slavs, Jews of every nation – encountered similar prejudice, of course, and for Asians and America's own blacks prejudice and restrictions were even more imaginative and cruel, but the Italians were widely regarded as something of a special case – more voluble and temperamental and troublesome than other ethnic groups. Wherever problems arose, Italians seemed to be at the heart of things. The widespread perception of Italians was that if they weren't fascists or bolsheviks, they were anarchists or communists, and if they weren't those, they were involved in organized crime.*

Even the *New York Times* declared in an editorial that it was 'perhaps hopeless to think of civilizing [Italians] or

---

* In fact – and this can't be said quickly enough – Italians were not unlawful. Italians in 1910 constituted 11 per cent of the immigrant population but accounted for just 7 per cent of foreign-born people in prison. As John Kobler notes, in terms of imprisonment rates per 100,000 of population, the Italians came twelfth out of seventeen nationalities.

keeping them in order, except by the arm of the law'. University of Wisconsin sociologist E. A. Ross insisted that crime in Italy had fallen only 'because all the criminals are here'. This was precisely the prejudice that Ruth Snyder and Judd Gray hoped to exploit when they created a pair of imaginary Italian anarchists as the supposed murderers of her husband.

For working-class Italians, assimilation was often a forlorn hope. Millions lived within but quite separate from the rest of America. It is a telling point that after twelve years in the country Sacco and Vanzetti still barely spoke English. The transcript of their trial shows that both men often did not fully understand questions put to them or what was being said by others. Even when they grasped the gist of matters, they struggled to express themselves. As someone remarked, it was not so much that they spoke English with an Italian accent as that they spoke Italian using English words. Here is a short specimen of Sacco trying to explain from the witness stand how he could be an anarchist and yet claim to love America:

> When I came to this country I saw there was not what I was thinking before, but there was all the difference, because I been working in Italy not so hard as I been work in this country. I could live free there just as well. Work in the same condition but not so hard, about seven or eight hours a day, better food. I mean genuine. Of course over here is good food, because it is bigger country, to any of those who got money to spend, not for the working and laboring class, and in Italy is more opportunity to laborer to eat vegetable, more fresh, and I came in this country.

Poor command of English was widely regarded as proof that Italians were lazy and irremediably backward. Many Americans were sincerely bewildered and affronted (not altogether without reason, it must be said) to think that the nation had flung open its doors to the tired and poor of Europe only to have that generosity repaid with strikes, the planting of bombs and the fomenting of rebellions. Sacco and Vanzetti became the living symbols of that ingratitude. A common view among Americans at the time was that even if they were innocent of the Braintree crimes, they still deserved to be punished. As the foreman of the jury in their case reportedly remarked early in the trial, 'Damn them, they ought to hang anyway.'

Five days after indictments were handed down against Sacco and Vanzetti in Massachusetts, a horse-drawn wagon pulled up outside the head offices of J. P. Morgan & Co. at the corner of Broad and Wall Streets in Manhattan. The driver, it is supposed, tethered the horse and departed sharply, for a few moments later the cart exploded with a force that rocked the district and blew out windows on the thirty-second floor of a building more than a block away. The bomb was a particularly vicious one: packed with shrapnel, it was designed to maim and was detonated when the street was packed with lunchtime office workers. Thirty people were killed instantly and several hundred injured. The heat of the blast was so intense that many of the victims suffered severe burns on top of any other injuries. A clerk at J. P. Morgan was decapitated at his desk by a sheet of flying glass, but no senior members of the firm – the presumed principal targets – were among the victims. J. P. Morgan himself was out of the country.

The other Morgan partners – including Charles Lindbergh's future father-in-law, Dwight Morrow – were meeting in a room that had no windows on the blast side of the building, so were securely shielded. At the end of the day, the casualty totals were 38 dead and 143 gravely injured. Among the luckiest people outside was Joseph P. Kennedy, father of the future president, who was close enough to be blown off his feet but far enough away not to be seriously hurt.

Morgan as a point of pride opened for business the next day. Rewards of $100,000 were offered for information leading to a conviction, but no one came forward who could describe the bomber or offer any other useful leads. Detectives and federal officials interviewed every blacksmith east of Chicago and visited more than four thousand stables in the hope of identifying the horse, cart or horseshoes involved in the bomb. The shrapnel had been made from sash weights, so they contacted every sash-weight dealer and manufacturer in America to try to find where the slugs came from. For three years detectives worked on the case. Not a single helpful fact emerged. No one was ever charged.

In 1991, the historian Paul Avrich, in *Sacco and Vanzetti: The Anarchist Background*, probably the most exhaustive book ever written on the case, declared that he had it on good (but unspecified) evidence that the bomber was Mario Buda, the man who had been with Sacco and Vanzetti on the evening of their arrest. At the time, however, Buda was not known to the police in New York and was not suspected or interviewed. Whether part of the bombing or not, he returned to Naples in a curious hurry soon after the bomb went off.

It later also emerged that Nicola Sacco had been close friends with Carlo Valdinoci, and that Valdinoci's sister had come to live in Sacco's house after her brother died in the Palmer house-bombing in Washington. Sacco and Vanzetti, it seems, may not have been quite so innocent as history has wished to make them.

The trial of Sacco and Vanzetti for the murders and payroll robbery at South Braintree began on 31 May 1921, Judge Webster Thayer presiding once again. Thayer was a gaunt, pale figure in his sixties. He had a hawk nose, thin mouth and white moustache. He was only five feet two inches tall, but had been a star athlete in his youth and had nearly become a professional baseball player. He went through life with a small chip on his shoulder because he was a butcher's son in a state where pedigree counted for a lot.

The trial lasted almost seven weeks, heard from about a hundred and sixty witnesses and produced over two thousand pages of testimony. According to the state's case, Sacco and another, unidentified man did the hold-up and shooting. No attempt was made to track down or identify the other gunman, or any of the other participants in the robbery. The state seemed oddly content to pin the whole thing on Sacco and Vanzetti. Vanzetti, even in the worst scenario, was merely a passenger in the getaway car, and only one witness confidently put him there. Forty-four others swore they saw him elsewhere that day – selling fish in Plymouth, for the most part – or declared him not to have been among the culprits. A group in Providence, known as the Morelli gang, actually had a history of robbing shoe factories, but the police did not investigate them. None of the robbery money was ever found or in any way connected to Sacco or Vanzetti. The prosecution offered no theories as to what had become of it.

Much of the testimony against the accused was pretty dubious. Lewis Pelzer, a factory worker, testified that he saw Sacco shoot Berardelli, but he had originally told police that he had dived under a table when he heard gunfire and hadn't seen anything. Three of his co-workers testified that he had never looked out of the window.

Mary Splaine, a key witness, said she looked out of a window just as the getaway car sped away. Her view lasted for no more than three seconds and was from a distance of between sixty and eighty feet, yet at the trial she was able to recount sixteen details about Sacco's appearance, including the shade of his eyebrows and the length of his hair at the neck. She even stated with certainty Sacco's height, even though she had only ever seen him seated in a moving automobile. Thirteen months earlier, she had failed to identify Sacco at all when viewing him in person from close range. Sacco had once briefly worked at the Rice and Hutchins factory, and several of its employees remembered him, but none except Mary Splaine said that Nicola Sacco was one of those present.

Just one witness placed Vanzetti at the scene at the time of the murder – as a passenger in the getaway car. None suggested that he fired a gun or was otherwise directly involved.

In his summing-up to the jury, Judge Webster Thayer laid great stress on what the legal profession called 'consciousness of guilt' – Sacco and Vanzetti's suspiciously evasive behaviour under questioning. Innocent people, Thayer stressed, did not need to fabricate answers. Ergo, they were guilty. The jury agreed. After five and a half hours of deliberation on 14 July 1921, it pronounced Sacco and Vanzetti guilty. The sentence was death by electrocution.

It cannot be said that the state rushed to execute them. Appeals went on for six years. Sacco and Vanzetti's defence team submitted seven motions for retrial on the grounds that Judge Thayer was biased and the trial not fair, and lodged two further appeals with the Massachusetts Supreme Court. All were denied. In 1925, Celestino Madeiros, a native of the Azores who was on death row for another crime, issued a confession. 'I hear by confess to being in the South Braintree shoe company crime and Sacco and Vanzetti was not in said crime,' he wrote. Under questioning, Madeiros proved vague about crucial details of the Braintree robbery – the time of day it took place, for instance – and Thayer dismissed the confession as untrustworthy, which in fact it was. Thayer also issued a detailed 25,000-word statement explaining why he had rejected all calls for a retrial.

The first signals of angry dissent arose not in America, but in France. On 20 October 1921, a bomb was sent to Ambassador Myron Herrick in a package disguised to look like a gift. By remarkable good fortune the package was inadvertently activated by one of the few people in Paris who could recognize it for what it was and had the forbearance to respond accordingly. Herrick's English valet, Lawrence Blanchard, had worked with bombs in the First World War and recognized the whirring sound within the package as a Mills hand grenade. He hurled the package into the ambassador's bathroom an instant before it detonated. The explosion destroyed the bathroom and felled Blanchard with a piece of shrapnel to the leg, but he was otherwise unhurt. Had Herrick opened the package himself, another ambassador would have greeted Lindbergh in Paris in 1927.

A few days later, another bomb (possibly an accidental detonation) at a Sacco–Vanzetti rally killed twenty people. In the following two weeks bombs exploded at American embassies or consular offices in Lisbon, Rio de Janeiro, Zurich and Marseilles.

In America, writers and intellectuals were the first to protest the convictions – notably the novelists Upton Sinclair and John Dos Passos, the short-story writer Katherine Anne Porter, the poet Edna St Vincent Millay, the critic Lewis Mumford, the newspaperman Heywood Broun, and several members of the Algonquin Round Table, including Dorothy Parker and Robert Benchley. Most of them were at one time or another arrested and charged with 'loitering and sauntering' – an offence peculiar to Boston, it seems. Benchley additionally swore that he had overheard Thayer boasting in the golf club at Worcester, Massachusetts, that he would 'get those bastards good and proper', which agitated liberal opinion further.

Petitions appealing for a retrial poured in from abroad. One had almost half a million signatures, another more than 150,000. Streets and cafés throughout the world were renamed for the two Italians. In Argentina, a brand of cigarettes was called Sacco y Vanzetti, as was a popular tango.

The involvement of intellectuals and foreigners stirred sharp resentment in some quarters. Working men, mostly Irish, held counter-demonstrations in Boston, calling for the swift execution of the two Italians. According to the writer Francis Russell, who lived through the period as a boy in Boston, public opinion was mostly against Sacco and Vanzetti. In particular, middle-class Republicans believed in their guilt. Senator William Borah of Idaho, chairman of the Committee on Foreign Relations, said 'it would be a national humiliation, a shameless, cowardly compromise of national courage, to pay the slightest attention to foreign protests', which he called 'impudent and wilful'.

The real turning point for many was when future Supreme Court justice Felix Frankfurter, then a law professor at Harvard, looked into the case and became convinced that Sacco and Vanzetti had been railroaded. Frankfurter detailed his objections in the March 1927 issue of the *Atlantic Monthly*. 'I assert with deep regret, but without the slightest fear of disproof, that certainly in modern times Judge Thayer's opinion stands unmatched for discrepancies between what the record discloses and what the opinion conveys,' he wrote. 'His 25,000-word document cannot accurately be described otherwise than as a farrago of misquotations, misrepresentations, suppressions, and mutilations . . . The opinion is literally honeycombed with demonstrable errors, and a spirit alien to judicial utterance permeates the whole.'

Frankfurter systematically and persuasively demolished the case against Sacco and Vanzetti, but his findings were not welcomed by the Boston establishment. Many Harvard alumni demanded that he be fired. Colleagues and old friends snubbed him. He found that when he walked into a room or restaurant some people would get up and leave. The article, it was said, cost Harvard $1 million in donations.

But elsewhere anger and a sense of injustice seemed to be on the increase. Among those who asked for a new trial were Berardelli's widow. The conservative *Boston Herald*, which had previously supported execution, reversed its opinion after reading Thayer's statement.

No one gave more attention to the case than Massachusetts Governor Alvan T. Fuller. Fuller appears to have been a thoroughly decent man. He began adult life as a bicycle salesman, then went to Paris and brought back two of the first automobiles ever imported into North America. Eventually he became sole New England distributor for Packard at a time when Packards were the best cars in the country. The relationship made him a millionaire many times over. He lived in a Boston mansion and collected eighteenth-century English paintings – Gainsboroughs and Romneys in particular. In fourteen years as an elected official, he never took a paycheque.

On 10 May 1927 – just at the time that Nungesser and Coli went missing – a bomb was mailed to Fuller, but luckily was intercepted and defused. In the same month, Fuller appointed a commission of three worthies – Abbott Lawrence Lowell, president of Harvard; Samuel Stratton, president of MIT; and Robert Grant, a retired judge – to consider formally whether Sacco and Vanzetti had been given a fair trial and should be executed. They were not young. Grant was seventy-five, Lowell seventy-one and Stratton sixty-six.

Fuller at the same time made a private study of the case. He read every word of the transcript. He had all the physical evidence – pistols, bullets, articles of clothing – sent to his house so that he could examine them. He called in and personally questioned all of the eleven surviving jurors (one had died) as well as witnesses from both trials. He several times devoted twelve- to fourteen-hour days to doing nothing else but studying the Sacco–Vanzetti case.

He twice interviewed Sacco and Vanzetti and even the hapless Celestino Madeiros, as well as members of their families. Fuller found himself particularly taken with Vanzetti. In prison Vanzetti had studied English by corres-pondence course and his language skills had improved enormously. In his later years in prison he wrote many moving and articulate letters and essays, and struck every-one with his sensitivity and intelligence. Vanzetti's lawyer, Fred Moore, said he had never met a man of such 'splendid gentility'. Governor Fuller, after their first meet-ing, came out gushing, 'What an attractive man!'

On the day of Lindbergh's visit to Boston in July, Fuller went first to Charlestown Prison to meet with the con-victed men. He spent fifteen minutes each with Sacco and Madeiros, but a full hour with Vanzetti. It was clear to everyone that Fuller wished not to execute the men, Vanzetti in particular.

At about the time of Lindbergh's visit, the Lowell Commission, as it was known, revealed its findings. It con-cluded that Sacco was guilty beyond any doubt, Vanzetti probably so, and that there were no grounds for a reprieve. Anger among liberals was almost immeasurable. Heywood Broun called it 'legalized murder' and wrote: 'It is not every prisoner who has a president of Harvard University throw the switch for him.'

That was that for Sacco and Vanzetti. On 3 August, Fuller announced with implicit regret that he could find no grounds for clemency and that the executions must proceed. Sacco and Vanzetti would be taken to the electric chair the following week.

The news did not cause quite the stir that might have been predicted, and this was almost entirely because President Coolidge in far-off South Dakota had just dumbfounded the nation with an unexpected announcement of his own.

Chapter 21

THE SECOND OF August was a cold, wet day in South Dakota. The thirty or so members of the presidential press corps were surprised to find themselves summoned to Rapid City High School for a special announcement at noon. Ushered into a classroom, they were even more surprised to find President Coolidge sitting at a teacher's desk. It was the fourth anniversary of Warren Harding's death and so also of Calvin Coolidge's assumption of the presidency. Coolidge looked inscrutably pleased about something.

The reporters were instructed to form a line. As each man filed past the desk, Coolidge handed him a two-inch by nine-inch strip of paper bearing the message: 'I do not choose to run for President in nineteen twenty-eight.' That was all. The decision caught everyone by surprise. 'A bolt from the blue would not be too extravagant a term to describe the Coolidge cryptogram,' wrote Robert Benchley in the *New Yorker*. Even Grace Coolidge, the first lady, was apparently unaware of her husband's decision, and learned the news afterwards from one of those present.

391

Coolidge spoke just five words at the press conference: 'Is everyone here now?' before it started and 'No' when asked if he would comment further on his announcement. Then the reporters rushed out to break the news to the world. The message itself was either ten words or twelve words long, depending on whether one counted 'nineteen twenty-eight' as one word or three – no one could agree – but the correspondents filing reports from the Western Union office in Rapid City sent nearly 100,000 words that day and the next.

Why Coolidge decided not to run is a question that has fed speculation for over eighty years. Probably there were many reasons. Neither he nor his wife had any fondness for Washington, particularly in the sapping mugginess of summer, which was why he was pleased to take such a long vacation in 1927. Nor was it as if he had a great programme to see through. Whatever mark Calvin Coolidge was going to leave on the world was unlikely to be altered by another four years in office. Coolidge also seems to have enjoyed a certain prescience regarding the economy. 'Poppa says there's a depression coming,' Grace Coolidge remarked to an acquaintance soon after her husband announced his decision.

But there was one other reason, nowhere noted at the time, that may have stood out above all others. Calvin Coolidge was depressed, chronically so. The reason was a family tragedy for which he blamed himself. Three years earlier, on the last day of June 1924, Coolidge's two sons, John and Calvin Junior, had a game of tennis on a White House court. Calvin Junior wore sneakers without socks and developed a blister, which became infected. Within a day or so, he was running a high fever and was drifting in and out of delirium. On 3 July, the day before his father's birthday, he was hurriedly admitted to Walter Reed General Hospital.

Coolidge wrote to his father: 'Calvin is very sick . . . He blistered his toe and infection got into his blood. The toe looks all right but the poison spread all over his system . . . Of course he has all that medical science can give but he may have a long-sickness with ulcers, then again he may be better in a few days.' In fact, three days later the boy was dead.

Coolidge had been president for just over eleven months and had been nominated to run for president in his own right just two weeks earlier. Coolidge and his wife were devastated. All interest in affairs of state seemed to drain out of the president. 'When he went the power and the glory of the Presidency went with him,' Coolidge wrote later.

Coolidge was convinced that his role as president was entirely responsible for his son's death. He wrote in his autobiography, 'If I had not been President he would not have raised a blister on his toe, which resulted in blood-poisoning, playing lawn tennis in the South Grounds . . . I do not know why such a price was exacted for occupying the White House.' The final sentence of Coolidge's auto-biography was strangely heartfelt: 'It costs a great deal to be President.'

Among the nation's press, the question concerning the president's announcement was not why he decided not to run, but why he chose such an ambiguous phrase as 'I do not choose to run' as opposed to a more direct 'I choose not to run' or 'I have decided not to run'. Many saw it not as an outright refusal to run but almost as the very opposite – a reluctant willingness to be drafted if that was the will of the people. The humorist Will Rogers put it succinctly in his popular newspaper column:

> I think Mr Coolidge's statement is the best-worded acceptance of a nomination ever uttered by a candidate. He spent a long time in the dictionary looking for that word 'choose,' instead of 'I will not.' It don't take much political knowledge to know that a man can get more votes running on the people's request than he can running on his own request. Mr Coolidge is the shrewdest politician that ever drew government salary.

The person in America most excited by the announcement was Herbert Hoover, who saw himself as the clear front-runner to succeed Coolidge even if the rest of the nation did not, or at least did not necessarily. Hoover was holidaying in the redwood forests of northern California when the news broke and was as puzzled as everyone else by Coolidge's choice of words. 'The word "choose" has various connotations in its New England usage,' he reflected later. 'I determined at once to say nothing until I could have a talk with the President.' According to Hoover's memoirs of 1952, he waited till both he and Coolidge were back in Washington in September, though other sources say they met sooner. When at last they caught up, Hoover, looking for clarity and perhaps even a kind of blessing, asked if Coolidge thought he should run. To which all Coolidge would say was 'Why not?'

If Coolidge secretly hoped that he would be implored by his party to stay on, that never happened, and if it bothered him he never indicated it. All that can be said is that he declined to endorse Hoover or any other candidate on the grounds that people should make up their own minds. He also, at once, looked much more relaxed and even amiable than he had in a long time.

Within a couple of days he was happily allowing himself to be inducted into the Sioux Indian nation as an honorary chief with the name of Womblee Tokaha, or Leading Eagle. For this ceremony he was presented with a large feathered headdress, which he proudly donned for photographs. He looked ridiculous, but somehow enchantingly so. The nation was delighted.

So high were Coolidge's spirits that five days later he cheerfully travelled twenty-three miles into difficult back country to dedicate a seemingly hare-brained scheme on behalf of one of the most fantastically obstreperous men of the twentieth century. The scheme was Mount Rushmore. The man was Gutzon Borglum.

Mount Rushmore was a granite outcrop so off the beaten track that no one had even noticed it until 1885, when one Charles Rushmore of New York happened to pass by on horseback and bestowed his name upon it. The idea for a mighty carved monument there of four presidents' heads originated with the state historian, Doane Robinson, who saw it as a way of attracting tourists. It would be, as *Time* magazine epically described it, 'the largest piece of sculpture ever wrought in the Christian Era'. The notion was eccentric, to put it mildly. The project had no secure funding and no government support at any level. There was no certainty that anyone could actually carve a mountainside, and the site was unreachable by road, which meant that people would struggle to see it anyway.

Just one man on earth had the necessary skills and experience to carry out the project, but he was also one of the most hot-tempered, quixotic and maddening individuals ever to grasp a jackhammer. He was also, as it turned out, the perfect choice.

In the summer of 1927, Gutzon Borglum was sixty-one years old. Nearly all the details of his life must be treated with a certain caution since Borglum liked to change them as time went along. He occasionally awarded himself a new year or month of birth and frequently claimed achievements that were not his to claim. In his *Who's Who* entry he declared himself an aeronautical engineer. He was not. Though born in Idaho, at Great Bear Lake, in 1867, he sometimes claimed, for no evident reason, to be from California. He listed two different women as his mother, though there was a certain justification for this. His father, a Danish-born Mormon, had married two sisters. One gave birth to Borglum, but then withdrew from the family, and the other sister raised him as her own. Fiery-tempered and barrel-chested, he was pathologically pugnacious. 'My life,' he once reflected, 'has been a one-man war.'

Borglum grew up mostly in Nebraska. As a young man, he worked as a machinist and apprentice lithographer, but then decided to pursue an interest in art. He took lessons from a woman in Los Angeles named Lisa Putnam, and eventually married her, even though she was eighteen years his senior. Together they moved to Paris, where Borglum trained as a sculptor (one of his teachers was Auguste Rodin). Borglum lived in Europe for eleven years before he abandoned his wife and returned to the United States, where he quickly established himself as a sculptor.

During the First World War, and evidently from out of nowhere, Borglum developed an obsession with inefficiencies in the aircraft industry. Without encouragement or authorization, he conducted inspections of several factories, during the course of which he actually uncovered some significant failings. President Woodrow Wilson asked him to write a report, and on the strength of this Borglum secured an office in the War Department Building in Washington, DC. Eventually Borglum made such a nuisance of himself that Wilson dismissed him, even though he actually held no position to be dismissed from.

When the war was over, Borglum persuaded the United Daughters of the Confederacy to let him carve a tableau 400 feet high and a quarter of a mile long into the face of Stone Mountain, near Atlanta, to celebrate the heroism and bravery of the Confederacy. Stone Mountain had certain resonances. It was where the Ku Klux Klan was reborn in 1915. Borglum was a member of the Klan himself for a time. With financial support from the United Daughters, Borglum undertook a great deal of preparatory work, but eventually he fell into dispute with the women and departed abruptly in 1925, leaving behind stacks of interesting sketches and unpaid bills. The Daughters had him charged with malicious mischief and two counts of larceny, but by this time Borglum was already in South Dakota, where Doane Robinson had invited him to come and have a look at Rushmore.

For Borglum, it was love at first sight. Rushmore had a

noble profile and durable surface. Geologists estimated that it would erode at a rate of no more than one inch per one hundred thousand years. In fact, this estimate proved to be true only in parts; Borglum would have to resort to a great deal of ingenuity and adaptability to realize his dream.

The budget was set at $400,000, which included a fee for Borglum of $78,000. In addition to the sculpture itself, Borglum envisioned a monumental 'Hall of Records' cut into the cliff behind the presidents' heads, reachable by a grand staircase from below. It would hold the Declaration of Independence and Constitution.

Sculpting a mountainside was much more a matter of engineering and pyrotechnics than of artful chiselling. Most of the features were magically blasted from the rock. Even the most delicate finishing work was done with pneumatic drills. The ambition was staggering. The four faces that greet the visitor today are each more than sixty feet high. The mouths are eighteen feet wide, the noses twenty feet long. You could insert a car lengthwise into each eye socket.

The possibility of a miscalculated blast turning one of the presidents into a noseless sphinx kept interest high, and the fact that Borglum looked and acted at least slightly mad, and was always difficult to work with, ensured constant press attention. In fact, mistakes did happen. Jefferson's nose developed an ominous crack, so the face had to be 'reset' at a different angle and many feet further into the stone. Finding sufficient runs of good stone was one of the biggest challenges. The orientations of the four heads – each looking in a different direction, Jefferson tucked almost impishly behind Washington – was dictated by the availability of workable stone. Most of Washington's face is about thirty feet in from the original surface. Jefferson's is twice that. Altogether, Borglum and his workers removed 400,000 tons of rock to create their heroic composition.

The greatest problem was financing. The frugal legislature of South Dakota declined to appropriate a penny for the project. Private contributors proved only slightly more generous. In consequence, work often came to a standstill. In the end, most of the cost was borne by the federal government, but even so it took fourteen years to complete the job, about twice as long as necessary in terms of just getting the work done. Among those donating money was Charles Rushmore, now a wealthy lawyer in New York, who sent $5,000.

For his subjects Borglum selected Washington, Jefferson, Lincoln and – to widespread consternation – Theodore Roosevelt, who was chosen, it seems, not for his greatness but because he and Borglum had once been chums.

On the day of the dedication, all this lay some way in the future. A road was now under construction but wasn't anywhere near finished, which meant that the audience of about 1,500 people had to trek two miles up a steep track to attend the ceremonies. President Coolidge made that part of the trip on horseback. He was dressed in a business suit, but wore his cowboy hat and boots. Upon arriving, Mr Coolidge impressed everybody by drinking from a communal dipper. As part of the ceremonies, engineers laid explosives into the bases of trees lining his approach route and gave him a 21-stump salute. Speeches were made and a flag was raised, and then Borglum was lowered on a rope on to the face of Rushmore, where he bored some holes with a pneumatic drill. Borglum's brief labours didn't produce anything recognizable, but it did represent the symbolic beginning of work and everyone went away happy.

Borglum and Coolidge got along fine. Borglum intended to include beneath the heads of the presidents a vast inscription, called 'The Entablature', which would encapsulate in 500 words the history of the United States, carved in letters so large that they could be read three miles away. At the dedication ceremony, Borglum impulsively offered the task of drafting it to Coolidge, who accepted with uncustomary enthusiasm.

Coolidge gave the matter much thought and effort over the following months, but when at last he submitted his compositions they proved to be embarrassingly unusable. Most read more like preparatory notes than considered text. Here was Coolidge on the Constitution: 'The constitution – charter of perpetual union of free people of sovereign states establishing a government of limited powers – under an independent President, Congress and Court, charged to provide security for all citizens in their enjoyment of liberty, equality and justice under the law.' The Entablature proposal was quietly dropped, to Coolidge's supreme annoyance. But in the summer of 1927 all that was in the future, too, and the president and Borglum parted great friends.

Back at the game lodge, waiting on Coolidge's desk on his return from Mount Rushmore was an appeal for clemency for Sacco and Vanzetti. He ignored it.

Charles Lindbergh's tour continued. On 10 August, he flew into Detroit, where Henry and Edsel Ford took time off from designing and testing the new Model A to go up for short spins in the *Spirit of St Louis* – an honour accorded few others. Although the Ford company manufactured planes, neither Henry nor Edsel had ever been up in an aeroplane before. Because there wasn't a passenger seat, Henry Ford, like all passengers, had to sit on the armrest, more or less doubled up. Back on the ground, Henry boasted that he had 'handled the stick' for a while, and looked awfully pleased with himself. Asked by newsmen about progress on the secret new car, Edsel said that things were going so well that it was ready to go into production. It isn't clear if he was being optimistic or deluded, but in either case he was quite wrong. Production was still some months off.

After a day off in Detroit, spent mostly with his mother, Lindbergh continued west across Michigan and onwards to Illinois on 13 August. Among those who may well have turned out to watch him pass over, and possibly even joined the crowds at Benton Harbor where Lindbergh made a brief stop, were the Anti-Saloon League's Wayne B. Wheeler and his wife and her father, who were vacationing together at the Wheelers' lakeside cottage at Little Sable Point on Lake Michigan.

What is known is that that evening, while Mrs Wheeler was preparing to cook dinner at the cottage, her oil stove exploded as she lit it and she was drenched from head to toe in flaming oil. Mrs Wheeler's 81-year-old father rushed in from a neighbouring room and suffered a fatal heart attack at the sight of his daughter in flames. Wayne Wheeler, who had been resting upstairs, arrived a moment later. He stifled the blaze with a blanket and summoned an ambulance, but his wife's burns were too severe and she died that night in hospital. The shock of the incident was more than Wheeler could bear. Three weeks later, he suffered a heart attack of his own and died.

With Wheeler gone, Prohibition lost its spirit and momentum, as well as its chief fundraiser. Within three years, the Anti-Saloon League would be so hard up that it would have to cancel the newspaper subscription at its Washington office. Within six years, Prohibition was dead.

On 18 August, an act more important than anyone at the time appreciated, both in symbolic terms and practical ones, took place in Cleveland, Ohio, when the last piece of steel framework was hoisted into place on the massive new Union Terminal project. There had never been anything quite like it. As well as a spanking new railway station, the complex incorporated a hotel, post office, department store, shops, restaurants and a fifty-two-storey office building, the tallest building erected in America that year (and second tallest anywhere until the Chrysler Building went up). All the component parts of the project were physically interlinked, something that had never been done before.

The project was as notable for who built it as for what it was. The developers were brothers Oris and Mantis Van Sweringen. Of all the business titans America produced in the 1910s and '20s, none were more extraordinary or are now more forgotten. Born into modest and challenging circumstances in Cleveland – their father was a drunkard who rarely worked – they started off as small-time property developers, but they plugged away and branched out into other areas until by the 1920s they were two of the richest men in America. They were also by a long shot two of the strangest.

No one knew where their strange first names came from. Their parents had evidently just liked the sounds and made names out of them. The brothers were pale and small and inseparable. In the words of their biographer, they were 'almost wholly dependent on each other'. They lived in a fifty-four-room mansion but slept side by side in twin beds in the master bedroom. They didn't smoke, drink or stay up late. They were pathologically shy. They took no part in public life and avoided having their pictures taken. They never named any of their projects after themselves. They didn't attend the topping-out ceremony for the Union Terminal complex on 18 August or the dinner afterwards.

Oris was three years older than Mantis and essentially ran the business while Mantis ran his life. Mantis packed his brother's bags, looked after his pocket money, kept track of his appointments. Oris slept a great deal; twelve hours a night was usual. Mantis sometimes rode horses, but otherwise neither had any known interests. They never took vacations.

Their estate, called Daisy Hill, spread over 477 acres. The house had eighty telephone lines to keep them in touch with their business empire. Among the other rooms in the house were two dining rooms where no guest was ever entertained, a gym that was forever undisturbed, and twenty-three bedrooms that never received a visitor. They had no friendships, though Mantis did eventually fall for a widow named Mary Snow and enjoyed a relationship with her, which he somehow kept secret from Oris. A field on the property was used sometimes for polo matches and more occasionally as an airstrip. According to the brothers' biographer, Herbert H. Harwood, Jr, Charles Lindbergh landed there once and gave Mantis a ride while Oris remained on the ground and fretted, but Harwood didn't say when this was. It wasn't the summer of 1927.

If Mantis didn't invent the leveraged buyout, he became one of its first great masters. Essentially the brothers borrowed heavily to acquire a business, then used existing businesses as collateral to borrow and acquire still more. The enterprise was a tangled network of interconnected holdings, which by the late 1920s consisted of 275 separate subsidiaries. They had so many companies that they struggled to come up with original names for them all, so that, for instance, they owned a Cleveland Terminals Building Company, a Terminal Building Company and a Terminal Hotels Company. They bought the Nickel Plate Railroad for $8.5 million, but put up just $355,000 of their own money – and all of that was borrowed from the Guardian Bank of Cleveland (which eventually went out of business without being repaid a penny). They had built this colossus with a personal investment of less than $20 million, nearly all of it borrowed. Nobody did leveraged buyouts better than the Van Sweringens.

Mantis's real passion, however, was railways. The industry was incredibly fragmented: in 1920, America had almost 1,100 different railway companies. Many lines went from nowhere much to nowhere much, either because the towns or industries along the way never developed as expected or because the original builders never managed to extend the lines to the main metropolises. The Lake Erie & Western ran from Sandusky, Ohio, to Peoria, Illinois; the Pere Marquette wandered confusedly around the upper Midwest, as if looking for a lost item. These forlorn lines – 'orphans' as they were known in the trade – were generally pretty easy to acquire and the Van Sweringens did so with enthusiasm. They loved to acquire railways.

Within eight years the pair had built up the third largest railway empire in the country. By 1927 they controlled almost 30,000 miles of rail line, about 11 per cent of the national total, with routes stretching from the Atlantic Ocean to Salt Lake City. Along the way they also scooped up warehouses, ferries and the Greenbrier resort hotel in West Virginia. At their peak, they had 100,000 employees and assets of between $2 billion and $3 billion. Their personal wealth was put at something over $100 million – from almost nothing ten years earlier.

While building their empire, they also quietly but significantly changed the world. At a place called Turkey Ridge outside Cleveland they built a new town from scratch and called it Shaker Heights. Shaker Heights was the first planned dormitory community in America, and as such it became the model on which nearly all other suburbs were built. In like manner, the Union Terminal complex neatly anticipated the modern American shopping mall.

Unfortunately, their empire was essentially an inverted triangle. If any part of it at the bottom failed, the whole mighty edifice would come tumbling down, and that is just what happened. Though they could have no idea of it at the time, the topping out of the Union Terminal complex on 18 August was in every sense the high point of their careers.

When the Great Depression came they were desperately exposed. Their money was nearly all in railways and real estate – two of the most vulnerable places to put it – and they were grossly overextended in any case. They had bought Missouri Pacific stock at $101, but by the early 1930s it was trading at $1.50. They were unable to pay off bonds that came due or interest on loans. The Missouri Pacific and the Chicago & Eastern Illinois failed and brought the whole precarious enterprise down with them.

In the end, nobody better personified the giddy recklessness and folie de grandeur of the 1920s than the Van Sweringens. The stress and disappointment proved too much for Mantis, who died of heart failure aged fifty-four in 1935. Oris sat with him for the last ninety minutes of his life. Mantis was conscious, but they didn't exchange a word. Mantis's estate was valued at $3,067.85, half of which consisted of seven horses. Lost without his brother, Oris died eleven months and ten days later of heart failure of his own. His estate was worth even less than his brother's.

They were buried in a shared grave in Cleveland's Lake View Cemetery. The gravestone records their names and their dates of birth and death beneath a single word: 'Brothers'.

CHAPTER 22

THE SUCCESSFUL FLIGHTS across the ocean of the *America*, *Columbia* and *Spirit of St Louis* had a galvanizing, if not always entirely realistic, effect on expectations for the future of aviation.

Almost at once people began to dream of ways of converting the summer's heroics into practical actions. In Paris, Charles Levine briefly attracted the attention of reporters by announcing that he would launch a regular passenger airline service between America and Europe, and would invest $2 million of his own money in the venture. How he would safely convey passengers in both directions when no plane was yet capable of a successful westward crossing was a matter he failed to explain. As with so many Levine schemes, it was quickly forgotten.

Edward R. Armstrong, a Canadian-born engineer, approached the problem from the opposite direction. Rather than try to increase the range and load-carrying capacity of planes, his idea was to cut the distances they needed to fly by building a string of floating landing fields – eight in all – at 350-mile intervals across the Atlantic.

These 'seadromes' would each be 1,100 feet long, weigh 50,000 tons, and be anchored to the ocean floor by steel cables. All would have restaurants, gift shops, lounges and viewing decks. Some would have hotels. The cost of each platform would be $6 million. A trip from New York to London, Armstrong calculated, could be done in about thirty hours.

Armstrong formed the Armstrong Seadrome Development Company in 1927 and gradually secured financial backing. On 22 October 1929, he announced plans to begin work in sixty days. Unfortunately that was the week of the stock market crash and his financing fell apart. Armstrong continued for years to try to get his plan launched, reducing the number of proposed platforms to five and then three as planes became more powerful. Eventually, of course, they were not needed at all and his dream was never realized, but his seadromes did form the basis of modern offshore oil platforms. Armstrong died in 1955.

Two million people a year sailed between Europe and America in the 1920s, so the potential market for air passengers was considerable. From our modern time-harried perspective, ocean crossings look glamorous and romantic, but they were also time-consuming, uncomfortable in bad weather and sometimes seriously perilous. Fog was a frequent and dreaded danger in the days before radar. Most ships had a long record of unnerving near misses. 'There were many more close calls on the Western Ocean than passengers ever heard about,' writes John Maxtone-Graham in *The Only Way to Cross*. Collisions were not uncommon. On 15 July of this summer, just as the *Leviathan* carrying Byrd and his team was sailing nearby, the Holland America liner *Veendam* struck – essentially ploughed through – a Norwegian freighter, the *Sagaland*, near Nantucket at 4.40 in the morning. The *Sagaland* sank quickly with the loss of one life. The *Veendam* escaped serious damage and no one aboard was reported injured. It was nonetheless a sobering reminder of how dangerous ocean travel could be, for the ships collided in clear weather.

For all these reasons, knocking even a day off the crossing was an appealing proposition, which explains how it was that on 1 August Clarence Chamberlin accepted an invitation from the United States Lines and reboarded the mighty *Leviathan* with the intention of trying to take off from its upper deck in an aeroplane. A rickety 114-foot-long runway had been erected to facilitate the launch, but whether that would be enough was anybody's guess. No plane had ever taken off from a ship at sea, and Chamberlin himself thought his chances of success were only slightly better than even. Shortly before his takeoff someone asked him if he knew how to swim. Chamberlin grinned and admitted that he did not.

Happily, swimming proved unnecessary. In a lull between rainstorms, Chamberlin climbed into a Fokker biplane and shot down the creaking runway and into the void beyond with just enough speed and lift to stay airborne. He circled the ship, gave a casual wave and headed for Teterboro, New Jersey, where he delivered 900 pieces of airmail and posed bashfully for pictures. Inspired by Chamberlin's example, the owners of the new passenger liner *Île de France*, launched that year, installed a catapult that could fling a six-passenger plane down a shorter runway and into the air, and for a few years passengers who were daring, wealthy and in a hurry could reach shore a day or so sooner than their fellow passengers.

As August opened, Charles Lindbergh was coming to the end of the second week of his long tour of America. So far he had had just one hitch, but it was quite a serious one. After Boston he had flown on to Portland, Maine, but had been unable to land because of fog. He circled for nearly two hours but then, running low on fuel, he had to look for somewhere safe to land. He grew separated from an escort plane and came down on Old Orchard Beach in Maine. Luckily, a man named Harry Jones offered pleasure flights for tourists from the beach – it is just possible that someone had told Lindbergh about this before he took off, in case he did run into trouble – and Jones had a hangar there with tools, which he was happy to let Lindbergh use.

Almost at once a crowd collected as word got around that Lindy had landed on the beach. People crept up to the hangar and watched him working. 'He never looked at the crowd, nor did he betray the slightest consciousness of an audience,' wrote a young woman named Elise White, who was present. By the time Lindbergh finished tinkering with his plane, the crowd had grown so large that he needed a megaphone to address it. He asked the people to clear a space so that he could depart, but instead they pressed forward to look at the plane more closely 'and he threw the megaphone down in disgust', related a slightly startled Miss White. This was not the Charles Lindbergh that they had read about.

It's easy to understand Lindbergh's frustration. His plane was a sensitive instrument and the possibility of some witless gawker damaging it was a real and constant concern. The sight of people pawing his plane or leaning on it or waggling its moving parts was naturally horrifying to Lindbergh. He now essentially fled. Within moments of people coming forward, he was in the plane and proceeding with it on to the beach, trusting that people would scatter as he advanced. Luckily, they did. Lindbergh taxied to the far end of the beach, turned the plane into the wind and raced forward. 'It moved smoothly over the sand and in no distance at all – hardly more than a hundred yards – it was in the air,' wrote Miss White. 'He tipped and banked and turned swooping low over the beach then rose like a silver winged bird against the blue sky.' Thirty minutes later he was in Portland and facing new hordes of people whose most earnest desire was to crowd in on him and his beloved craft.

It is impossible to imagine what it must have been like to be Charles Lindbergh in that summer. From the moment he left his room in the morning, he was touched and jostled and bothered. Every person on earth who could get near enough wanted to grasp his hand or clap him on the back. He had no private life any more. Shirts he sent to the laundry never came back. Chicken bones and napkins from his dinner plate were fought over in kitchens. He could not go for a walk or pop into a bank or chemist's. If he went into a men's room, people followed. Cheques he wrote were rarely cashed; recipients preferred to frame them instead. No part of his life was normal, and there was no prospect that it ever would be again. As Lindbergh was discovering, it was a lot more fun to get famous than to be famous.

His tour consisted of sixty-nine overnight stops and thirteen 'touch' stops, where Lindbergh landed long enough to greet officials and say a few words, but did not otherwise linger. He also flew by request over scores of small towns, but only if they agreed to paint their town name on a rooftop for the benefit of other aviators. In communities where he could not land he dropped leaflets that read:

> Greetings. Because of the limited time and the extensive tour of the United States now in progress to encourage popular interest in aeronautics, it is impossible for the *Spirit of St Louis* to land in your city. This message from the air, however, is sent you to express our sincere appreciation of your interest in the tour and in the promotion and extension of commercial aeronautics in the United States.

It thereupon urged every citizen, as a matter of national urgency, to work for 'the establishment of airports and similar facilities', so that the United States could take 'its rightful place' as the world leader in commercial aviation.

From the start his receptions were chaotic. Excited onlookers and even members of the official greeting parties tended to rush forward to greet the plane as it was still taxiing. This was profoundly unnerving to Lindbergh. He had once seen a man sliced in two by a spinning propeller. Because he had no forward visibility, every landing was effectively blind. At least twice – in Kansas City and Portland, Oregon – he couldn't land at the intended destination because of crowds on the runway, and had to set down on nearby farmland. Elsewhere, batteries of guns fired in salute of his arrival produced drifting smoke that obscured his visibility further. All in all, he faced more dangers flying around America than he ever had on his flight to Paris.

To try to keep to schedules, Lindbergh was often driven at high speed along his parade routes, a matter that dismayed spectators and alarmed Lindbergh since onlookers here, too, were inclined to step into the road for a better look.

An entirely typical day was Lindbergh's visit to Springfield, Illinois, on 15 August, where he arrived in early afternoon having flown from Chicago by way of Mooseheart, Aurora, Joliet and Peoria. In the one hour and forty-one minutes he was on the ground at Springfield, Lindbergh did the following: made a brief speech at the airfield, was presented to about a hundred local officials, invited to admire and review the 106th Illinois Cavalry and placed in an open-top car for a five-mile dash past 50,000 cheering people waving flags, laid a wreath at the tomb of Abraham Lincoln, and was taken to the local arsenal where he was presented with a gold watch and bathed in a succession of rambling, overwrought speeches. Here is a sampling of the florid tribute paid him by Mayor J. Emil Smith:

> As he sailed through the silver of that summer dawn, the stars watched with a still delight to see a child of earth so brave riding the air, a comrade of cloud and wind and foaming wave. And as he neared his goal the sun, the sea and the huge unfettered spaces hailed him a victor and chanted to him, 'Well done.'

All that made the Springfield stop a little different was

its extreme familiarity: this had been one of Lindbergh's working airfields during his stint as an airmail pilot. Indeed, he had chosen the site of the field just fifteen months earlier.

In conclusion, the mayor announced that they were renaming the airfield Lindbergh Field in his honour – an irony that cannot have been lost on young Charles since just the previous year the citizens of Springfield had over-whelmingly defeated a bond proposal to build a decent airfield in the town. That they had any field at all was thanks only to the local chamber of commerce, which provided modest funding to give the city the most basic facilities.

After his ceremonies, Lindbergh was rushed back to his waiting plane for an onward flight to St Louis, where he faced more presentations, more crowds and yet another evening banquet. Lindbergh was under such constant pressure on the ground that he found the flying between cities the most restful part of his tour, and sometimes introduced long detours into his itineraries to give himself some peace. Where he could – over lakes, for instance, or level ground – he often flew just fifteen feet or so above the surface, which increased the sense of speed and thrill, but narrowed his margin for recovery to zero if anything went wrong. He was given two days a week off, which must have been a blessed relief, but even then he was far from home and constantly in the company of strangers.

Charles Levine was now the only Atlantic flyer still in Europe and he showed no inclination yet to come home. He poked around for the rest of the summer. He travelled to Italy, where he met the Pope and declared Mussolini the greatest statesman in the world. Returning to Paris, he made the papers for getting into a fistfight with a fellow American near the Opéra. 'I never saw the man before, but he insulted me and I took a crack at him,' Levine said. 'I used to be a boxer,' he added significantly. The cause of the outburst was never explained, but was rumoured to involve a woman.

Levine also announced plans to fly home with Maurice Drouhin, one of the two French pilots whose endurance record Chamberlin and Acosta had beaten in Levine's plane in April. This would present an interesting challenge since Drouhin spoke no English and Levine no French. Levine several times announced takeoff dates, but each one came and passed. Then abruptly in late August Levine collected his plane from the hangar at Le Bourget and took off in it. Some hours later, officials at Croydon Aerodrome in London were astonished to see the plane approaching in a decidedly erratic fashion. The *Columbia* was a famous aeroplane, so they recognized it at once, but it was obvious that whoever was flying it was either in-competent or incapacitated. This was a matter of some alarm: Croydon was a busy airport, with regular passenger flights to Paris and elsewhere, and controllers had only limited means to alert other aircraft to stay back. The *Columbia* circled the airport four times, once almost crash-ing into the control tower.

Finally, it came in to land at a steep and awkward angle, and hit the ground so hard that it bounced high into the air again before slamming heavily back to earth and rolling to a halt. Out from it stepped a beaming Charles Levine. It was the first time he had ever flown solo. It trans-pired that he had travelled 130 miles further than necessary to get there. Levine said he had just had a whim to go up alone. Soon afterwards, however, news reached London that Levine had in fact taken off just ahead of a writ from Drouhin, who was complaining bitterly that Levine owed him 80,000 francs in wages. The hangar manager at Le Bourget also reported that he had never been paid. Levine had evidently also failed to tell his wife that he would be leaving her behind in Paris. (Their marriage did not long outlast the summer.)

To avoid arrest now, Levine had to give a formal undertaking that he would never under any circumstances attempt to fly over British soil again. Levine was nothing if not irrepressible, and within a few days he announced plans for another Atlantic flight, this one from Cranwell Aerodrome in Lincolnshire with Captain Walter Hinchliffe, a senior pilot of Imperial Airways. In the days that followed, Levine constantly contradicted himself about whether he and Hinchliffe would fly to America westward over the Atlantic or eastward across Asia and the northern Pacific. In the event, they didn't go anywhere and the papers lost interest in both of them.

Drouhin did eventually get some of his back pay, but didn't have long to enjoy it. He died the next year in a crash during a test flight at Orly. Hinchliffe didn't fare any better. He vanished at about the same time while trying to fly the Atlantic with a female companion.

With the Atlantic conquered, attention turned to the Pacific – specifically, the 2,400 miles of challenging emptiness that lay between California and Hawaii. In the immediate aftermath of Lindbergh's flight, James D. Dole, a Massachusetts native who had amassed a fortune growing and canning pineapples in Hawaii, announced a new challenge, to be called the Dole Pacific Race, with $35,000 in prize money. Dole's event was to be a proper race, with competitors all taking off at the same time (or as nearly as possible) from the municipal airfield in Oakland, California. The race was scheduled for August, but was overtaken by events considerably before then. On 29 June, two Army flyers successfully flew in a Fokker from Oakland to Oahu in twenty-six hours. It was an extraordinary achievement – hitting Hawaii was a real feat of navigation – and the two pilots, Lt Lester J. Maitland and Lt Albert F. Hegenberger, deserve to be remembered, but unfortunately they weren't even much noticed then because their success occurred at exactly the moment that Commander Byrd and his team were splashing down at Ver-sur-Mer. Two weeks after the Maitland–Hegenberger flight, two more pilots, Ernest Smith and Emory Bronte, also flew from Oakland to Hawaii – though only just. Virtually out of fuel, they crash-landed into a tree on Molokai, but somehow emerged unscathed. They had beaten Maitland and Hegenberger's time by fourteen minutes. So by 16 August, when the Dole race got under way, the competitors had absolutely nothing to prove.

Staging it as a race considerably heightened the dangers. It increased pressure on pilots to take off whether or not their aircraft were fully ready, and then to push those planes to their limits in order to beat others reasonably presumed to be doing likewise. A race – particularly a well-publicized race with a big prize – tended to attract flyers who were more eager than skilful. Hawaii was a tiny target in a vast ocean, and reaching it stretched even the most experienced pilots to the limits of their capabilities.

The whole enterprise was a recipe for catastrophe, and catastrophic it proved.

Three competitors died in crashes before they even reached Oakland. Another plane crashed in the sea as it approached the Oakland airfield; the two occupants escaped without serious injury but their plane was lost. Another plane was not allowed to depart after it became clear that the pilot had no idea how much fuel he needed to reach Hawaii and didn't have a fuel tank nearly big enough. It was obvious that several of the hopeful competitors were dangers to themselves.

By the day of the race, the number of planes taking part had been reduced to eight, and four of those were scratched before takeoff or turned back soon after. Of the four planes that set off, two made it to Hawaii and two more were lost en route. One of those never seen again was a plane carrying a pretty 22-year-old schoolteacher from Flint, Michigan, named Mildred Doran, who was not a pilot but simply accompanying others to add glamour and interest for the press. When word got back that six people, including Miss Doran, were missing, a pilot named William Erwin took off from Oakland to look for them, but he disappeared, too. A great sea search – the greatest in history, it was claimed – was mounted, involving thirty-nine warships and nineteen civilian ships, but nothing was found. The Navy reported, a bit sourly, that it had burned 383,550 gallons of fuel looking for lost flyers. Altogether, ten people died in the Dole race. The whole thing was widely criticized. Byrd called it 'hasty and ill-advised', and many echoed his sentiments.

Despite the disaster of the Dole race, people were suddenly announcing daring and risky flights all over the place. Paul Redfern, the son of the dean of Benedict's College, a school for black students in Columbia, South Carolina, announced a plan to fly from Brunswick, Georgia, to Rio de Janeiro in a Stinson Detroiter aeroplane. Redfern was an unlikely hero. He had been crazy about planes all his life – so much so that he often wore an aviator's goggled helmet even when on the ground and just going about his daily business – but his academic training was as a musician. His experience as a pilot consisted of a couple of years of barnstorming at county fairs and working as a spotter of illegal stills for the government. The same age as Lindbergh, he was small and slight (he weighed just 108 pounds) and had a nervous-looking face, but then he had a lot to be nervous about. He was proposing to fly 4,600 miles – further than anyone had flown before – over ocean and jungle, into a realm far beyond the range of reliable maps and weather reports.

He packed as if he didn't really expect to make it. He took with him fishing tackle, rifle and ammunition, quinine, mosquito nets, surgical kit, spare boots and much else that would only be of use if he crash-landed in the jungle. For his short-term needs he packed twenty sandwiches, four pints of coffee, a pound of milk chocolate and two gallons of water. On 25 August, he took off.

Aviation experts quoted by the Associated Press said that it would take him at least sixty hours to reach Rio. Before he had even cleared the Caribbean he was lost, and dropped a message to a Norwegian freighter, the *Christian Krohg*, asking for directions. The message bounced off the deck and into the sea, but amazingly a Norwegian seaman dived in and retrieved it. The message said: 'Point ship to nearest land, wave flag or handkerchief once for each 100 miles. Thanks, Redfern.'

The ship obliged and Redfern with a snappy salute departed. It was the last anyone ever saw of him, though for years afterwards missionaries and other visitors to the interior of Dutch Guiana passed on reports of a white man living among the Indians. According to these reports, the Indians treated the man as a divinity because he had dropped in on them from the sky. The white man, it was said, had taken a wife and now lived in contentment with the natives. Several expeditions plunged into the jungle to try to find Redfern. At least two men lost their lives in the quest, but he was never found. In 1938, at the request of Redfern's wife – that is, his one certain wife, back in America – Redfern was declared officially dead by a court in Detroit.

Scarcely less improbable, but miraculously more success-ful, was a flight undertaken by Edward F. Schlee, a Detroit businessman, and William S. 'Billy' Brock, a cheerful, conspicuously portly former airmail pilot. They set out to beat the round-the-world record of 28 days, 14 hours and 36 minutes made the previous year by two other Detroit men using aeroplanes, trains and ships, but this time they intended to do it exclusively by air.

Schlee, the son of German immigrants, had been an engineer for Henry Ford, but in 1922 he left Ford and opened a petrol station. Then he opened another. Within five years he had more than a hundred petrol stations. He also owned a small airline called Canadian American Airways, through which he employed Brock. Schlee was thirty-nine years old in the summer of 1927, Brock thirty-one. Brock had already been in the news that summer for dashing by air from Detroit to the Black Hills to deliver a new collie to Grace Coolidge, the president's wife, after her previous pet ran off.

Although neither Brock nor Schlee had any experience of distance flying, they set themselves the ambitious goal of circling the world in just fifteen days. Their plane was a Stinson Detroiter powered by a Wright Whirlwind engine. They took off the day after Redfern, and for the next two and a half weeks their exploits gripped the world – largely because they were so constantly and thrillingly operating at the very edge of their competence. They successfully flew the Atlantic – a notable achievement in itself, of course – but had no idea where they were when they got to the other side. Passing over a beach crowded with holiday-makers, they dropped a message asking the name of the locality. A man with a stick obligingly traced the name 'SEATON' in the sand and pointed to a Union Jack flutter-ing over the promenade. With their location fixed, they proceeded to a triumphant reception in London. They took off from Croydon just hours before Levine flew in, rather more erratically, from Paris, then made their way in stages across Europe to Constantinople before continu-ing on to Calcutta, Rangoon, Hanoi, Hong Kong and Shanghai. They were finally forced down by a typhoon on Kyushu in Japan. They had covered 12,795 miles in nine-teen days, but were still 9,850 miles from home. Bad weather and the daunting breadth of the Pacific made them decide to end their quest while they were still ahead, and they returned by ship to a hero's welcome. The trip took more out of them than they seem to have realized. At a banquet in Detroit upon his return, Schlee got up to speak, read the first five words of his speech and collapsed as the events of recent weeks caught up with and overwhelmed him.

Things did not get better for Schlee after that. In the summer of 1929 he was nearly killed when he was hit by a spinning propeller, which struck his head and amputated his right arm at the shoulder, leaving him much diminished. Just three months after that, he lost everything in the Wall Street crash. In 1931, his plane, *Pride of Detroit*, was auctioned by order of the sheriff's department as part of a debt judgement. It was bought by a man named Floyd M. Phinney for just $700. Schlee died in 1969 'in obscure poverty'. Brock, too, did not fare well. He died of cancer in 1932.

And still people kept flying. In Britain, an unlikely 62-year-old woman, Princess Löwenstein-Wertheim, stepped forward as yet another figure to attempt the first east-to-west crossing. The daughter of the Earl of Mexborough, she had grown up in London as Lady Anne Savile, but had married, at the rather advanced age of thirty-one, Prince Ludwig Karl zu Löwenstein-Wertheim-Freudenberg of Germany. Widowed after just two years, the princess used her considerable inheritance to indulge a passion for aviation. In 1912 she became the first woman to cross the English Channel by air – albeit as a passenger. Soon after, again as a passenger, she flew from Egypt to France. When, in 1927, a dashing captain named Leslie Hamilton expressed a desire to cross the Atlantic from east to west, she funded the flight on the understanding that she would accompany them. With Lt Col. Frederick Minchin as co-pilot, they took off from an airfield near Salisbury in Wiltshire. The princess wore a stylish hat and an ocelot coat, as if they were off for cocktails at the Savoy. They were sighted over Ireland and again from a ship about halfway across the Atlantic, but they never reached America and no trace of them was ever found.

At about the same time, a plane called *Old Glory*, owned by William Randolph Hearst, took off from Old Orchard Beach in Maine – the beach where Lindbergh had made his recent unscheduled landing in the *Spirit of St Louis* – heading for Rome. *Old Glory* was piloted by Lloyd Bertaud, the man who had taken out an injunction against Charles Levine in May after Levine failed to provide contracts and insurance as promised. Accompanying Bertaud as co-pilot was James DeWitt Hill and along for the ride as a passenger was Philip A. Payne, editor of Hearst's *Daily Mirror*. Just three and a half hours after take-off they issued an urgent, unexplained SOS. They were never seen again. A few hours later, two Canadian airmen, Capt. Terrence Tully and Lt James Medcalf, took off from Newfoundland, bound for London in a plane called the *Sir John Carling*. They were never heard from again either.

CHAPTER 23

H. L. MENCKEN CALLED it 'the one authentic rectum of civilization', but for most people Hollywood was a place of magic. In 1927, the iconic 'HOLLYWOOD' sign on the hillside above the city actually said 'HOLLYWOODLAND'. It had been erected in 1923 to advertise a property development and had nothing to do with motion pictures. The letters, each over forty feet high, were in those days also traced out with electric lights. (The 'LAND' was removed in 1949.)

Los Angeles in 1927 was America's fastest growing city, and its richest when measured per capita. The population of greater Los Angeles, including the unincorporated communities of Beverly Hills and Santa Monica, had more than doubled in a decade to almost 2.5 million, and those lucky citizens were 60 per cent better off than the average American elsewhere. And what accounted for much of that was southern California's most celebrated industry: motion pictures.

By 1927, Hollywood was producing some 800 feature films a year, 80 per cent of the world's total output, plus some 20,000 short features. Movies were America's fourth largest industry, employing more people than Ford and General Motors put together, and generating over $750 million for the economy – four times more than was earned by all sports and live entertainments combined. Twenty thousand cinemas sold 100 million tickets a week. On any given day, one sixth of all Americans were at the pictures.

It seemed crazy that such a huge and popular business could be struggling, but it was. The problem was that turnover was so rapid that few individual pictures made much profit. Programmes were sometimes changed three or even four times a week, so there was a constant need for more product. Studios were churning out as many as four new films a week, a rate that was clearly incompatible with quality. When somebody pointed out to MGM chief Irving Thalberg that it was wrong to put a beach scene into a movie set in Paris since Paris patently is not on any coastline, Thalberg looked at the person in astonishment. 'We can't cater to a handful of people who know Paris,' he replied.

As audiences became more discerning in where they sat, if not always over what they watched, cinema owners built bigger, more sumptuous cinemas in the hopes of coaxing in more people at higher prices. Big cinemas began to appear from about 1915 (a reminder that while Europe was at war America was at the pictures), but the golden age of the picture palace was the 1920s. Cinemas were built on a scale that was truly epic, with auditoriums that could seat 2,000 or more patrons in an atmosphere of opulence greater than any they had experienced before. People, it was said, went to Loew's cinemas just to enjoy the well-appointed toilets.

Architects borrowed freely and imaginatively from any culture that had ever built on a grand scale – Persian, Moorish, Italian Renaissance, Baroque, Meso-American, gilded French. Egyptian became especially popular after the discovery of the tomb of King Tutankhamun in 1922. At the Tivoli in Chicago the marbled lobby was said to be an almost exact copy of the king's chapel at Versailles, except presumably for the smell of popcorn.

The problem was that movies alone couldn't fill such a large volume of seats. Cinema owners had to provide extra attractions – musical performances, newsreels, serials, a comic turn, perhaps a magician or other novelty act, dance demonstrations, a round or two of a popular game called Screeno. Some of the big cinemas spent as much as $2,800 a week on orchestras alone. Increasingly, the film became a minor feature of the entire package.

In 1927, an industry insider named Harold E. Franklin produced a book with a dull title but a worrisome message. *Motion Picture Theater Management* outlined with clinical precision the grim economics of motion picture screening. Rent on a typical new movie palace took roughly a third of gross receipts, and advertising swallowed up half as much again. Orchestras lopped another 15 per cent off the intake, and live entertainers typically took about 7 per cent more. When all the fixed costs of staff salaries, utility bills, maintenance, property taxes and so on were factored in, the profit in even the best-case scenario could never be more than a sliver of overall takings.

Despite the economic risks – indeed, folly – of building ever larger cinemas, owners somehow persuaded themselves that the answer was to keep doing so. The first half of 1927 alone saw the opening of Grauman's Chinese Theatre in Los Angeles, where patrons could enjoy movies from within the sanctum of a faux Buddhist pagoda; the 3,600-seat Norshore in Chicago, whose interiors were a confection of costly rococo; the similarly ornate and gleaming 3,100-seat Proctor's Eighty-Sixth Street Theatre in New York; and the granddaddy of them all, the vast, bejewelled Roxy Theatre on Fiftieth Street at Seventh Avenue in New York. Everything about the Roxy was without parallel. It seated 6,200 people. The dressing rooms could accommodate 300 performers. A 118-piece orchestra made every movie a symphonic as well as a visual experience. An organ so massive it needed three men to play it provided musical interludes. Fourteen Steinway pianos were on permanent standby. The air in the theatre was cooled and freshened by giant machines in the basement. Drinking fountains dispensed ice-cold water – a thrilling novelty. The Roxy even boasted its own 'hospital' where, as the literature proudly noted, 'even a major operation can be performed if necessary'. So dazzling was the infrastructure that even *Scientific American* sent a reporter to write a feature. A cartoon in the *New Yorker* showed a child in the lobby asking her mother in hushed awe, 'Mama, does God live here?'

Building the cinema was estimated to have cost between $7 million and $10 million. The money came from a film producer named Herbert Lubin, who was effectively bankrupted by the project, but the name and vision came from Samuel Lionel Rothafel – known to one and all as 'Roxy'. A Minnesotan, Rothafel grew up in Stillwater, twenty miles east of St Paul, the son of a shoemaker, and was headed for a career in professional

427

baseball when he was unexpectedly sidetracked (through a romantic entanglement) into cinema management. He quickly distinguished himself as a showman with a particular gift for rescuing troubled operations. The idea of combining movie presentations with live shows was a Roxy invention. The most notable fact about Roxy himself was that he didn't actually like movies. He lived in an apartment hidden above the cinema's five-storey-high rotunda.

The opening of the new Roxy was such a momentous occasion that President Coolidge and Vice-President Charles Dawes both sent congratulations (though Coolidge in his predictably odd way praised Rothafel for some equipment he had donated to the Walter Reed Hospital in Washington and never mentioned the cinema).

The new Roxy took in $127,000 in its first week, but such business could never be sustained.* The *New Yorker*, in the Talk of the Town column in the summer of 1927, noted that just three New York cinemas – the Paramount, the Roxy and the Capitol – offered 70,000 seats a day.

While the cinemas were struggling to maintain their audiences, things were not going terribly well on the production side of the business either. The previous November unions representing the craft trades – painters, carpenters, electricians and the like – had secured something called the Studio Basic Agreement, which granted

---

* A little-noticed fact was that the Roxy was sold almost at once to the Fox film company for a whopping $15 million. The purchase contributed significantly to Fox's bankruptcy in the following decade.

them important and costly concessions. The studios were now terrified of being squeezed similarly by actors and writers. With this in mind, thirty-six people from the creative side of the industry met for dinner at the Ambassador Hotel in Los Angeles in January 1927 and formed a kind of executive club to promote – but even more to protect – the studios. It was a reflection of their own sense of self-importance that they called it the International Academy of Motion Picture Arts and Sciences, elevating films from popular entertainment to something more grandly artistic, scientific and, literally, academic. In the second week of May, while the world fretted over the missing airmen Nungesser and Coli, the academy was formally inaugurated at a banquet at the Biltmore Hotel in Los Angeles. (The idea of having an awards ceremony was something of an afterthought, and wasn't introduced until the academy's second-anniversary dinner in 1929.)

Then came a stunning setback. On 9 July, the Federal Trade Commission ordered an immediate end to the system known as block booking, wherein cinemas were required to take all or most of a studio's output, not just its more desirable features. Block booking had sustained Hollywood for years. Under it, exhibitors might be compelled to take as many as fifty dreadful to mediocre pictures in order to get perhaps two or three more promising ones. The FTC ruling threw everything into uncertainty, and left the film industry in the exceedingly odd position of being hugely successful and gravely imperilled at the same time.

Something radical was needed to put the movie business back on track. In Los Angeles, a tiny, somewhat ragtag studio named Warner Brothers stood ready to provide it with a novel picture with sound called *The Jazz Singer*.

It is a painful irony that silent movies were driven out of existence just as they were arriving at a kind of glorious summit of creativity and imagination, so that some of the best silent movies were also some of the last. Of no film was that more true than *Wings*, which opened on 12 August at the Criterion Theatre in New York, with a dedication to Charles Lindbergh.

The film was the conception of John Monk Saunders, a bright young man from Minnesota who was also a Rhodes scholar, gifted writer, handsome philanderer and drinker, not necessarily in that order. In the early 1920s, Saunders met and became friends with the film producer Jesse Lasky and Lasky's wife, Bessie. Saunders was an uncommonly charming fellow, and he persuaded Lasky to buy a half-finished novel he had written about aerial combat in the First World War. Fired with excitement, Lasky gave Saunders a record $39,000 for the idea and put him to work on a script. Had Lasky known that Saunders was sleeping with his wife, he might not have been quite so generous.

Lasky's choice for director was unexpected but inspired. William Wellman was thirty years old and had no experience of making big films – and at $2 million *Wings* was the biggest film Paramount had ever undertaken. At a time when top-rank directors like Ernst Lubitsch were paid $175,000 a picture, Wellman was given a salary of $250 a week. But he had one advantage over every other director in Hollywood: he was a First World War flying ace and intimately understood the beauty and enchantment of flight as well as the fearful mayhem of aerial combat. No filmmaker has ever used technical proficiency to better advantage.

Wellman had had a busy life already. Born into a well-to-do family in Brookline, Massachusetts, he had been a high school dropout, a professional ice hockey player, a volunteer in the French Foreign Legion and a member of the celebrated Lafayette Escadrille air squadron. Both France and the United States had decorated him for gallantry. After the war he became friends with Douglas Fairbanks, who got him a job at the Goldwyn studios as an actor. Wellman hated acting and switched to directing. He became what was known as a contract director, churning out low-budget westerns and other B movies. Always temperamental, he was frequently fired from jobs, once for slapping an actress. He was a startling choice to be put in charge of such a challenging epic. To the astonishment of everyone, he now directed one of the most intelligent, moving and thrilling pictures ever made.

Nothing was faked. Whatever the pilot saw in real life the audiences saw on the screen. When clouds or exploding dirigibles were seen outside aeroplane windows they were real objects filmed in real time. Wellman mounted cameras inside the cockpits looking out, so that audiences had the sensation of sitting at the pilots' shoulders, and outside the cockpit looking in, providing close-up views of the pilots' reactions. Richard Arlen and Buddy Rogers, the two male stars of the picture, had to be their own cameramen, activating cameras with a remote-control button.

Filming was done outside San Antonio, Texas. The scale of the production was vast and complex. Whole battlefields were scrupulously recreated on the plains of Texas. Wellman deployed as many as 5,000 extras and sixty aeroplanes in some scenes – an enormous logistical exercise. The army sent its best aviators from Selfridge Field in Michigan – the very men with whom Lindbergh had just flown to Ottawa – and stunt flyers were used for the more dangerous scenes. Wellman asked a lot of his airmen. One pilot was killed, another broke his neck, and several more sustained other serious injuries. Wellman did some of the more dangerous stunt-flying himself. All this gave the movie's aerial scenes a realism and immediacy that many found almost literally breathtaking. Wellman captured features of flight that had never been caught on film before – the shadows of planes moving across the earth, the sensation of flying through drifting smoke, the stately fall of bombs and the destructive puffs of impact that follow.

Even the land-bound scenes were filmed with a thoughtfulness and originality that set *Wings* apart. To bring the viewer into a Parisian nightclub, Wellman used a boom shot in which the camera travelled through the room just above table height, skimming over drinks and between revellers, before arriving at the table of Arlen and Rogers. It is an entrancing shot even now, but it was rivetingly novel in 1927. '*Wings*,' wrote Penelope Gilliatt simply in the *New Yorker* in 1971, 'is truly beautiful.' *Wings* was selected as best picture at the very first Academy Awards ceremony in 1929. Wellman wasn't even invited to the ceremony.

Despite its entrancing aerial sequences and affecting story of bravery, camaraderie and loss, many people went to *Wings* not to thrill at the aerial acrobatics but to gaze in admiration and longing at its female lead, the enchanting Clara Bow.

Above: The sculptor Gutzon Borglum views a model for his presidential sculptures on Mount Rushmore – a monumental and seemingly hare-brained project dedicated in summer 1927 and only completed 14 years later.

Right: Bartolomeo Vanzetti, fish vendor (*left*), and Nicola Sacco, shoemaker – two Italian immigrants whose convictions for murder and death sentences made them an international *cause célèbre*. Their guilt or innocence is still a matter of dispute.

Left: Robert G. Elliott, America's top executioner and a master of the difficult art of administering death by electrocution. He would execute, among many others, Sacco and Vanzetti in the summer of 1927, and the next year Ruth Snyder and Judd Gray.

Right: On 29 August, following the execution of Sacco and Vanzetti, their funeral procession through Boston attracted many thousands of viewers – quite a different gathering from the ones greeting Lindbergh.

Right: Nineteen twenty-seven
was a great year for movies. One
of the best was William Wellman's
Wings, a thrilling and technically
groundbreaking epic about First World
War air combat that won the first
Academy Award and featured the famed
'It Girl' Clara Bow.

Below: While it was by no means the
first 'talking picture', *The Jazz Singer*,
starring the singer Al Jolson, was the
production that made sound movies real
to a mass audience and ended the silent
era – in the process saving Hollywood
from financial ruin.

Cinemas that showed those
films were constructed
on the scale of palaces, as
this interior shot of New
York's famed Roxy Theatre
demonstrates. Its opening
in 1927 was so momentous
an occasion that President
Coolidge sent a telegram
of congratulations to its
builder.

Two of the oddest business titans America ever produced were the brothers Mantis and Oris Van Sweringen (**right**). Inseparable and reclusive, they made a fortune in railways and property and built Shaker Heights, the first planned suburban community, and Cleveland's Union Terminal (**above**), at the time the second tallest building in America.

Al Capone, the famed Chicago gangster. In 1927 his murderous mob flourished in the most politically corrupt city in the country and grossed more than $100 million.

Capone's eventual downfall came at the hands of Mabel Walker Willebrandt, the chief federal Prohibition prosecutor who developed the novel theory that he could be prosecuted for evading taxes.

Above: The 1920s was a decade justly noted for financial chicanery. Dapper Charles Ponzi's famed 'scheme' involved postal reply coupons. By 1927 he resided in Charlestown Prison with his fellow Italian immigrants Sacco and Vanzetti.

Above right: Albert B. Fall (*left*), former secretary of the interior, and Edward Doheny, an oil tycoon, outside the Washington, DC, courtroom where they stood trial in 1927 for their roles in the Teapot Dome bribery and corruption scandal.

Right: Texas Guinan, the premier nightclub hostess of the era, being led into a paddy wagon after a police raid on one of her many speakeasies. Her genial expression here speaks volumes about the trivial and temporary nature of her arrest.

Perhaps the nuttiest pastime in an era of nutty fads was the 'sport' of flagpole-sitting. Its undisputed champion was 'Shipwreck' Kelly, seen here atop the St Francis Hotel in Newark, New Jersey, where he remained for 12 days in June 1927.

Left: The archetypal figure of the era was the flapper – style-conscious women who flouted conventional mores to smoke, drink, consort with the opposite sex and dance the Charleston just about anywhere.

For people who liked music with their illegal booze, Harlem was the place to go. Its premier establishment was the famed Cotton Club, where such black musical geniuses as Duke Ellington, Cab Calloway and Fats Waller performed for a whites-only clientele.

The memorably named Kenesaw Mountain Landis, a federal judge in Chicago who became commissioner of baseball after the famed 'Black Sox' series-fixing scandal of 1919 and who may or may not have 'saved baseball'.

Nineteen twenty-seven saw the first primitive television broadcasts, but the real 'father of television' was the lone and luckless inventor Philo T. Farnsworth, who in September of that year perfected the cathode ray tube system that eventually made television a practical reality.

Above: Alas for Farnsworth, his eventual 165 patents could not prevent the radio pioneer David Sarnoff, founder of the Radio Corporation of America, from stealing his ideas and making television a commercially viable product.

Left: Automotive titan and anti-Semitic crackpot Henry Ford. His efforts to replace his company's fabled Model T with a new Model A in 1927 dealt the Ford Motor Company a setback from which it never fully recovered.

Left: Charles Lindbergh stopped on his cross-country barnstorming tour on 11 August to meet Henry Ford, who took a short flight with Lindbergh in the *Spirit of St Louis,* claiming to have 'handled the stick'.

Below: Henry Ford's most ambitious, and ultimately foolish, project was Fordlandia, a model American community built in the jungles of Brazil to produce the rubber his cars required reliably and cheaply. The incompetence of his managers and the harsh conditions of the Amazon eventually doomed the venture.

Perhaps the most sensational sporting event of 1927 was the heavyweight title bout between Jack Dempsey and Gene Tunney at Chicago's Soldier Field on 27 September before 150,000 people. Here Dempsey, having knocked down Tunney, finally makes it to a neutral corner during the still-controversial 'Long Count'.

Bow was just twenty-two years old in 1927, but already a Hollywood veteran. Her background could not have been tougher. She was born into poverty in the Bay Ridge district of Brooklyn and was raised by a mother who was frequently drunk and always dangerously unstable. Once as a child Clara awoke to find her mother holding a knife to her throat. (Eventually Mrs Bow was committed to an asylum.)

Bow arrived in Hollywood in 1923, having won a photographic competition, and quickly became a star. She was universally adored by colleagues. She routinely put in fifteen-hour days, and often went from one movie straight into another. She made fifteen films in 1925 alone, thirty-five altogether between 1925 and 1929. Once she worked on three films at the same time. Her talent as an actress, and no doubt as a person, was an ability to convey an array of emotions, from demure innocence to shameless lust and back again, in a single winsome glance. 'She danced even when her feet were not moving,' the studio mogul Adolph Zukor once said of her. 'Some part of her was always in motion, if only her great rolling eyes. It was an elemental magnetism, an animal vitality, that made her the centre of attraction in any company.'

Her personal life was rather less successful. She was dazzlingly promiscuous. According to Wellman, during the filming of *Wings* Bow had relationships (not all necessarily consummated – but not necessarily not, as it were) with Buddy Rogers, Richard Arlen, a stunt pilot, two pursuit pilots 'and a panting writer'. At one point in the 1920s, she was engaged to five men in four years. In the same period she had liaisons with many others. Once, according to Roger Kahn, her boyfriend came home and realized there was someone hiding in her bathroom. 'Come on out so I can knock your teeth out, you yellow son of a bitch!' the boyfriend yelled. The door opened and out stepped a sheepish Jack Dempsey. She spent much of the summer of 1927 draped like a wet towel over Gary Cooper, whom she had met on the set of *Wings*, in which he had a small part as a doomed airman.

Bow was originally billed as the 'Brooklyn Bonfire', then as the 'Hottest Jazz Baby in Films', but in 1927 she became, and would for evermore remain, 'the It Girl'. 'It' was first a two-part article and then a novel by a flame-haired English novelist named Elinor Glyn who was known for writing juicy romances in which the main characters did a lot of undulating ('she undulated round and all over him, twined about him like a serpent') and for being the mistress for some years of Lord Curzon, former viceroy of India. 'It,' as Glyn explained, 'is that quality possessed by some few persons which draws all others with its magnetic life force. With It you win all men if you are a woman – and all women if you are a man.' Asked by a reporter to name some notable possessors of 'It', Glyn cited Rudolph Valentino, John Gilbert and Rex the Wonder Horse. Later she extended the list to include the doorman at the Ambassador Hotel in Los Angeles.

It the novel was a story in which the two principal characters – Ava and Larry, both dripping with 'It' – look at each other with 'burning eyes' and 'a fierce gleam' before getting together to 'vibrate with passion'. As Dorothy Parker summed up the book in the *New Yorker*, '*It* goes on for nearly three hundred pages, with both of them vibrating away like steam-launches.'

The motion picture was completely different.

Although Glyn received a screen credit for *It*, the story as filmed bore no relation to anything she had ever written. All that remained of Glyn's earlier effort was the title. In the film, Bow played the part of Betty Lou, a lively and good-natured department store salesgirl who decides to woo and win the store's dishy owner, one Cyrus Waltham.

The movie was an enormous hit in 1927. With *Wings*, it confirmed Bow as Hollywood's leading female star. She received 40,000 letters a week – more than all the people in a fair-sized town. In the summer of 1927, her career seemed set to go on indefinitely. In fact, it was nearly at an end. Winsome and enchanting as she was to behold, her Brooklyn accent was the vocal equivalent of nails on a blackboard, and in the new world of talking pictures, that would never do.

Considering that moving pictures and recorded sound had both independently existed since the 1890s, it took a surprisingly long time for anyone to work out how to put them together. The problem was twofold. First was the matter of sound projection. Nothing existed that would allow clear, natural-sounding speech to be played to an auditorium full of people, particularly in the new cavernous spaces of the 1920s. Equally intractable was the challenge of synchronization. Designing a machine that could match voices and moving lips precisely defeated all attempts at solution. As events demonstrated, it was easier to fly a man across the Atlantic than to capture his voice on film.

If talking pictures could be said to have a father, it was Lee De Forest, a brilliant but erratic inventor of electrical devices of all types. (He had 216 patents.) In 1907, while searching for ways to boost telephone signals, De Forest invented something called the thermionic triode detector. De Forest's patent described it as 'a System for Amplifying Feeble Electric Currents' and it would play a pivotal role in the development of broadcast radio and much else involving the delivery of sound, but the real developments would come from others. De Forest, unfortunately, was forever distracted by business problems. Several companies he founded went bankrupt, twice he was swindled by his backers, and constantly he was in court fighting over money or patents. For these reasons, he didn't follow through on his invention.

Meanwhile, other hopeful inventors demonstrated various sound-and-image systems – Cinematophone, Cameraphone, Synchroscope – but in every case the only really original thing about them was their name. All produced sounds that were faint or muddy, or required impossibly perfect timing on the part of the projectionist. Getting a projector and sound system to run in perfect tandem was basically impossible. Moving pictures were filmed with hand-cranked cameras, which introduced a slight variability in speed that no sound system could adjust to. Projectionists also commonly repaired damaged film by cutting out a few frames and re-splicing what remained, which clearly would throw out any recording. Even perfect film sometimes skipped or momentarily stuttered in the projector. All these things confounded synchronization.

De Forest came up with the idea of imprinting the sound directly on to the film. That meant that no matter what happened with the film, sound and image would always be perfectly aligned. Failing to find backers in

America, he moved to Berlin in the early 1920s and there developed a system that he called Phonofilm. De Forest made his first Phonofilm movie in 1921 and by 1923 he was back in America giving public demonstrations. He filmed Calvin Coolidge making a speech, Eddie Cantor singing, George Bernard Shaw pontificating, and DeWolf Hopper reciting 'Casey at the Bat'. By any measure, these were the first talking pictures. However, no Hollywood studio would invest in them. The sound quality still wasn't ideal and the recording system couldn't quite cope with multiple voices and movement of a type necessary for any meaningful dramatic presentation.

One invention De Forest couldn't make use of was his own triode detector tube because the patents now resided with Western Electric, a subsidiary of AT&T. Western Electric had been using the triode to develop public address systems for conveying speeches to large crowds or announcements to fans at baseball stadiums and the like. But in the 1920s it occurred to some forgotten engineer at the company that the triode detector could be used to project sound in cinemas as well. The upshot is that in 1925 Warner Brothers bought the system from Western Electric and dubbed it Vitaphone. By the time of *The Jazz Singer*, it had already featured in theatrical presentations several times. Indeed, the Roxy on its opening night in March 1927 played a Vitaphone feature of songs from *Carmen* sung by Giovanni Martinelli. 'His voice burst from the screen with splendid synchronization with the movements of his lips,' marvelled the critic Mordaunt Hall in the *New York Times*. 'It rang through the great theatre as if he had himself been on the stage.'

Despite Hall's enthusiastic praise, the Vitaphone technology was actually already obsolescent. Vitaphone's sound was recorded on to discs, as on a record album, and one motor turned both projector and phonograph together, which kept them in synch so long as the disc and film were both positioned exactly right and started at precisely the same instant, which was always easier said than done. Where the system shone was in providing rich, vibrant sound with enough amplitude to fill the largest auditorium, and that is what audiences found miraculous.

Vitaphone sound itself was soon overtaken by better sound systems, all of which were based on De Forest's original concept of imprinting sound directly on to film. Had De Forest been more focused, he would have died a much wealthier man.

The Jazz Singer was by no means the first sound movie. It wasn't even the first talking picture – but that was a nicety lost on its adoring audiences. For most people, *The Jazz Singer* would be the picture that made talking pictures real.

The Jazz Singer was originally a Broadway play by Samuel Raphaelson which originated as a short story called *The Day of Atonement*. Warner Brothers decided to make it into its first talking production because they had the eager participation of Al Jolson, then one of the performing world's greatest stars.

Jolson was born Asa Yoelson, the son of a rabbi, in Lithuania, in 1885 or 1886 (he was never clear about this) and came to the United States with his family when he was about four. At the age of nine, he ran away from home and worked at odd jobs, including in a circus. Eventually juvenile authorities found him working in a bar in

Baltimore and deposited him in the St Mary's Industrial School for Boys – the same school that would become home to Babe Ruth the following decade. Unlike Ruth, Jolson stayed just a short while.

Jolson was not an adorable person. His idea of a good joke was to urinate on people, which may go some way to explaining why he had four wives and no friends. But he had a wonderful voice and, by all accounts, a powerful stage presence, and he became America's most popular performer. Warner Brothers knew it was lucky to get him.

It has often been written that Warner Brothers was so broke before the making of *The Jazz Singer* that Al Jolson had to lend the company money to pay for sound equipment, but that seems not to have been the case at all. Warner Brothers was a small studio, but not a destitute one. In fact, in 1927 it had the biggest star in Hollywood after Clara Bow – the performing dog Rin Tin Tin. This beloved German shepherd starred in one successful movie after another – four in 1927 alone – and in one poll was voted the most popular performer in America. According to Susan Orlean in her biography of the dog, Rin Tin Tin was also voted the Academy Award for best actor before the new motion picture academy had second thoughts about what that said about the talents of its human stars and insisted that it go to a person, Emil Jannings.

The great irony of all this is that apparently Rin Tin Tin wasn't one dog but many. In 1965, Jack Warner confessed to a reporter that his studio, fearful of the loss of the real Rin Tin Tin, had bred eighteen lookalikes and had substituted them freely in the making of the films. It was also said by many of those who worked with him that the original Rin Tin Tin was the most ill-tempered animal they had ever encountered. At all events, whether Rin Tin Tin was one dog or several, the franchise made Warner Brothers wealthy.

The Jazz Singer did, however, represent a considerable gamble. It cost $500,000 to make and, at the time of its filming, could be shown in just two cinemas in the world. Jolson, for all his star quality, was himself a gamble. He had never acted in front of a camera before. There was no point. He had no talent that suited silent movies. But now he shone.

The Jazz Singer took four months to shoot. The sound portion of the filming was all done in just two weeks between 17 and 30 August. It took such a short time because there was so little sound to be recorded. Altogether the movie had just 354 spoken words, nearly all coming from Jolson. The dialogue was not terribly polished, to say the least. A sample: 'Mama, darling, if I'm a success in this show we're gonna move from here. Oh, yes, we're gonna move up in the Bronx. A lot of nice green grass up there and a whole lotta people you know. There's the Ginsbergs, the Guttenbergs, and the Goldbergs. Oh, a whole lot of Bergs, I don't know 'em all.' (Accounts vary as to whether Jolson's words were spontaneous or scripted.)

As Jolson was filming his talking sequences in Los Angeles, 400 miles to the north in Sacramento Buster Keaton was filming what may be the single most memorable scene in any silent film – certainly one of the most perfect comic scenes, not to mention most dangerous. It was the scene in *Steamboat Bill Jr.* in which the front wall of a house falls on to Keaton, but he survives because he is standing in the space of an open window. To make the scene maximally thrilling – and it truly is – the window was made just two inches wider than Keaton on either side. Had the wall warped or buckled slightly or the point of impact been fractionally miscalculated, Keaton would have been killed. Perhaps nothing says more about silent movies and those who performed in them than that actors routinely risked their lives for the sake of a good joke. That didn't happen in talking pictures.

Steamboat Bill Jr. was one of Keaton's finest movies, but it was a failure at the box office. By the time it came out, people were already abandoning silent pictures. At the time he filmed *Steamboat Bill Jr.*, Keaton was earning well over $200,000 a year. By 1934, he would be bankrupt.

Talking pictures were the salvation of Hollywood, but that salvation came at very considerable cost – in anxiety for stars and producers, in new equipment costs for studios and cinemas, in job losses for thousands of musicians whose accompaniments were no longer needed. The greatest fear for the industry in the beginning was that sound movies would prove to be a passing fad – an unnerving possibility given the amount of investment necessary to get into talking pictures. Every cinema in the country that wanted to show sound movies had to invest between $10,000 and $25,000 in equipment. For the studios, a fully equipped sound stage cost a minimum of half a million dollars – and that was assuming the studio could even acquire the necessary recording equipment since demand very quickly outran supply. One desperate producer, unable to get hold of sufficient sound-recording equipment, seriously considered filming his movie as normal in California but with the sound recorded, via telephone line, on equipment in New Jersey. Luckily, he managed to acquire some sound equipment and didn't have to discover, as he most assuredly would have, that his long-distance scheme could never result in decent reproduction.

Once equipped, studios often discovered that they had to find new, quieter locations and quieter working conditions within those locations. 'When a scene is to be shot, the carpenters have to suspend their hammering, and the scene painters must stop singing at their work,' explained one observer earnestly. Delivery trucks couldn't sound their horns or rev their engines. Doors could not be slammed. Even the most carefully muffled sneeze could spoil a scene. At first, many pictures were shot in the dead of night to minimize the complications of background noise.

Another mighty blow was the loss of foreign markets. More than a third of Hollywood's income came from abroad. For a silent movie to be sold overseas, it simply needed new title cards inserted, but, pending the invention of dubbing and subtitles, sound movies could only be shown where people spoke the language in which the movie was made. One solution was to make multiple versions of a movie, using a single set but with up to ten different troupes of actors from different language groups filming one version after another.

All of these problems were of course overcome, and talking pictures quickly enjoyed success beyond anyone's wildest hopes. By 1930, virtually every cinema in America had sound. Movie audiences jumped from 60 million in 1927 to 110 million in 1930. Warner Brothers' worth shot up from $16 million to $200 million. The number of cinemas it owned or controlled went from one to seven hundred.

Talkies at first were often called 'speakies', though sometimes they were also called 'dialogue pictures'. For some time, what exactly constituted sound movies was a matter of uncertainty. Eventually a consensus arose. A picture that offered recorded music but no talking was said to be 'With Sound'. If it additionally had some sound effects, it was said to be 'With Sound and Effects'. If it had any recorded speech at all, it was a 'Talking Picture'. If it was a proper movie, with a full range of speech and sounds, it was an 'All-Talking Picture'. The first true all-talking picture was *The Lights of New York* in 1928, but such was the sound quality still that it came with subtitles as well.

Variety in the summer of 1927 noted that some four hundred aliens were working as actors or in other creative positions in Hollywood, and that more than half of all leading roles were taken by performers of foreign birth. Pola Negri, Vilma Bánky, Lya De Putti, Emil Jannings, Joseph Schildkraut, Conrad Veidt and many others from Germany or central Europe were big stars, but only so long as the public couldn't hear their accents. Universal and Paramount were both dominated by German stars and directors. Universal was said, only half in jest, to have German as its official language.

A few European actors – Peter Lorre, Marlene Dietrich, Greta Garbo – adjusted to or even thrived in the new sound regime, but most actors with foreign accents found themselves unemployable. Jannings, winner of the first Academy Award for acting, returned to Europe and spent the war years making propaganda films for the Nazis. Behind the scenes Europeans still thrived, but onscreen movies were now a thoroughly American product.

Though the significance of this wasn't much noticed in America, globally the effect was profound. Moviegoers around the world suddenly found themselves exposed, often for the first time, to American voices, American vocabulary, American cadence and pronunciation and word order. Spanish conquistadores, Elizabethan courtiers, figures from the Bible were suddenly speaking in American voices – and not just occasionally but in film after film after film. The psychological effect of this, particularly on the young, can hardly be overstated. With American speech came American thoughts, American attitudes, American sense of humour and sensibilities. Peacefully, by accident, and almost unnoticed, America had just taken over the world.

Chapter 24

Robert G. Elliott was not a murderous person by nature, but he proved, no doubt to his own surprise, to be rather good at killing people. A well-groomed, silver-haired man with a pipe and a thoughtful, learned air, he might in other circumstances have been a college professor. He certainly had the brains for it. Instead, in 1926, at the age of fifty-three, he became America's top executioner.

Elliott grew up in a prosperous family on a large farm in upstate New York. He studied mathematics and physics at Brockport Normal School (now the State University of New York at Brockport), but his passion was electricity, and he decided as a young man to become an electrical engineer. This was at a time in the late nineteenth century when electrical transmission was an exciting new technology. Elliott was employed setting up municipal lighting plants across New York and New England when he was sidetracked into the challenge of electrocuting criminals. This, too, was a new thing, but it wasn't going well.

Electrocution seemed, on the face of it, a quick, humane way of putting people to death, but in practice it proved to be neither neat nor straightforward. If the voltage was too low or not applied long enough, the victim was often dazed but not killed, and merely reduced to a gasping wreck. If a more ferocious jolt was given, the results tended to be unpleasantly dramatic. Blood vessels sometimes burst and, in one gruesome instance, a victim's eyeball exploded. At least once, the subject was slowly roasted alive. The smell of cooking flesh was 'unbearable', recalled one of those present. Electrocution, it became clear, was a science that required careful, professional management if it was to be done efficiently and relatively humanely. This is where Robert Elliott came in.

Called in as a consultant for an execution in New York State, and having read about the suffering and failures so far, Elliott realized that the trick of a successful execution was to adjust the application of electricity continuously and judiciously throughout the process, rather as an anaesthetist controls the flow of gas to a surgical patient, so that the subject was rendered first unconscious and then lifeless in a progressive and comparatively peaceful manner.

He performed his first two executions in January 1926, and proved so adept at it that soon states all over the east were commissioning him. It wasn't that Elliott found any satisfaction in killing people – quite the reverse – but that he had an ability, more or less unique, to dispatch them gently. In 1927, he was executing people at the rate of about three a month, at $150 a time, and was in all but name the official executioner for New York and New England.

Because of the lack of specialist equipment, Elliott had to make his own. Each victim was fitted with a piece of headgear that he adapted from leather football helmets bought at his local sporting-goods store. It is a macabre image, but an accurate one, to think of Sacco and Vanzetti going to their deaths dressed in the style of footballer Red Grange.

For all the fuss and heartfelt lamentations among pro-testers and editorial writers about the unfair trial and unjust fate of Sacco and Vanzetti, the evidence suggests that the majority of Americans thought the two men were probably guilty, and most of the rest didn't really care. According to the author Francis Russell, by 1926 most people couldn't have said whether Sacco and Vanzetti were still alive or not. The newspaperman Heywood Broun was certain that the average man 'cared nothing about the issue'. He despaired that his own newspaper, the *World*, carried more coverage of the Snyder–Gray case than it did of Sacco and Vanzetti. Even those who supported Sacco and Vanzetti weren't always terribly sympathetic. Katherine Anne Porter was shocked when, in passing, she expressed hope to the communist Rosa Baron that a pardon would be granted, and Baron snapped back: 'Pardoned – what for? They are no earthly use to us alive.'

Somewhat surprisingly, Sacco and Vanzetti were not the most notorious inmates in Charlestown Prison in the summer of 1927. That distinction belonged to a fellow immigrant who had rather faded from the news but whose name has, ironically, lived on more powerfully than those of Sacco and Vanzetti in the decades since. He was Charles Ponzi, and eight years earlier he had attracted the world's attention, and made himself an eponym, by devising a scheme designed to make people a lot of money very quickly.

Ponzi was a dapper and diminutive fellow, barely five feet tall. Originally from Parma, he came to the United States in 1903 at the age of twenty-one and worked at various jobs, from busboy to office clerk to vegetable wholesaler. But in 1919, while living in Boston, he concocted a scheme – in itself perfectly legal – to make a profit by trading in international postal reply coupons. These coupons were invented as a way to help people or businesses send or receive letters or parcels from abroad. The system was meant to facilitate small-scale exchanges between countries. Ponzi realized that he could buy coupons in Europe with depressed European currencies, then redeem them in America for booming US greenbacks. For every dollar invested, he could get back up to $3.50.

Promising investors a 50 per cent return on their investment every ninety days, Ponzi launched his scheme in autumn 1919, and by the following spring – at exactly the time that Parmenter and Berardelli were being gunned down in Braintree and Sacco and Vanzetti arrested in Brockton – Ponzi was being overwhelmed with eager clients. Thousands of people gathered daily outside his offices in Boston's North End trying to thrust money into his care. Often it was their life's savings. So much money flowed in that Ponzi literally couldn't bank it fast enough. It was packed into shoeboxes and stuffed in desk drawers. In April he took in $120,000, in May $440,000, in June $2.5 million, in July over $6 million, mostly in bills in small denominations.

The problem with Ponzi's system was that individual

coupons were worth only very small sums – 5 cents typically – so it would have been necessary to exchange truly monumental volumes of coupons to make a reasonable return. Ponzi didn't even try. It was much simpler to pay off early investors with funds paid in by more recent ones. As long as money kept flowing in, the scheme worked fine, but you didn't need to be a financial wizard to see that the arrangement couldn't be indefinitely sustained. Ponzi, alas, genuinely believed it could. He opened branch offices all around New England to take in yet more money, and embarked on an ambitious programme of expansion and diversification. At the time of his downfall, he was negotiating to buy a steamship line, a bank and a chain of cinemas, all in the sweetly delusional belief that he was a legitimate business titan in the mould of John D. Rockefeller. Ponzi, it is worth noting, personally benefited little from his artful manipulations. He bought a nice house and a new car with his investors' money, but otherwise his greatest financial indulgence was to donate $100,000 to an orphanage.

Ponzi's grand plans began to unravel when a newspaperman asked the Post Office's coupon-redemption department how it was coping with such an influx of business, and learned that there was no influx of business. It turned out that Ponzi had cashed in only $30 worth of postal coupons. All the rest was money taken from one lot of investors and given to another. Altogether, it is thought, Ponzi ended up some $10 million in the hole, equivalent to more than $100 million today. About 40,000 people had invested with him.

From beginning to end, Ponzi's scheme lasted just eight months. Ponzi was charged, convicted and sent to a federal prison for three and a half years. Upon his release, he faced additional state charges in Massachusetts, but absconded to Florida while out on bail. Florida was in the midst of its celebrated property boom, and Ponzi, irrepressible, very nearly succeeded in setting up a bogus real estate scheme there. He offered real land, but failed to tell investors that it was all deep seabed. In the summer of 1927, he was back in prison at Charlestown awaiting deportation.

If most Americans were indifferent to the fate of Sacco and Vanzetti, a shadowy handful showed that they were not. On the evening of 5 August, two New York subway stations, a church in Philadelphia and the home of the mayor of Baltimore were noisily rent with bombs. One person was killed and several injured in the subway bombings. The Baltimore bombing puzzled many because Sacco and Vanzetti had no connection with that city, and the mayor, William F. Broening, had never expressed a view one way or another on the case.

As ever, the police were clueless as to the perpetrators. For a time the chief suspect in New York was a man, identified only as a dental assistant, who was caught peering into St Paul's Cathedral in New York in what police thought was a suspicious manner. When searched he was found to be carrying an anarchist leaflet. He was arrested and held without bail. His fate beyond that is not known, but he was not charged with any of the bombings. No one was.

Sacco and Vanzetti's execution was scheduled for the night of 10 August, the day that President Coolidge dedicated Mount Rushmore. Outside, angry crowds thronged the streets and mounted police strained to maintain order. 'The air seemed charged with electricity,' Robert G. Elliott noticed as he arrived in the early evening. Machine guns had been placed along the prison walls, and those manning them were authorized, it seems, to fire into the crowd if things got ugly. Inside, Sacco, Vanzetti and a third condemned inmate, Celestino Madeiros – the young man whose confession to the Braintree robbery Judge Thayer had dismissed in 1925 – were given their last meals and offered last rites. Madeiros had nothing to do with the Sacco and Vanzetti case. He was just part of a job lot, and was being put to death now for the murder of a bank clerk in another robbery.

At about 11 p.m., the witnesses assembled and Elliott readied his apparatus, but just thirty-six minutes before the scheduled execution a reprieve arrived from Massachusetts Governor Alvan Fuller, granting the condemned men's defence team – which was essentially the lone, harried lawyer Fred Moore – twelve days to find a court prepared to grant a retrial or hear new evidence. Madeiros, though unconnected, got a stay, too, for convenience's sake.

More bombs went off. The home of one of the jurors, in East Milton, Massachusetts, was blown up in the middle of the night of 16 August. Happily, no one was killed. Across the country in Sacramento, California, a bomb blew the roof off a cinema. Why Sacramento and why a cinema were questions no authority could answer.

Fred Moore could find no one to come to Sacco and Vanzetti's rescue. Supreme Court Justice Louis D. Brandeis, the most likely saviour, had to recuse himself because of 'personal relations with some of the people interested'. His wife had formed a sympathetic friendship with

Sacco's wife, Rose. Chief Justice William Howard Taft refused to cross the border from his summer home in Canada to make a ruling. Justice Harlan Fiske Stone likewise declined to come ashore from his cottage off the Maine coast.

On the evening of 22 August, Sacco's wife and Vanzetti's sister went to the Massachusetts State House to plead with Governor Fuller. Fuller spent an hour and a half with the women, but would not change his position. 'My duties are outlined by law,' he said sadly. 'I am sorry.' The executions would proceed, as required by law, from midnight.

Once again, the crowds assembled – though this time they were noticeably smaller and more subdued. The familiar steps were repeated. The witnesses gathered anew. Elliott laid out his equipment. The clock was watched as the minutes slowly ticked by. At last the time came. Madeiros was selected to go first and came into the execution chamber in a semi-stupor – a consequence, bizarrely, of overeating. Charlestown solemnly observed the tradition of giving a condemned prisoner whatever he wanted for his last meal, and Madeiros had evidently gone to town. Elliott worked with brisk efficiency. Madeiros was strapped into the electric chair at 12:02 and declared dead seven minutes later.

Sacco was next. He refused last rites and walked the seventeen steps from his cell to the execution chamber unaided, but was noticeably pale. As he was being strapped into the chair, he cried out in Italian, 'Long live anarchy!' then added in English, 'Farewell, my wife and child, and all my friends!' (In fact, Sacco had two children; the error was attributed to nerves.) An unfortunate delay arose at this point because the head covering he was to wear could not be found. As Elliott and other officials searched for it, Sacco continued jabbering nervous farewells to friends and relatives. The headgear was found wedged under Madeiros's body on a stretcher in a corridor and was hastily retrieved and plonked on Sacco's head.

'Good evening, gentlemen,' Sacco called in a slightly startled tone at this. Finally, and quietly, he uttered the words 'Farewell, mother,' and the switch was thrown. He was pronounced dead at 12:19:02.

Vanzetti, the final victim, also refused last rites. He had four more steps to traverse and proceeded with calmness and dignity. He shook hands with his guards, then turned to the warden, William Hendry, and shook his hand, too. 'I want to thank you for everything you have done for me, Warden,' Vanzetti said. Hendry was too overcome to reply. Then Vanzetti turned to the witnesses and in a clear voice and in good English said: 'I wish to tell you that I am innocent, and that I never committed any crime, but sometimes some sin. I thank you for everything you have done for me. I am innocent of all crime, not only of this, but all. I am an innocent man.' As an afterthought he added, 'I wish to forgive some people for what they are now doing to me.' He took the chair and sat calmly and silently as he was strapped in and his head was covered. A moment later the switch was thrown. 'There was complete silence in the room, except for the crackling, sputtering sound of the current,' Elliott wrote in his 1940 memoir, *Agent of Death*. Vanzetti was declared dead at 12:26:55, less than eight minutes after Sacco.

In America, reaction to the executions was surprisingly muted. In New York, crowds received the news in 'mournful silence', according to the *Times*. In Boston, all was eerily subdued. People waited for official confirmation, then quietly dispersed into the night. To most people, further protests seemed pointless. Troops and police were stood down. By the next day, city life had returned to normal.

Elsewhere it was a different story. Protests broke out across the world – in Buenos Aires, Mexico City, Sydney, Berlin, Hamburg, Geneva, Leipzig and Copenhagen. Many demonstrations turned violent. Nine people were killed in Germany. In London, protesters and police clashed in Hyde Park. Forty people were injured, some requiring hospitalization. In Havana, the US embassy was bombed. In Geneva, rioters attacked the Palace of the League of Nations even though the United States was not a member, and broke windows in shops and hotels. In the confusion, shots were fired and one man was killed. In Berlin, New York Mayor Jimmy Walker, on a goodwill tour of Europe, was threatened with physical violence by the city's communists. Nowhere for several days was it safe to be an American.

The French were particularly impassioned. Parisians, who until recently had been turning out in joyous droves to greet Lindbergh, Byrd, Chamberlin and Levine, now poured through the streets of the city looking for Americans to beat up. Where Americans were scarce, the mobs turned on prosperous-looking natives. Patrons of many pavement cafés were assaulted and in some cases savagely beaten just for looking intolerably bourgeois. Several cafés were wrecked in pitched battles between customers and rioters. Elsewhere in the city, the roaming mobs turned on anything with an American theme –

cinemas showing American films, American hotels, stores that sold American goods. According to the London *Times* correspondent, the rioters particularly targeted American shoe stores for some reason. To the disgust of many, the mobs also desecrated the Tomb of the Unknown Soldier. In trying to restore order, some two hundred policemen were injured. Some were stabbed.

Time magazine took the opportunity to indulge in a little anthropological bigotry. 'In South America,' it noted, 'the volatile – and indolent – inhabitants of Paraguay and Argentina were easily persuaded to stop all work . . . Swiss radicals were comically violent; Britons vaguely, Germans stupidly; Frenchmen hysterically violent.'

On the day of the execution, the Coolidges travelled by train west to Wyoming and Yellowstone National Park, where they spent several days enjoying the scenery, watching geysers and being entertained by bears, which in those days were encouraged to beg at the roadside. The president managed to fit in a little fishing, too. He issued no opinions about the Sacco and Vanzetti executions, or anything else.

Were Sacco and Vanzetti innocent? Across such a distance of time, it is impossible to say anything with certainty, but there are grounds for suspecting that they were not perhaps as innocent as they made themselves out to be. There was for a start their close friendship with Carlo Valdinoci, the most notorious of bombers. They were also self-declared disciples of Luigi Galleani, the most militant and implacable of anti-American radicals. Galleani was a swashbuckling figure. He had been jailed in Italy for radical activities but escaped – reportedly after seducing the warden's wife – and settled in America, where he immediately began calling for the violent overthrow of the government. Galleani published a radical journal called *Cronaca Sovversiva* (*Chronicle of Subversion*), which had a small but devoted readership of about four or five thousand. A regular contributor was Bart Vanzetti. Galleanists are thought to have been behind most or all of the notable bombings in this period. Vanzetti was widely rumoured to be a maker of bombs, if not necessarily a deliverer of them. The historian Paul Avrich states that Vanzetti was 'probably involved' in the bombing at Youngstown, Ohio, that killed ten policemen, and was certainly part of the small cell responsible for it.

Many people closely involved in the case, then and later, concluded that Sacco and Vanzetti were certainly guilty of *some*thing. The novelist Upton Sinclair, who was wholly sympathetic to both men, came to believe that they had been involved in bomb-making at the very least. Katherine Anne Porter was forced to a similar conclusion after long discussions with people inside the anarchist movement. According to several accounts, Sacco and Vanzetti's own lawyer, Fred Moore, believed that Sacco was guilty of the Braintree killings and Vanzetti probably so. That view was shared by their fellow anarchist Carlo Tresca, who knew both men well. Francis Russell, who wrote two books on the case, long believed in their innocence ('these men were not the stuff of criminals, either in their natures or their habits'), but eventually he concluded that they were guilty. The private papers of Harvard's president and head of the review commission, A. Lawrence Lowell, opened in 1977, showed that he, too, had hoped to find the men innocent but had been persuaded of their guilt by the evidence. A dispassionate examination of the records indicates that the jurors in both trials were not obviously bigoted and that Justice Thayer, whatever his beliefs outside the court, conducted a fair trial.

No one spent more time investigating Sacco and Vanzetti and the sinister world in which they operated than the late Paul Avrich, a professor at City University of New York. In his 1991 work, *Sacco and Vanzetti: The Anarchist Background*, Avrich asked rhetorically whether Vanzetti could have been involved in the Braintree hold-up, and wrote: 'Though the evidence is far from satisfactory, the answer almost certainly is yes. The same holds true for Sacco.' Even if innocent of that crime, Avrich believed, they were almost certainly guilty of other murderous acts, including the bombings that led to the Palmer raids of 1919. That, he said, was 'a virtual certainty'.

Ballistics tests in the 1920s were basic and fairly easy to disbelieve, but more scrupulous tests in the modern era showed that the bullet that killed Berardelli was indeed fired from Sacco's gun – or else the evidence had been tampered with in a way that requires a substantial edifice of conspiracy.

The last word on the matter should perhaps be left to Avrich. 'It is frustrating to ponder,' he wrote in 1991, 'that there are still people alive – the widow of Sacco among them – who might, if they chose, reveal at least part of the truth.' None ever did. They are all dead now.

Chapter 25

As he became famous, Babe Ruth discovered that celebrity had a distinct downside, notably that he couldn't go into many public places without being bothered, occasionally dangerously so. In 1921 he was drinking in a speakeasy in New Jersey when a drunken customer started to harass him. They exchanged words and stepped outside. Harry Hooper, a fellow ballplayer who was drinking with Ruth that night, emerged from the men's room to find Ruth gone. Looking outside, he discovered Ruth standing stiffly with a gun held to his head. Luckily Hooper's timely arrival frightened Ruth's harasser and he fled into the night. After that, Ruth limited his drinking to the safety of his residence.

By 1927 that residence was the Ansonia Hotel, a wonderfully vast and eccentric Beaux Arts palace on Broadway between Seventy-Third and Seventy-Fourth Streets. The Ansonia was an apartment hotel – a popular new concept in the 1920s – which meant that it combined the spaciousness and permanence of an apartment with the conveniences of a hotel: maid service, concierge desk, daily replenishment of towels and so on. According to various accounts, the Ansonia featured a lobby fountain with a live seal and a 'roof farm' where the management kept cows and chickens to provide milk and eggs for favoured residents. It had three restaurants, including one that could seat 550, and the world's largest indoor swimming pool in the basement. Pneumatic tubes shot messages from the front desk to any desired residence.

The Ansonia's thick walls provided superlative sound-proofing, which made it attractive to musicians – Enrico Caruso and Arturo Toscanini were among its distinguished residents – but it was also popular with writers, theatrical people, ballplayers and others of a slightly vagabond nature. The novelist Theodore Dreiser lived there for some time. The impresario Florenz Ziegfeld had a thirteen-room suite on one floor where he lived with his wife and a smaller suite one floor above where he kept his mistress.

The Ansonia also featured in baseball's darkest episode. It was there, on 21 September 1919, that a group of gamblers ostensibly led by the mobster Arnold Rothstein (though he always vehemently denied it) met with some underpaid members of the Chicago White Sox and agreed to fix the World Series. Ruth was not living there at that time. In 1926 he moved into an apartment that was eight, eleven or twelve rooms in size, depending on which of his biographers you decide to credit. Whatever its dimensions, it was an exceptionally comfortable place.

Ruth in 1927 was the best-paid player in baseball and proud of the fact. Before the season he had held out for a more generous contract, which Jacob Ruppert was loath to grant given Ruth's advancing age and abdomen, and Ruppert's own financial setbacks in Florida from the previous autumn's hurricane. Eventually, Ruppert caved in and gave Ruth a three-year contract at $70,000 a year, and acted as if he had been almost mortally wounded by it. The newspapers made great play of how enormous Ruth's salary was. On his pay, newsmen calculated, Ruth could buy a new car every week or a new house every month. By baseball standards, Ruth's salary *was* enormous – nearly half the Yankees' total payroll and more than the totals earned by the next five best-paid players in the club combined. This, however, was more a reflection of how modestly compensated baseball players were in the 1920s than of how fabulously rich Ruth had become.

Compared with other celebrities, particularly Hollywood stars, baseball players' earnings were modest indeed. Ruth's salary of $1,350 a week compared with $4,000 to $5,000 for Clara Bow and Buster Keaton, $15,000 for Tom Mix, $20,000 for Douglas Fairbanks, and a truly satisfying $30,000 for Harold Lloyd. All these paled when compared in turn with the sums earned by mobsters like Arnold Rothstein and Waxey Gordon, who were said to take in $200,000 a month. What Ruth almost certainly didn't know was that even Graham McNamee, the radio broadcaster, was on a higher salary than he was. It would be wrong to say that Ruth was paid appallingly, but he certainly wasn't paid a penny too much.

Ruth made the bulk of his money off the playing field. In the winter of 1926–7, he is estimated to have brought home nearly a quarter of a million dollars from newspaper columns that he didn't write, endorsements for products that he was mostly unacquainted with, a short but lucrative vaudeville tour, and his beloved movie, *Babe Comes Home*. Despite all that, he still had to borrow

$1,500 from Ruppert to pay his 1927 tax bill. Money and Ruth were never in each other's company long.

On 8 August, the Yankees departed on their longest trip of the season – to Philadelphia, Washington, Chicago, Cleveland, Detroit and St Louis for three to four days each; back to New York for a single make-up game against the Red Sox; then on to Philadelphia and Boston for six days more. In addition, Ruppert managed to squeeze in a side trip to Indianapolis on 15 August for an exhibition game against a minor league team there. Exhibition games were highly lucrative to Ruppert and he packed them in whenever he could. Altogether, in thirty days the Yankees would travel 3,700 miles, play twenty-seven games and make a dozen separate train journeys, several of them long.

Babe Ruth quite liked road trips. They gave him a change of scene and a chance of sex with new acquaintances. They also provided a welcome breather from the complexities of his personal life, which had become uncomfortably numerous. Ruth had fallen for a model and actress named Claire Merritt Hodgson. A native of Georgia, Miss Hodgson had – to put it mildly – a full and lively past. Married at fourteen, a mother at sixteen, a widow at twenty-three, she had come north seeking fame and fortune, and somehow had discovered a taste for ballplayers. Among her several reputed conquests the most notable was Ty Cobb. Ruth, however, adored her and they were soon all but living together. Exactly when and how he broke the news of his new relationship to his existing wife – still living on their rural estate in Massachusetts – is unknown, but it was some time after the disastrous World Series of 1926, which was the last time they were ever seen in public together. In short, Ruth's life by 1927 had grown awfully complicated. As the author Leigh Montville has written: 'He now had a wife, a full-time mistress, a farm, an apartment, a mistress's apartment, an adopted daughter [and] an adopted family.' So the chance to get away from all that for a while had a certain appeal.

Miller Huggins, the Yankees' manager, loved road trips, too, though for entirely different reasons. It wasn't that he longed to be close to his players, or they to him – surprisingly little affection flowed in either direction – but because it gave him a chance to indulge his favourite pastime, which was to visit roller rinks and just sit and watch. Huggins didn't skate himself, but his dream was one day to own a rink of his own. As far as anyone could tell, watching people roller-skate was the only thing in life that gave him pleasure.

Huggins was an oddity. He was for a start quite small – sources rarely agree on just how small, but in the region of five foot four or five – and so boyishly built that he was sometimes mistaken for the batboy. Forty-eight years old in 1927, he had grown up in Cincinnati. His parents were English immigrants; his father had been an excellent cricketer. Huggins studied law at the University of Cincinnati, where one of his professors was William Howard Taft, the Supreme Court chief justice who was at the present moment declining to intervene in the Sacco and Vanzetti case.

To the delight and pride of his parents, Huggins qualified as a lawyer in 1902, but then dismayed them by declining to practise. Instead he took up professional baseball, which in 1902 was only about two steps up from working in a brothel, or so at least it must have seemed to his parents. For the next dozen years Huggins performed competently if not outstandingly as an infielder for the Cincinnati Reds and St Louis Cardinals before eventually becoming player-manager and then just manager of the latter. When invited to take over the Yankees in 1917, he was sceptical and reluctant. The Yankees were a mediocre team and he viewed it as a demotion. But he won pennants in 1921, '22, '23 and '26 and by midsummer 1927 was clearly headed for another. Though not loved by his players, particularly Ruth, who fought with him endlessly and called him 'the Flea', Huggins treated them well and trusted them to make the right decisions on the field, unlike John McGraw of the Giants who considered his players 'incapable of thought'. With Ruth, his forbearance was at times close to saintly.

In New York he lived with his sister and an aunt in an apartment near Yankee Stadium. He never married. Nor did he ever realize his dream of owning a roller rink. Though no one could know it yet, in August 1927 Huggins was just two years away from death.

The poorer players of the team – which is to say most of them – looked forward to road trips because most of their expenses were covered and they received an allowance of $4 a day in road money, which meant they could either lead the life of Riley or live frugally and pocket the rest as savings. Over a season's worth of road trips, that could mount up to a fair sum for a player like Julie Wera on $2,400 a year.

Trains in the 1920s had names, not numbers, which endowed them with a certain air of romance and adventure: *Broadway Limited*, *Bar Harbor Express*, *Santa Fe*

De Luxe, Empire State Express, Texas Special, Sunrise Special, Sunset Limited. After Lindbergh's flight, the Pennsylvania Railroad relaunched its service between St Louis and the east coast and called it, all but inevitably, the *Spirit of St Louis*. Sometimes, it must be said, the names were more romantic than the journeys. The *Scenic Limited*, from St Louis to Pueblo, Colorado, was mostly across northern Kansas, which was not many people's idea of topographical sumptuousness, even in Kansas. Some names were flatly misleading. The New York, Chicago & St Louis Railroad didn't actually go to the stated terminals, but plied more modestly between Chicago and Buffalo. The *Atlantic Limited* likewise never sniffed salt air, but confined itself to a daily run across northern Minnesota and Michigan.

Some trains were renowned for their lack of comfort – in California, the *Gold Coast* was familiarly known as the 'Cold Roast' – but most made a reasonable effort at providing a quality service, and the best offered real splendour. The finest of all was the *Twentieth Century Limited*, which left Grand Central Station in New York at 6 p.m. each evening bound for Chicago. The *Limited* had a barber and ladies' hairdresser, bathrooms with hot baths, laundry facilities, an observation car with writing tables and complimentary stationery, even a stenographer for taking dictation. It was capable of covering the 960 miles in eighteen hours, but after several crashes, including one in 1916 in which twenty-six people died, a slightly more cautious trip of twenty hours became the scheduled norm. Even so, the *Twentieth Century Limited* was still the fastest and most comfortable form of travel not just in America, but anywhere on earth.

The most extraordinary feature of rail travel was how

much choice there was. Although the Van Sweringen brothers had done much to consolidate the industry, it was still bewilderingly fragmented. A customer in 1927 could buy a ticket on any of 20,000 scheduled services from any of 1,085 operating companies. Different companies frequently used different terminals, tracks and ticketing systems, none of which necessarily coordinated with anyone else's offerings. Seven different rail lines served Cleveland alone.

Trains went where each company's tracks dictated, which meant they didn't always take the shortest or fastest routes. The *Lake Shore Limited* from New York to Chicago travelled for its first 150 miles north towards Canada before abruptly turning left at Albany, as if suddenly remembering itself. Long-distance trains commonly divided or amalgamated en route in a complicated minuet that allowed them to connect with other services. The *Suwanee River Special* set off daily from St Petersburg, Florida, bound for Chicago, but at various points along the way cars were unhooked and reattached to other trains heading for Buffalo, Cleveland, Detroit and Kansas City. The *Lake Shore Limited* paused at Albany to take on cars from Boston and Maine and again at Buffalo to collect cars from Toronto, while at Cleveland some cars were split off and sent south to Cincinnati and St Louis while the main train continued west to Chicago. For passengers, the possibility of waking up in Denver or Memphis when one was expecting Omaha or Milwaukee added a frisson of uncertainty to every long journey, while the shuntings and recouplings in the wee hours meant that almost no one got a good night's sleep. The romance of travel wasn't always terribly evident to those who were actually experiencing it.

To keep customers distracted, and to generate extra income in a crowded market, nearly all trains put a great deal of emphasis on their food. Although galleys had barely room to flip a pancake, the cooks turned out an extraordinary range of dishes. On Union Pacific trains, for breakfast alone the discerning guest could choose among nearly forty dishes – sirloin or porterhouse steak, veal cutlet, mutton chop, wheatcakes, broiled salt mackerel, half a spring chicken, creamed potatoes, cornbread, bacon, ham, link or patty sausages, and eggs in any style – and the rest of the day's meals were just as commodious. Overnight passengers on the *Midnight Limited* between Chicago and St Louis could even partake of a lavish (and literal) 'midnight luncheon' while rattling through the lonely night.

The Yankees travelled in special cars hooked on to the end of a regular train, partly to keep fans from disturbing the ballplayers but also to keep the ballplayers from disturbing normal people, for the players' car was easily the rowdiest on any train. Trains in the 1920s lacked cooling systems and in hot weather the players generally sat around in their underwear. Babe Ruth had a private compartment, as did Huggins. The rest of the team shared curtained enclosures with upper and lower berths – 'rolling tenements', as they were drolly known. When Ruppert was with the team, an extra car was hooked on for him alone. On all road trips, there was a lot of time to talk, play cards and fool around. Ruth played a great deal of bridge or poker, betting wildly on the latter. The more serious or scholarly among the players read or wrote letters. Benny Bengough practised the saxophone.

The Yankees divided into two social sets on the road.

There was the party set of Ruth, Bob Meusel, Waite Hoyt and Bengough, and the quiet set (sometimes called the movie set) of those who behaved. These included Earle Combs, Wilcy Moore, Cedric Durst, Ben Paschal, Herb Pennock and Lou Gehrig.

Also frequently joining the lively crowd was *New York Times* reporter Richards Vidmer. Ballplayers didn't normally fraternize with reporters, but they always made an exception for Vidmer because he was an attractive, youthful, athletic person, much like themselves, but with a life and background more exciting and dashing than any five players could boast together. The son of a brigadier general, Vidmer had grown up all over the world and moved comfortably in high circles. It was Vidmer, it may be recalled, who watched President Harding urinate in a White House fireplace. Vidmer trained as an aviator in the First World War, married the daughter of the Rajah of Sarawak, one of the richest men in the Far East, and played both golf and baseball professionally before taking up journalism. High-spirited and irresistible to women, he was the inspiration for a very popular novel, *Young Man of Manhattan*, whose author, Katharine Brush, was a former amour.

Vidmer was also perhaps the most memorably dreadful sportswriter ever. In an interview given many years after he retired, Vidmer cheerfully admitted that he rarely turned up at a ballpark before the third or fourth inning of a game, and sometimes not till the fifth or sixth. He wrote text that was at once excruciating and unreliable. Here he is describing a day in which Gehrig hit two home runs while Ruth had none: 'Whereas Ruth and the other Yanks left the field after five hours of baseball in varying degrees of dejection, the laddie that's known as Lou pranced off in high glee, kicking his heels hilariously and whistling a merry tune.' Among the many demonstrative acts in which Lou Gehrig never indulged we can comfortably number prancing in glee and kicking his heels. In Vidmer's hands, a Ruth clout wasn't a home run, it was a 'sapient sock', and the ball in flight wasn't a ball in flight but 'animated leather'. The Tigers became 'the Jungle Cats', the left arm 'the port turret'. The Yankees were always 'the Hugmen' (after Miller Huggins). When Ruth hit his 400th career homer Vidmer wrote a moving piece about how an usher tried to take the ball from a boy in the bleachers, but the boy wouldn't yield it because he wanted to give it to the Babe himself, and that when Ruth learned of this he invited the boy to the clubhouse. There he graciously accepted the gift and gave the boy half a dozen shiny new autographed balls in return. 'I had the story exclusive,' Vidmer confided years later, 'since I'd made it up.'

Like nearly all sportswriters, he never wrote anything suggesting the least impropriety on the part of any player, which in the case of Babe Ruth meant suppressing a great deal. Apart from not wanting to imperil a good friendship, there was a practical reason for his tactfulness. Major league teams paid the expenses of travelling sportswriters, which had a powerful effect on their loyalty. They were in essence PR men for the team.

No visiting team had ever been more popular than the Yankees were in the summer of 1927. Twenty thousand turned out on a Friday afternoon in Chicago to watch them play the White Sox, ten times the number that came to watch the Sox play the fourth-place Athletics three days later. The Yankees drew 21,000 in Cleveland, 22,000 in

Detroit, even 8,000 in lowly, fanless St Louis – all on week-days. On Labor Day, in Boston as the Yankees' long road trip finally drew to a close, an estimated 70,000 people turned up at Fenway Park – far more than it could hold – even though the home-town Red Sox were a magnificent forty-nine games out of first place.

All the fans in all the cities were drawn by the same thing – the chance to see Babe Ruth in the flesh, and ideally to watch him swat a ball into the firmament. That Ruth was locked in a seesaw battle with the youthful upstart Lou Gehrig for the home run championship brought the kind of excitement that made people crush their hats in distraction. There really had never been any-thing like it. At mid-August, Gehrig – impossibly, unprecedentedly – led Ruth by 38 home runs to 36. But Ruth came back with towering clouts in Chicago on 16 and 17 August to draw level. Gehrig went one up again on 19 August against the White Sox, but Ruth matched that the next day in Cleveland to put them even again at 39.

By now people were practically having heart attacks. On 22 August, Ruth hit his fortieth; Gehrig tied with him two days later. Ruth hit his forty-first and forty-second home runs on 27 and 28 August in St Louis. Gehrig came back with a three-run shot in St Louis on 29 August. Two days later, back in New York against the Red Sox, Ruth hit the last home run of the month for either player. As August ended, Ruth had 43 home runs, Gehrig had 41. Their 84 home runs compare with 28 all season for the Red Sox, 26 for the Indians. No team other than the Yankees had ever hit 84 home runs in a season before – and this was with the season only four fifths over.

Ruth, it had to be said, was nowhere near on course to

beat his record of 59 home runs from 1921, but he might with luck get to 50 – only the third time that he, or anyone, had reached that eminent milestone. If Gehrig stayed hot he might get to 50, too. So as August ended, September had the prospect of being a pretty exciting month for baseball. In fact, no one could begin to guess just how exciting it was about to get.

As the Yankees proceeded from city to city through the Midwest at ground level, Charles Lindbergh covered much the same territory from the air. From Detroit, he went on to Chicago, St Louis, Kansas City, Wichita and St Joseph, Missouri, then back north to Moline, Milwaukee and Madison before at last heading to Minnesota for what was expected to be a triumphant homecoming. Alas, it didn't work out quite that way. First, he received news that George Stumpf, his well-meaning but not very useful assistant at Roosevelt Field before the flight to Paris, had just been killed in a plane crash in Missouri. Stumpf had gone up as a passenger with a military pilot named C. C. Hutchinson, who was showing off to some people at a lake resort near St Louis when his plane clipped a flagpole and crashed. Hutchinson was thrown clear and not seriously injured. Stumpf was crudely garrotted by a wire that became twisted around his neck.

In Minneapolis and St Paul, Lindbergh was rushed at such speed along the parade route that to most onlookers he was nothing more than an impassive blur. To people who had stood for hours with excited children, this was a matter of bitter disappointment. 'No parade at all would be preferable to one in which the hero is not to be satisfactorily seen,' grumbled the *Minneapolis Tribune* in an editorial.

Newspapers had begun to report that pickpockets and burglars were following Lindbergh around the country to take advantage of the distractions that his visits brought. In Chicago, during the Lindbergh parade armed gunmen strolled into a jewellery store on State Street and casually robbed it of $85,000 in cash and goods. Now came the dismaying news that souvenir hunters had broken into Lindbergh's family home in Little Falls, unoccupied since his father's death, and taken books, photographs and other irreplaceable personal items. Perhaps for this reason, Lindbergh wore a look of grim resolve for much of his visit to his home town, though it may have been simple exhaustion. In any case, he listened politely but without emotion as six long-winded speakers, including the Swedish consul in Minneapolis, heaped praise upon him before he returned to his plane and with a look of clear relief took off for Fargo and points west. His trip was barely one third over. Little wonder he looked dazed.

His tour, however, was having much greater effect than he probably realized. Papers everywhere lovingly recorded his flying times between cities: Grand Rapids to Chicago, 2 hours 15 minutes; Madison to Minneapolis, 4 hours; St Louis to Kansas City, 3 hours 45 minutes. For anyone who had ever travelled between any such pairs of places, these were magical times. Moreover, Lindbergh repeated these feats day after day, safely, punctually, routinely, without fuss or sweat, as if dropping in by air were the most natural and sensible way in the world to arrive at a place. The cumulative effect on people's perceptions was profound. By the end of the summer, America was a nation ready to fly – quite a turnaround from four months earlier when aviation for most people simply meant barnstormers

471

at county fairs and the like, and the United States seemed unlikely ever to catch up with Europe. Whether Lindbergh knew it or not, his tour of America had a far more transformative effect on the future of aviation than his daring dash to Paris ever could.

The great irony is that by the time America was ready to take to the air properly, Charles Lindbergh would no longer be anybody's hero.

September
Summer's End

―――――

'A few Jews add strength and character to a country. Too many create chaos. And we are getting too many.'

Charles Lindbergh

CHAPTER 26

O F ALL THE labels that were applied to the 1920s – the Jazz Age, the Roaring Twenties, the Age of Ballyhoo, the Era of Wonderful Nonsense – one that wasn't used but perhaps should have been was the Age of Loathing. There may never have been another time in the nation's history when more people disliked more other people from more directions and for less reason.

Bigotry was casual, reflexive and well nigh universal. At the *New Yorker*, Harold Ross forbade the use of the term 'toilet paper' on grounds of taste (it made him queasy), but he had nothing at all against 'nigger' and 'darkie'. In the week before Lindbergh's flight to Paris, the *New Yorker* ran a cartoon with the immortally dismal line 'Niggers all look alike to me.'

George S. Kaufman as a young man lost his job on a newspaper in Washington when the owner came in one night and said, 'What's that Jew doing in my city room?' Bert Williams, a black comedian who was described by W. C. Fields as 'the funniest man I ever saw', was beloved by millions and rich enough to rent a de luxe apartment in

Manhattan, but was allowed to live there only if he agreed to confine himself to the service entrance and freight elevator when coming and going. At the Supreme Court, Justice James C. McReynolds was so prejudiced against Jews that he refused to speak to fellow justice Louis Brandeis, and made a point of studying papers or even reading a newspaper when Brandeis was addressing the court. He was similarly rude to Mabel Walker Willebrandt because of her sex.

Nothing better captured the expansive spirit of detestation in the period than the resurgence of the Ku Klux Klan. Until recently moribund, the Klan burst on to the national stage in the 1920s with a vigour and breadth of appeal that it had never had in its postbellum heyday. The Klan hated *everybody*, but it did so in ways strategically contrived to reflect regional biases, so that it focused on Catholics and Jews in the Midwest, Orientals and Catholics in the Far West, Jews and southern Europeans in the east, and blacks everywhere. At its peak, the Klan had five million members (some sources say eight million), and seventy-five members of Congress either belonged to or were openly associated with it. Several cities elected Klan mayors. Oklahoma and Oregon had Klan governors. In Oregon the Klan nearly succeeded in getting Catholic schools outlawed, and in many places Catholics were forbidden places on school or hospital boards and Catholic-owned businesses were boycotted.

For many, the Klan became almost as much a social organization as a political one. In Detroit, thousands of happy citizens attended a Christmas rally outside city hall where a Santa Claus dressed in Klan regalia distributed presents to children by the light of a burning cross. In

Indiana, a Klan picnic rally – or Klonklave, as they were numbingly known – featured a jousting tournament with men in Klan robes, and a tightrope walker, also in full regalia, carrying a cross in one hand and an American flag in the other, while doing stunts on a high wire.

Under the leadership of a flabby junior high school dropout named David C. Stephenson, the Klan especially thrived in Indiana. The state boasted 350,000 members; in some communities up to half the white men were fee-paying Klansmen. Fired up by Stephenson and his minions, Indianans became peculiarly receptive to wild anti-Catholic rumours. Many in the state believed that Catholics had poisoned President Harding and that priests at Notre Dame University in South Bend were stockpiling armaments in preparation for a Catholic uprising. In 1923 the most surreally improbable rumour of all emerged – that the Pope planned to move his base of operations from the Vatican City to Indiana. According to several accounts, when residents of the town of North Manchester heard that the Pope was on a particular train, 1,500 of them boarded it with a view to seizing the pontiff and breaking up his conspiracy. Finding no one recognizably papal, the mob turned its attentions to a travelling corset salesman, who was nearly dragged off to an unhappy fate until he managed to convince his tormentors that it was unlikely that he would try to stage a coup armed with nothing but a case of reinforced undergarments.

The Klan's downfall was unexpectedly sudden, and it was the plump and unlovely Stephenson who brought it about. In March 1925, he took out on a date a young woman of good character named Madge Oberholtzer. To the extreme distress of her parents, Madge didn't come home that night or the following night. When eventually Stephenson returned her, the young woman was in a dreadful condition. She had been beaten and savagely abused. Skin had been torn from her breasts and genitals. Her doctor and family learned that Stephenson had grown drunk and violent after collecting her, had forced her to go to a hotel and there brutally and repeatedly raped her. In shame and desperation, Oberholtzer had swallowed a fatal dose of mercuric chloride. By the time she reached home doctors could do nothing for her. She took two weeks to die.

Stephenson was confident that his position as Klan head in Indiana would protect him from prosecution, and was astonished when he was convicted of kidnap, rape and second degree murder, and sentenced to life in prison. In revenge he released documents that exposed corruption at the highest levels in Indiana. The mayor of Indianapolis and the head of the Republican Party in the state were both jailed for taking payoffs. The governor should have been but escaped on a technicality. The entire Indianapolis City Council was dismissed and fined, and a prominent judge was impeached. The whole affair was so squalid and disgusting that Klan membership everywhere collapsed, and the Klan retreated into the shadows of American life. It was never a national force again.

Remarkably, the Ku Klux Klan was not the most dangerous outpost of bigotry in America in the period. That distinction belonged, extraordinary though it is to state, to a coalition of academics and scientists. Since early in the century, a large number of prominent and learned Americans had been preoccupied, often to the point of obsessiveness, with the belief that the country was filling up with dangerously inferior people and that something urgent must be done about it.

Dr William Robinson, a leading New York physician, spoke for a vociferous minority when he declared that people of an inferior nature 'have no right in the first instance to be born, but having been born, they have no right to propagate their kind'. W. Duncan McKim, also a physician and author of *Heredity and Human Progress*, proposed that 'the surest, the simplest, the kindest, and most humane means for preventing reproduction among those whom we deem unworthy of the high privilege, is a gentle, painless death'.

The problem, as most saw it, was twofold. America was producing far too many defectives through careless and unrestricted breeding, while at the same time introducing almost limitless volumes of additional inferiority through unrestricted immigration from backward nations.

Nearly everyone had an especially dreaded race. The writer Madison Grant disdained Jews because of their 'dwarf stature, peculiar mentality and ruthless concentration on self-interest'. Frank J. Loesch, a member of a presidential commission on crime reform, thought the problem was Jews and Italians together, 'with the Jews furnishing the brains and the Italians the brawn'. Charles B. Davenport, one of the most eminent scientists of his day, was more expansively dubious and listed Poles, Irish, Italians, Serbians, Greeks and 'Hebrews' as less intelligent and reliable, more susceptible to depravity and crimes of violence, than people of sound Anglo-Saxon or Teutonic stock. These were not people, in Davenport's view, who could be lifted out of their bad habits, but were immutably condemned by their genes to be troublesome, destructive and dull. They were creating an America that was 'darker in pigmentation, smaller in stature [and] more given to crimes of larceny, kidnapping, assault, murder, rape, and sex immorality'. Madison Grant called it 'race suicide'.

All these views were bundled together into the smart new science of eugenics, which may be simply defined as the scientific cultivation of superior beings. In most of the world, eugenics was an innocuous goal – a well-intentioned wish to produce healthier, stronger, smarter people – but in America eugenics took on a harsher cast. It led to the sinister belief that procreation should somehow be regulated and directed. As an official of the American Eugenics Society observed: 'Americans take more care over the breeding of cattle and horses than of their own children.' Eugenics was used to justify the introduction of restrictive covenants on where people could live, enforced deportations, the suspension of civil liberties, and the involuntary sterilization of tens of thousands of innocent people. It resulted in the severe curtailment of immigration and its virtual elimination from certain parts of the world. It even led eventually, but more or less directly, to the downfall of Charles Lindbergh, the pilot who once could do no wrong.

The bible of negative eugenics, as they became known in America, was the fearsome and popular *Passing of the Great Race* by Madison Grant, a New York lawyer (by training, though he never practised) and naturalist (by practice, but without training), which was first published in 1916. Grant took it as read that the only really good group of humans was what he called the 'Nordic race', by which he meant essentially all northern Europeans except the Irish. Europe divided into three tiers of being – Nordic, Alpine and Mediterranean – which grew progressively more degenerate as one moved south.

One obvious problem with Grant's theory was that he had to explain how such wretched people had managed to produce the Athens of Plato and Socrates, the Roman Empire, the Renaissance and so many other marvels of antiquity. Grant's explanation was that in ancient Greece and Rome the ruling class was composed of Nordic Achaeans, who weren't really Mediterranean at all, but were northern Europeans who had drifted south. All the great Renaissance artists, Grant maintained, were 'of Nordic type . . . largely of Gothic and Lombard blood'. All others – the real Italians – were dull, stunted and shifty, and were genetically condemned to remain forever so.

Grant believed that any degenerate genes introduced into the general population would not be diluted and made safe, but would permanently taint the whole. 'The cross between any of the three European races and a Jew is a Jew,' he grimly explained.

Although none of this was compatible with even the small amounts of genetics that were understood at the time, it appears that Grant was saying exactly what a lot of people wanted to hear. His book was praised by the *American Historical Review*, *Yale Review* and *Annals of the American Academy of Political and Social Science*. Henry Fairfield Osborn, head of the Natural History Museum in New York and the country's leading anthropologist, wrote the introduction.

Among others supporting Grant's views, in whole or in part, were the Yale economist Irving Fisher, the Harvard neuropathologist E. E. Southard, A. Lawrence Lowell of Harvard – the man whose committee condemned Sacco and Vanzetti to death – the birth control activist Margaret Sanger, and Herbert Hoover, who had a lifelong antipathy to people with brown skin. In 1909, in a report for his employers, Hoover declared that black and Asian labourers should be avoided because they suffered from 'a low mental order' and a pathological 'lack of coordination and inability to take initiative'. Stressing his own first-hand experience, Hoover concluded that 'one white man equals from two to three of the colored races, even in the simplest forms of mine work such as shoveling or tramming'. If Hoover modified these views in later years, he gave no evidence of it. In 1921, he was patron of a eugenics conference hosted by the Natural History Museum in New York and inspired by *The Passing of the Great Race*.

For a time, the principles of negative eugenics were practically inescapable. At the Sesquicentennial Exhibition in Philadelphia in 1926, the American Eugenics Society had a stand with a mechanical counter showing that a person of inferior nature was born somewhere in the United States every forty-eight seconds, while 'high-grade' persons came along only once every seven and a half minutes. The relative rates at which the counters revolved showed all too dramatically how swiftly the nation was being overwhelmed with inferiority. It was one of the most popular displays at the exhibition.

The spiritual headquarters for the eugenics movement in America was the Eugenics Record Office, opened in 1909 in Cold Spring Harbor on Long Island's North Shore, and largely funded by the sort of wealthy people who wanted more innately superior beings like themselves and fewer of any other kind. (The property abutted the estate of the Tiffany family of jewellery renown.) The first director was Charles Davenport, a Harvard-trained biologist. Davenport believed eugenic explanations could be found for every aspect of the human condition – obesity, criminality, propensity to lie or cheat, even love of the sea. Under Davenport, the ERO also made several studies of the deleterious effects of racial interbreeding. As he explained: 'One often finds in mulattoes ambition and drive combined with low intelligence, so that the hybrid is unhappy, dissatisfied with his fate and rebellious ... A hybridized people are a badly put together people and a dissatisfied, restless, ineffective people.' Davenport argued not just for the sterilization of the inferior and faulty, but for their castration, in order to remove desire as well as reproductive ability, just to be on the safe side.

Davenport, however, was the soul of enlightened compassion compared with his young protégé Harry H. Laughlin, who may have been the most lamentable person to achieve scientific respectability in America in the twentieth century. Born in 1880 in Oskaloosa, Iowa, Laughlin trained at the North Missouri State Normal School, and worked as a teacher and school administrator after college, but developed an interest in breeding and enrolled at Princeton to study biology. In 1910 he met Davenport, who was so taken with Laughlin's zeal and devotion to eugenic purification that he made him superintendent of the Eugenics Record Office.

Laughlin's credo was simple: 'To purify the breeding stock of the race at all costs.' As Edwin Black notes in *War Against the Weak*, Laughlin's plan of attack was threefold: 'sterilization, mass incarceration and sweeping immigration restrictions'. In furtherance of these goals, Laughlin created the imposingly named, ferociously vengeful Committee to Study and to Report on the Best Practical Means of Cutting Off the Defective Germ Plasm in the American Population, which had the self-assigned task of eradicating reproductive inferiority from America once and for all. Laughlin's committee was chaired by David Starr Jordan, president of Stanford, and included scientists and academics from many of America's best universities – Harvard, Princeton, Yale and the University of Chicago, among others.

The committee also included a brilliant but eccentric French surgeon, Alexis Carrel, from the Rockefeller Institute in New York. Carrel's extreme views on eugenics – which were in some respects little short of mad – would contribute significantly, even dangerously, to Charles Lindbergh's opinions, but mercifully that was still some way off.

Laughlin, meanwhile, was tireless in his efforts to root out and limit human inferiority wherever it arose. The House Committee on Immigration and Naturalization appointed him its expert adviser and assigned him the task of determining the comparative degeneracy of various ethnic groups. To persuade the members of how urgently reforms were needed, Laughlin filled the committee chamber with photographs of drooling mental defectives, all identified as recent immigrants, beneath a banner reading 'Carriers of the Germ Plasm of the Future American Population'.

Congress could not resist the authority of the committee or Laughlin's horrifying propaganda, and it quickly pushed through the 1921 Dillingham Immigration Restriction Act followed by the 1924 National Origins Act. Together these ended America's open-door immigration policy. By 1927, more people were being deported from Ellis Island than were coming in through it.

That more or less settled the problem of imported inferiority, but left the issue of home-produced backwardness, of which there was a separate abundance.

Laughlin and his supporters turned their attention to that challenge with, if anything, even more enthusiasm. They conducted tests on large blocks of people and repeatedly produced unnerving results. They reported that up to 80 per cent of all prisoners and half of servicemen were feeble-minded. New York alone was calculated to contain as many as 200,000 mentally subnormal people. Altogether, it was believed, about one third of the American population was dangerously backward.

The solution, in Laughlin's view, was sterilization on a massive scale. He believed in sterilizing not merely the insane and mentally deficient, but also orphans, tramps, paupers, the hard of hearing and the blind – 'the most worthless one-tenth of our present population', as he put it with a certain conspicuous absence of compassion.

In 1927, the question of how freely the state could exercise the power of sterilization came to a head in a legal case known as Buck vs Bell. The case focused on a seventeen-year-old girl in Virginia named Carrie Buck, who was deemed to be of low intelligence and had recently given birth to an illegitimate child, in consequence of which she was now confined in the Virginia Colony for Epileptics and Feeble-Minded at Lynchburg. Her mother was already an inmate there. In 1924 Carrie

Buck was selected for sterilization by the colony's superintendent, Dr John H. Bell (hence Buck vs Bell).

The heart of the case was that not only was Carrie Buck
mentally incompetent, but so were her mother and
daughter – three straight generations of defectives. The
family, it was argued, was clearly incapable of producing
other than mental defectives and ought to be sterilized for
its own good and the good of society. The evidence against
the family was hardly overwhelming. Laughlin, the state's
chief witness, pronounced against the Bucks without ever
having met or examined any of them. He declared that
Carrie Buck came from a 'shiftless, ignorant and worthless
class' of Southerner and should be rendered incapable of
producing more of her kind on grounds of class alone.

The charge of simple-mindedness against Vivian, the
daughter, was made purely on the word of a social worker
who examined the child once and thought there was
something 'not quite normal' about her, but she freely
added: 'I should say that perhaps my knowledge of the
mother may prejudice me in that regard.' The child was just
six months old at the time; no tests then existed for determining the mental capabilities of such a young person. In
fact, Vivian was later shown to have normal, possibly even
above average, intelligence. She died of an intestinal disorder aged just eight, but her performance at school to that
point was entirely capable, and once she even made the
honour roll. Carrie Buck herself was clearly not retarded in
any meaningful sense, if at all. She read newspapers every
day and enjoyed the new craze for crossword puzzles. An
academic who later interviewed Buck described her as 'not
a sophisticated woman [but] neither mentally ill nor
retarded'.

Nonetheless, when given the new Stanford version of the Binet–Simon test, which eventually became the modern IQ test (and it is interesting to reflect that the IQ test was invented not to determine how smart people are but how stupid), Carrie Buck was held to have a mental age of nine while her mother didn't quite make it to eight. Officially they both fell into the classification of 'moron'.

The case came before the US Supreme Court in the spring of 1927. The court ruled by a vote of eight to one that Buck should be sterilized. The majority opinion was written by 86-year-old Oliver Wendell Holmes, Jr – a man of such long life that he had fought as an infantryman in the Civil War.

Holmes summarized the situation concisely: 'Carrie Buck is a feeble-minded white woman. She is the daughter of a feeble-minded mother in the same institution, and the mother of an illegitimate feeble-minded child.' He agreed with Laughlin that sterilization was necessary in society 'to prevent our being swamped with incompetence'. Then he gave his solution: 'It is better for all the world, if instead of waiting to execute degenerate offspring for crime, or to let them starve for their imbecility, society can prevent those who are manifestly unfit from continuing their kind. The principle that sustains compulsory vaccination is broad enough to cover cutting the Fallopian tubes.'

Then came the ringing conclusion that has been quoted ever since: 'Three generations of imbeciles are enough.'

Only one justice, Pierce Butler, dissented from the majority view, and he did not offer a written opinion to explain his dissent. Holmes was supported by all the other justices, who included Chief Justice and former US President

William Howard Taft and the liberal Louis D. Brandeis.

Thanks to this ruling, states now had the right to perform surgery on healthy citizens against their will – a liberty never before extended in any advanced country. Yet the case attracted almost no attention. The *New York Times* gave it a small mention on page nineteen. The *News Leader* of Richmond, Virginia, where the matter was a local story, didn't report it at all.

Slowly sentiment began to turn against negative eugenics. Many serious geneticists, like Thomas Hunt Morgan of Columbia University, would have nothing to do with it, and in the summer of 1927 Harvard quietly declined a gift to endow the university with a chair in the subject.

Harry H. Laughlin, however, seemed unstoppable. He became increasingly – and in retrospect very oddly – hostile to epileptics, insisting that they must either be sterilized or by some means confined during their reproductive years. The oddity in this is that it is now known that Laughlin was secretly an epileptic himself. He sometimes had seizures at Cold Spring Harbor, which his colleagues overlooked or covered up even as they were condemning sufferers elsewhere.

In the 1930s, Laughlin sowed the seeds of his downfall as he began to establish warm relationships with Germany's newly emergent Nazis, some of whom came to Cold Spring Harbor to study American methods and findings. In 1936, the University of Heidelberg awarded Laughlin an honorary degree for his commitment to race purification. The following year Laughlin and Cold Spring Harbor became US distributors of a Nazi documentary called *The Hereditarily Diseased*, which argued that it was foolishly sentimental to keep retarded people alive.

This was more than many people could countenance. At a convention of the American Jewish Congress in New York, the keynote speaker, Bernard S. Deutsch, attacked Laughlin in the bitterest terms. 'Dr. Laughlin's "purification of race" theory is as dangerous and as spurious as the purified Aryan race theories advanced by the Nazis, to which it bears suspicious resemblance,' Deutsch said. The Carnegie Institution, the Eugenics Record Office's chief source of funding, appointed Herbert Spencer Jennings, a respected geneticist from Johns Hopkins University, to review Laughlin's work. Jennings found that Laughlin had falsified data, manipulated findings to support racist conclusions and generally perpetrated scientific fraud for over a quarter of a century. Laughlin was forced to step down from the ERO and it was effectively closed in 1938. Laughlin retired to Missouri, but a huge amount of damage had been done.

Altogether at least 60,000 people were sterilized because of Laughlin's efforts. At the peak of the movement in the 1930s, some thirty states had sterilization laws, though only Virginia and California made wide use of them. It is perhaps worth noting that sterilization laws remain on the books in twenty states today.

In late September 1927, Carrie Buck, her legal options exhausted, was scheduled for sterilization and the procedure was carried out the following month. Her sister was sterilized as well, but without knowing what was happening. She was told she was being treated for appendicitis.

CHAPTER 27

I<small>N THE SPRING</small> of 1927, just before the Snyder–Gray trial consumed the world's attention, an arresting story appeared as the second lead on page one of the *New York Times*. As an indication of its significance, the *Times* gave it seven stacks of headlines. It said:

F<small>AR</small>-O<small>FF</small> S<small>PEAKERS</small> S<small>EEN</small>
<small>AS</small> W<small>ELL AS</small> H<small>EARD</small> H<small>ERE</small>
<small>IN A</small> T<small>EST OF</small> T<small>ELEVISION</small>

L<small>IKE A</small> P<small>HOTO</small> C<small>OME TO</small> L<small>IFE</small>

Hoover's Face Plainly
Imaged as He Speaks
in Washington

T<small>HE</small> F<small>IRST</small> T<small>IME IN</small> H<small>ISTORY</small>

Pictures are Flashed by Wire
and Radio Synchronizing
with Speaker's Voice

Commercial Use in Doubt

But AT&T Head Sees a New
Step in Conquest of Nature
After Years of Research

The accompanying report described how reporters and officials at AT&T's Bell Telephone Labs on Bethune Street in Manhattan had watched in astonishment as a live image of Commerce Secretary Herbert Hoover in Washington materialized before them on a glass screen about the size of a modern Post-it note.

'More than 200 miles of space intervening between the speaker and his audience was annihilated,' marvelled the anonymous reporter. Listeners could even hear Hoover's speech. 'Human genius has now destroyed the impediment of distance,' the commerce secretary intoned with gravity and pomp.

'As each syllable was heard, the motion of the speaker's lips and his changes of expression were flashed on the screen in the demonstration room,' explained the *Times* man. 'It was as if a photograph had suddenly come to life and begun to talk, smile, nod its head and look this way and that.'

Mr Hoover was then succeeded by a comedian named A. Dolan, who first told some stories in an Irish brogue, then quickly changed into blackface and returned with 'a new line of quips in negro dialect'. This, too, was deemed visually excellent.

It appears, however, that the reporter may have been carried away by the emotion of the moment because the AT&T equipment was not capable of projecting really clear

491

images. Realizing this, AT&T abandoned all attempts to conquer television soon afterwards, and left the field open to others, of whom there were many.

As a theoretical notion, television had been around for some time. As far back as 1880, a French engineer named Maurice Leblanc saw that images could be sent a bit at a time because the eye retains an image for about a tenth of a second and thus can be fooled into seeing intermittent images as whole ones. It's why we see movies as a continuous show rather than as thousands of individual frames. That considerably simplified the challenge of transmission.

Four years later, a German named Paul Nipkow invented a system using a spinning disc to scan images on to a sensor through holes placed at calculated intervals around the disc. It was a tricky proposition and Nipkow failed to make it work, but his disc became the standard on which nearly all subsequent attempts at creating television were based. The term *television* itself was coined by a Franco-Russian inventor, Constantin Perskyi, for the Paris Exhibition in 1900, though many other names were used for various devices in the early days – iconoscope, radio-visor, electric eye, even electric telescope.

By the 1920s four parties were thought to be close to breakthrough: teams at Bell Laboratories and General Electric in the United States and the individuals Charles Francis Jenkins in Baltimore and John Logie Baird in Britain.

For all the effort and anticipation, no one knew quite what television would be good for. The general assumption was that the applications would mostly be practical. *Scientific American*, in an article entitled 'Motion Pictures by Radio', foresaw television as a crime prevention device. 'A criminal suspect might appear simultaneously in a thousand police headquarters for identification,' it supposed. AT&T saw it not as an entertainment medium, but as a way of allowing people on telephones to see each other.

Only Charles Francis Jenkins saw clearly what TV could offer. 'The new machine will come to the fireside . . . with photoplays, the opera and a direct vision of world activities,' he predicted. Though forgotten now – he doesn't even have an entry in the *American Dictionary of National Biography* – Jenkins was an accomplished inventor. He owned over four hundred patents, several of them for successful devices, some of which we use yet. If you have ever had a drink from a conical paper cup, you have used a Jenkins product. But one invention that was never going to work was his radiovisor, as he called it. Even if he got it working, which he did not, it could only ever transmit forty-eight lines of image, not enough to show objects as anything other than shadowy blurs. It would be like trying to identify objects through frosted glass.

But this was the deliriously upbeat 1920s, and although Jenkins did not have a product to sell, or anything more than a vague (and ultimately unrealizable) hope that his system could be developed into something commercially appealing one day, he formed a corporation, which was soon valued at more than $10 million.

Much the same sort of inflated optimism attended the efforts of John Logie Baird, a Scotsman based in London. From an attic flat in Soho, Baird created a stream of mostly useless inventions, including inflatable shoes and a safety razor made of glass (so it wouldn't rust). His private life was equally unorthodox in that he and another man shared the affections of a woman who had once been Baird's girlfriend, was now the second man's wife, and who found it impossible to choose between the two. In true British fashion, the arrangement to share was agreed between all three over a cup of tea.

As an inventor Baird was inspired and indefatigable, but always painfully short of funds. Most of his working models were assembled from salvaged oddments and other scraps. His first Nipkow disc was the lid of a ladies' hatbox. His lenses were made from bicycle headlights. Wondering if he might get a better resolution of his images if he shone them through a real human eye, he called at the Charing Cross Ophthalmic Hospital and asked if they had any eyes they could spare. A doctor, thinking him a qualified anatomist, gave him one. Baird took the eye home on the bus, but discovered that the optic nerve was useless without a blood supply, and anyway when he clamped the eyeball into his contraption he made such a gruesome mess of it that it made him ill and he put it all in the bin.

Still he persevered and in 1925, in his lab, Baird managed to transmit the world's first recognizable image of a human face. Baird was an accomplished publicist – one of his stunts was to place a working TV in a window of Selfridges department store, drawing crowds great enough to stop traffic – and that brought a rush of financing. By 1927, Baird was at the head of a company that had nearly two hundred employees. He was not a good company man and hated having to answer to a board of directors. Developing a particular dislike for Sir Edward Manville, the pompous chairman imposed on him by his principal investors, Baird had a lab built with an intentionally narrow entrance. The portly Manville, on his first visit, got stuck and had to be pushed through from behind. As Baird recalled proudly, 'he lost several buttons from his waist-coat and dropped his cigar and tramped on it in the process' and never visited the lab again.

The inescapable shortcoming of a Nipkow system, as Baird found to his unending frustration, was that it required a pair of large, noisily whirring discs – one to send and one to receive a signal – and could produce at best only a small image. A four-inch-square picture would require spinning discs six feet across – not something that many people would want in their living rooms. The discs could be dangerous, too, as a visiting scientist to Baird's lab painfully discovered when he leaned too close and his long white beard was yanked into the workings.

The reality that Baird and all the others involved with mechanical television could never overcome was that spinning discs simply could not provide the clarity of image necessary to make television a commercial pro-position. In practical terms it was impossible to produce more than about sixty lines of imagery, and the viewing screen could never be larger than about the size of a drinks coaster. Nevertheless, Baird persevered and by the summer of 1927 had about as good a working model as his system could provide.

On 8 September, slightly less than five months after the Bell Labs presentation with Herbert Hoover, the *New York Times* reported another exciting demonstration of television, this time from England. As reporters looked on, Baird used his mechanical system to send a live image of himself more than two hundred miles from Leeds to

London. His image was clear, but it was also frustratingly small at just two and a half inches by three; and when magnified to a larger size through a special lens it lost all clarity.

In fact, unknown to Baird, the *New York Times* and everyone else in the world at large, television had actually had its real birth one day earlier in far-off California when a young man with the resplendent name of Philo T. Farnsworth, the greatest inventor of whom most people have never heard, used cathode ray tubes and an electron beam to produce an image that genuinely had the promise to make television an enchanting reality.

Philo Farnsworth, 'the forgotten father of television', was born in 1906 in a log cabin in Utah. His parents, pious Mormons, moved the family to a farm in Idaho not long afterwards, and it was there, in the idyllic surroundings of the Snake River Valley, that young Philo spent a happy childhood. He was uncommonly bright and devoured everything he could find on science and technology. In the summer of 1921, while ploughing his father's field, the fifteen-year-old Philo had a scientific epiphany. He had been reading Einstein's theory on electrons and the photo-electric effect, and now it occurred to him that beams of electrons could be scanned on to a screen in a back-and-forth pattern exactly as he was ploughing his father's field, one line at a time in alternating directions. Within months he had devised a workable plan for transmitting images electronically. He made a sketch of it, which he showed to his high school chemistry teacher, Justin Tolman. Luckily for Farnsworth, Tolman was so impressed that he kept the drawing. It would later confirm Farnsworth's priority for the invention.

Lacking financing, Farnsworth left the idea undeveloped and instead finished high school, married his sweetheart and enrolled at Brigham Young University in Salt Lake City. One day he fell into a chance conversation with two young businessmen from San Francisco, who were so impressed with his ideas that they offered to invest $6,000 – which is to say, their entire joint savings – in the project, and to help him secure a bank loan. With this, Farnsworth set up a small lab on Green Street in San Francisco. He was still just twenty years old – too young, as he discovered, to sign the contract on the bank loan.

Farnsworth filed his first patents for television in January 1927. Building a working television system was an almost ridiculous challenge. Parts couldn't be bought off the shelf – most of them didn't exist, except in Farnsworth's fertile brain – so nearly every glowing valve and gently thrumming tube had to be designed and built from scratch. Farnsworth and a small team he assembled worked feverishly, and by early September were ready to transmit the first image ever using electronic apparatus. The image was only a simple horizontal line and Farnsworth only sent it as far as the next room, so it didn't have the romance and awe of Baird's or AT&T's creations. But it did have one thing the rival inventions didn't have: a future.

At the heart of Farnsworth's system was something called an image-dissector camera, which allowed him to paint (as it were) pictures across a screen by scanning them in electronically one line at a time – and to do it so quickly that the eye is fooled into thinking it is seeing a series of continuous images. Even in its earliest versions Farnsworth's system had 150 lines, giving it a crispness that no mechanical system could ever achieve.

Although the wider world knew nothing of Farnsworth's invention, people who understood electronics soon learned of it and came to marvel at his work. One visitor was the physicist Ernest Lawrence, who was overjoyed to behold a part of Farnsworth's device called the 'multipactor', which concentrated electron beams and fired them in bursts, multiplying their intensity. Inspired, Lawrence returned to Berkeley and produced the world's first particle accelerator.

Eventually, Farnsworth had 165 patents, including for all the important elements of modern television, from scanning and focusing images to projecting live pictures across great distances. But the one thing he didn't have was any way of making the whole enterprise commercial.

Enter David Sarnoff.

Sarnoff's world was radio. From a technical point of view he didn't know the first thing about television – he didn't actually know that much about radio – but he had two qualities that Farnsworth signally lacked: commercial acumen and vision. He was the one person in the world who could transform television from an interesting laboratory novelty into something that everyone would want to have within ten feet of his sofa.

Sarnoff was born in a poor village in rural Russia, in what is now Belarus, but moved with his family to the lower East Side of New York in 1900 when he was nine. He could not have been more of a yokel; before his trip to America he had never seen a paved road. Now he was in the most colossally dynamic city on earth. Sarnoff learned English, quit school at fourteen and went out to make his mark on the world. He landed a job as an office boy at American Marconi, the telegraph company, and there became an adept wireless operator. Throughout his life he claimed to have been the first person to receive and relay onwards the news of the *Titanic*'s sinking, from an office in Wanamaker's department store. According to Sarnoff's own version of events – and Sarnoff's versions of events often only loosely intersected with what actually happened – he stayed at his post for seventy-two hours and more or less single-handedly coordinated rescue efforts.

In 1919, American Marconi was bundled into a new company called Radio Corporation of America. Sarnoff – young, ambitious, instinctively opportunistic – quickly became master of the new medium. He made radio popular and profitable – two things that were by no means assured in 1920. Radio at the time was an exciting novelty, but a radio set was also a costly investment and people weren't at all sure that it was worth the outlay, particularly if the only available programming was provided by a local bank or insurance broker or poultry farm.

Companies that made radios didn't care what people listened to, or whether they listened at all, once the radios were bought. Sarnoff, remarkably, seems to have been alone in seeing that if there wasn't anything worth listening to, they wouldn't buy radios. He realized that to succeed radio needed to be organized, professional, and above all entertaining. As a demonstration of radio's potential, he arranged to broadcast the Dempsey– Carpentier prize fight on 2 July 1921. Sarnoff reasoned that if people realized that they could listen to exciting events live as they happened, they would flock to radio. To that end, he had loudspeakers erected at various locations where people could listen to the fight for free. Ten thousand listeners packed into Times Square and other demonstrations were laid on elsewhere. In the event, a technical fault meant there was no live broadcast from ringside. Instead the details of the fight were relayed by ticker tape to a Manhattan studio where an announcer recreated the fight from sketchy details and a great deal of imagination. That is what the crowds heard. It didn't matter. They *thought* they were hearing the fight live. The idea of being able to know what was happening as it happened seemed to many an almost impossible miracle.

Radio now took off. At the time of the Dempsey–Carpentier fight, one American home in five hundred had a radio. Within five years, the proportion was one in twenty. By the end of the decade, saturation would be nearly total. Never before had a consumer product gained universal acceptance so quickly.

To improve broadcast standards, and secure RCA's dominance of the industry, Sarnoff persuaded his masters to join with Westinghouse and General Electric to form a radio network, the National Broadcasting Company. NBC's successful broadcasts of big events – not least Lindbergh's arrival in Washington in June 1927 – were so impressive that they inspired the creation of a second network, the Columbia Broadcasting System, which began broadcasting now, in September 1927. Its principal investor was the Columbia Phonograph Corporation, which wanted to sell more phonograph albums.

Network broadcasting proved to be extremely expensive. Radio was unique among entertainment media in that it didn't charge for content. Once someone bought a radio, he could listen to all the programmes he wanted in perpetuity for free. On top of that, the programming was dismayingly ephemeral. Movies could be shown again, plays could be performed over and over, but a radio play or concert or variety show was broadcast once and then was gone for ever. Even if it could be recorded, nobody wanted to hear the same programmes night after night, so radio had constantly to generate new material at often quite staggering costs. NBC executives were horrified to discover that their two regular opera programmes were costing the network $6,000 a week. It was so hard to make a profit that some insiders wondered whether radio had a commercial future.

The obvious solution, selling advertising, was curiously slow to take hold. In the beginning, programmes, if they had any commercial content at all, just mentioned the name of a sponsor, without making any kind of overt sales pitch. Commercial radio also had to contend with the stout opposition of Herbert Hoover, who as secretary of commerce controlled the air waves. Hoover believed that radio should apply itself to noble, sober purposes. 'If a speech by the President is to be used as the meat in a sandwich of two patent medicine advertisements, there will be no radio left,' he declared, and threatened to take away licences from the worst abusers. Luckily, however, by the summer of 1927 Hoover was so busy with other matters – the Mississippi flood at first, then getting himself elected president – that he lost the will or ability to follow through.

Sarnoff was only too happy to take advantage of this. He found, as he suspected, that listeners didn't mind advertisements at all. By its second year on air, NBC was selling over $10 million worth of ads a year. By the early 1930s, radio advertising was worth over $40 million a year in a market that was greatly shrunken by the Great Depression. Newspaper advertising fell by a third and magazine ads by closer to a half as radio advertising took off. Nearly 250 daily newspapers folded in the decade after the birth of network radio. Listening to the radio became the thing that every household did, and David Sarnoff could legitimately take the credit for almost all of that. By 1929, just before the stock market crash, RCA stock was 10,000 per cent higher than it had been just five years before, and David Sarnoff was the darling of the radio industry.

And in the midst of all this, he discovered television. In 1929, Sarnoff attended a conference of radio engineers in Rochester, New York, and there saw a presentation by a clever inventor named Vladimir Zworykin. Like his compatriot Igor Sikorsky, the aircraft designer, Zworykin had grown up rich in Russia, but had fled to America following the country's revolution. Although Zworykin spoke almost no English on arrival, he landed a job with Westinghouse in Pittsburgh and so impressed the directors that he was soon given his own lab.

Zworykin perceived the possibility of electronic television in exactly the way that Farnsworth did. Television was what he talked about in Rochester and it transfixed Sarnoff. Sarnoff saw at once the future of television as an even greater potential medium for entertainment and wealth creation for RCA, and now threw himself behind its development with an almost alarming enthusiasm.

Zworykin told Sarnoff that he could deliver a working system in two years for a cost of $100,000. Sarnoff hired him and provided him with everything he could need. As matters turned out, it would cost RCA more than $50 million to get a working system together – an incredible gamble for an unproven technology. Worse, Sarnoff discovered that the most vital patents, and much of the attendant insight, resided with a young man with the improbable name of Philo Farnsworth in San Francisco.

For Farnsworth, things were not going so well. Broadcasting a clear image of a line was one thing, developing it into a fully fledged entertainment system was quite another. Even a fairly basic set-up would require millions of dollars of investment, which Farnsworth clearly didn't have. Learning of his progress, Zworykin paid him a visit. Farnsworth, thinking RCA wished to license his patents, happily showed Zworykin everything, including how to make an image dissector, the apparatus at the very heart of his system. Thanks to this help, RCA now quickly developed an image dissector of its own. Sarnoff airily informed Farnsworth that RCA didn't actually want or need his patents – this was a lie – but that it was generously prepared to offer him $100,000 for everything: patents, diagrams, working models and all the contents of his lab. Farnsworth dismissed the offer as the insult that it was.

Increasingly desperate for funds, Farnsworth sold out to the Philadelphia Storage Battery Company, better known as Philco, and moved east. It was not a happy relationship. Farnsworth hated being a salaried employee. When his infant son died, Farnsworth requested time off to take the boy back to Utah to bury him in the family plot. Philco refused to give him leave, and the two parted ways soon after. Philco meanwhile became convinced that RCA was trying to bribe or blackmail its employees into giving away trade secrets. It filed a suit charging RCA operatives with plying Philco employees with 'intoxicating liquors at hotels, restaurants and nightclubs'. The case was settled out of court.

All this made Farnsworth increasingly paranoid and stressed. From the confidently beaming youth of a year or two before, he became a gaunt and driven-looking figure. Even his hair looked angry. He argued with his original investors and flatly refused to collaborate with any out-siders. Eventually, he ended up with a lawsuit against RCA for patent infringement.

Sarnoff couldn't bear to come second at anything and never hesitated to crush those who challenged him. When Edwin H. Armstrong, an electrical engineer, invented FM radio, which provided clearer, stronger signals than AM radio, Sarnoff did all in his power to have it suppressed by getting the Federal Communications Commission to restrict available bandwidth for it. Armstrong sued and found the wrath of RCA coming down upon him. RCA's lawyers tied him up in court for years. The battle cost Armstrong his health and every penny he owned. In 1954, despondent and broke, he committed suicide.

Now RCA waged much the same sort of battle against Farnsworth. It maintained that Farnsworth could not have conceived of electronic television in 1922 on the grounds that a fifteen-year-old schoolboy could hardly have come up with an idea that had eluded the most brilliant minds of science and technology for years. Luckily for Farnsworth, his old chemistry teacher, Justin Tolman, was able to produce his original sketch. That, and the fact that Farnsworth possessed the relevant patents, left the court in no doubt. In 1935, it ruled that Farnsworth was 'the undisputed inventor of television' – a stunning victory for the lone inventor.

RCA essentially ignored the ruling. At the 1939 New York World's Fair it demonstrated a working television that was entirely dependent on Farnsworth patents, for which it had neither made payment nor secured permission. After years of further wrangling, RCA finally agreed to pay Farnsworth $1 million and a royalty on every television sold. However, Farnsworth's most valuable patents ran out in the late 1940s, just as TV was about to take off, so he never got anything like the full measure of wealth to which he was rightly entitled.

In 1950, Sarnoff secured a promise from the Radio and Television Manufacturers Association of America that it would refer to him henceforth as 'the Father of Television' and to Vladimir Zworykin as 'the Inventor of Television'. Farnsworth was effectively expunged from the record.

Farnsworth retired to Maine and descended into alcoholism. He died in March 1971, drunk, depressed and forgotten. He was sixty-four years old. The *New York Times*, in its obituary, referred to him not as the inventor of television, but as a 'pioneer in the design of television'. Sarnoff died later that same year at the venerable age of eighty.

After television, Vladimir Zworykin helped to invent the electron microscope. He survived Sarnoff and Farnsworth by eleven years, dying in 1982 the day before his ninety-third birthday. In an interview in 1974, he claimed never to watch television because it was so mindless, and said that his greatest contribution to television technology was the invention of the off switch.

In fact, the off switch was invented by Philo Farnsworth and was part of his earliest patent.

Chapter 28

M OST OF US, given a pad of paper, a pencil and a few minutes to think, could come up with a reasonably respectable list of writers who were at work in the 1920s: F. Scott Fitzgerald, Ernest Hemingway, William Faulkner, James Joyce, Virginia Woolf, T. S. Eliot, Gertrude Stein, Dorothy Parker, Ezra Pound and so on.

It is unlikely, however, that many of us would think to include the name of Harold Bell Wright. Yet Wright was more popular than any of the people on the list above and may well have had greater lifetime sales than all of them put together. In 1925 when the first printing of his novel *A Son of His Father* came off the presses in Chicago, it filled twenty-seven railway boxcars. His 1911 book *The Winning of Barbara Worth* was so beloved that fans named a hotel, a road and a school after it. Wright's books were sentimental and predictable – they invariably concerned a person who had been buffeted by life's travails, but then found happiness and success through hard work and Christian fellowship – but people couldn't get enough of them.

Much the same could be said of a great many other

writers whose names have long since slipped into obscurity. Cosmo Hamilton, Arthur Somers Roche, Coningsby Dawson, T. S. Stribling, Hervey Allen, Stark Young, Hermann Keyserling, Warwick Deeping, Thyra Samter Winslow, Knut Hamsun, Julia Peterkin, Gene Stratton-Porter, Zona Gale and Mazo de la Roche all enjoyed greater sales, and often greater fame, than any of the better remembered authors of the 1920s.

None, however – not even Harold Bell Wright at full, emotive throttle – could begin to compare with the success of two other American authors whose books sold and sold for decades. They were Zane Grey and Edgar Rice Burroughs and they were almost certainly the two most popular authors on the planet in the twentieth century.

They had a good deal in common. Both were from the Midwest, both came comparatively late to professional writing – Grey at thirty, Burroughs at thirty-five – and even later to success, and both were by almost any measure pretty terrible writers. The wonder is not that they are no longer widely read, but that they ever were. Of Grey, the critic Burton Rascoe wrote: 'It is difficult to imagine any writer having less merit in either style or substance than Grey and still maintaining an audience at all.' Burroughs was largely spared such insults because as a pulp writer he wasn't deemed worthy of even scornful notice. But the world devoured their output. Nobody knows how many books they sold – estimates range, rather wildly, from 25 million apiece up to 60 million or so if translations, posthumous publications and book-length magazine publications are counted in. Whatever the actual total, for both it was unquestionably a gratifyingly large number.

Grey, in an interestingly secretive way, was much the

more intriguing of the two. Newspaper and magazine profiles in his lifetime portrayed him as a pleasant and unassuming dentist from Ohio who wrote adventure stories in his spare time, hit pay dirt in 1912 with *Riders of the Purple Sage*, then cranked out a succession of highly popular books, mostly westerns, over a period of nearly thirty years. He invented, or at the very least cornered the market in, many of the conventions of the genre – the black-hearted villain, the bullied rancher and his chaste, pretty daughter, the strong, silent cowboy 'whose heart belongs to no female save his warm-nosed mare', as one writer once nicely put it.

But Grey had a great secret. In private, he was spectacularly libidinous. An ardent outdoorsman, he often went on long trips into the wilderness with attractive, high-spirited young women – his wife's two young cousins, friends of the family, casual acquaintances – and slept with them all. Sometimes he took as many as four at a time away with him. Occasionally he brought them home with him afterwards. As his biographer Thomas H. Pauly reports: 'There exists an enormous, totally unknown cache of photographs taken by Grey of nude women and himself performing various sexual activities, including intercourse . . . These photographs are accompanied by ten small journals, written in Grey's secret code, that contain graphic descriptions of his sexual adventures.'

In between these invigorating breaks Grey lived quietly with his wife, a woman of stoic temperament, in Lackawana, Pennsylvania, and later Altadena, California, and wrote two or sometimes three books a year. He produced some ninety-five books altogether, and left so many manuscripts when he died, suddenly of a heart attack in

1939, that Harper & Brothers was still publishing new Zane Grey books fourteen years later. At his peak he earned $500,000 a year. In 1927, he made just under $325,000. For purposes of comparison, F. Scott Fitzgerald, in his best year, earned $37,599.

Edgar Rice Burroughs had a tamer life than Grey – but then, after all, who didn't? – but wrote racier stuff. Three years younger than Grey, Burroughs was born in 1875 into a well-off family in Chicago, but he was something of a black sheep and struggled to find a role for himself in life. He went west as a young man and tried storekeeping, ranching, panning for gold and working as a railway policeman, all without success, before he discovered he had a knack for writing stories. In 1912, at the age of thirty-six, he produced his first hit, *Tarzan of the Apes*.

Burroughs was no hack. He used pulp fiction plots, but wrote with a certain panache, as if he didn't quite understand the genre. Here are the opening lines to *Tarzan of the Apes*:

> I had this story from one who had no business to tell it to me, or to any other. I may credit the seductive influence of an old vintage upon the narrator for the beginning of it, and my own sceptical incredulity for the balance of the strange tale.

It is perhaps not Tolstoy, but it is certainly far removed from the usual simply worded, straight-into-the-action openings of most cheap fiction of the day. In a career that lasted almost forty years, Burroughs produced some eighty books, including twenty-six Tarzan novels, a great deal of science fiction and a few westerns. All his efforts were characterized by exhilarating action, lightly clad females and an unwavering attachment to eugenic ideals. Tarzan himself could have been the poster boy for the eugenics movement. *Tarzan*, as many readers will surely know already, is the story of an aristocratic English infant who is left orphaned in the African jungle and is brought up by apes. Fortunately, because he is white and Anglo-Saxon, he is innately brave, strong, decisive and kind, instinctively ethical, and clever enough to solve any problem. He even teaches himself to read – quite a feat considering that he speaks no human language and doesn't know what a book is when he first sees one. Thank goodness for racial superiority.

The creation or maintenance of superior beings is something that preoccupied Burroughs throughout his career. Nearly all his outer space books are concerned with the breeding of master races on Mars or Venus.* In *Lost on Venus*, he writes admiringly of a society in which 'no defective infant was allowed to live' and citizens who were 'physically, morally or mentally defective were rendered incapable of bringing their like into the world'. Back on earth, writing as himself in an article in the *Los Angeles*

---

* Putting advanced societies on nearby planets wasn't in itself a preposterous notion in 1927. The March issue of *Scientific American*, no less, contained an article solemnly speculating on whether Mars contained a civilization superior to our own. (It also had an article suggesting that humans might be evolving into a race of one-eyed Cyclopeans.) Other respectable publications posed similar questions about Venus, where it was supposed that the inhabitants lived in some kind of tropical paradise beneath thick Venusian clouds.

Examiner, he insisted that the world would be a better place if all 'moral imbeciles' were systematically eliminated. He even titled one of his books *Bridge and the Oskaloosa Kid*. Oskaloosa was the birthplace of Harry H. Laughlin.

As time went on, Burroughs became increasingly slapdash. He recycled plots and was often arrestingly careless with his prose. His lone novel of 1927, *The War Chief*, begins:

> Naked, but for a G-string, rough sandals, a bit of hide, and a buffalo headdress, a savage warrior leaped and danced to the beating of drums.

Four paragraphs later we get:

> Naked, but for a G-string, rough sandals, a bit of hide, and a buffalo headdress, a savage warrior moved silently among the boles of great trees.

Occasionally he just slipped into drivel. Here is a Martian warrior named Jeddak whispering sweet nothings to Thuvia, Maid of Mars, in a book of that title in 1920:

> Ah, Thuvia of Ptarth, you are cold even before the fiery blasts of my consuming love! No harder than your heart, nor colder is the hard, cold ersite of this thrice happy bench which supports your divine and fadeless form!

Such passages could run on for some time. It hardly seemed to matter. People were still devotedly buying his stuff when he died in California of a heart attack in March 1950, aged seventy-four.

Among serious writers of fiction, only Sinclair Lewis enjoyed robust sales in the summer of 1927. *Elmer Gantry* was far and away the best-selling fiction work of the year. A satire on evangelist preachers, it was roundly condemned across the nation, especially by evangelist preachers. The fundamentalist preacher Billy Sunday, apprised of its content, called on God 'to strike Lewis dead', which doesn't seem terribly Christian of him. The Reverend C. S. Sparkes of the Congregational Church of Sauk Centre, Minnesota, Lewis's own home town, bitterly contrasted Lewis with the saintly Charles Lindbergh, saying that Lewis possessed a mind 'that is dead – dead to goodness and purity and righteousness', while Lindbergh was 'clean in mind and soul'.

Elmer Gantry was banned in several cities – in Boston, selling it was made an indictable offence, as opposed to just a misdemeanour, as an indication of how severely disagreeable it was – but of course such prohibitions merely made the book seem more juicily desirable to those who could get it. The novel sold 100,000 copies on its first day of publication, and was cruising towards 250,000 by the end of summer – numbers that not even Grey and Burroughs could count on.

Elmer Gantry was the fifth in a string of critical and commercial successes for Lewis that made him the most admired writer of his day. The others were *Main Street* (1920), *Babbitt* (1922), *Arrowsmith* (1925) and *Mantrap* (1926). In 1930, he would be the first American awarded a Nobel Prize in literature. Not everyone was a fan. Ernest

Hemingway, in a letter to his editor, said: 'If I wrote as sloppily and shitily as that freckled prick I could write five thousand words a day year in and year out.' Though Lewis had no sense of it just yet, 1927 would mark the apex of his career trajectory. His later novels would fall out of fashion and he would end up an alcoholic, so racked with delirium tremens that he would be confined in a straitjacket.

Hemingway produced no novel in 1927. He was mostly preoccupied with personal affairs – he divorced one wife and wed another in Paris in early summer, just about the time Lindbergh was flying in – but did come out with a volume of short stories, *Men Without Women*. Dorothy Parker in the *New Yorker* called it 'a truly magnificent work . . . I don't know where a greater collection of stories can be found,' but the book didn't stir the same public excitement as Hemingway's debut novel of the previous year, *The Sun Also Rises*. Also well received, but not runaway commercial successes, were *The Bridge of San Luis Rey* by a new writer named Thornton Wilder, and *Mosquitoes* by another newcomer, William Faulkner.

F. Scott Fitzgerald, the other American literary giant of the age – to us, if not to his contemporaries – produced no book in 1927. Instead he made his first trip to Hollywood, lured by a commission to write the screenplay for a movie called *Lipstick*. The fee was $3,500 up front with a further $12,000 on acceptance, but in the event his script was deemed inadequate and turned down, so the bulk of the fee was never paid. Fitzgerald also had a screen test, but he didn't do well at that either. In the end, the trip to California cost him far more than he earned. Fitzgerald was fading fast in 1927. *The Great Gatsby*, published two years earlier, had been a failure. Unsold stacks of the book sat in the warehouse of Charles Scribner's Sons, his publisher, and would still be there when Fitzgerald died, broke and all but forgotten, in 1940. Not until the 1950s would the world rediscover him.

The publishing industry was in a state of interesting flux in 1927, and that was largely owing to a longstanding prejudice. Traditionally, publishing was closed to Jews (except at menial and dead-end levels). All the old firms – Harper & Brothers, Scribner's, Doubleday, Houghton Mifflin, Putnam's – were solidly white and largely Protestant, and their output tended to be carefully conservative. That began to change in 1915 when a young Jewish man named Alfred A. Knopf, the son of an advertising executive, started the imprint that still bears his name. Knopf brought America the works of Sigmund Freud, Franz Kafka, Jean-Paul Sartre, Albert Camus, André Gide, D. H. Lawrence, E. M. Forster, Thomas Mann and many others. The preponderance of foreign authors was explained simply by the fact that many American literary agents would not deal with a Jewish publisher.

All this cast the conservatism of the old-line WASP publishers into sharp relief. Charles Scribner's Sons, a family firm founded in 1846, boasted for years that it never published a word that would make a maiden blush, but now found itself struggling to keep up with changing mores. In early 1927, when Maxwell Perkins, its most celebrated editor, was working on Hemingway's afore-mentioned volume of short stories, he felt he had to alert Charles Scribner II, the firm's head, that it contained certain words that might shock him. Perkins was so old-school that he could not bring himself to utter the actual words, but wrote them down. One word he couldn't even write down. (It was never recorded what the words were or whether any or all of them made it into the finished book.)

Interestingly, although Scribner's was squeamish about publishing profanities, it had no hesitation in 1927 in publishing one of the most virulently racist books of the decade, *Re-forging America*, by the amateur eugenicist Lothrop Stoddard. Mr Stoddard's previous book with Scribner's, *The Rising Tide of Color Against White World Supremacy*, hints a little more clearly at where he stood on matters. In *Re-forging America*, Stoddard argued that America should create a 'bi-racial' society, by which he meant not one in which people mingled harmoniously, but rather the very opposite: one in which whites and non-whites were kept separate from cradle to grave so as not to risk cross-contamination to the detriment of either. The book was favourably reviewed in several places.

While Knopf was carving out a lucrative niche for itself among foreign authors, another new Jewish firm was finding great success by discovering – or in some cases rediscovering – American writers. The firm was Boni & Liveright, named for brothers Albert and Charles Boni and for Horace Liveright, and for a short while it was perhaps the most interesting and dynamic publishing house in America. The Boni brothers had until recently run the Washington Square Bookshop, a leftist hangout on MacDougal Street, and Liveright was a bond salesman. Although the three founders didn't have a lot of expertise in publishing, the firm quickly made a name for itself.

The men squabbled endlessly and by the early 1920s

both Bonis had departed, leaving Liveright (pronounced, incidentally, 'live-right', not 'liver-right') as sole head. In the three years 1925 to 1927, he produced what was perhaps the most dazzling parade of quality books ever to emerge from a single publishing house in a concentrated period. They included *An American Tragedy* by Theodore Dreiser, *Dark Laughter* by Sherwood Anderson, *In Our Time* by Ernest Hemingway (who then eloped to Scribner's), *Soldiers' Pay* by William Faulkner, *Enough Rope* by Dorothy Parker, *Crystal Cup* by Gertrude Atherton, *My Life* by Isadora Duncan, *Education and the Good Life* by Bertrand Russell, *Napoleon* by Emil Ludwig, *The Thibaults* by Roger Martin du Gard (forgotten now, but he was soon to win a Nobel Prize), *The Golden Day* by Lewis Mumford, three plays by Eugene O'Neill, volumes of poems by T. S. Eliot, Ezra Pound, E. E. Cummings, Edgar Lee Masters and Robinson Jeffers, and a work of cheery froth by Hollywood screenwriter Anita Loos called *Gentlemen Prefer Blondes*. Purporting to be the diary of a dizzy golddigger named Lorelei Lee, *Gentlemen Prefer Blondes* wasn't great literature, but it sold and sold and sold. James Joyce was said to be enchanted by it.

Liveright was a great publisher but a terrible businessman. He gave advances that were too indulgent, employed far more people than he needed to and paid them more than he should have. Because of his bad business decisions, Boni & Liveright made profits of just $1,203 in 1927 and was in serious danger of going out of business.

Liveright exacerbated matters considerably by investing heavily, and generally unsuccessfully, in the stock market and on Broadway. In 1927 he found temporary salvation from an unlikely source. He brought over from

London a play that had been a big success there: *Dracula*. For the American production, he selected a little-known Hungarian actor named Bela Lugosi. Although Lugosi had been in America for six years, he still spoke little English and learned his lines phonetically, without really under- standing what they meant, which gave him interesting diction. Lugosi had started his career playing romantic leads, but in 1926 he played a villain in a small but memorably named movie called *The Devil in the Cheese*. On the strength of that, it seems, he landed the role of Dracula. On 19 September, it opened at the Shubert Theatre in New Haven, Connecticut. After a successful two- week tryout, it had its formal premiere at the Fulton Theatre in New York on 5 October, just before Lugosi's forty-fifth birthday. In what may have been the best idea he ever had, Liveright hit on the gimmick of having a nurse stand by at each performance to help those who fainted, to emphasize just how terrifying an experience *Dracula* was. The ploy worked brilliantly. *Dracula* was a huge hit and ran for a year in New York, then toured for two years more, making Liveright a lot of money when he most needed it.

It was also the making of Bela Lugosi, for Lugosi essentially did nothing else for the rest of his career but play Dracula. He starred in the 1931 movie and a great number of sequels. He also changed wives often – he was married five times – and became addicted to narcotics, but professionally he did almost nothing else for almost thirty years. Such was his devotion to the role that when he died in 1956, he was buried dressed as Count Dracula.

For Horace Liveright, *Dracula* proved a reprieve, not a solution. The firm went under in 1933, but by then its good work was done. Thanks almost entirely to Knopf and

Liveright, American publishing was vastly more cosmopolitan and daring by the late 1920s than it had been just
a dozen or so years before.

After an uninspiring spring and summer, Broadway was
stirring promisingly at last. Two plays of lasting note were
in rehearsals in September. One was *Funny Face* with music
and lyrics by George and Ira Gershwin. Starring Fred and
Adele Astaire and Betty Compton, mistress of Mayor
Jimmy Walker, it would be a great hit and would run for
250 performances. Among its songs were 'My One And
Only' and ''S Wonderful'. Jemmied into it in a burst of
topical exuberance was a role featuring a 'Lindbergh-esque
aviator'. (The 1957 film version was completely different
and cut the aviator. It also preserved just four of the original songs.)

Far more influential was a complex musical about life
on a Mississippi riverboat. Called *Show Boat*, it would
change musical theatre for ever. As one theatre historian
has put it: 'The history of the American Musical Theatre,
quite simply, is divided into two eras – everything before
Show Boat and everything after *Show Boat*.'

Show Boat was based on a novel from the previous year
by Edna Ferber, who had just recently – and quite late in
life – become extremely successful as a writer. Forty-two
years old in the summer of 1927, she was from Appleton,
Wisconsin, the daughter of a Jewish shopkeeper. She was
small and round, never married or had a partner, and
carried a sharp tongue. Once the camp author Michael
Arlen, seeing Ferber in a double-breasted jacket, said,
'Why, Edna, you look almost like a man,' to which Ferber
replied, 'Why, Michael, so do you.' Thanks to her wit, she

was welcomed to the Algonquin Round Table, the informal luncheon club of wits who gathered every weekday in the Algonquin Hotel, and professionally embraced by George S. Kaufman, the most successful comedic playwright of the day. They collaborated extremely successfully on a string of comedies.

However gifted Ferber was with comedy, her skills as a novelist have not weathered well. The novel *Show Boat* is 'a kind of hilarious anthology of bad writing', in the candid words of John Lahr. In evidence of her propensity to write 'like a teenager on diet pills', he cites this passage: 'The Mississippi itself was a tawny tiger, roused, furious, bloodthirsty, lashing out with its great tail, tearing with its cruel claws, and burying its fangs deep in the shore to swallow at a gulp land, houses, trees, cattle, humans, even . . .' But it was a different age, and many found the book enchanting. Among its greatest fans was the composer Jerome Kern. He all but begged Ferber to let him make it into a musical. Ferber was doubtful that it could be done, but allowed him to try. The result was what a theatre historian has called 'perhaps the most successful and influential Broadway musical play ever written'.

Kern was born in New York City in 1885 (the same year as Edna Ferber) into a prosperous household. His father was a successful businessman, and young Jerome was well educated. He trained in musical theory and composition at the New York College of Music, though he spent his early years working in Tin Pan Alley. His original speciality was creating new songs for imported plays – interpolations, as they were known in the trade – but soon he was cranking out original scores. Kern might never have become famous. He was booked to sail on the *Lusitania* in

May 1915 on its last fateful voyage, but overslept and missed its departure.

It was an extraordinarily busy time on Broadway. An average of fifty new musicals a year opened in the 1920s. Kern was amazingly prolific. In 1917 alone, he wrote the music for five plays, and a number of incidental songs as well. But he also developed ambitions. In the same year he wrote: 'It is my opinion that the musical numbers should carry the action of the play and should be representative of the personalities of the characters who sing them.' This was, improbable though it may seem today, a revolutionary notion, and it was *Show Boat* that would make it a reality.

Kern could have done with a hit. He had already had one notable failure in 1927. *Lucky* had opened on 22 March to mixed reviews and closed two months later (on the day Lindbergh landed in Paris). The play apparently had one wonderful song, 'Spring Is Here', but Kern neglected to get it published and it is now lost. Of Kern's most recent five plays, just one, *Sunny*, had been a real hit. The others had mostly been disappointing. *Dear Sir* closed after just fifteen performances. So *Show Boat* was both a crucial production for him and a bold gamble, too.

It had a complicated plot, it covered a span of forty years and it addressed the highly sensitive issue of race – not the obvious makings of a night of light-hearted entertainment. *Show Boat* began rehearsals in the second week of September, almost three months ahead of its scheduled opening on Broadway, which was much, much earlier than would normally be the case, but its epic production numbers required careful preparation.

With music by Kern, book and lyrics by Oscar

Hammerstein II, choreography by Sammy Lee and sets by Joseph Urban, *Show Boat* debuted at the National Theatre in Washington on 15 November, then moved on to Philadelphia, and finally opened on Broadway at the new Ziegfeld Theatre on 27 December. *Rio Rita*, the play Charles Lindbergh never quite saw, had to move out to make room for it. The reception everywhere was ecstatic.

As Lahr put it in 1993: 'Nothing like it had ever been seen on the American stage.' It marked the birth of the integrated musical, by which is meant simply that all the elements of a musical – script, songs, dance, sets – contributed to a coherent whole, exactly what Kern had been calling for as far back as 1917.

Show Boat was racy stuff in every sense of the word. It involved miscegenation and relations between blacks and whites, and dealt sympathetically with the plight of black people in the South. It had a chorus of ninety-six, equally divided between blacks and whites, and was the first production in the history of American theatre in which blacks and whites sang together on stage. Just three years earlier, when authorities learned that Eugene O'Neill's play *All God's Chillun* proposed to show black and white children playing together as if that were normal, the district attorney for Manhattan sent the police to stop it. So for that reason alone the play was tremendously exciting. For people inclined to be enlightened, this was a breakout moment.

The play contained six songs that are still widely known today – 'Ol' Man River', 'Can't Help Lovin' Dat Man', 'Bill', 'Make-Believe', 'Why Do I Love You' and 'You Are Love'. 'Ol' Man River' turned out to be uncannily like an existing song called 'Long-Haired Mamma', published earlier that year. The composer, Maury Madison, thought so, too, and sued Kern. They settled out of court.

The substance of the play itself was anything but an automatic hit. As well as miscegenation, it seriously looked at gambling and broken marriages. It was also extremely long, not finishing until after 11.30 p.m. But people flocked to it. Several members of the audience were moved literally to tears. From the beginning *Show Boat* was a smash hit, grossing $50,000 a week during the course of its run.

It was a memorable week for Edna Ferber. The night after *Show Boat* opened, a play she co-wrote with George S. Kaufman, *The Royal Family*, had its premiere. A comedy that deftly parodied the famously temperamental and self-important Barrymore acting clan, it was an immediate hit and ran for ten months. The Barrymores were eminently worthy of parody. John Barrymore once left a stage to punch an electrician who had not focused a light on him properly, and if someone coughed while he was emoting, he would stop and call out to the audience, 'Would someone please throw that seal a fish?' Ethel Barrymore did her best to get the play stopped, but failed.

Although Ferber and Kaufman squabbled endlessly and often bitterly, they wrote three great comedies together – *The Royal Family*, *Dinner at Eight* and *Stage Door* – before breaking up in permanent rancour. When Kaufman was near death, Ferber came to visit him and thought they had achieved a reconciliation. As she left, Kaufman called her back and said, 'Edna, are you going to the funeral?'

'What funeral?' she asked.

'Yours. You're dead, Edna, dead!' he cried, and fell back on the pillows. He never spoke to her again.

Altogether eighteen plays opened on Broadway in the

week that *Show Boat* premiered – eleven of them on the day after Christmas, making it the busiest single night in the history of Broadway. Theatre seemed to be enjoying its greatest triumph, but in fact tough times lay ahead. Talking pictures were about to change the world of entertainment profoundly, not just by stealing audiences from live theatre, but, even worse, by stealing talent. Talking pictures needed actors who were comfortable with the spoken word and writers who could create real dialogue. An enormous exodus was about to begin. Spencer Tracy, Clark Gable, Humphrey Bogart, Fredric March, Bette Davis, W. C. Fields, James Cagney, Claudette Colbert, Edward G. Robinson, Leslie Howard, Basil Rathbone, Claude Rains, Cary Grant, Paul Muni, Paulette Goddard and many more who could be seen in 1927 on Broadway would all shortly decamp to Hollywood. American theatre would never be the same again.

When *Show Boat* went on the road in 1929, it didn't do very well at all. Everybody was at the talkies.

CHAPTER 29

O F ALL THE figures who rose to prominence in the 1920s in America, none had a more pugnacious manner, finer head of hair or more memorable name than Kenesaw Mountain Landis.

Landis was a slight figure – he weighed no more than 130 pounds and stood just five and a half feet tall – but a commanding presence. Sixty-one years old in the summer of 1927, he had a wizened face and parchment skin beneath a white mane. The radical journalist John Reed described Landis as having 'the face of Andrew Jackson three years dead'.

Born and raised in Millville, Ohio, he owed his curious name to a bizarre circumstance. His father, a surgeon for the Union Army in the Civil War, lost his leg at Kennesaw Mountain, Georgia, and, oddly, decided to commemorate the event by naming his son after the site (but with a slight adjustment of spelling).

Landis trained as a lawyer in Chicago, then by chance and good fortune landed a plum job as personal assistant to Walter O. Gresham, US secretary of state under President Grover Cleveland. As reward for diligent service to the nation, Landis was made a federal judge in Illinois in 1905. There he distinguished himself by his many rash and startling judgements.

He gained national attention by charging Kaiser Wilhelm of Germany with murder after the sinking of the *Lusitania* (on the grounds that he had killed a resident of Illinois). In his most famous case, he fined Standard Oil $29 million – an audacious sum – for violating antitrust laws. Soon afterwards, an appeals court threw Landis's judgement out, which is what often happened with Landis decisions. According to one authority, Landis had more cases reversed on appeal than any other judge in the federal system.

Wherever legal news was being made, Landis was uncannily present. He presided over the early stages of the famous libel suit between Henry Ford and the *Chicago Tribune*. (The trial was then moved to Michigan, outside his jurisdiction.) During and after the First World War, Landis became particularly noted for prosecuting radicals. He sentenced Victor Berger, a socialist congressman from Wisconsin, to twenty years in prison for criticizing the war in a newspaper editorial. Later he said that he would far rather have stood Berger in front of a firing squad. That sentence was later overturned.

He held a group trial for 101 Wobblies who were collectively charged with 17,022 crimes. Despite the complexity of the case, under Landis's expert guidance the jury took less than an hour to find every one of the defendants guilty. Landis dispensed total sentences of over 800 years and fines totalling $2.5 million – enough to finish the Industrial Workers of the World as a national force.

In the same period, Landis took charge of an antitrust case between the existing major leagues and the upstart Federal League. For years the American and National Leagues had enjoyed monopoly powers, which allowed them to impose a contractual submissiveness on players through the reserve clause, but the Federal League threatened all that by offering better pay and the chance of free agency. Landis permanently endeared himself to American and National League team owners by deferring a ruling for so long that the Federal League owners eventually ran out of money, gave up and disbanded.

With the Federal League out of the way, the baseball owners were able to return to treating their players appallingly. They renounced all agreements made during the Federal League's existence, refused to deal further with a new players' union, and cut salaries everywhere. All this created quite a lot of ill will among the players, and nowhere more so than with the Chicago White Sox, whose owner, Charles Comiskey, was famed for his miserly instincts. Comiskey charged players for laundering their uniforms. He promised an infielder named Bill Hunnefield a $1,000 bonus if Hunnefield stayed healthy enough to play in 100 games, then benched him for the remainder of the season when he got to 99.

In 1919, seven members of the White Sox, with names that could almost have been supplied by central casting – Chick Gandil, Happy Felsch, Swede Risberg, Lefty Williams, Eddie Cicotte, Fred McMullin and the great Shoeless Joe Jackson – agreed to throw the World Series against the Cincinnati Reds for fairly modest payoffs. The 'Black Sox' conspirators were not, by and large, terribly bright. Risberg had just a third-grade education and was a borderline psychotic; he threatened to kill anyone who blew the whistle on the fix, and was deemed just about unbalanced enough to do so. Jackson had never been to school at all and couldn't read or write. Several of the conspirators seemed not quite to understand what was expected of them. Jackson batted .375 in the series and had a record eight hits, one of them a surprise bunt in the tenth inning of a tied game that he beat out with great hustle. Gandil won a game with a walk-off hit. In the end, the White Sox did lose the series, 5 games to 3, but seemed to struggle to do so. One reason for this, it has been suggested, is that the Reds were in on a separate fix and were doing *their* utmost to lose, too.

Nearly every baseball insider, it seems, knew what was going on. When the scandal broke, the major league owners invited – in fact, all but beseeched – Landis to become baseball's first commissioner. Landis agreed on the understanding that he be given dictatorial powers and a written undertaking from the owners that they would never question his judgements. He set up office in the People's Gas Building in Chicago behind a door that had a single word on it: 'Baseball'.

The seven conspirators plus another player, Buck Weaver, who didn't take part in the fix but knew about it and didn't report it, were put on trial in the summer of 1921. A fact not often remembered is that the jury found all eight not guilty, then went out with them to a restaurant to celebrate. One reason the players were cleared was that it was not actually illegal to fix a baseball game, so they could only be charged with wilfully defrauding the public and injuring Comiskey's business, and the jurors decided that that case was not proved. The point was academic because Landis banned them for life anyway.

Landis at first kept his federal judgeship even though it was illegal for him to do so. For entirely understandable reasons, judges were not permitted to receive money from private interests. Eventually Landis was compelled to give up his role as judge, an outcome that may have affected history more than is appreciated because Landis was also a vigorous defender of Prohibition – a novel position to take in Chicago in the 1920s. He handed out prison sentences of up to two years to people found guilty of purveying even small amounts of liquor. On his very last day as a judge, in early 1922, he sentenced a small-time Chicago saloonkeeper to a year in jail and a $1,000 fine for selling two glasses of whisky. Had Landis stayed on the bench, Chicago might not have remained the world's most comfortable place to be a criminal. Whatever Kenesaw Mountain Landis did for baseball, he may actually, if inadvertently, have done even more for Al Capone.

Chicago in 1927 was both the second largest city in America and the fourth largest in the world. Outside America, only London and Paris were grander. But it was also famous, in the words of an editorial in the *Chicago Tribune*, for 'moronic buffoonery, barbaric crime, triumphant hoodlumism, unchecked graft, and a dejected citizenship'.

What the *Tribune* editorialist didn't say – obviously couldn't say – was that a certain portion of that buffoonery resided with the paper's own proprietor, Robert Rutherford McCormick.

McCormick was born, in 1880, into a family that was rich and unhappy in roughly equal measure. Through his father he was related to Cyrus McCormick, inventor of the mechanical reaper, which brought a lucrative connection to the farm-equipment company International Harvester, and on his mother's side he stood heir to the *Chicago Tribune*. His mother was so disappointed that Robert was a boy that she dressed him as a girl and called him Roberta until he was old enough to go to school. Whether for this reason or some other, McCormick didn't discover sex until he was well into his thirties. Then he became something of a satyr and, among other transgressions, stole his first wife from a cousin.

He had a boyish enthusiasm for warfare and was delighted beyond words to be made a colonel in the Illinois National Guard without ever having done anything to merit it other than to exist as a rich person. For the rest of his life he insisted on being addressed as 'Colonel'. When his wife died he had her buried with full military honours, a distinction to which she was not remotely entitled (or very probably desirous of). When the First World War broke out, McCormick served briefly in France. His one battlefield experience was at Cantigny, which so moved him that he made that the name of his estate at Wheaton, Illinois, upon his return to civilian life.

With another cousin, Joseph Medill Patterson, Mc Cormick ran the *Chicago Tribune* from 1910. Although Patterson was an avowed socialist and McCormick was just an inch or so to the left of fascism, they worked surprisingly well together, and the paper prospered, doubling its circulation in their first decade of management. In 1919, the cousins launched the tabloid *New York Daily News*. Remarkably, for the first six years of its existence they ran it from Chicago. Eventually Patterson went off to New

York to focus on the *Daily News*, leaving McCormick in sole charge of the *Tribune*.

Under McCormick, the *Tribune* achieved its era of greatest importance. By 1927 its circulation was 815,000, almost double what it is today. The company owned paper mills, ships, dams, docks, some 7,000 square miles of forests, and one of the country's earliest and most successful radio stations, WGN (short for 'World's Greatest Newspaper'). It also had interests in real estate and banks.

As the years passed, McCormick became increasingly eccentric. When the president of the Lake Shore Bank, which he controlled, displeased him, McCormick demoted him to running a vegetable stand outside his estate. He insisted that the *Tribune* always refer to Henry Luce, founder of *Time* magazine, whom he loathed, as 'Henry Luce, who was born in China but is not a Chinaman'. He developed a private theory that men at the University of Wisconsin wore lace underwear and dispatched a reporter to find out if that was true. (Coincidentally, this was just at the time that Charles Lindbergh was a student there.) For reasons never explained, McCormick kept eastern time at Cantigny, but didn't tell guests, so first-time visitors often arrived at dinner to find the dishes being cleared away.*

In addition to Henry Luce, McCormick deeply detested Henry Ford, immigrants and Prohibition. But above all else he hated Chicago's mayor, William Hale Thompson.

---

* In 1927, McCormick had not yet settled on his most celebrated idiosyncrasy – namely a devotion to simplified spelling. That would begin in 1934, when he would introduce to the *Tribune* such novel spellings as *fate, burocracy, iland* and *lam*, among a large and ever-changing corpus. The *Tribune* maintained the practice for forty-one years.

Thompson was an oaf from head to toe and ear to ear, but his supporters never held that against him. 'The worst you can say about Bill is that he's stupid,' remarked one cheerfully. Thompson was supported because he never got in the way of corruption or the making of money. Born two years before the Great Fire of Chicago in 1871, Thompson grew up rich. His father made a fortune buying property cheaply from distressed owners after the fire and selling it at great profit as Chicago rebuilt. Young Thompson grew into a strapping lad – he was six feet four inches tall and so known to all as Big Bill – but not an especially promising one. He dropped out of school and went west, working as a ranch hand and cowboy, but in 1899 after the death of his father he returned to Chicago and took over the family business. Despite a lack of brains or aptitude, in 1915 he was elected mayor, and for the next eight years presided serenely as the city became the most resplendently corrupt and lawless in the nation.

Chicago was to corruption what Pittsburgh was to steel or Hollywood to motion pictures. It refined and cultivated it, and embraced it without embarrassment. When a mobster named Anthony D'Andrea was killed in 1921, eight thousand people attended the funeral. The cortège was two and a half miles long. The honorary pallbearers included twenty-one judges, nine lawyers and the Illinois state prosecutor.

Gangsters enjoyed almost total immunity in the city. When three men came to the home of an underworld figure named Patsy Lolordo and shot him dead on his own sofa, they left fingerprints all over the room. Mrs Lolordo knew the men and said she was prepared to give evidence against them. Police investigated but decided, with regret, that they couldn't find enough evidence to proceed. In 1927, the state of Illinois had never successfully prosecuted a single mobster for anything.

It was a city where the chief of police, George Shippy, could shoot and kill an innocent man who was trying to deliver a package to his house because the man looked Jewish, and Shippy thought he might be delivering a bomb. The deceased, it turned out, was just an innocent deliveryman trying to do his job. Shippy was not charged.

Thompson, his work done, retired as mayor in 1923, but his admirers, fearful of the kinds of things Prohibition enforcer Emory Buckner was doing in New York – padlockings and so on – persuaded Thompson to run again in 1927, just to be on the safe side. By Chicago standards the election was peaceful. There were just two bombings, two shootings, two election officials beaten and kidnapped, and twelve declared cases of intimidation of voters. Al Capone donated $260,000 to Thompson's campaign. He or someone in his camp is often credited with coining the droll slogan 'Vote early and vote often.' In fact, the phrase was decades old in 1927, but Capone certainly understood the sentiment. According to the official tally, slightly more than one million votes were cast in a city with almost exactly that number of registered voters.

Thompson had run on a novel platform. He had vowed to repeal Prohibition, keep America out of the League of Nations and end crime in Chicago. The first two he had no power to do; the third he had no intention of doing. He also claimed, for reasons not easily discerned, that King George V of Britain was planning to annex Chicago, and promised that if elected he would find the king and 'punch him in the snoot'. His first action on re-election was to set about removing all treasonous works from the city's schools and libraries. Thompson appointed a theatre owner and former billboard changer named Sport Hermann to purge the city's institutions of any works that were less than '100 per cent American'. Hermann appointed a body called the Patriots' League to decide which books were sufficiently objectionable to be discarded, but admitted when pressed that he had read none of the books that he was proposing to burn – it is entirely possible that he had never read a book of any kind – and further admitted that he couldn't remember the names of any of the people advising him. Just to make sure that no possible element of self-inflicted risibility was over-looked, Hermann announced that the bonfire would be lit by the Cook County executioner.

Remarkably, all this got a lot of support. William Randolph Hearst's *Herald and Examiner* backed Thompson's campaign, and hoped that other cities would clear their library shelves, too. The Ku Klux Klan likewise saluted the clear-out and suggested that the city next turn its attention to any books that were favourably inclined towards Jews or Catholics. The head of the Municipal Reference Library announced that he had independently destroyed all books and pamphlets in his care that struck him as dubious. 'I now have an America First library,' he said proudly.

In such a world as this, Al Capone looked sane and practically respectable. He liked to insist that he was really just a businessman. 'I make my money by supplying a public demand,' he said at a press conference in 1927. (And it is notable that Al Capone held press conferences.) 'Ninety per cent of the people of Cook County drink and gamble, and my offence has been to furnish them with those amusements. Whatever else they may say, my booze has been good and my games have been on the square.' In 1927, he headed an organization that turned over $100 million a year. He may have approached matters from a wayward angle, but Al Capone was one of America's great success stories.

He was born Alphonse Capone in January 1899 in Brooklyn. His father was a conscientious citizen and never, as far as is known, broke the law. He was a barber and eventually owned his own shop – a proud achievement for a poor immigrant. He never learned English.

Al was the Capones' fourth son, and the first one born in America. His eldest brother, Vincenzo, ran away to the west in 1908 at the age of sixteen. The Capones got one letter from him the following year, from Kansas, then heard nothing more from him ever again. In fact, Vincenzo had become a Prohibition agent known as Richard 'Two Gun' Hart. He had named himself after the cowboy star William S. Hart, and dressed like him, too, in outsized Stetson, with a tin star on his breast and a pair of loaded holsters around his waist. In the summer of 1927, extraordinarily enough, he was in South Dakota and working as a personal bodyguard to President Coolidge.

Young Al, needless to say, followed a rather different career path. Expelled from school for striking a teacher (she hit him first, he always carefully explained), he became a protégé of a Brooklyn racketeer named Johnny Torrio. A mild, delicate person, Torrio was the man who put the organized into organized crime. He was adept at gaining control of particular trades or businesses. All the ice deliverymen in a borough, say, would pay a commission to

Torrio and in return would be granted a monopoly in a particular district, allowing them to raise their prices. Anyone who challenged their monopoly was likely to find his office dynamited, his legs broken, his building condemned by the city, or any of a number of other undesirable outcomes. Torrio at his peak controlled two hundred separate associations, from the Soda Dispensers and Table Girl Brotherhood to the Bread, Cracker, Yeast and Pie Wagon Drivers' Union. Even shoeshine boys paid him $15 up front and $2 a month thereafter.

In 1920, for reasons that have never been convincingly explained, Torrio decided to leave Brooklyn and start all over again in Chicago. As a first move, he knocked off a mobster there named Big Jim Colosimo (who in some accounts is described as Torrio's uncle and in others simply as an associate) and took over his operations. Things went well for some time, but then territorial tensions arose. On a cold afternoon in January 1925 Torrio was helping his wife carry bags of shopping from their car into their house when two men from a rival gang approached and shot him five times at close range. Torrio survived, but decided he had had enough. He turned all the Chicago operations over to Al Capone. And so began America's most famous era in lawlessness.

The two most striking features of Capone's reign were how youthful he was and how short it was. Capone was just twenty-six – Lindbergh's age at the time of his Paris flight – when he took over from Torrio, and his career as a top mobster really only lasted from the spring of 1925 to the end of 1927. As late as early 1926, newspapers in Chicago were giving Capone's name as Caponi or Caproni. A *Chicago Tribune* reporter in the summer of 1926 dubbed him 'Scarface', and it was then that the legends began.

A reporter for *Time* magazine colourfully and imaginatively claimed that Capone had been 'branded on one swart cheek' – *Time* really couldn't get enough of that word 'swart' – 'by the razor memento of the Neapolitan Camorra'. In fact, Capone got his scars one evening at a Coney Island bar when, drunk, he leaned across to a girl and said, 'Honey, you have a nice ass, and I mean that as a compliment.' Unfortunately, the young woman was with her brother, who felt honour-bound to do something emotional, and he slashed Capone across the face with a knife, leaving him with two livid scars on his left cheek and a fainter one along the neck. Capone was always self-conscious about the scars and did all he could to disguise them, including coating his face in talcum powder.

Capone was no doubt capable of violence, but it is perhaps worth noting that the well-remembered scene in which he beats to death two dinner guests with a baseball bat was entirely made up. It appeared in a 1975 book called *The Legacy of Al Capone* by a writer named George Murray. In half a century, no one else had ever mentioned it – and beating guests to death at a dinner table is not something other guests would forget to mention. Capone has also many times been credited with the line 'You can get a lot farther with a smile and a gun than you can get with just a smile,' but it appears he probably never said that either.

Chicago in the 1920s was not really as violent as reputation has it. With 13.3 murders per 100,000 of population, it was indubitably more homicidal than New York with 6.1, Los Angeles with 4.7 or Boston with just 3.9, but it was less dangerous than Detroit at 16.8, or almost any city in the South. New Orleans had a murder rate of 25.9 per 100,000, while Little Rock's was 37.9, Miami's 40, Atlanta's 43.4, Charlotte's 55.5, and Memphis was miles ahead of everyone with a truly whopping rate of 69.3. The average in America today, you may be surprised and comforted to hear, is 6 per 100,000.

One thing Chicago did have was a special attachment among its gangsters for the Thompson submachine gun, or Tommy gun as it was more affectionately known. The gun was named after General John Taliaferro Thompson, director of US arsenals, who spent much of the First World War developing it. His idea was to make a portable machine gun light enough to be carried by a single soldier. Thompson's gun was wondrously lethal. It could fire up to a thousand rounds a minute and drill holes through armoured vehicles. In a demonstration, it cut through quarter-inch steel plate and felled a tree almost two feet thick. Unfortunately, by the time Thompson had the gun ready for production the war was over and the army didn't want it. Police forces didn't want it either because it was so lively that it was impossible to aim accurately. Fire from a Thompson was all but randomly distributed, which made it ideal for hoodlums – and made hoodlums very scary people once they started pulling the trigger. Illinois imposed no restrictions on the sale of Tommy guns, so they were available to the general public in hardware stores, sporting goods stores and even drugstores. The wonder is that the death tolls in Chicago weren't higher.

What Chicago also had in unusual abundance throughout Prohibition was beer. Most cities didn't. Beer required corruption on an epic scale. You can't hide a brewery, so to produce and distribute beer without attracting legal enquiries required the disbursement of a great deal of hush money, and there was hardly a uniformed city employee who didn't share in the benefits. A steady stream of police and officials visited Capone's headquarters at the Metropole Hotel each day to pick up their payoffs and instructions. The police force of Chicago became in effect Capone's private army. Goodness knows what Kenesaw Mountain Landis would have made of that if he had been left in his position as a federal judge.

Prohibition may be the greatest gift any government ever gave its citizens. A barrel of beer cost $4 to make and sold for $55. A case of spirituous liquor cost $20 to produce and earned $90 – and all this without taxes. By 1927, Capone's organization – which, interestingly, had no name – had estimated receipts of $105 million. The scale of his operations unquestionably makes him one of the most successful businessmen in American history.

Many people, it seems, were very happy to look at it that way. When students at Northwestern University's Medill School of Journalism (named for Robert McCormick's grandfather) were asked in 1927 to name the ten most outstanding people in the world, they chose Charles Lindbergh, Richard Byrd, Benito Mussolini, Henry Ford, Herbert Hoover, Albert Einstein, Mahatma Gandhi, George Bernard Shaw, the golfer Bobby Jones, and Al Capone.

For Capone, 1927 was an exceptionally good year. Profits were flowing in, Chicago's gangs were mostly at peace, and Capone increasingly found himself a person of importance. When newspaper deliverymen threatened a crippling strike in Chicago, it was to Capone, not Big Bill

Thompson, that the proprietors turned for help. Capone got the strike called off and was invited to a meeting of the owners, chaired by Robert McCormick, so that they could express their gratitude.

'McCormick wanted to pay me afterward,' Capone said later, 'but I told him to give the money to a hospital.' McCormick's version of the story was rather different. 'I arrived late at a publishers' meeting,' he recorded briskly in a memoir. 'Capone walked in with some of his hoodlums. I threw him out.' Whatever in fact transpired, there was no strike, and the newspapers of Chicago for ever after went easy on Capone.

As the summer of 1927 wound to an end, Al Capone was the world's favourite gangster. In a couple of weeks 150,000 people would pack into Soldier Field in Chicago to watch the Dempsey–Tunney rematch. The place would be full of celebrities, but it would be Al Capone that everyone in the stadium would crane to see. At the age of twenty-eight, he appeared to be on top of the world. In fact, time was about to run out for him. Within months he would be gone from Chicago and his empire would be crumbling around him.

CHAPTER 30

Lou Gehrig, in his quiet, methodical, all but invisible way, was having a fantastic year. As the second week of September began, he had 45 home runs, 161 runs batted in, and a .389 batting average. As his biographer Jonathan Eig notes in *Luckiest Man*, Gehrig could have stopped there, with almost a month of the season still to play, and had one of the best seasons ever. In fact, he did essentially stop there.

His mother was unwell with a goitre and needed surgery. Gehrig was beside himself with anxiety. 'I'm so worried about Mom that I can't see straight,' he confided to a teammate.

'All his thoughts were on Mom,' the sportswriter Fred Lieb wrote later. 'As soon as he finished the game, he would rush to the hospital and stay with her until her bedtime.' Gehrig hit just 2 more home runs the rest of the season. His heart wasn't in the game. All he could think about was his beloved momma.

Babe Ruth, meanwhile, began knocking balls out of

parks as if hitting tee shots at a driving range. Between 2 and 29 September he hit 17 home runs. No one had ever done anything like that in a single month.

The Yankees seemed incapable of doing anything wrong. On 10 September, they beat St Louis for the twenty-first time in a row – the most consecutive victories by one team over another during a single season. On 16 September, Wilcy Moore, who was such a bad batter that players would come out of the locker room and vendors would pause in their transactions to watch the extra-ordinary sight of him flailing at empty air with a piece of wood, miraculously connected with a ball and sent it over the right-field wall for a home run, an event that nearly gave Babe Ruth a heart attack. On the mound, Moore scattered seven hits to push his record to 18 and 7 as the Yanks beat the White Sox 7 to 2.

In the midst of this, almost unnoticed, the Yankees clinched the pennant. They had been in first place every day of the season – the first time that had ever happened. Their position was so commanding that they could lose all fifteen of their remaining games and the second-place Philadelphia Athletics could win all seventeen of theirs, and the Yankees would still come out on top. In point of fact, the Yankees won twelve of their last fifteen games even though they didn't need to. They couldn't help themselves.

Ruth was majestically imperturbable. On 16 September he was called into court in Manhattan, charged with the alarming crime of punching a cripple. The reputed victim, Bernard Neimeyer, claimed that on the evening of 4 July he had been walking near the Ansonia Hotel when a man accompanied by two women accused him of making an inappropriate remark and punched him hard in the face. Neimeyer said he didn't recognize his assailant, but was told by onlookers that it was Babe Ruth. Ruth, in his defence, said that he had been having dinner with friends at the time, and produced two witnesses in corroboration. In court, Neimeyer seemed to be a little crazy. The *Times* reported that he frequently 'rose excitedly to his feet, waving a book of notes which he added to from time to time as the hearing proceeded. He was often cautioned by the clerk of the court not to talk so loudly.' The judge dismissed the case to general applause. Ruth signed a bunch of autographs, then went to the ballpark and hit a home run, his fifty-third.

Two days later, in a doubleheader against the White Sox, he swatted his fifty-fourth, a two-run shot in the fifth inning. Three days after that, on 21 September, Ruth came to the plate in the bottom of the ninth inning against Detroit. The bases were empty and the Tigers were up 6 to 0, so Sam Gibson, the Tigers' pitcher, didn't need to throw him anything good, and dutifully endeavoured not to. Ruth caught one anyway, and hefted it deep into the right-field stands for his fifty-fifth homer. A new record was beginning to seem entirely possible.

The next day Ruth hit one of his most splendid home runs of the season. In the bottom of the ninth inning with Mark Koenig on third and the Yankees trailing 7 to 6, Ruth came to the plate and lofted his fifty-sixth home run high into the right-field bleachers for a walk-off 8–7 victory. As Ruth trotted around the bases – carrying his bat with him, as he often did, to make sure nobody ran off with it – a boy of about ten rushed in from right field and joined him on the base paths. The boy grabbed on to the bat with both hands, and was essentially carried around the bases and into the dugout, where Ruth quickly vanished down the runway, pursued by yet more jubilant fans. The game was the Yankees' one hundred and fifth victory of the season, tying the American League record for season victories.

Beyond Yankee Stadium, the world hardly noticed. Halfway across the continent in Chicago something much more exciting was about to happen.

It was the Dempsey–Tunney rematch. Chicago was even more abuzz than it had been for Lindbergh's recent visit. People poured into the city in numbers never before seen. It was impossible to find a hotel bed, hard enough to get a seat in a restaurant. Chartered trains streamed in from every point of the compass – from Akron, Pittsburgh, Atlanta, the distant west. In three days, more than a hundred extra trains arrived in the city. Scheduled trains were made longer – in some cases much longer. The *Twentieth Century Limited* that pulled in on fight day was three times its normal length. Among the arriving multitudes were Al Jolson, Charlie Chaplin, Douglas Fairbanks, Harold Lloyd, Florenz Ziegfeld, Gloria Swanson, Walter Chrysler, Ty Cobb, nine US senators, ten state governors, mayors beyond counting and business potentates from all over. David Sarnoff was there to make sure the radio hook-ups were all in order. The Marquess of Douglas and Clydesdale, a British adventurer who would shortly become the first man to fly over Mount Everest, attended as the guest of Gene Tunney, as did the British writer Somerset Maugham.

Popular sentiment was overwhelmingly with Dempsey.

Tunney had all the makings of a hero – he was clean-living, intelligent, polite, reasonably good-looking – but, like Lou Gehrig, he lacked the chemistry that stirred affection. He had grown up poor in Greenwich Village, the son of Irish immigrants, and weighed just 140 pounds when he took up boxing professionally. Even when he had built himself up to 190 pounds, he lacked power. He made up for it through deft feinting and jabbing. As Tunney explained it, Dempsey was a fighter but he was a boxer – something much more scientific. He won his bouts by out-thinking his opponents and wearing them down. The strategy nearly always worked. In sixty-six professional bouts Tunney was beaten just once, by Harry Greb in 1922. No one had ever knocked him off his feet.

Tunney promoted himself as an intellectual and a gentleman. He didn't drink or swear and refused to advertise cigarettes, but he made a lot of money endorsing other things – cars, hats, shoes, pyjamas and walking sticks, among much else. He had an unfortunate tendency to pomposity. He liked to carry a book around with him. When asked what it was, he would reply casually, 'Oh, just a copy of the *Rubáiyát* that I am never without.' This was largely why most people couldn't stand him. The typical fight fan, as Paul Gallico of the *Daily News* put it, 'wanted to see the book-reading snob socked back to Shakespeare'.

One serious concern with staging the fight in Chicago was the city's reputation for corruption. Al Capone had long been a Dempsey admirer. He hated Tunney's refined mannerisms. 'A fucking pansy' was how he characterized him. Capone let word get out that he would make sure Dempsey didn't lose this time. Dempsey was horrified to learn this and wrote to Capone pleading with him not to interfere. 'If I beat Tunney, or Tunney beats me in true sportsmanship, it will prove who really deserves to be champion,' Dempsey explained. The next day he received three hundred roses and an unsigned card saying, 'To the Dempseys, in the name of sportsmanship.' Capone reportedly bet $50,000 on Dempsey to win, and bought one hundred of the best seats in the stadium at $40 a seat.

On fight day Tunney and Dempsey both jogged five miles, then relaxed. Tunney passed the time examining rare manuscripts in a library with his new pal Somerset Maugham. Dempsey's pastimes were not noted, but presumably were a little less intellectually ambitious.

By early evening, Soldier Field was steadily filling and the atmosphere was growing electric. People spent most of the time before the fight picking out celebrities at ringside – though fans in the most distant seats, it must be said, could barely see the ring, never mind those gathered around it. Some seats were over seven hundred feet from the action.

The most enlivening pre-fight moment was when Al Capone arrived, in overcoat and fedora, encircled as always by a protective ring of burly men. 'Nothing smaller than a fieldpiece could penetrate his double-walled fortress of meat,' wrote the *New Yorker* later. Accompanying Capone as special guest was Damon Runyon.

The crowd was put at 150,000 – enough to fill Yankee Stadium twice over. Six thousand ushers attended to the throngs. Each wore an armband saying 'Tunney–Dempsey Boxing Exhibition' – a touch of gentility insisted on by Tunney. Never before had so many sports fans packed into a single space.

In the centre of it all – a small, bright opening in an

ocean of heads and enshrouding darkness – was the ring. Bathed in the light of forty-four 1000-watt lamps, the ring was twenty feet to a side, the largest size allowed, which gave Tunney more room to escape. A crucial feature of the Dempsey–Firpo fight had been that Dempsey was able to stand over Firpo and clobber him anew each time Firpo tried to haul himself to his feet. It was this that led the Tunney camp to insist on the rule of retiring to a neutral corner after a knockdown – a consideration that would give boxing its greatest moment of controversy before the night was out.

The National Broadcasting Company linked eighty-two stations to form a national broadcast. More people listened to the fight that night than had witnessed any other event in history. For Lindbergh's homecoming in June, the audience had been 30 million. This time it would be 50 million. As ever, Graham McNamee's was the warm voice to which nearly half the nation turned.

The most striking feature of the fight was its lateness. The scheduled starting time was 9.45 p.m. in Chicago – 10.45 p.m. on the east coast – and proceedings were running about fifteen minutes late when the two robed competitors finally emerged, to a stupendous and appreciative roar from the crowd, and climbed into the intensely bright ring. Both fighters looked calm and prepared.

The referee, Dave Barry, gave the customary lecture at the centre of the ring, the men retired to their corners, a bell clanged, and the most eagerly anticipated fight in America to that time – possibly ever – began. Dempsey came out swinging and hit so hard that McNamee said he could see the ring trembling. But Tunney dodged and danced expertly, and Dempsey's blows mostly fell harm-lessly against his arms.

Tunney at the same time began picking Dempsey to pieces – jabbing and parrying, then dancing away. The strategy had a devastating cumulative effect. Dempsey's face became more and more swollen with each passing round – eventually, it seemed, with each passing blow. Cuts opened above his eyes and he bled from the mouth. But still he marched on, 'tirelessly, relentlessly, savagely, viciously, desperately', in the words of *New York Times* reporter James P. Dawson.

Tunney was cruising to victory when, in the seventh round, Dempsey stopped him in his tracks, and brought 150,000 people to their feet, with a sudden, violent flurry of punches that left Tunney sitting on the canvas in a help-less daze, his left arm resting on a rope. He was almost certainly no more than a punch or two away from oblivion. 'I am free to say I found the canvas a pretty com-fortable place just then,' Tunney joked to reporters afterwards, but he was in serious trouble and 50 million people in America knew it. At least ten radio listeners, it was later reported, dropped dead from heart attacks during the seventh round, though surely any such figure was drawn from thin air.

Dempsey, his blood up, failed to withdraw immedi-ately to a neutral corner as required, but hovered, waiting to clobber Tunney when he rose again. The referee, Barry, had to shoo him back to neutral territory before starting the count. This gave Tunney a few precious extra moments to recover. How many exactly has been a matter of intense debate ever since, but it was something in the region of five or six seconds.

At the count of nine, Tunney clambered back to his feet and, with surprising lightness, managed to dance his way out of further trouble. In fact, he had little idea what was going on. 'I was oblivious . . . and had to be told later on what happened,' he admitted years later.

Dempsey had blown his chance. The exertion left the former champ exhausted. In the next round, Tunney floored him with a sudden sharp hook of his own. Dempsey bounded back up, but he seemed to have little left. Tunney dominated easily thereafter and won on a unanimous decision.

Dempsey supporters have always felt that their hero was cheated, as did Dempsey himself. 'Intentionally or otherwise, I was robbed of the championship,' he told reporters in his dressing room immediately after the fight. 'I am not an alibi artist, but I know down in my soul that I knocked Tunney out tonight and what's more chased him all around the ring and should have won on points at least.'

According to Roger Kahn in his 1999 biography of Dempsey, *A Flame of Pure Fire*, the referee didn't enforce the neutral-corner rule when Dempsey went down. Kahn said he was 'consumed by outrage' when he first reviewed footage of the two key moments of the fight. 'Two knockdowns, one round apart, and two different sets of rules. The explanation, I believe, is not complicated. In my tape of Chicago 1927, I am looking at a crooked referee,' Kahn wrote.

In fact, a viewing of the footage – now available to everyone with access to the internet – is not nearly so clear cut. When Tunney fell in the seventh round, Barry pushed Dempsey out of the way, clearly ordering him back to his corner, then turned and began the count immediately while Dempsey was still withdrawing. Barry could hardly have acted more quickly or decisively. In the following round when Dempsey fell, Barry didn't send Tunney to a neutral corner because there wasn't time. Dempsey jumped up immediately, like someone rebounding off a trampoline, and began swinging again before the referee could step forward or even raise his arm.

The long count was unfortunate, but no one was to blame for it more than Jack Dempsey. Tunney chose to look at the bigger picture. 'We have fought twenty rounds and I think I beat him in nineteen of them,' he told reporters.

Tunney earned $990,000 for the fight, which someone calculated included $7,700 for time spent horizontal during the long count. Dempsey made just under $450,000. Tunney was eager for yet another rematch, but Dempsey declined. He never fought again. Tunney had just one more fight himself. He shunned the obvious challenger, Jack Sharkey, and instead fought a New Zealander named Tom Heeney at Yankee Stadium. Tunney won in eleven rounds and made $500,000 for his efforts, but what was most notable about the fight was that only half the tickets were sold. Boxing without Dempsey was not the draw it had been. The promoters lost over $150,000.

In early September, from South America there came an intriguing story. A French engineer named Roger Courteville, while making a journey by car from Rio de Janeiro to Lima – the first coast-to-coast crossing of South America by motorized vehicle, in itself an extraordinary story –

announced that en route, along a lonely track in Mato Grosso state, he had come upon the missing English explorer Percy Fawcett, last seen hunting for the fabled lost city of Z in the jungles beyond Fordlandia. At the time of their encounter, Courteville didn't realize who Fawcett was, so didn't report his discovery.

In accounts he later wrote for the *New York Times*, Courteville said that he was brought up short by the sight of a grey-haired white man, about sixty years old, sitting by a rutted track in the middle of nowhere. 'He was wearing shorts, a khaki shirt and old thick-soled shoes, which were tied to his stockingless feet by the fibers of swamp plants,' Courteville reported. 'His hands were shaking with fever.' Courteville particularly noted that the man's bare legs were swarming with mosquitoes. Courteville spoke to him in Portuguese but got no reply, then tried English. He asked the man why he allowed the mosquitoes to browse so freely on his legs.

'They are hungry, the poor devils,' the man replied flatly in an English accent. That, remarkably, was the extent of their conversation.

'The stranger, after the manner of Englishmen, was un-responsive and disinclined to talk about himself and his affairs,' Courteville went on. So, amazingly, Courteville got back in his car without making any effort to determine the man's identity, render assistance, or even to ask what he was doing there. He just drove on and casually reported the encounter to an official in Lima when he got there some months later.

The official got very excited because Fawcett was the most famous missing man in South America.

As it turned out, the man Courteville encountered

could not have been Fawcett. For one thing, Fawcett was bald and this man had long hair. So who he was and how he had got there were great mysteries. No one knew of any other Englishman who had gone into the jungle and not come out again.

Courteville's discovery, even though it wasn't Fawcett, stirred interest in Fawcett anew. A British-American adventurer named George Miller Dyott announced plans to lead a search party into the 50,000 square miles of tangled wilderness in which Fawcett might reasonably be supposed to be. Supported by ten mules, sixty-four bullocks and a small army of guides and porters, Dyott spent months hacking his way into the interior and nearly died himself, but didn't find Fawcett or Courteville's mysterious Englishman or anyone else who wasn't known to be there already. Then two more people, a Swiss man and a reporter from United Press International, embarked on a separate expedition, but were never heard from again at all. From England, Fawcett's wife said people should stop their searching. She told reporters that she was in touch with her husband telepathically, and that he was fine and would come out when he was ready. He never did.

On 2 September, en route to Cheyenne, Wyoming, Charles Lindbergh flew over Rapid City High School and the State Game Lodge where the Coolidges had made their home for the summer. President Coolidge came out and waved a handkerchief. Lindbergh dropped special messages at both places. The one at the game lodge was never found.

Seeing how tired Lindbergh had become, those responsible for his tour instituted a rule that he would provide no more than four and a half hours of personal appearances a day – two and a half hours of parades and speeches by day and two hours of banqueting at night. Everything would have to be compressed to fit into that timetable.

Newspapers continued to report his progress around the country, but with more of a sense of duty than of enthusiasm, and the stories nearly always now appeared on inside pages. Only occasionally did something mildly out of the ordinary happen. In Abilene, Texas, Lindbergh arrived to find that the organizers had fitted his parade vehicle with a throne. Embarrassed at such a display of grandeur, Lindbergh refused to sit in it, and it had to be removed. That was about as interesting as Lindbergh's tour got now.

With the Dempsey–Tunney fight concluded, sports fans turned their attention back to baseball and the question of whether Babe Ruth could break his home run record. It was getting awfully close. Ruth went two games, on 24 and 25 September, without a homer, which left him four short of the record with just four games to play.

On the first of those four games, on 27 September, Ruth got his fifty-seventh in style by hitting a grand slam off Lefty Grove of Philadelphia – one of only six home runs Grove gave up all season. Ruth didn't hit grand slams often: this was his first of the season and only the sixth of his career.

The Yankees had a day off on 28 September, and the rest clearly did Ruth good, for in his first at-bat the next day, at the start of a three-game series against the Washington Senators, he hit his fifty-eighth home run off

Horace 'Hod' Lisenbee, a rookie who was having a great year – the only good one he would ever have. Like Lefty Grove, Lisenbee gave up just six home runs all season. Two of them were by Ruth.

Ruth now needed just one more to tie his record. In the bottom of the fifth inning, he came to the plate with the bases loaded and two out. Senators manager Bucky Harris signalled to the bullpen to send in a right-hander named Paul Hopkins.

Hopkins was an unexpected choice, and no doubt caused many a spectator to turn to the nearest person with a scorecard for enlightenment. Hopkins had just graduated from Colgate University and had never pitched in the major leagues before. Now he was about to make his debut in Yankee Stadium against Babe Ruth with the bases loaded and Ruth trying to tie his own record for most home runs in a season.

Pitching carefully (as you might expect), Hopkins worked the count to 3 and 2, then tried to sneak a slow curve past Ruth. It was an outstanding pitch. 'It was so slow,' Hopkins recalled for *Sports Illustrated* seventy years later at the age of ninety-four, 'that Ruth started to swing and then hesitated, hitched on it and brought the bat back. And then he swung, breaking his wrists as he came through it. What a great eye he had! He hit it at the right second – put everything behind it. I can still hear the crack of the bat. I can still see the swing.' It was Ruth's fifty-ninth home run, tying a record that less than a month before had seemed hopelessly out of reach.

The ball floated over the head of the right-fielder, 37-year-old Sam Rice, who is largely forgotten now but was one of the great players of his day and also one of the most mysterious, for he had come to major league baseball seemingly from out of nowhere.

Fifteen years earlier, Rice had been a promising youngster in his first season in professional baseball with a minor league team in Galesburg, Illinois. While he was away for the summer, his wife moved with their two small children on to his parents' farm near Donovan, Indiana. In late April, a tornado struck near Donovan, killing seventy-five people. Among the victims were Rice's wife, children, mother and two sisters. Rice's father, himself seriously injured, was found wandering in shock with one of the dead children in his arms. He died nine days later in hospital. So, at a stroke, Rice lost his entire family. Dazed with grief, he drifted around America working at odd jobs. Eventually he enlisted in the navy. While playing for a navy team his remarkable talents became apparent. Clark Griffith, owner of the Washington Senators, somehow heard of this, invited him for a trial, and was impressed enough to sign him. Rice joined the Senators and in his thirties became one of the finest players in baseball. No one anywhere knew of his personal tragedy. It didn't become public until 1963, when he was inducted into the Hall of Fame.

After Ruth's homer, Hopkins struck out Lou Gehrig to end the inning, then retired to the bench and burst into tears. It was one of just eleven major league appearances Hopkins ever made. He missed the whole of the 1928 season with an injury and retired with a record of no wins and one loss after the 1929 season. He returned to his home state of Connecticut, became a successful banker and lived to be ninety-nine.

* * *

The last day of September was sultry in New York. The temperature was in the low 80s and the air muggy when, in the next to last game of the season, Ruth came to the plate in the bottom of the eighth against Tom Zachary, a 31-year-old left-hander from a tobacco farm in North Carolina. Though a pious Quaker, Zachary was not without guile. One of his tricks was to cover the pitching rubber with dirt so that he could move closer to home plate – sometimes by as much as two feet, it has been claimed. In 1927 he was in his tenth season. He gave up just six home runs all year. Three of them were to Ruth.

It was Ruth's fourth trip of the day to the plate. He had walked once and singled twice and had come nowhere near a home run. The score was tied 2–2. There was one out and one man on – Mark Koenig, who had tripled.

'Everybody knew he was out for the record, so he wasn't going to get anything good from me,' Zachary told a reporter in 1961. Zachary wound up, eyed the runner, then uncorked a sizzling fast ball. It went for a called strike. Zachary wound up and threw again. This pitch was high and away, and Ruth took it for a ball. For his third pitch, Zachary threw a curve – 'as good as I had', he recalled. Ruth hit the ball with what was effectively a golf swing, lofting it high into the air in the direction of the right-field foul pole. The 8,000 fans in Yankee Stadium watched in silence as the ball climbed to a towering height, then fell for ages and dropped into the bleachers just inches fair. Zachary threw down his glove in frustration. The crowd roared with pleasure.

Ruth trotted around the bases with his curiously clipped and delicate gait, like someone trying to tiptoe at speed, then stepped out of the dugout to acknowledge the applause with a succession of snappy military salutes. Ruth was responsible for all four runs that day. The *Times* the next day referred to the score as 'Ruth 4, Senators 2'.

A little-known fact was that the game in which Babe Ruth hit his sixtieth home run was also the last game in the majors for Walter Johnson, the greatest pitcher of the age. No one threw harder. Jimmy Dykes, then of the Athletics, recalled in later years how as a rookie he was sent to the plate against Johnson, and never saw Johnson's first two pitches. He just heard them hit the catcher's mitt. After the third pitch the umpire told him to take first base.

'Why?' asked Dykes.

'You've been hit,' explained the umpire.

'Are you sure?' asked Dykes.

The umpire told him to check his hat. Dykes reached up and discovered that the cap was facing sideways from where Johnson's last pitch had spun the peak. He dropped his bat and hurried gratefully to first base.

In twenty-one years as a pitcher, Johnson gave up only 97 home runs. When Ruth hit one off him in 1920, it was the first home run Johnson had yielded in almost two years. In 1927, Johnson broke his leg in spring training when hit by a line drive, and never fully recovered. Now, with his fortieth birthday approaching, he decided it was time to retire. In the top of the ninth inning, in his last appearance in professional baseball, he was sent in to pinch-hit for Zachary. He hit a fly to right field. The ball was caught by Ruth, to end the game, Johnson's career, and an important part of a glorious era.

In the clubhouse afterwards, Ruth was naturally exultant over his sixtieth homer. 'Let's see some son of a bitch try and top that one!' he kept saying. The general reaction among his teammates was congratulatory and warm, but in retrospect surprisingly muted. 'There wasn't the excitement you'd imagine,' Pete Sheehy, the team equipment manager, recalled many years later. No one expected Ruth to stop at sixty. It was assumed that he would hit at least one more the next day, and possibly reach even greater heights in years to come. Ruth after all had been the first to hit 30, 40, 50 and 60 homers. Who knew that he wouldn't hit 70 in 1928?

In fact, neither he nor anyone else would hit so many again for a very long time. In his last game of the season, Ruth rather anticlimactically went 0 for 3 with a walk. In his last at-bat he struck out. Lou Gehrig, however, did hit a home run, his forty-seventh of the season. That might seem a disappointing number after his earlier pace, so it is worth remembering that it was more than any other player had *ever* hit, apart from Ruth.

In banging out 60 home runs, Ruth outhomered all major league teams except the Cardinals, Cubs and Giants. He hit home runs in every park in the American League and hit more on the road than at home. (The tally was 32 to 28.) He homered off 33 different pitchers. At least 2 of his home runs were the longest ever seen in the parks in which they were hit. Ruth hit a home run once every 11.8 times at bat. He had at least 6 home runs against every team in the American League. He did all this and still batted .356 – *and* scored 158 runs, had 164 runs batted in, 138 walks, and even had 7 stolen bases and 14 sacrifice bunts. It would be hard to imagine a more extraordinary year.

Ruth and Gehrig between them came first and second in home runs, runs batted in, slugging percentage, runs scored, total bases, extra base hits and bases on balls.

Combs and Gehrig were first and second in total hits and triples. Four players – Ruth, Gehrig, Lazzeri and Meusel – each had more than 100 runs batted in. Combs was also third in runs scored and total bases, and Lazzeri was third in home runs. As a team, the Yankees had the American League's highest team batting average and lowest ERA. They averaged 6.3 runs and almost 11 hits per game. Their 911 runs were more than any American League team had ever scored in a season before. Their 110 victories were a league record, too. Just one player was ejected from a game all season and the team had no fights with other teams. Baseball has never fielded a more complete, dominant and disciplined team.

Babe Ruth's home run record stood until 1961 when Roger Maris, also of the Yankees, hit 61, though Maris had the advantage of a longer season, which gave him 10 more games and 50 more at-bats than Ruth in 1927. In the 1990s, many baseball players suddenly became immensely strong – some evolved whole new body shapes – and began to smack home runs in quantities that made a mockery of Ruth's and Maris's numbers. It turned out that a great many of this new generation of ballplayers – something in the region of 5 to 7 per cent, according to random drug tests introduced, very belatedly, in 2003 – were taking anabolic steroids. The use of drugs as an aid to hitting is far beyond the scope of this book, so let us just note in passing that even with the benefit of steroids most modern players still couldn't hit as many home runs as Babe Ruth hit on hot dogs.

Practically speaking, there's no saying when the summer of 1927 ended. October brought some of the most summery days of the year, with temperatures touching 85 in New York and rising into the high 90s elsewhere in the east. Autumn arrived gradually, on no particular date, as seasons generally do.

The Yankees met the Pittsburgh Pirates in the World Series (or *World*'s Series, as it was still commonly called), and beat them easily in four games, confirming in many people's minds that the Yankees were the best team ever.

Calvin and Grace Coolidge returned to Washington from the west and moved back into a refurbished White House. The president stood by his vow not to run for re-election. Herbert Hoover failed to secure Coolidge's endorsement, but made no secret of his wish to succeed him. In November, terrible floods ravaged much of New England, killing more than a hundred people. Coolidge declined to visit and sent Hoover instead.

The Jazz Singer played to huge crowds in New York, even at $10 a ticket. Samuel Raphaelson, who wrote the play on which the film was based, thought it was a terrible picture. 'I've seen very few worse,' he said, but most people disagreed. The actress May McAvoy, who also starred in the film, recalled later that she would stand in cinemas where it was showing and watch the audiences. When Jolson spoke, she said, people reacted with such rapture 'you'd have thought they were listening to the voice of God'. The movie cleared a profit of $1.5 million in its year of release.

The Holland Tunnel opened after five and a half years of construction, and work began in earnest on Mount Rushmore. In England, Dr Dorothy Cochrane Logan, an American doctor working in London, was charged with perjury for claiming to have swum the English Channel for a $5,000 prize when in fact she had mostly ridden across in the support vessel. That seems to have marked an end both to Channel swimming and to stunts generally. In Detroit, Henry Ford began hiring again as the company geared up for production of the new Model A.

Charles Lindbergh finished his long tour at last. In the final month he dashed through Oklahoma, Arkansas, Tennessee, Alabama, Mississippi, Louisiana, Georgia, Florida, South Carolina, North Carolina, Virginia, the District of Columbia, Maryland, New Jersey, Delaware and Pennsylvania before finally landing at Mitchel Field on Long Island on 23 October. In three months he had flown 22,350 miles, visited 82 cities, delivered 147 speeches, ridden 1,285 miles in parades, and been seen by an estimated 30 million people, about one quarter of the American populace. His last official engagement was a dinner in Manhattan in honour of Raymond Orteig.

And then – it must have seemed like a miracle – he was free. After five months of unceasing attention, it was all over. Except of course that it wasn't. It was never going to be over. Lindbergh was now attached to a fame that he could never get away from. He had little idea what he would do next. How he would fill the rest of his life was a problem that would, as it were, fill the rest of his life.

On 27 October, Lindbergh turned up unexpectedly at Curtiss Field, saying that he had 'not done much flying lately' – a curious declaration coming just four days after the finish of a 22,350-mile trip. The *Spirit of St Louis* was being serviced after the long tour, so Lindbergh asked if he could borrow a plane. The Curtiss ground crew gladly provided one, and Lindbergh spent a blissful hour alone and at peace in the sky.

Upon landing he found awaiting him the most

terrifying experience of the summer. Twenty chorus girls had just arrived at the airfield for a photo shoot. Their visit was entirely coincidental and had nothing to do with him, but they were naturally excited to learn that the world's most eligible bachelor was just the other side of a hangar door, and they gleefully laid siege to the building, peering through the grimy windows and calling through cracks in the door, beseeching him to come out so that they could tousle his hair and drape themselves over him. Lindbergh seriously looked as if he might die. Seeing his anguish, the airfield manager had a car brought round to the hangar's back door. Relieved and grateful, Lindbergh leapt in and sped off, narrowly averting an unendurable encounter with twenty cheerfully adoring young women.

It would probably have done no good to remind Lindbergh that he had just spent the summer meeting presidents and kings, addressing crowds so large that they filled whole landscapes, receiving tributes on a scale never before accorded a human being. At the end of it all the most famous man in the world was, it seems, still just a kid.

A reasonable question to ask, if not such an easy one to answer, is what was it about Charles Lindbergh and his 1927 flight to Paris that so transfixed the world? In good measure, clearly, it was Lindbergh himself – the fact that he was boyish and wholesome, that he did it alone, that he behaved with such modesty and aplomb in the immediate aftermath of the flight. To this could be added the pure enchantment of knowing that an ocean could now be crossed. The thought that an aeroplane could leave New York and reappear hours later in Paris or Los Angeles or Havana, as if rematerializing from thin air, seemed almost the stuff of science fiction.

For Americans, there was also the gratifying novelty of coming first at something. It is a little hard to imagine now, but Americans in the 1920s had grown up in a world in which most of the most important things happened in Europe. Now suddenly America was dominant in nearly every field – in popular culture, finance and banking, military might, invention and technology. The centre of gravity for the planet was moving to the other side of the world, and Charles Lindbergh's flight somehow became the culminating expression of that.

None of this, of course, explains 100,000 Parisians streaming across the grass at Le Bourget to greet the taxiing *Spirit of St Louis*, or four million turning out in New York, or all the renamed mountains and beacons and boulevards. All that can be said is that for some unknowable reason Lindbergh's flight brought the world a moment of sublime, spontaneous, unifying joy on a scale never before seen. Charles Lindbergh would for evermore be the touchstone for that feeling. It was of course an impossible obligation.

Nearly nine decades have passed since the summer of 1927, and not a great deal survives. The airfields of Long Island are long gone. Roosevelt Field closed in 1951. Today it is a 110-acre shopping centre, the biggest in New York State. The spot where Lindbergh and the others took off is marked by a plaque underneath an escalator near the Disney store. A statue called 'Spirit' commemorating Lindbergh's flight stands, forlornly, on a traffic island in the car park.

Not much survives even as memory. Many of the most notable names of the summer – Richard Byrd, Sacco and Vanzetti, Gene Tunney, even Charles Lindbergh – are rarely encountered now and most of the others are never heard at all. So it is perhaps worth pausing for a moment to remember just some of the things that happened that summer. Babe Ruth hit 60 home runs. The Federal Reserve made the mistake that precipitated the stock market crash. Al Capone enjoyed his last summer of eminence. *The Jazz Singer* was filmed. Television was created. Radio came of age. Sacco and Vanzetti were executed. President Coolidge chose not to run. Work began on Mount Rushmore. The Mississippi flooded as it never had before. A madman in Michigan blew up a school and killed forty-four people in the worst slaughter of children in American history. Henry Ford stopped making the Model T, and promised to stop insulting Jews. And a kid from Minnesota flew across an ocean and captivated the planet in a way it had never been captivated before.

Whatever else it was, it was one hell of a summer.

Epilogue

―――――――

'The country can regard the present with satisfaction and anticipate the future with optimism.'

Calvin Coolidge in his last State of the Union address, December 1928

ON 30 APRIL 1928, almost exactly one year after his first test flight in the *Spirit of St Louis*, Charles Lindbergh delivered his treasured plane – his *ship*, as he always called it – to the Smithsonian Institution in Washington. In its year's career, it had made 175 flights and been in the air for 489 hours and 28 minutes. It went on display in the Arts and Industries Building on the Mall on 13 May, one week before the first anniversary of the historic flight. Lindbergh insisted that the *Spirit of St Louis* never be exhibited elsewhere. It has never left the Smithsonian's care.

'I don't know why he was so insistent about that,' Dr Alex M. Spencer, a cheerful senior curator, tells me one day in 2011 when I visit. 'I don't imagine anybody asked him.'

Spencer and I are standing on a mezzanine overlooking the spacious entrance hall of the Smithsonian National Air and Space Museum. Directly before us, frozen for ever in imagined flight, the *Spirit of St Louis* hangs from the ceiling on thin wires. It looks small and unnervingly insubstantial. The absence of forward visibility is striking. It is hard to imagine Lindbergh folding himself into such a cramped space – even harder to imagine him squeezing in passengers like Henry Ford. It would have been extremely snug in there. At close range, it is also clear that the plane is covered in thin fabric, adding to its air of frailty. It is little wonder that Lindbergh fretted over people touching his beloved machine.

I have come to the museum to ask Spencer what difference, if any, Lindbergh's flight made to the history of aviation. 'Oh, lots!' he responds emphatically, and guides me to a neighbouring gallery, 'America in the Air', a vast cube of a room filled to a point just shy of crowdedness with gleaming vintage aeroplanes. To the uninstructed eye, the planes don't seem to have a great deal in common, but in fact they have been chosen for display with care. 'If you consider them in the order in which they were built, they tell quite a remarkable story,' says Spencer.

He points first to a Ford Tri-Motor dating from 1928. Grey and boxy, made of sheets of corrugated aluminium, it looks almost as if it might have been built in a home workshop by someone who didn't entirely understand aerodynamics. It is perhaps telling that Henry Ford declined ever to go up in one of his own machines.

'Now compare that with this plane,' Spencer says and moves us along to a Boeing 247-D. The Boeing is larger and strikingly sleeker. Every surface is attractively streamlined. The cantilevered wings are free of wires and struts, the engine cylinder heads are hidden beneath shiny cowlings, the engines themselves are built into the wings rather than just bolted on. This is clearly a plane from a new, more stylish era.

'And then came this,' says Spencer proudly, presenting his pièce de résistance, the Douglas DC-3. Created in

1935, launched in 1936, the DC-3 was the first truly modern airliner. It had twenty-one seats, could fly almost 1,500 miles and cruise at nearly 200 miles an hour. A passenger could board a DC-3 at 4 p.m. in New York and arrive in Los Angeles for breakfast the next morning. The age of modern air travel had truly begun.

'And this all happened in less than a decade,' Spencer says, indicating the full range of marvels around us. 'That's what Lindbergh's flight achieved.'

'But wouldn't it have happened anyway?' I ask.

'Sure,' Spencer agrees. 'But it wouldn't have happened so fast and it wouldn't have been so overwhelmingly American.'

Lindbergh's flight, it has been calculated, spurred as much as $100 million in aviation investments in America. In the mid-1920s, Boeing, a small manufacturer of aeroplanes in Seattle, had so little work that it sometimes built furniture just to keep going. Within a year of Lindbergh's flight it employed a thousand people. Aviation became to the 1930s what radio was to the 1920s. Lindbergh himself was tireless in his promotion of the industry. Barely had he finished his national tour than Dwight Morrow, newly installed as American ambassador in Mexico, asked him if he would make a goodwill visit to the country. It was an audacious request. Mexico was on the edge of revolution. Bandits had recently attacked a train travelling from Mexico City to Los Angeles and killed several passengers, including a young American schoolteacher named Florence Anderson. Morrow and his wife travelled in armoured vehicles. This was no place in which to have a lost airman come down.

Lindbergh accepted the invitation without hesitation, however, and immediately laid plans for a tour of Central America and the Caribbean that was nearly as ambitious, and often would prove even more hair-raising, than his trip around America. Remarkably, he would fund the trip himself.

On 13 December, just six weeks after finishing the US tour, Lindbergh took off from Bolling Field in Washington, DC, bound for Mexico City. The flight, though only two thirds the distance of his Paris trip, was nonetheless epic. Unable to find a good map of Mexico, he flew with one that was little better than a page torn from a high school geography book. So long as he kept to the Gulf Coast, he could hold his bearings, but once he turned inland at Tampico he had nothing to guide him but instinct. The only town he passed was not shown on his map, and the scattered rail lines he encountered didn't lead him anywhere productive. Eventually, he happened on a lonely eminence that he took to be Mount Toluca, and realized that he had gone considerably past his target. By the time he turned round and found his way to Valbuena Airfield, he had been in the air for 27 hours and 15 minutes and was hours late.

When Lindbergh's plane touched down at 2.30 in the afternoon, a crowd of 150,000 rushed forward in such jubilation that it picked up the plane and *carried* it to the hangar. Dwight Morrow, who had been waiting on a dais with President Plutarco Calles and an assortment of dignitaries since eight in the morning, was the most relieved man in the western hemisphere.

For the next two months, Lindbergh toured the region, often flying through wild weather or landing at dangerously inadequate airfields. Everywhere he was greeted by throngs and hailed as a hero. Roads and schools and rivers and cocktails and vast numbers of children were named after him. He visited Guatemala, Belize, El Salvador, Honduras, Nicaragua, Costa Rica, Panama, Colombia, Venezuela, the Virgin Islands, Puerto Rico, the Dominican Republic, Haiti, Cuba and the Panama Canal Zone, but he spent Christmas in Mexico City with the Morrows. Also there for the holidays was the Morrows' daughter Anne. She was a senior at Smith College in Northampton, Massachusetts – coincidentally, Calvin Coolidge's home town. Anne was shy, attractive, smart and wonderfully self-contained. Lindbergh was smitten. He had his first girlfriend. Soon they would be engaged. In sixteen months they would be married.

Upon his return to America, Lindbergh almost at once was summoned to heroic action again. An aeroplane flown from Ireland by two Germans and an Irishman had crash-landed in eastern Canada on a remote dot of land called Greenly Island off the coast of Labrador. It was the first successful east-to-west crossing of the Atlantic by plane, but now the airmen were stranded. To their aid flew Floyd Bennett and Bernt Balchen. Bennett, it may be remembered, was the flyer who had nearly been killed in the crash of Richard Byrd's *America* on its maiden flight almost exactly a year earlier. Bennett was either extraordinarily unlucky or not fully recovered because upon reaching Canada he collapsed with pneumonia. At news of this, Lindbergh rushed to the Rockefeller Institute to fetch a vial of serum, and flew with it through blizzard and gale to bring it to Bennett's bedside. Alas, it turned out that the serum was the wrong kind, and Bennett died. He was thirty-seven years old.

Through his exposure to the Rockefeller Institute, Lindbergh met Alexis Carrel, who would provide him with an enduring friendship and years of bad advice. 'Nobody in Charles Lindbergh's adulthood affected his thinking more deeply than Alexis Carrel,' wrote A. Scott Berg in his acclaimed 1998 biography of Lindbergh. A native of Lyons, Carrel was one of the most gifted surgeons of his day. As a medical student in France, he became celebrated for extraordinary feats of dexterity – tying two pieces of catgut together with the use of just two fingers or sewing five hundred stitches into a single sheet of cigarette paper. These were more than just amusing stunts, for his abilities with needle and thread led Carrel to devise helpful new methods for suturing. He invented a way of splicing arteries that kept the interior surface smooth and therefore clot-free, and in so doing saved countless lives. In 1906, he took up a position at the Rockefeller Institute, and six years later was awarded the Nobel Prize for Medicine – the first person in America to be so honoured. In the course of a long career, Carrel also performed the first coronary bypass operation (on a dog) and did pioneering work that helped pave the way for organ transplants and tissue grafts later.

He proved, however, to be a bundle of odd notions. He was convinced that sunlight was a bad thing, and maintained that the world's most backward civilizations were always where the tropical glare was brightest. He insisted that everything in his operating theatres, from gowns to dressings, be black. He flatly refused to engage with anyone who didn't please him at first glance.

Carrel became especially noted for his chilling views

on eugenics. He believed that people who were defective or backward should be 'euthenistically disposed of in gas chambers'. Such people, in his view, should be prepared to give up their lives for the greater good of humanity. 'The concept of sacrifice, of its absolute social necessity, must be introduced into the mind of modern man,' Carrel maintained.

Carrel outlined his views bluntly, if not always entirely coherently, in a best-selling book of 1935 called *Man the Unknown*. There he asked:

> Why do we preserve these useless and harmful beings? Those who have murdered, robbed while armed with automatic pistol or machine gun, kidnapped children, despoiled the poor of their savings, misled the public in important matters, should be humanely and economically disposed of in small euthanasic institutions supplied with proper gases. A similar treatment could be advantageously applied to the insane, guilty of criminal acts.

The solution to the earth's problems, Carrel maintained, was to create a 'High Council of Doctors' (which, he hinted, he stood ready to lead) whose chief role would be to ensure that the planet's affairs always remained in the control of 'the dominant white races'.

Carrel's views for a time enjoyed a surprisingly respectful following. When he spoke at the New York Academy of Medicine, 5,000 people jammed into a lecture hall designed to hold 700. Lindbergh was particularly enthralled. 'There seemed to be no limit to the breadth and penetration of his thought,' he marvelled.

Through Carrel, Lindbergh became interested in trying to make a machine that could keep organs alive artificially during surgery, and at length devised an instrument called a perfusion pump – 'a spirally coiled glass tube, resembling a hot water heater', as *Time* magazine described it. It was basically a kind of sophisticated filter. Carrel revelled in the publicity that Lindbergh's involvement brought – it coincided very conveniently with the publication of *Man the Unknown* – and persuaded journalists that the pump represented a historic breakthrough in medical science. *Time* featured the two men on its cover, with the apparatus proudly displayed between them. Lindbergh's perfusion pump was unquestionably a nifty device, but it is fair to say that it would never have attracted the attention it did if it had been invented by anyone else. In practice, it had few useful applications and no role at all in surgery. Although several perfusion pumps were built, it is believed that none were still in use by 1940.

In the wider world, Lindbergh was still mobbed almost everywhere he went. In the spring of 1928, he took a plane up for a spin from Curtiss Field on a Sunday, a day when sightseers now turned out in large numbers. When news spread through the crowd that Lindbergh was coming in to land, 2,000 people swarmed on to the runway in what the *Times* described as a frenzied stampede. Two women were injured, several children were separated from their parents, and many people were bruised or had clothing torn. Lindbergh was trapped in his plane for fifteen minutes. This was now his life. Even when he and Carrel travelled to Copenhagen to demonstrate the perfusion pump at a scientific conference, police had to erect barricades to keep back the crowds.

Finding privacy became an impossible quest. Lindbergh and Anne Morrow were married in May 1929, and for their honeymoon went sailing off the Maine coast on a borrowed thirty-eight-foot yacht. On their second day out, they were infuriated to find an aeroplane buzzing them while a photographer snapped pictures. Soon after that, a boat full of reporters and photographers began a relentless pursuit. 'For eight straight hours [they] circled about our boat,' Lindbergh recalled later with undimmed bitterness.

The Lindberghs steadfastly tried to live as normal a life as they could. Charles took positions with Trans-continental Air Transport, a forerunner of TWA, and Pan Am, and was on course to become a leading figure in the aviation industry when his and Anne's lives were disrupted in the most devastating manner possible. In early 1932, an intruder climbed through an upstairs window in their house near Hopewell, New Jersey, and kidnapped their infant child, Charles Augustus Junior. Though they paid a $50,000 ransom, two months later the child was found murdered.

Through all their worry and grief, the Lindberghs were immersed in the most grotesque media circus. Low-flying aeroplanes carrying sightseers at $2.50 a trip constantly flew over their house and made it impossible for them to go outside. Two photographers somehow got into the morgue in Trenton and took pictures of the dead baby. The pictures were much too horrible to be published, but they circulated privately and could be purchased for $5. When Bruno Hauptmann, a German immigrant, went on trial for the murder in the little town of Flemington, New Jersey, 100,000 people turned up on the first day. In

February 1935, Hauptmann was found guilty and sent for execution. His executioner was Robert G. Elliott.

By this time, Charles and Anne had had enough. They moved to Europe, first to Kent in England, then to a house on a tiny island off the north coast of Brittany. On a neighbouring island was the summer home of Alexis Carrel and his wife. The Lindberghs travelled around Europe a great deal, too, and developed an undisguised fondness for Germany. In 1936, Charles attended the Olympics in Berlin as a guest of the Nazis and clearly enjoyed himself immensely. Afterwards he wrote home to a friend that the Germans had 'a sense of decency and values which is way ahead of our own' – rather an extraordinary thing to write of Nazi Germany.

In 1938, Lindbergh accepted a medal from Hermann Goering, which many found offensive. Anne noted bitterly, and with justification, that the presentation was made at a dinner at the US embassy in Berlin, that Goering was a guest of the American government, that Lindbergh did not know he was to be honoured and did not want to cause a scene at a formal event. All this was so. On the other hand, even after Germany and America went to war, Lindbergh never returned the medal.

There is no evidence to suggest that Charles Lindbergh would ever have countenanced atrocities, but equally when a person speaks of the world as having too many of one kind of person, he is within hailing distance of those who do. What is certainly true is that both he and Anne were unapologetic admirers of Adolf Hitler. Anne described Hitler as 'a visionary who really wants the best for his country'. Lindbergh thought Hitler was 'undoubtedly a great man'. He acknowledged that the Nazis tended to be a little fanatical, but maintained, in a spirit of fairness, that 'many of Hitler's accomplishments would have been impossible without some fanaticism'.

The Lindberghs gave serious thought to moving to Germany. At the very moment that they were doing so, Germany underwent the notorious outburst known as Kristallnacht, when citizens across the nation attacked Jewish shops and property. ('Kristallnacht', or 'night of glass', refers to the broken glass they left behind.) Kristallnacht has an almost festive sound, as if it were a night of light-hearted pranks and merriment. In fact, it was state-countenanced terror. In his book *Hitlerland*, Andrew Nagorski recounts one incident in which a young boy was flung from an upstairs window into the street below. As the injured boy tried to crawl away, members of the crowd took turns kicking him. He was saved by a passing American. Kristallnacht horrified the world.

The Lindberghs were shocked, to be sure, but in their own peculiar way. Anne wrote in her diary: 'You just get to feeling you can understand and work with these people when they do something stupid and brutal and undisciplined like that. I am shocked and very upset. How can we go there to live?' Two things are pretty astonishing here. First, though Mrs Lindbergh is clearly troubled by this particular outburst ('something stupid and brutal and undisciplined'), she betrays no discomfort with the general German attitude to Jews. Second, in her own words, Kristallnacht didn't make living in Germany an intolerable proposition, but simply a challenging one.

For the first time, people began to wonder if Charles Lindbergh was really a suitable hero for the nation. Much worse was to come.

* * *

The Lindberghs, it was said, were offered a house in Berlin confiscated from Jews, but in the end elected to come home. Charles became closely involved with an organization called America First, which was formed to oppose American involvement in another European war. In September 1941, he travelled to Des Moines, Iowa, to deliver a speech, to be carried on national radio, explaining why he believed that war with Germany was wrong. A crowd of 8,000 jammed into the Des Moines Coliseum that evening. Lindbergh's speech was not scheduled to begin until 9.30 p.m., so that the audience could first hear a national radio address from the White House by Franklin Roosevelt. It is a forgotten fact, but America was already close to war by September 1941. German U-boats had recently sunk three American freighters and attacked a naval ship, the USS *Greer*. Many America First supporters maintained that the American ships had deliberately provoked the attacks, an assertion that many others found outrageous. All this meant that there was a good deal of tension in the air when Lindbergh rose at the conclusion of Roosevelt's broadcast and moved to a lectern at centre stage. In a voice often described as reedy, Lindbergh declared that three specific forces – the British, the Jews and Franklin Delano Roosevelt – were leading America to war by wilfully distorting the truth. 'I am speaking here only of war agitators, not of those sincere but misguided men and women who, confused by misinformation and frightened by propaganda, follow the lead of the war agitators,' he said.

Lindbergh's remarks were met by boos and applause in roughly equal measure. At each interruption he paused till the noise subsided. Not once did he look at the audience or take his eyes from his prepared text. The Jews, he went on, were a particularly malign influence because of their ownership and domination of 'our motion pictures, our press, our radio, and our government'. He conceded that Jews were right to be upset by the persecution of their race in Germany, but maintained that a pro-war policy had dangers not only for 'us' but also for 'them'. He didn't elaborate on why he thought that.

Britain, he said, was 'not strong enough to win the war that she declared against Germany'. Finally, he dropped in a piece of weird Carrelesque idealism. 'Rather than go to war with Germany,' he suggested, 'America should join with her and England to form a mighty "Western wall" of race and arms which can hold back either a Genghis Khan or the infiltration of inferior blood.' It was an extraordinary speech and it finished him as an American hero.

An editorial in the next morning's *Des Moines Register* tried to strike a judicious tone. 'It may have been courageous for Col. Lindbergh to say what was in his mind,' the *Register* wrote, 'but it was so lacking in appreciation for consequences – putting the best interpretation on it – that it disqualifies him for any pretensions of leadership in this republic in policy-making.'

Later that day came news that Germany had torpedoed the 1,700-ton freighter *Montana* off Greenland. All over America, people disowned Charles Lindbergh. Wendell Willkie, soon to be the Republican Party's choice for president, called Lindbergh's speech 'the most un-American talk made in my time by any person of national repute'. Lindbergh's name came off streets and schools and airports. Lindbergh Peak became Lone Eagle Peak. In

Chicago, the Lindbergh Beacon became the Palmolive Beacon. TWA stopped calling itself 'the Lindbergh Line'. Even Little Falls, his home town, painted out Lindbergh's name on its water tower. President Roosevelt said privately: 'I am absolutely convinced that Lindbergh is a Nazi.' Three months later, the Japanese attacked Pearl Harbor and America was at war.

Once America entered the war, Lindbergh supported the Allied cause wholeheartedly, but it was too late. His reputation would never recover. After the war, he became a devoted conservationist and did huge amounts of good work all over the planet, but without regaining the public's affection. A 1957 movie about his flight to Paris, starring Jimmy Stewart, was a failure at the box office. As the years passed, Lindbergh largely withdrew from public life. He died of cancer at his home on Maui in Hawaii at the age of seventy-two in 1974. He was so organized that he even had his own death certificate filled out in readiness. Only the time of death was left blank. He never retracted any part of the Des Moines speech.

Almost thirty years after his death, in 2003, it emerged that Lindbergh had had a far more complicated private life than previously thought. Between 1957 and his death, he had conducted a secret long-distance relationship with a German milliner, Brigitte Hesshaimer of Munich, with whom he had two sons and a daughter. The children told reporters that Lindbergh had been 'a mystery visitor who would turn up once or twice a year'. They knew he was their father, but thought his name was Careu Kent.

According to further reports, Lindbergh also had simultaneous relationships with Brigitte Hesshaimer's sister, Marietta, by whom he had two more children, and with a German secretary, identified only as Valeska, with whom he had yet two more children. All this extraordinary bonding was managed with such remarkable discretion that neither Lindbergh's American family nor his biographer A. Scott Berg had the least notion of it. Quite how Lindbergh managed it all is a story waiting to be told.

What can be said in the meantime is that the greatest hero of the twentieth century was infinitely more of an enigma and considerably less of a hero than anyone had ever supposed.

All this makes the subsequent lives of the other main figures in this story seem a little tame and anticlimactic, but here, in necessarily compressed form and approximately chronological order, is what became of them after the long summer of 1927.

Charles Nungesser and **François Coli**, the French airmen who started it all, were never seen again, but they were by no means forgotten. In November 1927 it was reported with some embarrassment that $30,000 that New York Mayor Jimmy Walker was supposed to present to Madame Nungesser in Paris had disappeared and could not be found. This was the Roxy Fund – the money that had been collected at the benefit concert at the Roxy Theatre that Lindbergh had briefly attended in June. Some $70,000 collected from elsewhere in America did turn up, but the New York City portion seems to have gone permanently astray.

Today, on a windy clifftop above the small and pleasant coastal resort of Étretat, in Normandy, there stands a white concrete memorial that looks rather like a giant pen nib thrust into the earth. Pointing towards

America, it marks the spot where the heroic French airmen took their leave of their native soil for the last time. It is the only memorial anywhere to that summer of remarkable flights.

A few miles to the west lies the village of Ver-sur-Mer, where **Commander Richard Byrd** and his team ditched in the sea. A small municipal museum contains the few surviving relics of that night, including a little piece of the aeroplane's fabric covering – all that remains of it now.

Byrd followed the Atlantic flight with two long expeditions to Antarctica – one of them generously, and a bit surprisingly, sponsored by Jacob Ruppert of the Yankees – and on the first of them flew (indisputably) over the South Pole. Byrd was promoted to rear admiral and spent the rest of his life comfortably basking in the role of hero. He died in 1957 at the age of sixty-eight.

Bernt Balchen, the unsung hero of the *America* adventure, accompanied Byrd on his South Pole flight. He went on to become a colonel in the US Air Force and had a distinguished career, though, as was noted earlier, he fell foul of the Byrd family because of suggestions in his autobiography that Byrd had not reached the North Pole in 1926 as claimed. Balchen died in 1973. **George Noville** accompanied Byrd on his second expedition. Noville Peninsula and Mount Noville, Antarctica, are both named after him. Noville died in 1963 in California. Little beyond that is known. **Bert Acosta**, the fourth member of the 1927 *America* crew, did not fare so well. He became a hopeless alcoholic and spent several spells in jail for vagrancy and for failing to maintain alimony payments. Seized with a burst of idealism during the 1930s, he pulled himself together enough to go to Spain and fly combat missions for the anti-fascist republicans, but after the war he returned to the United States and slipped back into dissolute habits. He died, more or less destitute, in 1954.

Also moving relentlessly downhill was the strange and enigmatic **Charles A. Levine**. In October 1927, after almost five months away, Levine came home. He was given a parade up Fifth Avenue, but almost no one turned up. At a luncheon at the Hotel Astor, Mayor Jimmy Walker made a direct reference to the poor treatment Levine had been given.

It subsequently became clear why Levine had lingered in Europe. The Justice Department was after him for up to $500,000 in unpaid taxes. This turned out to be the first in a lifetime of troubles for Levine. In 1931, police issued a warrant for him on charges of grand larceny after he failed to appear for questioning over irregularities concerning a $25,000 bank loan. Soon afterwards he was arrested in Austria and charged with planning to counterfeit money and casino gambling chips. Those charges were later dropped. In 1932 Levine received a suspended sentence for violating the Workmen's Compensation Law, and in 1933 he was charged with attempting to pass counterfeit money in New Jersey, though that charge too was later dropped. In 1937 he was convicted of smuggling two thousand pounds of tungsten powder into the United States from Canada, and served eighteen months in Lewisburg Penitentiary. In 1942, he was sentenced to 150 days in jail for helping to smuggle an illegal alien into the United States from Mexico. The fellow was a Jewish refugee, so it would seem to have been a reasonably humanitarian act, but the court, for whatever reason, did not see it so.

After that, Levine dropped from sight. In 1971, when *American Heritage* ran an article about the flight of the *Columbia*, Levine was listed as missing and of unknown whereabouts. In fact, he was living in impoverished obscurity. He died in Washington, DC, in 1991, aged ninety-four.

Levine's flying companion, **Clarence Chamberlin**, lived almost half a century after the summer of 1927 but without doing anything of particular note. He worked as an aviation consultant and for a time managed the new Floyd Bennett Field (named after the luckless airman) in Brooklyn, New York's first public airport, opened in 1930. He died in Connecticut in 1976 just before his eighty-third birthday.

Babe Ruth and **Lou Gehrig** finished off the autumn of 1927 with a barnstorming tour. Barnstorming – putting together a touring team of big-leaguers to play exhibition games – was highly lucrative. In a tour of twenty-one games, Ruth and Gehrig both made sums equal to their annual salaries as players.

Barnstorming matches tended to be good-natured but chaotic. Fans frequently ran on to the field to chase down grounders that reached the outfield, and an outfielder might very well find himself competing with a clutch of eager spectators to catch a fly ball. Thirteen of the twenty-one games in 1927 had to be abandoned early because the crowds were out of control. In Sioux City, Iowa, 2,000 fans rushed on to the field at one point, and Lou Gehrig was credited with saving the life of a man who was being trampled.

Barnstorming proved to be the undoing of Gehrig and

Ruth's friendship. To widespread astonishment, Gehrig in 1932 started going out with a young woman named Eleanor Twitchell. They were married the following year. In 1934, Eleanor accompanied Lou and several of his teammates on a post-season tour of Japan. On the ocean crossing, Eleanor disappeared for some time one afternoon. Lou, frantic that she might have fallen overboard, searched everywhere for her. Eventually he found her in Ruth's cabin. Eleanor and Ruth had been drinking. She was decidedly tipsy. Whatever else may have been going on in there is unknown, but for years rumours persisted that it was considerably more than conversational. When Yankees catcher Bill Dickey was asked about it years later, he acknowledged that 'something happened', but would be drawn no further. 'I don't want to tell you about it' is all he would say. What *is* known is that communication between Gehrig and Ruth ceased more or less completely from that day.

In early 1939, after playing nearly fourteen full seasons without missing a game, something went wrong with Lou Gehrig. He became clumsy and seemed to have no strength. After eight games he asked to be benched, ending his streak at 2,130 consecutive games, a record that would stand for half a century, and went to the Mayo Clinic in Rochester, Minnesota. There it was discovered that he was suffering from motor neurone disease, a gradually fatal condition. His career was over.

Shortly after his diagnosis was made public, the Yankees held a Lou Gehrig Appreciation Day. Awards were presented and tributes paid. Joe McCarthy, the Yankees' new manager, wept as he described Gehrig's virtues. Gehrig wasn't expected to speak – he was petrified of

585

crowds – but he stepped to the microphone and made what has long been considered the most moving speech ever given in a sporting context in America. He began:

> Fans, for the past two weeks you have been reading about the bad break I got. Today I consider myself the luckiest man on the face of the earth. I have been in ballparks for seventeen years and have never received anything but kindness and encouragement from you fans. Look at these grand men. Which of you wouldn't consider it the highlight of his career just to associate with them even for one day?

He spoke for no more than a minute, mostly to praise his teammates and family. It wasn't the words so much as the sincerity that moistened every eye in the park. When he finished he received an ovation greater and more heartfelt than any given before or since in Yankee Stadium. Babe Ruth stepped forward, whispered something in his ear and embraced him. It was the first time they had spoken in nearly six years. Just under two years later, on 2 June 1941, Gehrig was dead. He was thirty-seven years old.

Ruth had retired in 1935. He had wanted to be made manager of the Yankees, but Jacob Ruppert dismissed the idea out of hand. 'You can't even manage yourself,' he said woundingly. Ruth instead was traded to the Boston Braves, one of the worst teams in baseball. He played just twenty-eight games there, but finished with a Ruthian flourish. In his last game, against the Pirates on 25 May 1935, he hit three home runs. At the time he retired, he held fifty-six major league records.

On 13 June 1948, Babe Ruth made a farewell appearance at Yankee Stadium not unlike Gehrig's nine years earlier. He was dying of cancer and looked unmistakably frail. He wore a Yankees uniform, which hung loosely on his much reduced frame. He said a few words of thanks into a microphone set up at home plate, but his cancer made it difficult for him to speak.

He died two months later aged fifty-three. Harry Hooper, his old teammate, said Ruth was 'a man loved by more people and with an intensity of feeling that perhaps has never been equalled before or since'. Waite Hoyt put it more simply: 'God, we liked that big son of a bitch. He was a constant source of joy.'

Henry Ford at last produced his long-awaited Model A automobile in early December. To make sure that no one was unaware of this milestone event, the company placed full-page ads in 2,000 daily newspapers.

People flocked to showrooms to gaze in wonder at the novelty of a Ford that came in a range of exotic colours – Arabian Sand, Rose Beige, Gunmetal Blue, Niagara Blue and Andalusite Blue – and was reasonably stylish, well appointed and comfortable, for a price between $385 and $1,400 depending on features. In every city, Ford showrooms could be recognized at once by the crowds gathered around them. At least ten million people were estimated to have viewed the car in its first thirty-six hours on sale.

The initial reaction was highly favourable. Some 400,000 Model As were ordered in the first two weeks of December. What Ford didn't tell eager buyers was that production was still only running at about a hundred cars a day. So dealers, who had had no customers for months, now found they had plenty of customers but almost no cars to give them. The loss of goodwill was immense.

Ultimately, the Model A was no more than a modest success. It was discontinued after four years as it became evident that American car buyers now wanted annual model changes. In the 1930s Ford dropped to third place in market share, with barely half the sales of General Motors and less even than Chrysler. Its payroll fell from over 170,000 in 1929 to just 46,000 in 1932, and total production at Ford plants dropped from 1.5 million vehicles to just over 230,000. The company survived, of course, and has remained one of America's most important manufacturing concerns, but it would never again be the dominant force it once was.

Edsel Ford died of stomach cancer in 1943 at the early age of forty-nine, never having had much chance to get out from under his father's shadow. Henry Ford, growing rapidly senile, followed four years later, aged eighty-three. He never made it to Fordlandia, his rubber enterprise in Brazil.

Ruth Snyder and **Judd Gray** met their fate at Sing Sing in January 1928, one month after the Model A made its debut. Their executioner was the lethally ubiquitous **Robert G. Elliott**.

Snyder was sent to the chair first. 'When her eyes fell upon the instrument of death she almost collapsed,' Elliott recorded in his memoirs. 'The matrons tenderly assisted her to the chair, and, as she was placed in it, she broke down and wept. "Jesus, have mercy on me, for I have sinned," she prayed between sobs.' Elliott gently attached electrodes to her right leg and the nape of her neck and lowered a cloth bag over her head. For reasons unstated, she was spared the usual leather football helmet. Then Elliott stepped back and threw the switch. Two minutes later Ruth Snyder was dead. It was the first electrocution anywhere of a woman.

Gray immediately followed and walked to the chair with a businesslike briskness, as if this were a visit to the dentist. He wore a look of calm resolve and politely cooperated as he was strapped in and wired up. 'He was one of the bravest men I have ever seen go to death by law,' Elliott wrote. 'I felt extremely sorry for this man who had forsaken his wife and daughter for the woman who lay dead a short distance away. I believe nearly everyone in the room did.' Two minutes later, Gray was dead, too.

The next morning, readers of the *New York Daily News* were greeted with a sensational image. Filling the whole of the front page under the single word 'DEAD!' was a slightly blurred photograph of Ruth Snyder at the time of execution. Her head is covered, and she is obviously strapped in place, but otherwise looks reasonably comfortable. The photo was taken by a *Daily News* reporter named Tom Howard, who was present as an official witness and had sneaked in a miniature camera strapped to his shin. At the right moment, he had discreetly lifted up his trouser leg and activated the shutter by means of a wire running to his jacket pocket. The edition sold out within minutes of hitting the streets. Inside, the paper provided 289 inches of coverage on the execution. Even the *New York Times* gave the story 63½ inches – over five feet – of coverage.

Two months after the executions, Robert G. Elliott and his wife were slumbering peacefully in their home in Richmond Hill in Queens when they were blown out of bed by a tremendous explosion. Bombers – presumably

Sacco and Vanzetti sympathizers – had left an explosive device on their front porch. The upward force of the blast blew the roof more than thirty feet across the lawn, but remarkably the Elliotts were not injured. The house, however, had to be completely rebuilt. No one was ever caught for the bombing. Elliott lived on till October 1939, when he died of a heart attack aged sixty-five.

Herbert Hoover suffered a couple of frights on his road to the White House. In the autumn of 1927 his opponents, of whom there were many, began floating the notion that Hoover couldn't legally run because he hadn't been resident in America for the preceding fourteen years as the Constitution required. (The stipulation was put there by the founding fathers to make sure that the office could be held only by those who had remained loyally at home during the revolution.) Rumours also circulated that Hoover had once applied for British citizenship. (He hadn't.)

In the end, no one pursued the challenge and on 4 November 1928, on the first occasion in his life in which he ran for office, Hoover was elected President of the United States by a record margin. He received nearly two thirds of the popular vote and over 80 per cent of electoral votes. Among those endorsing him was Charles Lindbergh.

He took office in March 1929, and in October the stock market crashed. Hoover never recovered from that blow. In the three years following the crash, America's unemployment rate rose from 3 per cent to 25 per cent, while average household earnings fell by 33 per cent, industrial production by almost 50 per cent and the stock market by 90 per cent. Eleven thousand banks failed.

Hoover did quite a lot to try to stimulate the economy. He spent $3.5 billion on public works, including several projects for which we may thank him yet – notably the Golden Gate Bridge and Hoover Dam. He even donated his own salary to charity. As an aide to President Roosevelt once confessed, 'practically the whole New Deal was extrapolated from programs that Hoover started'. But nothing could overcome his absence of lovability. At the 1931 World Series, he was 'lustily' booed – the first time that that had ever happened to a president at a World Series game.

Having won the 1928 election by a record margin, Hoover lost the 1932 race by another record margin. He continued to work as hard after his presidency as during it. At one point, he wrote four books simultaneously, keeping a separate desk for each. He died in 1964 aged ninety and was buried at West Branch, Iowa, even though he had not lived there for more than eighty years. Today the Hoover presidential library at West Branch includes an excellent museum which houses, among much else, the television equipment on which he made his famous broadcast in April 1927.

Upon completion of his term, **Calvin Coolidge** retired with Grace to a rented house in Northampton, Massachusetts. He became a member of the board of the New York Life Insurance Company and faithfully attended the monthly board meetings in New York for a fee of $50 and reimbursement of his expenses. He also wrote his autobi-ography and a syndicated newspaper column. One afternoon just after New Year 1933, he went upstairs to shave. Grace found him on the floor of their bathroom dead of a heart attack. He was sixty years old. Most of his papers were destroyed soon after his death at his own request.

Benjamin Strong, governor of the Federal Reserve Bank of New York and the man who arguably gave the world the stock market crash and all the economic chaos that followed, didn't live to see any of it. He died in October 1928 at the age of fifty-five, overwhelmed by tuberculosis. Also not long surviving the summer of 1927 was **Myron Herrick**, US ambassador in Paris. He caught a chill while standing in the rain during the funeral of the French war hero Marshal Ferdinand Foch in March 1929 and died a few days later. He was seventy-four.

Six months after Herrick died, **Miller Huggins**, the Yankees' manager, developed a blotch under his eye and began to feel feverish. He went to St Vincent's Hospital in New York, and almost at once his condition grew critical. He was suffering from a skin infection called erysipelas (more commonly known as St Anthony's fire), which nowadays can be treated with antibiotics. In 1929, there were no effective treatments. Huggins died on 25 September 1929, aged fifty.

Dwight Morrow stepped down as ambassador to Mexico after three years in the job and came home to run for the Senate as a Republican from New Jersey. He stood on a platform opposing Prohibition and won by a landslide, but died suddenly in his sleep from a stroke on 5 October 1931, soon after taking office. He was fifty-eight years old.

Five months later, his grandson was kidnapped.

Six months after the Lindbergh-baby kidnapping, **Judge Webster Thayer** returned briefly to the news when his home was bombed, presumably by Sacco and Vanzetti supporters. Thayer spent the rest of his life living under police guard at his Boston club, though in fact he didn't have a great deal of life left. He died a little over six months later, aged seventy-five. **Alvan Fuller**, the other principal figure in the Sacco and Vanzetti case, retired as governor of Massachusetts in 1929 but lived under police guard for some years. After Myron Herrick's death, Fuller was considered for the position of ambassador to France, but was effectively vetoed by the French, who said they couldn't guarantee his safety. Instead he devoted the remaining twenty-nine years of his life to business and philanthropy. He died of a heart attack at a Boston cinema in 1958.

Jack Dempsey lost most of his fortune in the Wall Street crash. In 1935 he opened a restaurant on Broadway which was a New York institution for almost forty years before closing in 1974. Dempsey himself lived until 1983, dying at the age of eighty-seven.

Gene Tunney married an heiress from the Carnegie family, Polly Lauder, in 1929. She had never seen him fight. They honeymooned on the Adriatic island of Brioni, where Tunney 'walked, swam and talked' with George Bernard Shaw. Presumably he spent a little time with his bride as well. Tunney wrote some reminiscences, served on the boards of several large companies, and became 'a speaker of overwhelming authority and composure on any subject at all', as John Lardner recorded just a touch acidly in a *New Yorker* profile in 1950. His son John served as US Senator for California from 1965 to 1971. Tunney died in 1978 aged eighty-one.

The most successful of the 1920s boxers, however, was the wild bull **Luis Firpo**. Having arrived in America penniless, Firpo went home to Argentina $1 million richer after six years in the ring. He invested his fortune wisely and built up a business and ranching empire that eventually extended to an estate of over 200,000 acres. He was worth about $5 million when he died in 1960, aged sixty-five.

The tennis star **Bill Tilden** won the Wimbledon men's singles final for the last time in 1930 at the age of thirty-seven. After retiring from tennis, he pursued an acting career and toured successfully in the lead role in a revival of *Dracula*, the hit production of 1927. He also developed a tragic weakness for slim young boys. In 1947, he was sentenced to one year in jail in Los Angeles for interfering with a minor. Soon after his release, he was caught doing the same thing again and imprisoned a second time. He lost his few remaining friends and declined into a shabby, malodorous poverty. When he died in 1953 of a heart attack at the age of sixty, he had a net worth of $80.

Chicago Mayor Big Bill Thompson turned on **Al Capone** shortly after the Tunney–Dempsey fight in the belief – clearly delusional – that Capone was hurting his prospects for national political success, possibly as a presidential candidate for the Republicans. Shorn of protection, Capone moved to Florida in early 1928 and took up residence in Miami Beach. The next year he was arrested while changing trains in Philadelphia and sentenced to a year in prison for carrying a concealed weapon. In 1931, he was convicted of income tax evasion and given eleven years in prison.

Prison was not too tough for Capone. He had a bed with a sprung mattress and homemade meals were delivered to his cell. At Thanksgiving he was served a turkey dinner by a butler hired for the day. He was allowed to keep a stock of liquor and to use the warden's office to receive guests. The warden vehemently denied that Capone received preferential treatment, then was caught using Capone's car. In 1934, Capone's situation became considerably less attractive when Alcatraz opened in San Francisco Bay and he was part of its first intake. Capone was released in late 1939, by which point he was suffering acutely from late-onset syphilis. He died in Florida in 1947.

At just the time that Al Capone was entering Alcatraz, on the other side of the country **Charles Ponzi** was being deported to Italy. He moved to Brazil and died in poverty on a charity ward of a hospital in Buenos Aires in 1949.

Mabel Walker Willebrandt, the lawyer who devised the idea of going after criminals like Al Capone on the grounds of tax evasion, lived until 1963, dying in California just before her seventy-fourth birthday. After leaving government in 1929, she took a high-paying job as chief counsel for Fruit Industries Limited, a California company that grew grapes and was well known for helping people to make wine at home. This made Willebrandt look like a hypocrite (which indeed she was), and helped in a small but psychologically significant way to expedite the end of Prohibition.

A motion to repeal the Eighteenth Amendment came before Congress in early 1933. The House debated the bill for just forty minutes. In the Senate, as Daniel Okrent notes in his history of Prohibition, 'Of the twenty-two members who had voted for the Eighteenth Amendment sixteen years earlier and were still senators, seventeen voted to undo their earlier work.' In December 1933, Prohibition officially ended.

Also coming back into the news in 1933 was the all-but-forgotten aviator **Francesco de Pinedo**. After his return to Italy in 1927, Pinedo had resumed his career in Italy's air force, the Regia Aeronautica, and there imprudently plotted to depose the air minister, Italo Balbo. Learning of this, Balbo posted Pinedo to the furthest and most pointless outpost it was in his power to send him – Buenos Aires. Pinedo languished in obscurity until September 1933 when he turned up unexpectedly at Floyd Bennett Field in Brooklyn with a plan to fly solo to Baghdad, a distance of 6,300 miles.

Although this would be the furthest that anyone had ever flown, on the day of departure Pinedo arrived at the airfield dressed as if going out for a little light shopping – in blue serge suit, grey fedora hat and a light sweater. On his feet, it was noticed, he wore carpet slippers. The entire enterprise was patently misguided, but no one tried to stop him. As Pinedo's plane hurtled down the runway, it began to weave from side to side, then veered towards an administration building where a small crowd had gathered. It missed the crowd, but clipped a wing on some obstruction, tipped up on its nose and crashed into a parked car. Pinedo was thrown clear. According to some accounts, he rose from the tarmac and tried to get back into the plane – presumably in a state of confusion. Other witnesses said he remained motionless on the ground. At all events, before anyone could get to him the plane exploded. Pinedo perished in a giant fireball. What was going through his mind that morning and why he didn't abandon the takeoff when it was so clearly going wrong are questions that can now never be answered.

For the film industry, the transition from silent to talking pictures was faster than anyone ever thought possible. In June 1929, barely a year and a half after the debut of *The Jazz Singer*, of the seventeen cinemas on Broadway, just three were still showing silents. The Great Depression, however, hit the industry hard. By 1933, nearly one third of cinemas in America were shut and many of the studios were in trouble. Paramount was bankrupt; RKO and Universal were nearly so. Fox was struggling to reorganize and eventually would have to be rescued by a much smaller studio, Twentieth Century.

In New York in 1932, **Roxy Rothafel** opened Radio City Music Hall at the Rockefeller Center. (The famous Rockettes were originally the Roxyettes.) But his time was running out, too. In May, the Roxy Theatre went into receivership. Two years later, Rothafel was put in charge of the failing Mastbaum Theatre in Philadelphia. He reportedly spent $200,000 in ten weeks, but to no avail. The heyday of the great picture palaces was at an end. Rothafel died of a heart attack in a New York hotel in

1936. He was fifty-three years old. The Roxy Theatre was torn down in 1960.

Clara Bow, star of *Wings*, retired from acting in 1933 and became increasingly reclusive. She died in 1965, aged sixty. **William Wellman**, the director, made another sixty-five films before retiring in 1958. Many of his films were turkeys, but some were notable, among them *The Public Enemy* (1931), *The Ox-Bow Incident* (1943) and *The High and the Mighty* (1954). He died in 1975 aged seventy-nine. **John Monk Saunders**, the writer who conceived of *Wings*, didn't fare so well. He married the actress Fay Wray, but the marriage failed and his career went downhill because of drinking and drugs. He hanged himself in Florida in 1940.

Jerome Kern never had another hit on Broadway after *Show Boat*, though he tried several times. Eventually, like so many others, he moved to Hollywood. He died in 1945. **Oscar Hammerstein II** also seemed to have come to the end of his road with *Show Boat*. He went a dozen years without a hit, but then he teamed up with Richard Rodgers and between them they put together the greatest run of successes in the history of musicals: *Oklahoma!*, *Carousel*, *South Pacific*, *The King and I*, *Flower Drum Song* and *The Sound of Music*. Hammerstein died in 1960.

Jacob Ruppert, owner of the New York Yankees, suffered a heart attack in early 1939 and died nine days later at the age of sixty-nine. The world was astonished to find that he had left much of his estate, initially valued at between $40 million and $70 million, to a former showgirl named Helen W. Weyant. Miss Weyant confessed to reporters that she and Ruppert had had a secret friendship for many years, but insisted that it was no more than friendship. In the end, Ruppert's estate turned out to be worth just $6.5 million – the depression had severely hit his real estate holdings – and he had personal debts of $1 million on top. In order to pay the debts and his estate taxes, it was necessary to sell both the Yankees and the Ruppert brewery.

Also dying in 1939, following a long illness, was **Raymond Orteig**, the amiable hotelier who launched the Orteig Prize.

Gutzon Borglum didn't quite live to see Mount Rushmore completed. He died in March 1941, of complications following prostate surgery, just a few months before it was finished. He was seventy-three.

Montagu Norman, governor of the Bank of England and close friend of Benjamin Strong, suffered a bizarre accident in 1944 that brought his career to a close. While visiting his brother on his country estate in Hertfordshire, Norman went for a walk in fading light and appears to have tripped over a cow that was resting on the ground. The startled cow may have kicked Norman in the head in scrambling to its feet. Norman never fully recovered and died in 1950 aged seventy-eight.

Alexis Carrel was pushed out of his role at the Rockefeller Institute because his views were becoming too embarrassing. Carrel returned to France and started an institute that specialized in matters outside the scientific mainstream, including telepathy and water divination. He openly supported the Vichy regime and would almost certainly have been tried as a collaborator but died in 1944 before he could be brought to trial. He was seventy-one. At the Nazi war trials at Nuremberg after the war, Carrel's *Man the Unknown* was quoted in defence of Nazi eugenics practices.

Also dying in 1944 were two of Chicago's leading figures. The first to go was **Big Bill Thompson**, who died in March at the age of seventy-six. The following month, **Kenesaw Mountain Landis** took his earthly leave at the age of seventy-eight. Landis had spent most of the later part of his career fighting attempts to let blacks play in the major leagues. That ignoble battle was lost in 1947 when Jackie Robinson, the first black major league baseball player, took the field for the Brooklyn Dodgers.

Lindbergh's mother, **Evangeline Lodge Lindbergh**, died in 1954 from Parkinson's disease at the age of seventy-eight. His widow, **Anne Morrow Lindbergh**, produced five other children apart from the murdered Charles Junior, and became a successful and admired writer, mostly of memoirs. She died in 2001 at the ripe age of ninety-four, the last person of consequence to this story to have lived through that long, extraordinary summer.

Bibliography

Aberdare, Lord, *The Story of Tennis*. London: Stanley Paul, 1959.

Adair, Robert K., *The Physics of Baseball*. New York: Harper & Row, 1990.

Ahamed, Liaquat, *Lords of Finance: The Bankers Who Broke the World*. London: William Heinemann, 2009.

Allaz, Camille, *The History of Air Cargo and Air Mail From the Eighteenth Century*. London: Christopher Foyle Publishing, 2004.

Allen, Frederick Lewis, *The Lords of Creation: The Story of the Great Age of American Finance*. London: Hamish Hamilton, 1935.

——, *Only Yesterday: An Informal History of the 1920s*. New York: Perennial Library, 1964.

Allsop, Kenneth, *The Bootleggers: The Story of Chicago's Prohibition Era*. London: Hutchinson, 1961.

Almond, Peter, *Aviation: The Early Years*. Cologne: Könemann, 1997.

Amory, Cleveland, and Frederic Bradlee (eds), *Vanity Fair: A Cavalcade of the 1920s and 1930s*. New York: Viking Press, 1960.

Avrich, Paul, *Sacco and Vanzetti: The Anarchist Background*. Princeton: Princeton University Press, 1991.

Bak, Richard, *The Big Jump: Lindbergh and the Great Atlantic Air Race*. New York: John Wiley & Sons, 2011.

Balchen, Bernt, *Come North With Me: An Autobiography*. London: Hodder and Stoughton, 1959.

Baldwin, Neil, *Henry Ford and the Jews: The Mass Production of Hate*. New York: Public Affairs, 2001.

Barry, John M., *Rising Tide: The Great Mississippi Flood of 1927 and How It Changed America*. New York: Simon & Schuster, 1998.

Barton, Bruce, *The Man Nobody Knows: A Discovery of the Real Jesus*. Indianapolis: Bobbs-Merrill Co., 1925.

Baxandall, Rosalyn, and Elizabeth Ewen, *Picture Windows: How the Suburbs Happened*. New York: Basic Books, 2000.

Berg, A. Scott, *Goldwyn: A Biography*. New York: Ballantine Books, 1989.

——, *Lindbergh*. New York: Macmillan, 1998.

Bergreen, Laurence, *Capone: The Man and the Era*. New York: Simon & Schuster, 1994.

Berliner, Louise, *Texas Guinan: Queen of the Night Clubs*. Austin: University of Texas Press, 1993.

Best, Gary Dean, *The Dollar Decade: Mammon and the Machine in 1920s America*. Westport, CT: Praeger Publishers, 2003.

Bingham, Hiram, *An Explorer in the Air Service*. New Haven: Yale University Press, 1920.

Black, Edwin, *War Against the Weak: Eugenics and America's Campaign to Create a Master Race*. New York: Four Walls Eight Windows, 2003.

Blake, Angela M., *How New York Became American, 1890–1924*. Baltimore: Johns Hopkins University Press, 2006.

Blegen, Theodore C., *Minnesota: A History of the State*. Minneapolis: University of Minnesota Press, 1963.

Block, Geoffrey, *Enchanted Evenings: The Broadway Musical from Show Boat to Sondheim*. New York: Oxford University Press, 1997.

Boardman, Barrington, *From Harding to Hiroshima*. New York: Dembner Books, 1988.

Boorstin, Daniel J., *The Image, or What Happened to the American Dream*. New York: Atheneum, 1962.

Bordman, Gerald M., *Jerome Kern: His Life and Music*. New York: Oxford University Press, 1980.

——, *American Theatre: A Chronicle of Comedy and Drama, 1914–1930*. New York: Oxford University Press, 1995.

Boyle, Andrew, *Montagu Norman: A Biography*. London: Cassell, 1967.

Boyle, Kevin, *Arc of Justice: A Saga of Race, Civil Rights and Murder in the Jazz Age*. New York: Henry Holt, 2005.

Britton, Nan, *The President's Daughter*. New York: Elizabeth Ann Guild, 1927.

Brooks, John, *Once in Golconda: A True Drama of Wall Street 1920–1938*. New York: Harper & Row, 1969.

Brownlow, Kevin, *Behind the Mask of Innocence*. London: Jonathan Cape, 1990.

Budiansky, Stephen, *Air Power: From Kitty Hawk to Gulf War II: A History of the People, Ideas and Machines That Transformed War in the Century of Flight*. London: Viking, 2003.

Burroughs, Edgar Rice, *Thuvia: Maid of Mars*, London: Methuen and Co., 1920.

——, *The War Chief*. London: Methuen and Co., 1929.

——, *Tarzan of the Apes*. New York: Library of America, 2012.

Byrd, Richard Evelyn, *Skyward*. New York: G. P. Putnam's Sons, 1928.

Cahan, Richard, *A Court That Shaped America: Chicago's Federal District Court from Abe Lincoln to Abbie Hoffman*. Evanston: Northwestern University Press, 2002.

Cannadine, David, *Mellon: An American Life*. London: Allen Lane, 2006.

Carr, Steven Alan, *Hollywood and Anti-Semitism: A Cultural History up to World War II*. Cambridge: Cambridge University Press, 2001.

Carrel, Alexis, *Man the Unknown*. New York: Harper & Brothers, 1935.

Cerf, Bennett, *Try and Stop Me*. New York: Simon & Schuster, 1945.

Chamberlin, Clarence D., *Record Flights*. New York: Beechwood Press, 1942.

Chernow, Ron, *The House of Morgan*. London: Simon & Schuster, 1990.

——, *Titan: The Life of John D. Rockefeller, Sr.* Boston: Little, Brown and Co., 1998.

Churchill, Allen, *The Year the World Went Mad*. New York: Thomas Y. Crowell, 1960.

——, *The Literary Decade*. London: Prentice-Hall, 1971.

——, *The Theatrical 20's*. New York: McGraw-Hill, 1975.

Clark, Constance Areson, *God – or Godzilla: Images of Evolution in the Jazz Age*. Baltimore: Johns Hopkins University Press, 2008.

Clements, Kendrick A., *The Life of Herbert Hoover: Imperfect Visionary, 1918–1928*. London: Palgrave/Macmillan, 2010.

Clymer, Floyd, *Henry's Wonderful Model T, 1908–1927*. New York: McGraw-Hill Book Company, 1955.

Coben, Stanley, *Rebellion Against Victorianism: The Impetus for Cultural Change in 1920s America*. Oxford: Oxford University Press, 1991.

Cochrane, Dorothy, Van Hardesty and Russell Lee, *The Aviation Careers of Igor Sikorsky*. Seattle: University of Washington Press, 1980.

Cole, Wayne S., *Charles A. Lindbergh and the Battle Against American Intervention in World War II*. New York: Harcourt Brace Jovanovich, 1974.

Coolidge, Calvin, *Have Faith in Massachusetts: A Collection of Speeches and Messages*. London: John Lane/Bodley Head, 1923.

——, *The Autobiography of Calvin Coolidge*. London: Chatto & Windus, 1929.

Coombs, L. F. E., *Control in the Sky: The Evolution and History of the Aircraft Cockpit*. Barnsley: Pen and Sword Aviation, 2005.

Corn, Joseph J. (ed.), *Into the Blue: American Writing on Aviation and Spaceflight*. New York: The Library of America, 2011.

Coué, Emile, *Self Mastery Through Conscious Autosuggestion*. London: George Allen & Unwin, 1922.

Currell, Susan, *American Culture in the 1920s*. Edinburgh: Edinburgh University Press, 2009.

Currell, Susan, and Christina Cogdell (eds), *Popular Eugenics: National Efficiency and American Mass Culture in the 1930s*. Athens: Ohio University Press, 2006.

Dardis, Tom, *Firebrand: The Life of Horace Liveright*. New York: Random House, 1995.

Davis, Kenneth S., *The Hero: Charles A. Lindbergh and the American Dream*. Garden City, NY: Doubleday, 1959.

Dawidoff, Nicholas (ed.), *Baseball: A Literary Anthology*. New York: Library of America, 2002.

Deford, Frank, *Big Bill Tilden: The Triumphs and the Tragedy*. New York: Simon & Schuster, 1976.

Derr, Mark, *Some Kind of Paradise: A Chronicle of Man and the Land in Florida*. New York: William Morrow, 1989.

Dinnerstein, Leonard, and David M. Reimers, *Ethnic Americans: A History of Immigration* (fifth edn). New York: Columbia University Press, 2009.

Douglas, Ann, *Terrible Honesty: Mongrel Manhattan in the 1920s*. New York: Noonday Press/Farrar, Straus and Giroux, 1995.

Dumenil, Lynn, *The Modern Temper: American Culture and Society in the 1920s*. New York: Hill and Wang,1995.

Dyott, George M., *Man Hunting in the Jungle: The Search for Colonel Fawcett*. London: Edward Arnold, 1930.

Ehrmann, Herbert B., *The Case That Will Not Die: Commonwealth vs Sacco and Vanzetti*. London: W. H. Allen, 1970.

Eichengreen, Barry, *Golden Fetters: The Gold Standard and the Great Depression, 1919–1939*. New York: Oxford University Press, 1992.

Eig, Jonathan, *Luckiest Man: The Life and Death of Lou Gehrig*. New York: Simon & Schuster, 2006.

——, *Get Capone: The Secret Plot That Captured America's Most Wanted Gangster*. New York: Simon & Schuster, 2010.

Elliott, Robert G., with Albert R. Beatty, *Agent of Death: The Memoirs of an Executioner*. New York: E. P. Dutton & Co., 1940.

Engerman, Stanley J., and Robert E. Gallman, *The Cambridge Economic History of the United States* (Vol. 3). Cambridge: Cambrige University Press, 2000.

Evans, Harold, *The American Century*. New York: Alfred A. Knopf, 1999.

Everson, William K., *American Silent Film*. New York: Oxford University Press, 1978.

Eyman, Scott, *The Speed of Sound: Hollywood and the Talkie Revolution, 1926–1930*. New York: Simon & Schuster, 1997.

Faber, C. F., and R. B. Faber, *Spitballers: The Last Legal Hurlers of the Wet One*. Jefferson, NC: McFarland and Co., 2006.

Fisher, David E., and Marshall Jon Fisher, *Tube: The Invention of Television*. Washington, DC: Counterpoint, 1996.

Fitzgerald, F. Scott, *My Lost City: Personal Essays, 1920–1940*. Cambridge: Cambridge University Press, 2005.

Fogarty, Robert S., *The Righteous Remnant: The House of David*. Kent, Ohio: Kent State University Press, 1981.

Fogelson, Robert M., *Downtown: Its Rise and Fall, 1880–1950*. New Haven: Yale University Press, 2001.

Fokker, Anthony H. G., and Bruce Gould, *Flying Dutchman: The Life of Anthony Fokker*. London: George Routledge & Sons, 1931.

Ford, Henry, *My Life and Work*. London: William Heinemann, 1924.

Forden, Lesley, *The Ford Air Tours, 1925–1931*. New Brighton, Minnesota: Aviation Foundation of America, 2003.

Freedland, Michael, *Al Jolson*. London: W. H. Allen, 1972.

Frommer, Harvey, *Five O'Clock Lightning: Babe Ruth, Lou Gehrig and the Greatest Baseball Team in History, the 1927 New York Yankees*. New York: Wiley, 2007.

Furnas, J. C., *Great Times: An Informal Social History of the United States, 1914–1929*. New York: G. P. Putnam's Sons, 1974.

Gabler, Neal, *Walter Winchell: Gossip, Power and the Culture of Celebrity*. London: Picador, 1995.

——, *Walt Disney: The Biography*. London: Aurum Press, 2007.

Gage, Beverly, *The Day Wall Street Exploded: A Story of America in Its First Age of Terror*. Oxford: Oxford University Press, 2009.

Galbraith, John Kenneth, *The Liberal Hour*. London: Hamish Hamilton, 1960.

——, *Money: Whence It Came, Where It Went*. London: André Deutsch, 1975.

Gerstle, Gary, *American Crucible: Race and Nation in the Twentieth Century*. Princeton, NJ: Princeton University Press, 2001.

Gibbs-Smith, Charles H., *Aviation: An Historical Survey from Its Origins to the End of the Second World War*. London: Science Museum, 2003.

Goldberg, Alfred (ed.), *A History of the United States Air Force 1907–1957*. Princeton, NJ: D. Van Nostrand Co., 1957.

Goldman, Herbert G., *Jolson: The Legend Comes to Life*. New York: Oxford University Press, 1988.

Goldstein, Malcolm, *George S. Kaufman: His Life, His Theater*. New York: Oxford University Press, 1979.

Gordon, John Steele, *An Empire of Wealth: The Epic History of American Economic Power*. New York: Harper Perennial, 2005.

Gould, Stephen Jay, *The Flamingo's Smile: Reflections in Natural History*. New York: W. W. Norton, 1985.

Grandin, Greg, *Fordlandia: The Rise and Fall of Henry Ford's Forgotten Jungle City*. New York: Metropolitan/Henry Holt, 2009.

Grann, David, *The Lost City of Z: A Tale of Deadly Obsession in the Amazon*. New York: Vintage, 2010.

Grant, H. Roger (ed.), *We Took the Train*. DeKalb: Northern Illinois University Press, 1990.

——, *Railroads and the American People*. Bloomington: Indiana University Press, 2012.

Gregory, J. W., *The Menace of Colour*. London: Seeley, Service & Co., 1925.

Grey, Zane, *The Young Pitcher*. London: John Long, 1924.

Grossman, James R., Ann Durkin Keating and Janice L. Reiff (eds), *The Encyclopedia of Chicago*. London: University of Chicago Press, 2004.

Hackett, Alice Payne, *Seventy Years of Best Sellers, 1895–1965*. New York: R. R. Bowker, 1967.

Hamill, John, *The Strange Career of Mr Hoover Under Two Flags*. New York: William Faro, Inc., 1931.

Hamilton, Ian, *Writers in Hollywood 1915–1951*. London: Heinemann, 1990.

Hample, Zack, *The Baseball: Stunts, Scandals, and Secrets Beneath the Stitches*. New York: Anchor Sports, 2011.

Harwood, Jr, Herbert H., *Invisible Giants: The Empires of Cleveland's Van Sweringen Brothers*. Bloomington: Indiana University Press, 2003.

Hawes, Elizabeth, *New York, New York: How the Apartment House Transformed the Life of the City (1869–1930)*. New York: Alfred A. Knopf, 1993.

Helyar, John, *Lords of the Realm: The Real History of Baseball*. New York: Villard Books, 1994.

Higham, Charles, *Ziegfeld*. London: W. H. Allen, 1973.

Hobhouse, Henry, *Seeds of Wealth: Four Plants That Made Men Rich*. London: Macmillan, 2003.

Hokanson, Drake, *The Lincoln Highway: Main Street Across America*. Iowa City: University of Iowa Press, 1988.

Holden, Anthony, *The Oscars: The Secret History of Hollywood's Academy Awards*. New York: Little, Brown & Co., 1993.

Holtzman, Jerome, *No Cheering in the Press Box*. New York: Henry Holt, 1978.

Hoover, Herbert, *The Memoirs of Herbert Hoover: The Years of Adventure, 1874–1920*. London: Hollis and Carter, 1952.

——, *The Memoirs of Herbert Hoover: The Cabinet and the Presidency, 1920–1933*. London: Hollis and Carter, 1952.

Hoyt, Edwin P., *The Last Explorer: The Adventures of Admiral Byrd*. New York: John Day Company, 1968.

Hoyt, William G., and Walter B. Langbein, *Floods*. Princeton, NJ: Princeton University Press, 1955.

Hyman, Louis, *Debtor Nation: The History of America in Red Ink*. Princeton, NJ: Princeton University Press, 2011.

Hynd, Noel, *The Giants of the Polo Grounds: The Glorious Times of Baseball's New York Giants*. New York: Doubleday, 1988.

Jackson, Brian, *The Black Flag: A Look Back at the Strange Case of Nicola Sacco and Bartolomeo Vanzetti*. Boston: Routledge & Kegan Paul, 1981.

Jackson, Joe, *The Thief at the End of the World: Rubber, Power and the Seeds of Empire*. London: Viking, 2008.

Jackson, Kenneth T. (ed)., *The Encyclopaedia of New York City* (second edn). New Haven: Yale University Press, 2010.

Jenkins, Alan, *The Twenties*. London: Heinemann, 1974.

Jones, Maldwyn Allen, *American Immigration*. Chicago: University of Chicago Press, 1960.

Kahn, Roger, *A Flame of Pure Fire: Jack Dempsey and the Roaring '20s*. New York: Harcourt Brace and Co., 1999.

Kamm, Antony, and Malcolm Baird, *John Logie Baird: A Life*. Edinburgh: NMS publishing, 2002.

Katcher, Leo, *The Big Bankroll: The Life and Times of Arnold Rothstein*. London: Victor Gollancz, 1959.

Kennedy, Ludovic, *The Airman and the Carpenter: The Lindbergh Case and the Framing of Richard Hauptmann*. London: Fontana/Collins, 1986.

Kenrick, John, *Musical Theatre: A History*. New York: Continuum, 2008.

Kessner, Thomas, *The Flight of the Century: Charles Lindbergh and the Rise of American Aviation*. New York: Oxford University Press, 2010.

Kisseloff, Jeff, *You Must Remember This: An Oral History of Manhattan from the 1890s to World War II*. New York: Harcourt Brace Jovanovich, 1989.

Klingaman, William K., *1929: The Year of the Great Crash*. New York: Harper & Row, 1989.

Kobler, John, *Capone: The Life and World of Al Capone*. London: Michael Joseph, 1972.

Kostof, Spiro, *America by Design*. New York: Oxford University Press, 1987.

Kramer, Dale, *Heywood Broun: A Biographical Portrait*. New York: Current Books, 1949.

Lacey, Robert, *Ford: The Men and the Machine*. London: Heinemann, 1986.

——, *Little Man: Meyer Lansky and the Gangster Life*. London: Century, 1991.

La Croix, Robert de, *They Flew the Atlantic*. London: Frederick Muller Ltd, 1958.

Landesco, John, *Organized Crime in Chicago*. Chicago: University of Chicago Press, 1968.

Leighton, Isabel (ed.), *The Aspirin Age: 1919–1941*. New York: Simon & Schuster, 1949.

Lerner, Michael A., *Dry Manhattan: Prohibition in New York City*. Cambridge, Mass.: Harvard University Press, 2007.

Lindbergh, Anne Morrow, *The Flower and the Nettle: Diaries and Letters of Anne Morrow Lindbergh, 1936–1939*. New York: Harcourt Brace Jovanovich, 1976.

Lindbergh, Charles A., *The Spirit of St Louis*. New York: Charles Scribner's Sons, 1953.

——, *Autobiography of Values*. New York: Harcourt Brace Jovanovich, 1978.

Lingeman, Richard, *Sinclair Lewis: Rebel from Main Street*. New York: Random House, 2002.

Lochnar, Louis P., *Herbert Hoover and Germany*. New York: Macmillan, 1961.

Longyard, William H., *Who's Who in Aviation History*. Shrewsbury: Airlife, 1994.

Louvish, Simon, *Mae West: It Ain't No Sin*. London: Faber and Faber, 2005.

Loving, Jerome, *The Last Titan: A Life of Theodore Dreiser*. Berkeley: University of California Press, 2005.

Lowe, David Garrard, *Lost Chicago*. New York: Watson-Guptill Publications, 2000.

MacKeller, Landis, *The 'Double Indemnity' Murder: Ruth Snyder, Judd Gray, and New York's Crime of the Century*. Syracuse: Syracuse University Press, 2006.

Mackworth-Praed, Ben (ed.), *Aviation: The Pioneer Years*. London: Studio Editions, 1990.

Maltby, Richard, *Hollywood Cinema* (second edn). Oxford: Blackwell, 2003.

Mason, Herbert Molloy, *The Rise of the Luftwaffe, 1918–1940*. London: Cassell, 1975.

Maxtone-Graham, John, *The Only Way to Cross*. New York: Barnes & Noble, 1972.

Maxwell, Anne, *Picture Imperfect: Photography and Eugenics 1870–1940*. Brighton: Sussex Academic Press, 2008.

McCoy, Donald R., *Calvin Coolidge: The Quiet President*. New York: Macmillan, 1967.

McKinney, Megan, *The Magnificent Medills: America's Royal Family of Journalism During a Century of Turbulent Splendor*. New York: HarperCollins, 2011.

Meade, Marion, *Buster Keaton: Cut to the Chase*. London: Bloomsbury, 1996.

Meltzer, Allan H., *A History of the Federal Reserve (Vol. 1, 1913–1951)*. Chicago: University of Chicago Press, 2003.

Merz, Charles, *The Dry Decade*. Garden City, NY: Doubleday, Doran & Co., 1931.

Miller, Nathan, *New World Coming: The 1920s and the Making of Modern America*. New York: Scribner, 2003.

Milton, Joyce, *Loss of Eden: A Biography of Charles and Anne Morrow Lindbergh*. New York: HarperCollins, 1993.

Montague, Richard, *Oceans, Poles and Airmen: The First Flights over Wide Waters and Desolate Ice*. New York: Random House, 1971.

Montville, Leigh, *The Big Bam: The Life and Times of Babe Ruth*. New York: Doubleday, 2010.

Moore, Lucy, *Anything Goes: A Biography of the Roaring Twenties*. London: Atlantic Books, 2008.

Mordden, Ethan, *All That Glittered: The Golden Age of Drama on Broadway, 1919–1959*. New York: St Martin's Press, 2007.

Morone, James A., *Hellfire Nation: The Politics of Sin in American History*. New Haven: Yale University Press, 2003.

Morris, Peter, *A Game of Inches: The Stories Behind the Innovations That Shaped Baseball*. Chicago: Ivan R. Dee, 2006.

Mortimer, Gavin, *The Great Swim*. London: Short Books, 2009.

Murray, Robert K., *Red Scare: A Study in National Hysteria, 1919–1920*. Minneapolis: University of Minnesota Press, 1955.

Nagorski, Andrew, *Hitlerland: American Eyewitnesses to the Nazi Rise to Power*. New York: Simon & Schuster, 2012.

Nasaw, David, *Going Out: The Rise and Fall of Public Amusements*. New York: Basic Books, 1993.

Nash, George H., *The Life of Herbert Hoover: The Engineer, 1874–1914*. New York: W. W. Norton & Co., 1983.

——, *The Life of Herbert Hoover: The Humanitarian, 1914–1917*. New York: W. W. Norton & Co., 1988.

Nathan, Daniel, *Saying It's So: A Cultural History of the Black Sox Scandal*. Urbana: University of Illinois Press, 2003.

Nevins, Allan, and Frank Ernest Hill, *Ford: The Times, the Man, the Company*. New York: Charles Scribner's Sons, 1954.

——, *Ford: Expansion and Challenge, 1915–1933*. New York: Charles Scribner's Sons, 1957.

Norman, Barry, *Talking Pictures*. London: BBC Books/Hodder and Stoughton, 1987.

Okrent, Daniel, *Last Call: The Rise and Fall of Prohibition*. New York: Scribner, 2010.

Olson, Sherry H., *Baltimore: The Building of an American City*. Baltimore: Johns Hopkins University Press, 1980.

Orlean, Susan, *Rin Tin Tin: The Life and Legend of the World's Most Famous Dog*. London: Atlantic Books, 2011.

Pacyga, Dominic A., *Chicago: A Biography*. Chicago: University of Chicago Press, 2009.

Parrish, Michael E., *Anxious Decades: America in Prosperity and Depression, 1920–1941*. New York: W. W. Norton, 1992.

Pauly, Thomas H., *Zane Grey: His Life, His Adventures, His Women*. Urbana: University of Illinois Press, 2005.

Peretti, Burton W., *Nightclub City: Politics and Amusement in*

Manhattan. Philadelphia: University of Pennsylvania Press, 2007.

Pietila, Antero, *Not in My Neighborhood: How Bigotry Shaped a Great American City*. Chicago: Ivan R. Dee, 2010.

Pietrusza, David, *Judge and Jury: The Life and Times of Judge Kenesaw Mountain Landis*. South Bend, Indiana: Diamond Communications, 1998.

Pinedo, Francesco de, *Amerikaflug: Im Flugzeug Zweimal über den Ozean und über Beide Amerika*. Zürich: Rascher & Cie, 1928.

Pipp, E. G., *Henry Ford: Both Sides of Him*. Detroit: Pipp's Magazine, 1926.

Pisano, Dominick A., and R. Robert van der Linden, *Charles Lindbergh and the Spirit of St Louis*. Washington, DC: Smithsonian National Air and Space Museum, 2002.

Quint, Howard H., and Robert H. Ferrell, *The Talkative President: The Off-the-Record Press Conferences of Calvin Coolidge*. Amherst: University of Massachusetts Press, 1964.

Randel, William Peirce, *The Ku Klux Klan: A Century of Infamy*. London: Hamish Hamilton, 1965.

Rayner, Richard, *A Bright and Guilty Place*. London: Constable, 2010.

Reisler, Jim, *Babe Ruth Slept Here: The Baseball Landmarks of New York City*. South Bend, Indiana: Diamond Communications, 1999.

——, *Babe Ruth: Launching the Legend*. New York: McGraw-Hill, 2004.

Ribowsky, Mark, *The Complete History of the Home Run*. New York: Citadel Press, 2003.

Ritter, Lawrence S., *The Glory of Their Times: The Story of the Early Days of Baseball Told by the Men Who Played It*. New York: HarperCollins, 1992.

——, *Lost Ballparks: A Celebration of Baseball's Legendary Fields*. New York: Viking, 1992.

Root, Waverley, and Richard de Rochement, *Eating in America: A History*. New York: William Morrow & Co., 1976.

Russell, Francis, *Tragedy in Dedham: The Story of the Sacco–Vanzetti Case*. London: Longmans, 1963.
——, *Sacco & Vanzetti: The Case Resolved*. New York: Harper & Row, 1986.
Ruth, Babe (as told to Bob Considine), *The Babe Ruth Story*. New York: C. P. Dutton & Co., 1948.
Sampson, Anthony, *Empires of the Sky: The Politics, Contests and Cartels of World Airlines*. London: Hodder and Stoughton, 1984.
Sanders, James, *Celluloid Skyline: New York and the Movies*. London: Bloomsbury, 2002.
Schatz, Thomas, *The Genius of the System: Hollywood Filmmaking in the Studio Era*. New York: Henry Holt, 1988.
Schlesinger, Jr, Arthur M., *The Crisis of the Old Order, 1919–1933*. London: Heinemann, 1957.
Schwartz, Evan I., *The Last Lone Inventor: A Tale of Genius, Deceit and the Birth of Television*. New York: HarperCollins, 2002.
Seale, William, *The White House: The History of an American Idea*. Washington, DC: American Institute of Architects Press, 1997.
Shlaes, Amity, *Coolidge*. New York: HarperCollins, 2013.
Silver, Nathan, *Lost New York*. Boston: Houghton Mifflin, 1967.
Sinclair, Andrew, *Prohibition: The Era of Excess*. London: Faber and Faber, 1962.
Sklar, Robert, *Movie-Made America: A Cultural History of American Movies*. New York: Vintage, 1994.
Smelser, Marshall, *The Life That Ruth Built: A Biography*. Lincoln: University of Nebraska Press, 1993.
Smith, Page, *America Enters the World: A People's History of the Progressive Era and World War I*. New York: McGraw-Hill, 1985.
Smith, Rex Alan, *The Carving of Mount Rushmore*. New York: Abbeville Press, 1985.
Smith, Richard Norton, *An Uncommon Man: The Triumph of Herbert Hoover*. New York: Simon & Schuster, 1984.

——, *The Colonel: The Life and Legend of Robert R. McCormick, 1880–1955*. Boston: Houghton Mifflin, 1997.

Smith, Terry, *Making the Modern: Industry, Art, and Design in America*. Chicago: University of Chicago Press, 1993.

Sorensen, Charles E., with Samuel T. Williamson, *Forty Years With Ford*. London: Jonathan Cape, 1959.

Starr, Kevin, *Inventing the Dream: California Through the Progressive Era*. New York: Oxford University Press, 1986.

Stenn, David, *Clara Bow: Runnin' Wild*. London: Ebury Press, 1989.

Stern, Robert M., Gregory Gilmartin and Thomas Mellins, *New York 1930: Architecture and Urbanism Between the Two World Wars*. New York: Rizzoli, 1994.

Sullivan, Mark, *Our Times: The United States, 1900–1925* (6 vols). London: Charles Scribner's Sons, 1935.

Summers, Anthony, *Official and Confidential: The Secret Life of J. Edgar Hoover*. London: Victor Gollancz, 1993.

Taliaferro, John, *Tarzan Forever: The Life of Edgar Rice Burroughs, Creator of Tarzan*. New York: Scribner, 1999.

Tauranac, John, *Elegant New York: The Builders and the Buildings, 1885–1915*. New York: Abbeville Press, 1985.

Thomas, Henry W., *Walter Johnson: Baseball's Big Train*. Lincoln: University of Nebraska Press, 1995.

Thorn, John, and Pete Palmer, *Total Baseball: The Ultimate Encyclopedia of Baseball* (third edn). New York: Harper Perennial, 1993.

Toll, Robert C., *On With the Show: The First Century of Show Business in America*. New York: Oxford University Press, 1976.

Thurber, James, *The Years with Ross*. New York: Ballantine Books, 1972.

Tygiel, Jules, *Past Time: Baseball as History*. New York: Oxford University Press, 2000.

Van Creveld, Martin, *The Age of Airpower*. New York: Public Affairs, 2011.

Vincent, David, *Home Run: The Definitive History of Baseball's Ultimate Weapon*. Washington: Potomac Books, 2007.

Wade, Wyn Craig, *The Fiery Cross: The Ku Klux Klan in America*. New York: Simon & Schuster, 1987.

Wagenheim, Kal, *Babe Ruth: His Life and Legend*. New York: Henry Holt, 1992.

Walker, Stanley, *The Night Club Era*. Baltimore: Johns Hopkins University Press, 1933 (reprinted 1999).

Wallace, David, *Capital of the World: A Portrait of New York City in the Roaring Twenties*. Guilford, CT: Lyons Press, 2011.

Wallace, Graham, *The Flight of Alcock & Brown, 14–15 June 1919*. London: Putnam, 1955.

Ward, Geoffrey C. (with Ken Burns), *Baseball: An Illustrated History*. New York: Alfred A. Knopf, 1990.

Ware, Susan (ed.), *Forgotten Heroes*. New York: Free Press, 1998.

Watts, Jill, *Mae West: An Icon in Black and White*. Oxford: Oxford University Press, 2001.

Weigley, Russell F. (ed.), *Philadelphia: A 300-Year History*. New York: W. W. Norton & Co., 1982.

Weindling, Paul Julian, *Nazi Medicine and the Nuremberg Trials*. London: Macmillan, 2004.

Weintraub, Robert, *The House That Ruth Built: A New Stadium, the First Yankees Championship, and the Redemption of 1923*. New York: Simon & Schuster, 2011.

Whitehouse, Arch, *The Early Birds*. London: Nelson Publishing, 1967.

Williams, Ted, and John Underwood, *The Science of Hitting*. New York: Fireside/Simon & Schuster, 1971.

Wilmeth, Don B., and Christopher Bigsby, *The Cambridge History of American Theatre: 1870–1945*. Cambridge: Cambridge University Press, 1999.

Wilson, Edmund, *The American Earthquake: A Documentary of the Twenties and Thirties*. London: W. H. Allen, 1958.

Wohl, Robert, *The Spectacle of Flight: Aviation and the Western Imagination, 1920–1950*. New Haven: Yale University Press, 2005.

Yagoda, Ben, *Will Rogers: A Biography*. Norman: University of Oklahoma Press, 1993.

——, *About Town: The* New Yorker *and the World It Made.* New York: Da Capo Press, 2000.

Young, William, and David E. Kaiser, *Postmortem: New Evidence in the Case of Sacco and Vanzetti.* Amherst: University of Massachusetts Press, 1985.

Zeitz, Joshua, *Flapper: A Madcap Story of Sex, Style, Celebrity, and the Women Who Made Modern America.* New York: Three Rivers Press, 2006.

Zukowsky, John (ed.), *Building for Air Travel: Architecture and Design for Commercial Aviation.* Chicago: The Art Institute of Chicago, 1996.

Notes on Sources and Further Reading

Below are the principal sources used in this book, as well as suggestions for further reading. Full publication details for books can be found in the accompanying bibliography. Notes on individual citations and other sources used can be found at www.billbryson.co.uk.

General

The most entertaining and briskly informative account of the period remains *Only Yesterday* by Frederick Lewis Allen, originally published in 1931, but reissued many times since. Also excellent is Mark Sullivan's six-volume history, *Our Times*, though it goes only to 1925. More recent works of value include J. C. Furnas's *Great Times* and Nathan Miller's *New World Coming*. The only book specifically on 1927 of which I am aware is *The Year the World Went Mad* by Allen Churchill. A website containing an encyclopedic range of background information, including photographs and reprints of articles on Charles Lindbergh, is CharlesLindbergh.com. For the New York Yankees, a similar service is provided by the 'The Unofficial 1927 New York Yankees Home Page' at www.angelfire.com/pa/1927.

Prologue

Particularly valuable for the history of flight in the period were the similarly named *Aviation: The Early Years* by Peter Almond and *Aviation: The Pioneer Years* edited by Ben Mackworth-Praed. Very good on technical matters is L. F. E. Coombs's *Control in the Sky: The Evolution and History of the Aircraft Cockpit*. Much additional detail came from Graham Wallace's *The Flight of Alcock & Brown*, Robert de La Croix's *They Flew the Atlantic*, and the semi-official American *Aircraft Year Book*s for 1925–1930, published by the Aeronautical Chamber of Commerce of America, Inc. Hiram Bingham's *An Explorer in the Air Service*, though only incidentally useful for this volume, is a fascinating study of America's position with respect to military aviation in the First World War. For America's financing of the First World War, see *The House of Morgan* by Ron Chernow and *An Empire of Wealth* by John Steele Gordon.

Chapter 1

Details from the Snyder–Gray case come mostly from the *New York Times* and other contemporary accounts. A good general overview is provided in Landis MacKeller's *The 'Double Indemnity' Murder*. Other details come from *The American Earthquake* by Edmund Wilson and 'The Bloody Blonde and the Marble Woman: Gender and Power in the Case of Ruth Snyder', by Jessie Ramey in the *Journal of Social History*, Spring 2004. An interesting essay on the influence of the Snyder–Gray case on Hollywood is found in the October 2005 edition of the academic journal *Narrative*, 'Multiple Indemnity: Film Noir, James M. Cain, and Adaptations of a Tabloid Case', by V. P. Pelizzon and Nancy Martha West. Many of the details on the extraordinary quirks of Bernarr Macfadden come from a three-part series that ran in the *New Yorker* in October 1950.

Chapter 2

Lindbergh by A. Scott Berg is the standard biography. Kenneth S. Davis's *The Hero: Charles A. Lindbergh and the American Dream*, though more than fifty years old, is beautifully written and contains a great deal of detail not found elsewhere. Nothing, however, better captures the challenge and excitement of that summer than Lindbergh's own Pulitzer Prize-winning 1953 account, *The Spirit of St Louis*. Lindbergh offered a few additional observations on his life in *Autobiography of Values*, published shortly after his death. Technical details of Lindbergh's flight and a superlative analysis of its importance are provided by Dominick A. Pisano and R. Robert van der Linden in *Charles Lindbergh and the Spirit of St Louis*. All the titles mentioned here were of great help in this chapter and throughout the book.

Chapter 3

The definitive work on the Great Mississippi Flood of 1927 is *Rising Tide* by John M. Barry. Herbert Hoover's personal role in relief operations is neatly surveyed in 'Herbert Hoover, Spokesman of Humane Efficiency', *American Quarterly*, Autumn 1970. A more general book, but also excellent, is *Floods* by William G. Hoyt and Walter B. Langbein. Hoover's rise to greatness is chronicled by Kendrick A. Clements in *The Life of Herbert Hoover*; by George H. Nash in a two-volume work also called *The Life of Herbert Hoover*; and by Richard Norton Smith in *An Uncommon Man: The Triumph of Herbert Hoover*. Hoover himself left the exhaustive and surprisingly readable *The Memoirs of Herbert Hoover*. Details on the financial manoeuvrings of Andrew Mellon are largely taken from David Cannadine's elegant biography, *Mellon: An American Life*. The comments on Calvin Coolidge's work habits are found in Arthur M. Schlesinger's *The Crisis of the Old Order*; in Wilson Brown's 'Aide to Four Presidents', published in *American Heritage*, February 1955; in Donald R. McCoy's *Calvin Coolidge*; and in 'Psychological Pain and the

Presidency' by Robert E. Gilbert in *Political Psychology*, March 1998.

Chapter 4
Statistics on the comforts of American homes in 1927 come principally from the March and July 1927 issues of *Scientific American*. Other details come from *American Culture in the 1920s* by Susan Currell. For the state of American highways at the time, see *The Lincoln Highway* by Drake Hokanson. The situation at Roosevelt Field in May 1927 is well covered in 'How Not to Fly the Atlantic', *American Heritage*, April 1971, and in *The Big Jump* by Richard Bak and *The Flight of the Century* by Thomas Kessner.

Chapter 5
The case of United States vs Sullivan is discussed in 'Taxing Income from Unlawful Activities', Yale Law School Legal Scholarship Repository, Faculty Scholarship Series, Paper 2289, and in the March 2005 issue of the *Columbia Law Review*. Mabel Walker Willebrandt was the subject of an admiring profile in the *New Yorker* in the issue of 16 February 1929. Details of the American tour of Francesco de Pinedo come principally from contemporary reports in the *New York Times*, as do those of the murderous attack in Bath, Michigan, by Andrew Kehoe.

Chapter 6
Charles Lindbergh's flight to Paris remains one of the most written-about events of modern times, so details here are taken from many sources. I have at all times taken Lindbergh's own, meticulous *Spirit of St Louis* as the last word on the flight itself. For details of *Rio Rita* and other Broadway productions, see *American Theatre* by Gerald M. Bordman and *The Theatrical 20's* by Allen Churchill. The biographical details for Bill Tilden come mostly from Frank Deford's *Big Bill Tilden*. Myron Herrick was profiled in the *New Yorker* in the

issue of 21 July 1928. Little else has been written about him.

Chapter 7

The mania surrounding Lindbergh's successful flight is especially well captured in Kenneth S. Davis's *The Hero*. Other details are taken from 'Columbus of the Air', *North American Review*, September–October 1927; 'Lindbergh's Return to Minnesota, 1927', *Minnesota History*, Winter 1970; and 'My Own Mind and Pen', *Minnesota History*, Spring 2002; and from various contemporary newspapers in New York and London. Details of Lindbergh's reception in London come from various editions of *The Times* of London and from the *Illustrated London News*, 4 June 1927.

Chapter 8

Though not remotely reliable on many private matters, the most interesting and obviously personal account of Babe Ruth's life is *The Babe Ruth Story*, by Ruth himself with the help of the sportswriter Bob Considine. Also of note are *The House That Ruth Built* by Robert Weintraub, *The Big Bam* by Leigh Montville, *Babe Ruth: Launching the Legend* by Jim Reisler, and *The Life That Ruth Built* by Marshall Smelser. For details on Baltimore at the time of Ruth's upbringing, see *Baltimore: The Building of an American City* by Sherry H. Olson.

Chapter 9

One of the most fascinating books on America's national pastime is Robert K. Adair's *The Physics of Baseball* and one of the most delightful is Lawrence S. Ritter's oral history, *The Glory of Their Times*. Also providing much useful detail were *The Baseball* by Zack Hample, *Spitballers* by C. F. and R. B. Faber, *Baseball: An Illustrated History* by Geoffrey C. Ward (with Ken Burns), *Total Baseball* by John Thorn and Pete Palmer, *The Complete History of the Home Run* by Mark Ribowsky and *Past Time: Baseball as History* by Jules Tygiel.

Chapter 10

The flight of the *Columbia* and personality quirks of Charles A. Levine are well captured by Clarence D. Chamberlin in his autobiography, *Record Flights*, published in 1942 but still very readable. Other details of the flight and its aftermath come principally from the *New York Times*. A fascinating perspective on why there are no surviving copies of the movie *Babe Comes Home* is supplied by 'The Legion of the Condemned – Why American Silent Films Perished' by David Pierce, *Film History*, Vol. 9, No. 1, 1997.

Chapter 11

The idiosyncrasies of Dwight Morrow were examined by the *New Yorker* in a profile in the edition of 15 October 1927. Additional details can be found in *The House of Morgan* by Ron Chernow. The refurbishments to the White House in the summer of 1927 are discussed in *The White House: The History of an American Idea* by William Seale. The anecdote concerning President Coolidge's seasickness is from the *New Yorker*, 25 June 1927. A good survey of radio in the period is provided by 'Radio Grows Up', *American Heritage*, August–September 1983. Details on city life come from *Downtown: Its Rise and Fall* by Robert M. Fogelson. Gertrude Ederle and the craze for swimming the English Channel are discussed in *The Great Swim* by Gavin Mortimer.

Chapter 12

Two excellent studies of Prohibition are Daniel Okrent's *Last Call* and Michael A. Lerner's *Dry Manhattan*. Other details are taken from *Texas Guinan: Queen of the Night Clubs* by Louise Berliner and *The Night Club Era* by Stanley Walker. Many other details are taken from various issues of the *New Yorker*, which had an all-but-obsessive interest in alcohol and drinking throughout the thirteen years of Prohibtion.

Chapter 13
Richard Byrd's version of the flight of the *America* and associated events is related in his book *Skyward*, first published in 1928. He also wrote a long article titled 'Our Transatlantic Flight', published in *National Geographic* in September 1927. Sharply contrasting views by men who knew Byrd well are Anthony Fokker's *Flying Dutchman* and Bernt Balchen's *Come North With Me*. Additional perspective is provided by *Oceans, Poles and Airmen* by Richard Montague and *The Last Explorer* by Edwin P. Hoyt. The more sullen side of Charles Lindbergh's character was explored in a pair of profiles in the *New Yorker* on 20 and 27 September 1930.

Chapter 14
Though obviously biased and selective, *The Autobiography of Calvin Coolidge*, published in 1929, provides a clear, unvarnished account of the events of Coolidge's life. Other details come from *Calvin Coolidge: The Quiet President* by Donald R. McCoy and from the 2013 book *Coolidge* by Amity Shlaes. The latter provides an interesting revisionist view not just of Coolidge but also of Warren G. Harding. For a contrasting view of Harding, see *The President's Daughter* by Nan Britton, which remains breathtaking even today. An insider's account of Coolidge's foibles is found in 'Aide to Four Presidents', *American Heritage*, February 1955. Coolidge's mental state is interestingly dissected in 'Psychological Pain and the Presidency' by Robert E. Gilbert in *Political Psychology*, March 1998. Also of note is the essay 'Too Silent' in the *Review of Politics*, Spring 1999. More of Coolidge's odd disengagement from executive commitment is seen in 'Coolidge Refuses to Issue Proclamation Calling for Observance of Education Week', *New York Times*, 18 October 1927.

Chapter 15
The story of the meeting of the four central bankers on Long Island in the summer of 1927 is well told in *Lords of Finance*

by Liaquat Ahamed. Additional details come from *Once in Golconda* by John Brooks; *Golden Fetters: The Gold Standard and the Great Depression, 1919–1939* by Barry Eichengreen; and *A History of the Federal Reserve* by Allan H. Meltzer. Also very good, if a bit dated, is *The Lords of Creation: The Story of the Great Age of American Finance* by Frederick Lewis Allen. The rise and fall of the Gold Coast is interestingly surveyed in *Picture Windows: How the Suburbs Happened* by Rosalyn Baxandall and Elizabeth Ewen, and the story of America's addiction to consumer credit is well told by Louis Hyman in *Debtor Nation*.

Chapter 16

The most thorough (and enthusiastic) account of the 1927 Yankees is Harvey Frommer's *Five O'Clock Lightning: Babe Ruth, Lou Gehrig and the Greatest Baseball Team in History, the 1927 New York Yankees*. Conclusions on Lou Gehrig's character are drawn from Jonathan Eig's *Luckiest Man: The Life and Death of Lou Gehrig*, and from profiles of Gehrig in the *New Yorker*, 10 August 1929, and *Liberty*, 19 August 1933, as well as all of the other baseball books already cited. Very little has been written on the life of Jacob Ruppert, but a good profile can be found in the *New Yorker*, 24 September 1932.

Chapter 17

The story of Henry Ford's life and business is exhaustively covered in the two-volume *Ford* by Allan Nevins and Frank Ernest Hill, and more succinctly in Robert Lacey's *Ford: The Men and the Machine*. Neil Baldwin's *Henry Ford and the Jews* gives a scholarly take on Henry Ford's singular brand of anti-Semitism. An affectionate appraisal of the charms and idiosyncrasies of early Ford cars can be found in *Henry's Wonderful Model T* by Floyd Clymer. A more technical assessment is provided by Terry Smith in *Making the Modern: Industry, Art, and Design in America*. Perspective from men who knew Ford well is found in Charles E. Sorensen's *Forty Years With Ford* and E. G. Pipp's *Henry Ford: Both Sides of Him*.

Chapter 18
An indispensable account of the Ford Motor Company's adventures in Amazonia is Greg Grandin's *Fordlandia: The Rise and Fall of Henry Ford's Forgotten Jungle City*. For the story of rubber generally, Henry Hobhouse's *Seeds of Wealth* and Joe Jackson's *The Thief at the End of the World* are both good. For an absorbing account of Percy Fawcett's ill-judged jungle explorations, see *The Lost City of Z* by David Grann and *Man Hunting in the Jungle: The Search for Colonel Fawcett* by George M. Dyott.

Chapter 19
The Florida property boom and bust is extensively considered in *Some Kind of Paradise* by Mark Derr and two *American Heritage* articles, 'Bubble in the Sun', August 1965, and 'The Man Who Invented Florida', December 1975. The details of Jack Dempsey and his fights come principally from *A Flame of Pure Fire* by Roger Kahn, and from an occasional series in the *New Yorker* called 'That Was Pugilism', in particular from the issues of 19 November 1949 and 4 November 1950. Other details come from 'A Sporting Life', the *New Yorker*, 2 October 1999, and *American Heritage*, 'Destruction of a Giant', April 1977. The best account of Charles Lindbergh's tour around America is 'Seeing America With Lindbergh', *National Geographic*, January 1928. Details of the sesquicentennial exposition in Philadelphia come from *Philadelphia: A 300-Year History*, edited by Russell F. Weigley.

Chapter 20
Scores of books have been written on the Sacco and Vanzetti case. For general background, Francis Russell's *Tragedy in Dedham* and *Sacco & Vanzetti: The Case Resolved* are both excellent. For understanding the politics and motivations of

the two anarchists, Paul Avrich's 1991 study, *Sacco and Vanzetti: The Anarchist Background* is without compare. For an understanding of the mood of the nation in the post-First World War years, see *Ethnic Americans* by Leonard Dinnerstein and David M. Reimers, and *Red Scare: A Study in National Hysteria, 1919–1920*, by Robert K. Murray.

Chapter 21
The Carving of Mount Rushmore by Rex Alan Smith not only tells the story of Gutzon Borglum and his great monument, but also provides quite a lot of interesting detail on Calvin Coolidge's summer in South Dakota. The carving is also discussed in 'Mt Rushmore' in the *Smithsonian*, May 2006, and in 'Carving the American Colossus', *American Heritage*, June 1977. The effect on President Coolidge of his son's death is discussed in 'Psychological Pain and the Presidency', March 1998, and in 'The Presidency of Calvin Coolidge', *Presidential Studies Quarterly*, September 1999. The lives of the magnificently eccentric Van Sweringen brothers are comprehensively examined in *Invisible Giants* by Herbert H. Harwood, Jr.

Chapter 22
The *New York Times* ran perhaps 500 stories on long-distance flights in the summer of 1927, and the facts in this chapter are almost exclusively culled from those. Edward R. Armstrong's plans to build a string of floating platforms across the Atlantic Ocean are discussed in 'Airports Across the Ocean', in *American Heritage Invention & Technology*, Summer 2001. The pleasures and perils of ocean travel in the period are entertainingly considered in *The Only Way to Cross* by John Maxtone-Graham. A long account of Charles Lindbergh's visit to Springfield, Illinois, can be found in the October 1927 issue of the *Journal of the Illinois State Historical Society*.

Chapter 23

An excellent discussion of the filming of *Wings* can be found in Robert Wohl's *The Spectacle of Flight: Aviation and the Western Imagination, 1920–1950*. Details of Clara Bow's busy young life come from the aptly named *Clara Bow: Runnin' Wild* by David Stenn. Additional details on Bow in 1927 can be found in *Cinema Journal*, 'Making "It" in Hollywood', Summer 2003. Books on silent film and the transition to sound pictures are almost numberless, but of particular usefulness to this book were *American Silent Film* by William K. Everson, *The Speed of Sound: Hollywood and the Talkie Revolution, 1926–1930* by Scott Eyman, *The Genius of the System: Hollywood Filmmaking in the Studio Era* by Thomas Schatz, and *Movie-Made America: A Cultural History of American Movies* by Robert Sklar. The workings of Lee De Forest's triode detector were comprehensively explained in the March 1965 edition of *Scientific American*.

Chapter 24

The story of the career of Robert G. Elliott comes mostly from his 1940 memoir (written with Albert R. Beatty), *Agent of Death: The Memoirs of an Executioner*. The anger of the newspaperman Heywood Broun over the executions of Sacco and Vanzetti is taken from *Heywood Broun: A Biographical Portrait* by Dale Kramer. For Charles Ponzi, many interesting details, not found elsewhere, are given in a profile in the *New Yorker*, 8 May 1937. Details on the rioting in Europe come mostly from the *New York Times*, but also from the London *Times* of that week and the *Illustrated London News* of 3 September 1927.

Chapter 25

The Ansonia and other apartment hotels of the period are discussed in *Elegant New York* by John Tauranac and *New York, New York: How the Apartment House Transformed the Life of the City (1869–1930)* by Elizabeth Hawes. The literature on

American rail travel in the first decades of the twentieth century is surprisingly sparse. Two books that capture something of the romance, as well as the tedium, of rail travel then are *Railroads and the American People*, written by H. Roger Grant, and *We Took the Train*, edited by Grant. Also little written about was the Yankees' manager Miller Huggins. Much of the information here was drawn from a *New Yorker* profile in the 2 October 1927 issue. Charles Lindbergh's homecoming is well covered in 'Lindbergh's Return to Minnesota', *Minnesota History*, Winter 1970.

Chapter 26

America's peculiar affection for negative eugenics is particularly well treated in *War Against the Weak: Eugenics and America's Campaign to Create a Master Race* by Edwin Black and *Picture Imperfect: Photography and Eugenics 1870–1940* by Anne Maxwell. Also of interest, though focused on the following decade, is *Popular Eugenics: National Efficiency and American Mass Culture in the 1930s*, edited by Susan Currell and Christina Cogdell. The history of the Ku Klux Klan is covered in *The Fiery Cross* by Wyn Craig Wade; additional details were taken from 'Hooded Populism', *Reviews in American History*, December 1994. *Not in My Neighborhood* by Antero Pietila is very good on restrictive covenants. Other aspects of race hatred in America are dealt with in *Hollywood and Anti-Semitism* by Steven Alan Carr, and *Hellfire Nation* by James A. Morone. The unhappy outcome of eugenics in Germany is surveyed in *Nazi Medicine and the Nuremberg Trials* by Paul Julian Weindling. The case of Buck vs Bell is the subject of an excellent chapter in *The Flamingo's Smile* by the late Stephen Jay Gould.

Chapter 27

Two outstanding books on the invention of television are *The Last Lone Inventor: A Tale of Genius, Deceit and the Birth of Television* by Evan I. Schwartz and *Tube: The Invention of*

Television by David E. and Marshall Jon Fisher. The sad end of Philo T. Farnsworth is well treated in the *New Yorker*, 'A Critic at Large', 27 May 2002. John Logie Baird receives a sympathetic hearing in *John Logie Baird: A Life* by Antony Kamm and Malcolm Baird. Other details, particularly with respect to public demonstrations of television in the summer of 1927, come mostly from the *New York Times*.

Chapter 28
Two books by Allen Churchill, *The Literary Decade* and *The Theatrical 20's*, provide an excellent introduction to the worlds of books and theatre in the 1920s. Also offering good details and much insight on life in New York in the period is *About Town: The* New Yorker *and the World It Made* by Ben Yagoda. *Show Boat* is especially well treated in *Jerome Kern: His Life and Music* by Gerald M. Bordman and *Enchanted Evenings: The Broadway Musical from* Show Boat *to Sondheim* by Geoffrey Block. The life stories of America's two most popular authors of the period are recounted in *Tarzan Forever: The Life of Edgar Rice Burroughs, Creator of Tarzan* by John Taliaferro, and *Zane Grey: His Life, His Adventures, His Women* by Thomas H. Pauly. *Firebrand: The Life of Horace Liveright* by Tom Dardis is illuminating both on the publisher himself and on the literary firmament through which he moved.

Chapter 29
After decades of neglect, Kenesaw Mountain Landis finally received the recognition of a biography with David Pietrusza's excellent *Judge and Jury: The Life and Times of Judge Kenesaw Mountain Landis* in 1998. Some additional technical details come from *A Court That Shaped America: Chicago's Federal District Court from Abe Lincoln to Abbie Hoffman* by Richard Cahan. Chicago's greatest criminal is treated in *Capone: The Life and World of Al Capone* by John Kobler, *Capone: The Man and the Era* by Laurence Bergreen and *Get Capone* by Jonathan

Eig. The life of Robert R. McCormick is the subject of *The Colonel* by Richard Norton Smith and features prominently in *The Magnificent Medills* by Megan McKinney. The boorish mayor Bill Thompson is anatomized at length in 'The Private Wars of Chicago's Big Bill Thompson' in the *Journal of Library History*, Summer 1980. More general histories are Kenneth Allsop's *The Bootleggers*, John Landesco's *Organized Crime in Chicago*, and Dominic A. Pacyga's *Chicago: A Biography*.

Chapter 30
Descriptions of the last month of the 1927 baseball season are taken from the baseball books already cited. Of additional importance to this chapter was Henry W. Thomas's splendid and moving biography *Walter Johnson: Baseball's Big Train*.

Epilogue
A full survey of life in Nazi Germany, including the shocking events of Kristallnacht, can be found in *Hitlerland* by Andrew Nagorski. Anne Morrow Lindbergh's comments appear in *The Flower and the Nettle: Diaries and Letters of Anne Morrow Lindbergh, 1936–1939*. The news of Charles Lindbergh's serial infidelities from 1957 to some time shortly before his death was widely reported in 2003 after one of his German children took a DNA test that proved Lindbergh's paternity.

Acknowledgements

As ever, I am greatly indebted to a number of people and institutions for kindly assistance in the preparation of this book. In particular, I wish to thank Dr Alex M. Spencer, Dr Robert van der Linden and Dr Dominick Pisano of the Smithsonian National Air and Space Museum in Washington, DC; my saintly editors, Marianne Velmans, Gerry Howard and Kristin Cochrane; my British agent, Carol Heaton; my esteemed friend Larry Finlay; and my extraordinarily bright and diligent copy editors, Nora Reicherd and Deborah Adams, who between them saved me from a thousand careless mistakes, though of course any that remain are my own.

I am also most grateful to the ever helpful staff of the London Library; to Jon Purcell and his colleagues at the library of Durham University; to Bart Schmidt and colleagues at the Drake University Library in Des Moines; and to the staffs of the New York and Boston Public Libraries, the Lauinger Library at Georgetown University, and the library of the National Geographic Society in Washington, DC.

For advice, encouragement, introductions and occasional meals, I am most grateful to Keith and Win Blackmore, Jonathan and Rina Fenby, Tim and Elizabeth Burt, John and Anne Galbraith, Chris Higgins and Jenifer White, Anne Heywood, Larry and Lucinda Scott, Patrick Janson-Smith, Patrick Gallagher, Brad Martin, Oliver Payne, John and Jeri Flinn, Andrew and Alison Orme, Daniel and Erica Wiles, and Jon, Donna, Max and Daisy Davidson.

Special thanks go also to my children Catherine and Sam Bryson for their generous and extremely affordable research assistance, and, above all and as always, to my dear, long-suffering, imperturbable, all-forgiving wife, Cynthia.

Photo Acknowledgements

Ruth Snyder; Judd Gray; Babe Ruth kissing bat; Bath murders; Dwight W. Morrow; Lou Gehrig and Babe Ruth; Van Sweringen Brothers; Al Capone; Charles Ponzi; Albert Fall and Edward Donehey; Texas Guinan; Philo T. Farnsworth; Charles Lindbergh and Henry Ford: © Bettmann/CORBIS

Charles Lindbergh with goggles: Courtesy of the San Diego Air & Space Museum

Charles Lindbergh and Myron Herrick: Time Life Pictures/Time & Life Pictures/Getty Images

Charles Lindbergh at Croydon Aerodome: © TopFoto/The Image Works

Charles Lindbergh in Washington DC: The Art Archive at Art Resource, New York

Charles Lindbergh in New York City: Culver Pictures/The Art Archive at Art Resource, New York

Charles Nungesser and François Coli: Mary Evans Picture Library

Bert Acosta, Richard Byrd and other crew of the *America*: ©
AP Images; photo courtesy of Photography Collection,
Miriam and Ira D. Wallach Divison of Art, Prints and
Photographs, The New York Public Library, Astor, Lenox
and Tilden Foundations

America, in water; Clarence Chamberlin and others with
Columbia; Robert Elliot; Alvin 'Shipwreck' Kelly; Gene
Tunney and Jack Dempsey fight: AP Images

Francesco de Pinedo; Wayne Wheeler; Al Jolson: The
Granger Collection, New York

Babe Ruth: Louis Van Oeyen/Western Reserve Historical
Society/ Getty Images

Mississippi Flood: Courtesy of the Archives & Records
Services Division, Mississippi Department of Archives &
History

Herbert Hoover and Mississippi Flood children: Clifton R.
Adams/National Geographic Stock

Nan Britton and daughter; Sacco and Vanzetti funeral
procession: © Everett Collection/Superstock

Calvin Coolidge in cowboy costume: New York Times
Co./Archives Photos/Getty Images

Bankers Hjalmar Schacht, Benjamin Strong, Sir Montagu
Norman and Charles Rist: Federal Reserve Bank of New
York – Curating Section

Selling 'denatured' alcohol during Prohibition:
FPG/Hulton Archive/ Getty Images

PHOTO ACKNOWLEDGEMENTS

Gutzon Borglum in studio: The Library of Congress

Sacco and Vanzetti: New York Daily News Archive/New York Daily News/Getty Images

Clara Bow in *Wings*: PHOTOFEST

Roxy Theatre: Hulton Archive/Getty Images

Union Station area: Cleveland Union Terminal Collection, Michael Schwartz Library, Cleveland State University

Mabel Willebrandt: © CORBIS

Flappers; Cotton Club: © Underwood & Underwood/Corbis

Kenesaw M. Landis: Chicago History Museum/Archive Photos/Getty Images

David Sarnoff: G. Adams/Topical Press Agency/Getty Images

Henry Ford: Print Collection, Miriam and Ira D. Wallach Division of Art, Prints and Photographs, The New York Public Library, Astor, Lenox and Tilden Foundations

Fordlandia houses: From the collections of The Henry Ford, Photo ID p.1514.95; Digital Image ID p.1514.95/THF44286

Bill Bryson's bestselling travel books include *The Lost Continent*, *A Walk in the Woods* and *Notes from a Small Island*, which in a national poll was voted the book that best represents Britain. His acclaimed book on the history of science, *A Short History of Nearly Everything*, won the Royal Society's Aventis Prize as well as the Descartes Prize, the European Union's highest literary award. He has written books on language, on Shakespeare, and on his own childhood in the hilarious memoir *The Life and Times of the Thunderbolt Kid*. His last critically lauded bestseller was *At Home: A Short History of Private Life*. He was born in the American Mid-West, and lives in the UK.

Index